International Investment Law and Water Resources Management

Nijhoff International Investment Law Series

Series Editors

Dr. Eric De Brabandere (*Leiden University*)
Dr. Tarcisio Gazzini (*VU University Amsterdam*)
Dr. Stephan W. Schill (*University of Amsterdam*)
Prof. Attila Tanzi (*University of Bologna*)

Editorial Board

Andrea K. Bjorklund (*Montreal*) – Juan Pablo Bohoslavsky
(*El Bolsón, Río Negro*) – Chester Brown (*Sydney*) – David Caron (*London*) –
Patrick Dumberry (*Ottawa*) – Michael Ewing-Chow (*Singapore*) –
Susan D. Franck (*Lexington*) – Ursula Kriebaum (*Vienna*) –
Makane Mbengue (*Geneva*) – Catherine A. Rogers (*Carlisle*) –
Christian Tams (*Glasgow*) – Andreas Ziegler (*Lausanne*)

VOLUME 6

The titles published in this series are listed at *brill.com/iils*

International Investment Law and Water Resources Management

An Appraisal of Indirect Expropriation

By

Ana Maria Daza-Clark

BRILL
NIJHOFF

LEIDEN | BOSTON

Library of Congress Cataloging-in-Publication Data

Names: Daza-Clark, Ana Maria.
Title: International investment law and water resources management : an
   appraisal of indirect expropriation / by Ana Maria Daza-Clark.
Description: Leiden ; Boston : Brill Nijhoff, 2017. | Series: Nijhoff
   international investment law series ; VOLUME 6 | Includes index. |
   Includes bibliographical references and index.
Identifiers: LCCN 2016036679 (print) | LCCN 2016037313 (ebook) | ISBN
   9789004335295 (hardback : alk. paper) | ISBN 9789004335301 (E-books)
Subjects: LCSH: Water resources development--Law and legislation. |
   Investments, Foreign (International law) | International commercial
   arbitration. | Eminent domain (International law)
Classification: LCC K3498 .D39 2017 (print) | LCC K3498 (ebook) | DDC
   346.04/691--dc23
LC record available at https://lccn.loc.gov/2016036679

Typeface for the Latin, Greek, and Cyrillic scripts: "Brill". See and download: brill.com/brill-typeface.

ISSN 2351-9542
ISBN 978-90-04-33529-5 (hardback)
ISBN 978-90-04-33530-1 (e-book)

Copyright 2017 by Koninklijke Brill NV, Leiden, The Netherlands.
Koninklijke Brill NV incorporates the imprints Brill, Brill Hes & De Graaf, Brill Nijhoff, Brill Rodopi and
Hotei Publishing.
All rights reserved. No part of this publication may be reproduced, translated, stored in a retrieval system,
or transmitted in any form or by any means, electronic, mechanical, photocopying, recording or otherwise,
without prior written permission from the publisher.
Authorization to photocopy items for internal or personal use is granted by Koninklijke Brill NV provided
that the appropriate fees are paid directly to The Copyright Clearance Center, 222 Rosewood Drive,
Suite 910, Danvers, MA 01923, USA. Fees are subject to change.

This book is printed on acid-free paper and produced in a sustainable manner.

to Graham

Contents

Preface and Acknowledgements   IX
Abbreviations   XI

1   Introduction   1

2   The Special Nature of Water Resources   17

3   The Governance of Water Resources   35

4   Revisiting the Doctrine of the Police Power of States   64

5   Indirect Expropriation and International Investment Law   88

6   Water Management and Indirect Expropriation   115

7   The Nature of Property Rights over Water Resources
     The Role of Domestic Law   133

8   The Impact of Regulatory Measures on Foreign Investments
     The 'Quantitative' Approach   154

9   The Legitimacy of the Exercise of the Police Power of States
     The 'Qualitative' Approach   174

10   Conclusions   199

     Bibliography   215
     Index   245

Preface and Acknowledgements

In 2000 the residents of Cochabamba in Bolivia led an unprecedented protest that came to be known as the 'Cochabamba water war'. The trigger was the privatisation of the public water services provider – SEMAPA – and the sudden and extreme rise of water tariffs that came after a private foreign service provider took over. As a result, the government cancelled the concession contract it had made with Aguas del Tunari S.A., a foreign investor who would then initiate an investment treaty arbitration, alleging that Bolivia had failed to protect its investment in accordance with international treaty obligations.

The case was finally settled between Bolivia and the foreign investor and the rest is history. However, the repercussions of this event are significant, both to the legitimacy of the investment arbitration regime, as well as for advocates and water academics. As a former resident of Cochabamba I am no stranger to water shortages; yet, as a legal officer at the regulatory system for public utilities during the conflict, I have understood, with time, that the problem neither started with the privatisation process, nor would it end with the termination of a concession contract. During the course of writing this book, Cochabamba continues to suffer from water scarcity and still lacks the proper infrastructure to supply water services to its citizens.[1]

As it was eloquently put by the United Nations in 2006 'there is enough water for everyone. The problem […] is largely one of governance'.[2] In essence this is a book about governance and how international tribunals ought to allocate risk when governance fails, especially in the context of water resources-related disputes. While international investment law seeks stability, water law strives for adaptability. In the context of investment treaty arbitration, this tension plays out as a balance between the need for predictability on the one hand and the need for change on the other. However, the theoretical underpinnings and intrinsic interrelation between these two areas of law strike me as an unlikely friendship. It is difficult to get the balance right. For many years I have been interested in observing how these two regimes interact and whether they could achieve mutual supportiveness, from a developmental as well as legal

---

1 El sueño de Misicuni aún requiere más inversiones' available at: http://www.lostiempos .com/actualidad/local/20160410/sueno-misicuni-aun-requiere-mas-inversiones, visited on 10 July, 2016.

2 World Water Assessment Programme, 'The United Nations World Water Development Report 2: Water a Shared Responsibility,' (United Nations, 2009) 3.

perspectives. Yet, the absence of communication and exchange between epistemic communities weakens decision-making and prevents holistic solutions. Domestic public law experts (such as water lawyers) are not always aware that their decisions might have repercussion under international law and could become under the scrutiny of international arbitrators and judges. In turn, international investment tribunals often feel little connection to the domestic realities and pressures under which local decisions are adopted, nor do they have the mandate under international law to incorporate such considerations.

The focus of my work has been to determine the extent to which these two distinct communities might better understand one another. I have focused on the issue of indirect expropriation, as it allows for a comprehensive reflection of States' regulatory practice. While it is argued that expropriation has been largely studied, in the last ten years I have observed further developments which are worth close examination.

In this process I have been privileged with the opportunity to interact with both the investment law and water law communities, as a government official and later as an academic. The University of Dundee where I started this project, and the University of Edinburgh where I am concluding it, have been a source of enriching debate. Of course several other academic communities have had an impact on my ideas, stimulated my thinking and ultimately contributed to this work. I am indebted to colleagues, research assistants, family and friends around the world, especially to Dr Daniel Behn from the University of Oslo.

Abbreviations

CAA	Aguas de Aconquija from Argentina
BIT	Bilateral Investment Treaty
CAFTA	Central American Free Trade Agreement
COMESA	Common Market for an Eastern and Southern African Investment Agreement, Common Investment Area
DR-CAFTA	Dominican Republic-Central American Free Trade Agreement
ECT	Energy Charter Treaty
ECHR	European Court of Human Rights
EU	European Union
CETA	EU-Canada Comprehensive Economic and Trade Agreement
FET	Fair and Equitable Treatment
FAO	Food and Agriculture Organisation
FIPA	Foreign Investment Promotion and Protection Agreement
FTA	Free Trade Agreement
GATT	General Agreement on Tariffs and Trade
GATS	General Agreement on Trade in Services
GWP	Global Water Partnership
TEC	Global Water Partnership Technical Committee
GDP	Gross Domestic Product
HDI	Human Development Index
IWRM	Integrated Water Resources Management
ILC	International Law Commission
ICSID	International Centre for Settlement of Investment Disputes
ICC	International Chamber of Commerce
ICA	International Court of Arbitration
IISD	International Institute for Sustainable Development
IIA	International Investment Agreement
ITA	International Taxation Agreement
ITLOS	International Tribunal for the Law of the Sea
IWRA	International Water Resources Association
IUSCT	Iran–US Claims Tribunal
LCIA	London Court of International Arbitration
MTBE	Methyl tertiary-butyl ether
MDGS	Millennium Development Goals
MPI	Multidimensional Poverty Index

MAI	Multilateral Agreement on Investment
NIEO	New International Economic Order
NGO	Non-Governmental Organisation
NAFTA	North American Free Trade Agreement
OECD	Organisation for Economic Cooperation and Development
PCA	Permanent Court of Arbitration
PCIJ	Permanent Court of International Justice
PSNR	Permanent Sovereignty over Natural Resources
PDVSA	Petróleos de Venezuela S.A.
PSA	Product Sharing Agreement
PPP	Public Private Partnership
Helsinki Rules	Rules on the Uses of the Waters of International Rivers
S.A.	Sociedad Anónima
SCC	Stockholm Chamber of Commerce
TPP	Trans-Pacific Partnership
TTIP	Transatlantic Trade and Investment Partnership
UN	United Nations
UNCED	United Nations Conference on Environment and Development
UN Watercourses Convention	United Nations Convention on the Law of the Non-Navigational Uses of International Water Courses
UNICEF	United Nations Children's Emergency Fund
UNCTAD	United Nations Conference on Trade and Development
UNEP	United Nations Environment Programme
WWDR	United Nations World Water Development Report
UK	United Kingdom
US	United States
VCLT	Vienna Convention on the Law of Treaties
WHO	World Health Organisation
WTO	World Trade Organization
WWDR	World Water Development Report

CHAPTER 1

Introduction

1.1   Introduction

As the law evolves, expands and specialises, the overall normative coherence of particular legal orders can become more elusive. This increases the likelihood for potential conflict arising between different regimes or areas of law, such as water law and international investment law. On the one hand, water laws and policies are increasingly moving towards a holistic and adaptive approach to the management of water resources. International investment law, on the other hand, covers the obligation to protect foreign investment through stable and predictable legal environments, by means of international investment agreements.

To date, any conflict between the epistemic communities of water and investment law has been engaged, by necessity, in the context of disputes arising out of international investment obligations. International investment law, and not water law *per se*, constitutes the applicable law to decide potential conflicts between the regulation of water resources and the obligation to protect foreign investment. The proliferation of investment treaties has given rise to specific dispute settlement mechanisms granting jurisdiction to handle investment disputes. In contrast, the fields of international environmental and water law have somewhat less cohesive dispute settlement mechanisms embedded in their respective treaties.

At the end of the 1980s and during the early 1990s, the field of international investment law witnessed an explosion of Bilateral Investment Treaties (BITs) and other International Investment Agreements (IIAs).[1] By the early 2000s, there was an upsurge in the initiation of disputes granted jurisdiction under these BITs and Free Trade Agreements (FTAs) with investment chapters. International investment disputes allow a private foreign investor to initiate binding arbitration against the State hosting their investment. To date, these cases have been brought primarily under the International Centre for Settlement of Investment Disputes (ICSID) Convention or ad hoc arbitrations under the United Nations Commission on International Trade Law (UNCITRAL) arbitration rules. Increasingly, investment disputes are also brought under the rules of

---

1   UNCTAD reports that by July 2016, there is a total of 3316 IIAs, between BITs and other investment agreements. See UNCTAD, International Investment Agreements Navigator. Available at: http://investmentpolicyhub.unctad.org/IIA, last visited 5 July, 2016.

© KONINKLIJKE BRILL NV, LEIDEN, 2017 | DOI 10.1163/9789004335301_002

international arbitration centres such as the Permanent Court of Arbitration (PCA), the International Chamber of Commerce (ICC), the London Court of International Arbitration (LCIA), and the Stockholm Chamber of Commerce (SCC).[2]

During the period between the 1990s and the early part of the 2000s, international investment practitioners and commentators were well aware of the potential disputes arising from the exercise of regulatory prerogatives of host States in relation to the promises given to foreign investors. A vast number of academics and practitioners wrote extensively about political and regulatory risk.[3] Perhaps, having observed the Libyan nationalisation cases and the decisions coming out of the Iran – US Claims Tribunal (IUSCT), very few investment specialists believed that IIAs constituted a real threat to the regulation of the environment, health and safety. As Wälde *et al.* noted, as far back as the mid-1990s, Non-Governmental Organizations (NGOs) and other civil society actors might have adopted exaggerated views towards the scope of BITs and their effects over the police power of States.[4]

---

2   Up to July 2016 the number of investment treaty disputes reached 696. UNCTAD, Investment Dispute Settlement Navigator. Available at: http://investmentpolicyhub.unctad.org/ISDS, last visited July 1, 2016.

3   Thomas Wälde and Stephen Dow, 'Treaties and Regulatory Risk in Infrastructure Investment. The Effectiveness of International Law Disciplines versus Sanctions by Global Markets in Reducing the Political and Regulatory Risk for Private Infrastructure Investment,' *Journal of World Trade* 34, no. 2 (2000); Thomas Wälde and Todd Weiler, 'Investment arbitration under the Energy Charter Treaty in the light of new NAFTA precedents: Towards a global code of conduct for economic regulation,' *Transnational Dispute Management* 1(2004); Thomas Wälde and Abba Kolo, 'Environmental Regulation, Investment Protection and "Regulatory Taking" in International Law,' *International and Comparative Law Quarterly* 50, no. 4 (2001); Andrew Newcombe, 'The Boundaries of Regulatory Expropriation in International Law,' *ICSID Review* 20, no. 1 (2005); Vaughan Lowe, 'Regulation or expropriation?' *Current legal problems* 55 (2002); L. Yves Fortier and Stephen L. Drymer, 'Indirect Expropriation in the Law of International Investment: I know it when I see it, or Caveat Investor,' *ICSID review: Foreign investment law journal* 19, no. 2 (2004); Howard Mann, 'The Right of States to Regulate and International Investment Law,' in *Expert Meeting on the Development Dimension of FDI: Policies to Enhance the Role of FDI in Support of the Competitiveness of the Enterprise Sector and the Economic Performance of Host Economies, Taking into Account the Trade/Investment Interface, in the National and International Context* (Geneva 2002); Howard Mann and Konrad von Moltke, 'NAFTA's Chapter 11 and the Environment: Addressing the Impacts of the Investor-State Process on the Environment,' *International Institute for Sustainable Development, Publication Centre* (1999); M. Sornarajah, 'State responsibility and Bilateral Investment Treaties,' *Journal of World Trade Law* 20, no. 1 (1986).

4   Thomas Wälde and Abba Kolo, 'Environmental Regulation, Investment Protection and "Regulatory Taking" in International Law,' 814.

INTRODUCTION 3

Several commentators agreed with the view that regulatory measures aimed at protecting the environment, if adopted in good faith and following due process of law, would hardly be challengeable as violations of relevant provisions in IIAs.[5]

The opposite views challenge the legitimacy of the dispute settlement mechanism in investor-State arbitration, which permits a private foreign investor – a natural person or corporation – to sue a sovereign State before an international arbitral tribunal. Furthermore, the broad provisions on investment protection contained in IIAs have also been criticised. Given their broad scope they are perceived as biased in favour of investors.[6]

---

5 *Ibid.* See also Christoph Schreuer, 'The Concept of Expropriation under the ECT and other Investment Protection Treaties,' (2005); Gary H. Sampliner, 'Arbitration of Expropriation Cases under U.S. Investment Treaties: A Threat to Democracy or the Dog didn't Bark?' *ICSID Review: Foreign investment law journal* 18, no. 1 (2003).

6 Celine Levesque, 'Investment and Water Resources: Limits to NAFTA,' in *Sustainable Development in World Investment Law*, ed. Marie-Claire Cordonier Segger, Markus W. Gehring, and Andrew Newcombe, *Global Trade Law Series* (Alphen aan den Rijn: Kluwer Law International 2011); Howard Mann, 'Who Owns "Your" Water? Reclaiming Water as a Public Good under International Trade and Investment Law,' *International Institute for Sustainable Development* (2003); Howard Mann, 'International Economic Law: Water for Money's Sake,' *International Institute for Sustainable Development* (2004); Howard Mann, 'Implications of International Trade and Investment Agreements for Water and Water Services: Some Responses from Other Sources of International Law,' TDM (2006); Hugo A. Muñoz, 'La administración del agua y la inversión extranjera directa ¿Cómo se relacionan?' in *Estudios en homenaje al Dr Rafael González Ballar*, ed. Universidad de Costa Rica (UCR) (San Jose: Isolma S.A., 2009); Miguel Solanes, 'Water Services and International Investment Agreements,' in *Global Change: Impacts on Water and food Security*, ed. Claudia Ringler, Asit K. Biswas, and Sarah Cline, *Water Resources Development and Management* (Berlin/Heidelberg: Springer 2010); Miguel Solanes and Andrei Jouravlev, 'Revisiting Privatization, Foreign Investment, International Arbitration and Water,' *Serie Recursos Naturales e Infraestructura* 129 (2007); Attila Tanzi, 'On Balancing Foreign Investment Interests With Public Interests in Recent Arbitration Case Law in the Public Utilities Sector,' *The law and practice of international courts and tribunals: A Practitioners' Journal* 11, no. 1 (2012); Paul Stanton Kibel, 'Grasp on Water: A Natural Resource that Eludes NAFTA's Notion of Investment,' *Ecology Law Quarterly* 34, no. 2 (2007); Joseph Cumming and Robert Froehlich, 'NAFTA Chapter XI and Canada's Environmental Sovereignty: Investment Flows, Article 1110 and Alberta's Water Act,' *University of Toronto Faculty of Law Review* 65(2007); Vivien Foster and Tito Yepes, 'Is Cost Recovery a Feasible Objective for Water and Electricity? The Latin American Experience,' *World Bank Policy Research* Working Paper 3943 (2006); John D. Leshy, 'A Conversation About Takings and Water Rights,' *Texas Law Review* 83, no. 7 (2005); Fabrizio Marrella, 'On the changing structure of international investment law: The human right to water and ICSID arbitration,' *International Community Law Review* 12, no. 3 (2010); Stuart Orr, Anton Cartwright and Dave Tickner, 'Understanding water

One could argue that these two epistemic communities of investment lawyers and environmental/water lawyers do not look at the relationship between water and investment from the same angle. Perhaps they do not share the same values, and the interests to be protected are diverse. It was not too long ago that the investment arbitration regime saw as its mandate the application and enforcement solely of investment obligations, as purported in the relevant agreement, as a clear and strict one. In this light, Hirsh noted:

> thus far no arbitral tribunal has absolved a party to an investment dispute from its investment obligations (or significantly reduced its responsibility to compensate the injured investor).[7]

With reference to the standard of expropriation and compensation, the difficult task was, and still is, to ascertain when the legitimate exercise of the police power of the State, which does not entail compensation, has gone 'too far' and

---

risks A primer on the consequences of water scarcity for government and business,' (World Wildlife Fund, 2009); Carin Smaller and Howard Mann, 'A Thirst for Distant Lands: Foreign investment in agricultural land and water,' *International Institute for Sustainable Development. Foreign Investment for Sustainable Development Program* (2009); Paul Stanton and Jon Schutz, 'Two Rivers Meet: At the Confluence of Cross-Border Water and Foreign Investment Law,' in *Sustainable Development in World Investment Law*, ed. Marie-Claire Cordonier Segger, Markus W. Gehring, and Andrew Newcombe, *Global Trade Law Series* (Alphen aan den Rijn: Kluwer Law International, 2011); AquaFed, 'Bilateral Investment Treaties and the Right to Water: The case of the provision of public water supply and sanitation services. (Submission by AquaFed),' in *Office of the UN High Commissioner for Human Rights: Consultation on business and human rights: Operationalizing the 'Protect, Respect, and Remedy' framework on business and human rights* (Geneva 2009); Epaminontas E. Triantafilou, 'No Remedy for an Investor's Own Mismanagement: The Award in the ICSID Case Biwater Gauff v. Tanzania,' *International Disputes Quarterly. Focus: An Arbitrator's Perspective* Winter (2009); Jorge E. Vinuales, 'Access to Water in Foreign Investment Disputes,' *The Georgetown International Environmental Law Review* 21(2009); Jorge E. Vinuales, 'Iced Freshwater Resources: A Legal Exploration,' *Yearbook of International Environmental Law* 20, no. 1 (2011). See also Marie-Claire Cordonier Segger, Markus W. Gehring, and Andrew Newcombe, eds., *Sustainable Development in World Investment Law*, Global Trade Law Series (Alphen aan den Rijn Kluwer Law International, 2011); Edith Brown Weiss, Laurence Boisson de Chazournes, and Nathalie Bernasconi-Osterwalder, eds., *Fresh Water and International Economic Law* (Oxford; New York: Oxford University Press, 2005).

7 Moshe Hirsh, 'Sources of International Investment Law,' in *International Investment Law and Soft Law*, ed. Andrea K. Bjorklund and August Reinisch (Cheltenham, UK; Northampton, MA: Edward Elgar Pub., 2012), 13.

INTRODUCTION

therefore constitutes an act of expropriation. Academics and practitioners in the area of environmental law saw the implementation and continuity of environmental regulation as dependent on the decision of investment tribunals. For this reason, it is arguable that the environmental community might often see international economic law forums (such as investment treaty arbitration and the World Trade Organization (WTO) dispute settlement mechanisms) as a means of converting trade and investment tribunals into environmental tribunals. While this has certainly been the case in the context of investment arbitration, the WTO has faced similar challenges, stimulating to some extent cross-fertilization between the two regimes. In the context of the WTO, some academics have adopted an institutional perspective to illustrate the normative boundaries of the WTO in relation to the applicability or non-applicability of the other fields of law, in their intricate relationships:

> one of the phenomena we observe in relation to WTO law is jealousy on the part of environmentalists, labor rights advocates, human rights proponents and others due to the stronger enforceability and sanctions available with respect to violations of WTO law.[8]

It is incontestable that a balance between the protection of foreign investment and the protection of other societal values is needed to advance economic as well as human development. However, it is a reality that welfare objectives such as environmental, health and safety regulations often constitute the subject matter of investment and trade disputes; and that arbitral tribunals are called upon to scrutinise them. It follows that host States may have to repeal the measure as a way of restitution, or when this is not possible, pay compensation.[9] It should be noted, however, that in most cases, foreign investors seek compensation instead of restitution, because the relationship between investor and State is no longer one of trust and cooperation.

8   Joel P. Trachtman, 'Transcending "Trade and..." An Institutional Perspective,' *SSNR*. (2001). Available at: http://papers.ssrn.com/sol3/papers.cfm?abstract_id=271171, last visited March 21, 2016. In this article Professor Trachtman coins the term 'penance envy' to argue that not all international law has been created equal, and therefore some fields still lack institutions and enforcement mechanism.

9   This is the principle of reparation adopted in the case of *Chorzów Factory (Germany v. Poland) 1928 PCIJ (ser. A) No. 17*. For an account of remedies in International Law, see for instance Dinah Shelton, 'Righting Wrongs: Reparations in the Articles on State Responsibility,' *Symposium: The ILC's State Responsibility Articles. The American Journal of International Law* 96, no. 4 (2002).

6   CHAPTER 1

1.2 Initial Thoughts: Water and Investment

The core issues examined in this book pertain to the potential tensions that the protection of foreign investment has created in relation to water resources and its management. A regulatory measure seeking to protect, allocate or prioritise water resources may deprive the investor of his water entitlement, affecting the investment as a whole.[10] This action in turn could be considered as a *de facto* or indirect expropriation.[11] As discussed later in this book, these measures contrast with acts of direct expropriation of the investment, where a shift in ownership takes place, depriving the investor of the title and control over the property rights.

The application of standards of investment protection to secure long-term economic returns on investments, include water licences and permits (water rights) as production inputs from naturally variable water flows. The application of water management principles in turn requires a flexible legal framework to ensure sustainable availability and environmental protection. This approach involves an exploration of two potentially contradictory sets of concepts: *security* and *predictability*, which are at the core of international investment law; and *variability* and *adaptability*, which are inherent to the nature and management of water resources.

The argument develops on the basis of the police power doctrine, or the prerogative of States to regulate, because this doctrine has been consistently recognised by investment tribunals as a legitimate exercise of State's sovereignty. However, the notion of the police power needs to be revisited in the context of its foundations and underlying values. In order for the police power to be reasonably invoked and legitimately applied, there must be a dividing line between an act of indirect expropriation and the adoption of a legitimate regulation, which imposes reasonable burdens on investors.

---

10   A comparison could be drawn between 'investment,' as a complex project formed by contracts, licences, concessions, etc., and the 'bundle of rights' formed by sticks representing the enjoyment of each attribute of the property rights. The comparison of the 'investment' with a bundle of rights was proposed for instance in *ATA Construction, Industrial and Trading Company v. Hashemite Kingdom of Jordan*, ICSID Case No. ARB/08/2, Award of 18 May, 2012, para. 96.

11   This work will use the terms indirect expropriation, *de facto* expropriation, and takings indistinctively. However, one can refer to their different conceptions in Veijo Heiskanen (for instance), 'The Contribution of the Iran-United States Claims Tribunal to the Development of the Doctrine of Indirect Expropriation,' *International law FORUM du droit international: The Journal of the International Law Association International Law Forum du droit international* 5, no. 3 (2003).

INTRODUCTION

The first wave of investment disputes was characterised by the adoption of divergent approaches to the interpretation and application of investment treaty obligations in regard to indirect expropriation. At least that was the perception in *Methanex*[12] and *Metalclad*;[13] the first brought against the United States (US) and the second against Mexico.[14] However, it is safe to argue that as the investment arbitration regime matures, so does the arbitral practice; in the context of expropriation, it seems to be moving away from contradictory decisions towards relatively consistent awards.[15] It is also fair to argue that such developments may be attributed, among other factors, to increasing scrutiny that the investment arbitration regime has been subject to. After all, the public nature of the regime has enormous influence in the way States may conduct their policies and regulatory practice. This of course has equally vast implications on communities and other stakeholders.

The first wave of investment disputes and the developments in this fairly young investment arbitration regime has been an important stepping stone for the framework suggested in this book. It is believed that a sector-specific approach, tailored to the particular characteristics of the sector under dispute may further harmonise the manner in which arbitral tribunals assess investment disputes.[16] It is further argued that a sector-specific approach is appropriate for water-related disputes because special consideration is needed in relation to the unique nature of water in order to meet food, energy and water security. All of this should be viewed in the context of the current challenges

---

12   *Methanex Corp. v. United States of America*, UNCITRAL, Final Award of 3 August, 2005.

13   *Metalclad Corp. v. Mexico*, Arb (AF)/97/1, 5 ICSID Reports, 209.

14   A description of these cases, adopting different approaches to regulatory measures with an effect on investors' rights can be found in Rudolf Dolzer, 'New Foundations of the Law of Expropriation of Alien Property' *American Journal of International Law* 75(1981); Rudolf Dolzer, 'Indirect Expropriations: New Developments?' *New York University Environmental Law Journal* 11(2002); Rudolf Dolzer and Felix Bloch, 'Indirect Expropriation: Conceptual Realignments?' *International Law Forum du Droit International* (2003); Veijo Heiskanen, 'The Contribution of the Iran-United States Claims Tribunal to the Development of the Doctrine of Indirect Expropriation.'

15   Professor Andrea Bjorklund explored the increasing reliance of arbitral tribunals on previous decisions which indicates the emergence of a 'Jurisprudence *constante*.' See Andrea K. Bjorklund, 'Investment Treaty Arbitral Decisions as "Jurisprudence Constante,"' in *International Economic Law: The State and Future of the Discipline* ed. Colin B. Picker, Isabella D. Bunn, and Douglas W. Arner (Oxford: Hart, 2008).

16   It is noteworthy that this approach is not novel; the Energy Charter Treaty embraced the strategic importance of energy resources and devised an instrument to protect and promote trade and investment in the energy sector.

around increasing water scarcity and stiffer competition for limited water resources between users in various economic sectors.

1.3 Expropriation: From Political to Regulatory Risk

Resource rich States have had a tendency to swing between liberalisation and nationalisation. Latin American countries, for instance, have a long history of attracting and discarding foreign investment in the areas of natural resources and public services. Besides the obvious implication from the perspective of political and social stability, such changes impose large transaction costs on investors and citizens, who ultimately suffer the consequences of such political swings.[17] Traditionally, this type of expropriation was not difficult to identify, since States' political motives were clear at the outset; political risk is nothing new.[18] However, from the perspective of an investor, political risk is not the only risk that investors face in their host States. As Wälde noted, overt takings of property rights are being replaced by a different kind of interference, reflected in the use of States' regulatory powers and the manner in which such powers are exercised.[19] The attention has thus turned towards the issue of regulatory risk. This means that the emerging field of international investment

---

17 During the last century, Latin American countries such as Argentina, Bolivia, Ecuador and Venezuela have swung between privatisation and nationalisation, involving foreign investment in different fashions and periods. The nationalisation of Petróleos de Venezuela S.A. (PDVSA) accounts for a number of measures adopted by Venezuela to recover the control of oil resources. Likewise, Bolivia has nationalised the provision of water supply and sanitation services (in Cochabamba and La Paz), electricity distribution (in La Paz and Oruro) between 2000 and 2012, and several other economic sectors.

18 The negotiation of the Energy Charter Treaty is associated with the risks involved in the development of energy infrastructure that requires extensive amounts of investment capital, which accounted to high sunk costs. Such costs could only be recouped during long periods of time that placed foreign investors in a position where they faced periods of high political risk and instability. Indeed, policy developments in the host State could undermine the economic arrangements that attracted the investor in the first place. See Wälde and Weiler, 'Investment arbitration under the Energy Charter Treaty in the light of new NAFTA precedents: Towards a global code of conduct for economic regulation,' 430; Wälde and Dow, 'Treaties and Regulatory Risk in Infrastructure Investment. The Effectiveness of International Law Disciplines versus Sanctions by Global Markets in Reducing the Political and Regulatory Risk for Private Infrastructure Investment,' 3.

19 See Wälde and Dow, 'Treaties and Regulatory Risk in Infrastructure Investment. The Effectiveness of International Law Disciplines versus Sanctions by Global Markets in Reducing the Political and Regulatory Risk for Private Infrastructure Investment,' 4.

INTRODUCTION

law and arbitration is now mainly confronted with the challenge of identifying legitimate (non-compensable) regulation from breaches of international standards of protection; in this case, indirect expropriation.

International lawyers have extensively discussed the methodological difficulties of identifying regulation from expropriation.[20] There are, in fact, a number of initiatives in the academic literature that have contributed to the development of a more coherent approach. The Organisation for Economic Cooperation and Development (OECD) has extensively discussed the challenges around indirect expropriation,[21] and in recent years, institutions such as the International Institute for Sustainable Development (IISD) have followed suit with analysis on the best practices around indirect expropriation.[22] The United Nations (UN) Conference for Trade and Development (UNCTAD) has also published new developments regarding the issue.[23] These are just a few examples that illustrate that the distinction between indirect expropriation and regulation remains unclear.

1.4   The Return of the State: A New Generation of IIAS

Capital importing States have shown their dissatisfaction with international investment law and policy by using their power to denounce their investment treaties. Some of these States have also denounced the ICSID Convention. Moreover, traditionally capital exporting States, some of which saw themselves as respondents in a number of investment disputes, used their power in

---

20   See for instance Vaughan Lowe, 'Regulation or expropriation?'; Brigitte Stern, 'In Search of the Frontiers of Indirect Expropriation,' ed. W. Arthur Rovine, *Contemporary Issues in International Arbitration and Mediation The Fordham Papers 2007* (Brill, the Netherlands: Martinus Nijhoff Publishers, 2007).

21   See OECD, '"Indirect Expropriation" and the "Right to Regulate" in International Investment Law,' (Paris: Organisation for Economic Co-operation and Development, 2004); OECD Secretariat, 'Draft OECD Principles for International Investor Participation in Infrastructure,' in OECD *Global Forum on International Investment. Enhancing the Investment Climate: the Case of Infrastructure* (Istanbul, Turkey: OECD, 2006).

22   Howard Mann, 'The Right of States to Regulate and International Investment Law'; Suzy H. Nikièma, 'Best practices indirect expropriation,' (Winnipeg, Man.: International Institute for Sustainable Development, 2012); Mann, Howard 'The Final Decision in Methanex V. United States: Some New Wine in Some New Bottles,' International Institute for Sustainable Development (IISD) (2005).

23   UNCTAD, 'EXPROPRIATION: A Sequel. UNCTAD Series on Issues in International Investment Agreements II,' (New York, Geneva: United Nations, 2012).

a different manner; they have sought to renegotiate investment treaty provisions that – they perceived – as restraining the exercise of their police power.

A new generation of IIAs started to emerge, including provisions that delineated the assessment of regulatory practice.[24] It is important to note, however, that there is still an important number of IIAs which contain traditional provisions regarding expropriation and compensation. Distinctions between provisions in early IIAs and in the so-called second generation of IIAs, may still create some uncertainty, from an investor as well as host State's perspective, as to how tribunals should approach the exercise of regulatory powers.

Under the provisions of traditional IIAs (first generation), investors enjoyed protection against undue interference with their covered investment. The definition of 'investment,' included in most IIAs, covers an often non-exhaustive list of investment rights and property interests, including the right to use water resources under a licence or permit.[25] It is undeniable that a regulatory measure with an effect on an investor's property rights, understood broadly, diminishes the value of the investment. Yet, there is also some indication that host States stall and could stop the implementation of regulations designed to pursue general welfare objectives when subjected to arbitral disputes.

From that perspective, the obligation to protect foreign investment under IIAs, on one hand, may be perceived as hindering States' prerogative to

---

24   2004 and 2012 United States Model BITs, the 2004 Canadian Model BIT, the Dominican Republic-Central American Free Trade Agreement (CAFTA) and others, which will be discussed in the next chapters.

25   Mark Kantor provides an account of the changes observed in the US Model BITs 2004 and 2012. He argues that the protected investment under BITs is quite similar to the property rights covered by the Takings Clause in the United States. In this vein Kantor cites the *Florida Rock Industries, Inc. v United States*, which states:
      'Property interests are about as diverse as the human mind can conceive. Property interests may be real and personal, tangible and intangible, possessory and non-possessory. They can be defined in terms of sequential rights to possession (present interests – life estates and various types of fees – and future interests), and in terms of shared interests (such as the various kinds of co-ownership). There are specially structured property interests (such as those of a mortgagee, lessee, bailee, adverse possessor), and there are interests in special kinds of things (such as water, and commercial contracts).' in *Florida Rock Industries, Inc. v United States* (Florida Rock IV), 18 F. 3d 1560, 1572 fn 32 (Fed Cir 1994). As cited by Kantor in: Mark Kantor, 'Little Has Changed in the New US Model Bilateral Investment Treaty,' *ICSID review: Foreign investment law journal* 27, no. 2 (2012): 346. See also *Parvanov, Parvan, and Mark Kantor, 'Comparing U.S. Law and Recent U.S. Investment Agreements: Much More Similar Than You Might Expect,' in Yearbook on International Investment Law and Policy, edited by Karl P. Sauvant. New York: Oxford Unversity Press, 2010–2011.*

INTRODUCTION

regulate water resources. The regulation of water resources, on the other hand, may have expropriatory effects over the property rights of foreign investors, in breach of the IIAs' obligations.[26] International law recognises the police power of States when it is exercised in good faith and in a non-discriminatory manner. Under this premise, investors could not reasonably expect a static regulatory environment; yet, they will have legitimate expectations if the host State provided implicit or explicit assurances of certain levels of regulatory stability.

In this context, the question arises as to whether a State should bear the burden of risk for compromising the management of its water resources in order to comply with investment treaty obligations. Or whether a State should bear the burden of costs that involve the payment of compensation in favour of the investor for exercising its right to regulate its water resources. If the answer to the above inquiries is no, does this mean that the investor – and not the State – should bear these burdens?

Judge Higgins observed during her lectures at the Hague Academy of International Law:

> every time a judge decides whether compensation is not due, he is really deciding whether such losses shall be borne by the individuals on whom they happen to fall.[27]

Higgins, noting the development of the US jurisprudence on takings, expressed difficulties in appreciating the underlying policy that distinguishes a taking for the public purpose, which entails the right to compensation, from an 'indirect taking' through regulatory action, which does not.[28] The question is difficult and will depend on the interest at stake. There will be measures that fall within a narrow scope of the exercise of the police power (*strictu sensu*); such measures must be associated to the protection of welfare objectives e.g. environment, public health and morals. Other measures may fall within a broader exercise of the police power (*latu sensu*); those measures in turn may reflect host States' changes of public policy e.g. redistribution of welfare. It is clear, however, that each type of exercise of the police power must be subject to a different standard of review.

---

26   Muñoz, Hugo, 'La administración del agua y la inversión extranjera directa ¿Cómo se relacionan?' in *Estudios en homenaje al Dr Rafael González Ballar*, ed. Universidad de Costa Rica (San Jose: Isolma S.A., 2009).

27   See Rosalyn Higgins, 'The Taking of Property by the State. Recent Developments in International Law' *Recueil des Cours* (*The Hague Academy of International Law*) T. 176(1982), 277, 330–31.

28   *Ibid.*, 330–31.

Against this backdrop, it has been observed that the mere initiation of investment arbitration proceedings already constitutes a considerable burden for governments. In some cases, States have repealed their regulatory measures under the imminent possibility of being found in breach of an investment obligation. The anxieties of litigation may cause 'regulatory chill' on the side of host States' regulatory activity. Cases such as *Ethyl v. Canada*,[29] *SunBelt v. Canada*,[30] *Vattenfall v. Germany*,[31] illustrate this situation. In contrast, there have been cases where the host State justified the legitimate exercise of its police power successfully. Examples of such cases are *Methanex v. US, Chemtura v. Canada*,[32] *and S.D. Myers v. Canada*.[33] The prospect of an investment dispute relating to regulatory activity and the possibility that a host State will have to pay a large amount of compensation appears to go to the very core of State's sovereignty. Current negotiations of the Transatlantic Trade and Investment Partnership (TTIP) between the European Union (EU) and the US illustrate this point.[34]

---

29   In this case the Government of Canada imposed a ban on the importation of Ethyl products (gasoline additive MMT), the measure was challenged by the American investor claiming USD 251 million for losses arising from the expropriatory measure. See *Ethyl Corporation v. the Governments of Canada*, UNICTRAL, Award on Jurisdiction of 24 June, 1998.

30   In this case, the claimant sought restatement of the water export licences granted previously by British Columbia and payment of compensation for the loss of business opportunity. Alternatively, Sun Belt claimed compensation for permanent loss of business opportunity. See *Sun Belt v. Her Majesty the Queen (Government of Canada)*, under UNCITRAL Rules, Notice of Claim and Demand for Arbitration of 12 October, 1999.

31   *Vattenfall AB, Vattenfal Europe AG, Vattenfall Europe Generation AG v. Federal Republic of Germany*, ICSID Case No. ARB/09/6. This case will be further analysed in Chapter 6.

32   *Chemtura Corporation v. Canada*, UNCITRAL Award of 2 August, 2010.

33   *S.D. Myers, Inc. v. the Government of Canada*, UNCITRAL, Partial Award of 13 November, 2000. In this case, however, the claimant was granted compensation on grounds other than expropriation, namely national treatment and minimum standard of treatment.

34   Stephan Schill, 'The TTIP Negotiations: US versus EU Leadership in Global Investment Governance,' Kluwer Arbitration Blog, 5 March, 2016. Available at: http://kluwerarbitrationblog.com/2016/03/05/the-ttip-negotiations-us-versus-eu-leadership-in-global-investment-governance/, last visited 30 June 2016; Krista Hughes and Philip Blenkinsop, 'U.S. Wary of EU Proposal for Investment Court in Trade Pact.' Reuters (29 October 2015). Available at: http://www.reuters.com/article/us-trade-ttip-idUSKCN0SN2LH20151029, last visited 30 June 2016; Shawn Donnan, 'Transatlantic trade: Hard sell,' *Financial Times*, 8 June, 2014.

INTRODUCTION

The TTIP negotiations came after the second generation of IIAs emerged. These new treaties were arguably led by the US and its 2004 Model BIT, which embodied provisions clarifying the application of standards of protection; notably fair and equitable treatment and expropriation. They also reflect the contention of the US Congress, which asserts that US law, on the whole, provides already a high level of protection for investments. These modifications seek to ensure, as a consequence, that foreign investors in the US do not enjoy greater protection than US investors in the territory of the US.[35]

Despite the criticism and distrust that the investment regime stirred among capital importing States, practitioners of other areas of law and civil society, the second generation of IIAs indicate that states still endorse an international investment treaty and arbitration regime for the protection of foreign investment. The continuous increase in the number of IIAs, demonstrates that States still negotiate and conclude BITs, and increasingly also, FTAS.

1.5 A Framework to Identify Legitimate Regulation from Indirect Expropriation: Why Water Resources?

Each element of the environment is special in its own right, and the legal frameworks that regulate them reflect this fact. Yet, water – as will be illustrated in Chapters 2 and 3 – is unique; it is the combination of all its characteristics together that makes it this way. Perhaps the first and foremost distinct characteristic is that water has no known substitutes and its direct consumption is so essential to life that it is regulated as a *common good*[36] in most legal systems.

Rarely in the context of investment treaty arbitration have governments argued the importance of managing the *quality* of their water resources so as to pursue welfare goals. Perhaps, this is because the said spheres of regulation, which rest within the police power of States (*strictu sensu*), enjoy higher levels of deference. However, disguised acts of expropriation triggered by political agendas and social pressure, should not be ruled out. Special attention must be paid to the natural resources sector.

---

35 David Schneiderman, Constitutionalizing Economic Globalization: Investment Rules and Democracy's Promise, (Cambridge, U.K.; New York: Cambridge University Press, 2008), 74.

36 This work refers to water as a common good, generally as synonymous of common-pool resources. This term is used and explained by Elinor Ostrom and it is further developed and clarified in Chapter 3, Section 3.2.3.

Arguably most water-related disputes could arise out of the management of water resources and its effect on water rights.[37] While this work argues the importance of looking into the host State's domestic law, it acknowledges challenges of addressing all water legal systems. Yet, it is possible to identify commonalities across the board which may illustrate the precarious nature of water rights under most domestic laws. Essentially, the establishment of water rights systems are associated to the physical variability of water resources, which is different from other natural resources such as oil, gas, forests or land.

In order to bridge the fields of water and investment, Chapter 3 introduces a number of principles of water governance and resources management, as well as the regulation and appropriation of water rights at the national level. It is common ground that investors' property rights are acquired and shaped through the domestic legal systems of the host State, whereas the protection of such property rights occurs under the rules of international law. For this reason, it is relevant to understand how domestic laws incorporate current and potential challenges around water resources, embracing the increasing need for adaptive and integrated management.

In the context of international investment law, the provisions contained in the 2004 (and 2012) US Model BIT, replicated in several agreements of the new generation, provide further guidance on the determination of whether measures adopted by host States in exercise of their police power are legitimate. On the basis of these innovations in the law of international investment, this work aims to contribute to the literature by proposing a framework of analysis focusing on claims of indirect expropriation arising out of water regulatory measures. The criteria embedded in such a framework could also provide useful guidance to host States to test the legality of a regulatory measure that might potentially be deemed expropriatory. In so doing, the framework of analysis adopts a sector-specific approach, because water has inherent characteristics that make it different from other natural resources. This special nature is reflected, for instance, in the natural variability of water, which covers two aspects: unreliability and adaptability.

In this light, governments must adopt specific defences. Such arguments will direct the assessment of potential investment disputes to the core of the

---

37   The term 'water-related measures' refers, in this context, to the allocation, management, the regulation of uses and permits to use water resources, which may differ from the laws regulating the supply of water services, its infrastructure, operation costs, investment costs, and pricing, among others. The supply of water services may fall within the scope of the law of water resources, predominantly regarding allocation and use of water resources.

INTRODUCTION

regulatory measure, providing improved clarity of the governmental measure and the circumstances of its adoption. There might also be disputes over water quantities in which governments may be required to justify the need for allocating or reallocating water resources in a different manner than originally planned. In such cases, the examination of the issue may fall within a broader sphere of regulatory prerogative – different from the protection of public health, environment and safety – which calls for stricter scrutiny of the measure at issue.

There exist reasonable challenges to the strict application of IIA provisions, in spite of the broader implications on stakeholders and economic sectors within the host State. However, there are also challenges as to whether a systemic approach to the interpretation and application of investment agreements can be sustained, and how far it should be taken.[38] Most of the literature discussing the relationship between international investment law and other areas of law such as environmental law, human rights, labour law, etc. focus on the desirability to reconcile IIAs obligations of investment protection with other societal values or welfare objectives. Some of these welfare objectives constitute obligations enshrined in other international agreements and declarations, requiring complex methods of incorporation into investment agreements.[39] Among the methodologies put forward to assist both the parties to the dispute and arbitrators in deciding such disputes, the literature covers the principle of systemic integration of IIAs with other relevant rules of international law, such as environmental agreements, human rights obligations, labour standards and trans-boundary watercourses agreements, under Article 31(3)(c) of the Vienna Convention on the Law of Treaties (VCLT).[40] Further, some authors propose

---

38 See for instance *Glamis Gold, Ltd v. United States of America,* Award under UNICTRAL Rules of 8 June, 2009, and the analysis of Professor Michael Reisman of the systemic approach adopted by the tribunal in that dispute. W. Michael Reisman, "'Case Specific Mandates" versus "Systemic Implications": How Should Investment Tribunals Decide? The Freshfields Arbitration Lecture' *Arbitration International* 29, no. 2 (2013).

39 Those values maybe focused on human rights, the environment, indigenous rights, health, safety, security, water resources, and sustainable development. There are many societal concerns that are potentially affected by the operations of foreign investors, whether such an effect is attributable to the investor or not.

40 For authoritative writings in the area of treaty interpretation see Campbell McLachlan, 'The principle of systemic integration and Article 31(3) (C) of the Vienna Convention' *International and comparative law quarterly* 54, no. 2 (2005); Diane A. Desierto, 'Conflict of Treaties, Interpretation, and Decision-Making on Human Rights and Investment During Economic Crises,' *TDM* 1(2013); William W. Burke-White and Andreas Von Staden, 'Investment Protection in Extraordinary Times: The Interpretation and Application of

that investment dispute resolution should resort to analytical frameworks to address conflict of laws in trade and international investment law.[41] Water lawyers observe the asymmetric relations between investors and States, under the assumption that the interests of investors are widely protected by investment tribunals with detrimental effects to States. This approach advocates for the application of general principles of law accepted by relevant legal systems.[42] A specific analysis of these approaches is beyond the scope of this work; nonetheless, it does not disregard their assistance to arbitrators when applying the proposed framework of analysis.

In addition, it is appropriate to clarify that the supply of water services is not the focus of this work because the provision and regulation of water services has more in common with the regulation of other network infrastructure for the delivery of public utilities. Yet, one cannot ignore the sensitivities and feeling of entitlement that water inspires in users and communities as evidenced by past disputes over water service investments.

The analysis of water-related measures, in the context of investment arbitration, considers the large number of IIAs of the first and second generation that are currently in force. The second generation of IIAs, as argued earlier, develops important clarifications in the interpretation of the provisions linked to indirect expropriation and the prerogative of States to regulate. Such clarifications may elucidate a sense of obligation of States and investors towards an emergent standard of review that defers to the exercise of regulatory prerogatives. Therefore, the scope of analysis does not cover a conflict preventive approach, it rather aims to assist the investor-State dispute settlement mechanism to progress into a more predictable and consistent method of assessment.

Non-Precluded Measures Provisions in Bilateral Investment Treaties,' *University of Pennsylvania Law School Public Law and Legal Theory Research Paper Series* No. #07-14 (2007); Bruno Simma and Theodore Kill, 'Harmonizing Investment Protection and International Human Rights: First Steps Towards Methodology,' in *International Investment Law for the 21st Century Essays in Honour of Christoph Schreuer*, ed. Ursula Kriebaum Christina Binder, August Reinisch, and Stephan Wittich (Oxford, New York: Oxford University Press, 2009); J. Romesh Weeramantry, *Treaty Interpretation in Investment Arbitration* (Oxford, U.K.: Oxford University Press, 2012).

41 The work of Pauwelyn in the context of the potential conflicts between WTO law and other societal values constitutes an important example. See Joost Pauwelyn, *Conflict of norms in public international law: How WTO law relates to other rules of international law* (Cambridge, UK; New York: Cambridge University Press, 2003).

42 See Miguel Solanes and Andrei Jouravlev, 'Revisiting Privatization, Foreign Investment, International Arbitration and Water.'

CHAPTER 2

The Special Nature of Water Resources

2.1 Introduction

Water is essential to life of humans, animals and plants, it is also pivotal to any economic undertaking, and what is more it has no possible substitutes. As the Ohio Supreme Court of the United States (US) eloquently stated:

> water is a *sine qua non* of the happiness, health, welfare, and agricultural and industrial progress of the state. Its absence or presence makes the difference between a desert and a garden. It is essential to preserve life of both man and beast, and industrial progress and development depend in a tremendous measure upon an adequate underground water supply.[1]

One cannot address issues of water scarcity from a policy or legal perspectives, without exploring the nature of water and the growing pressures affecting its sustainability. This chapter discusses the nature of water resources by exploring its physical characteristics, as well as its social, economic and environmental aspects.[2]

Pressures over water resources are often the effect of economic globalisation and trade. As will be discussed later in this chapter, economic development and wealth generate further demand for water to produce water intensive products. These products range from foodstuffs, clothing, information technology products and transport. Increased production and demand pose challenges on the long-term sustainability and availability of water resources.

2.2 The Unique Nature of Water Resources

Whether water is unique may be contested in different contexts. Admittedly, water is not the only element essential to sustain life; air and energy are also

---

1 The Court was confronted to the question of whether an environmental amendment was to be applied to groundwater resources. See *State v. Martin, 168 Ohio St. 37, 151 N.E.2d 7 (1958)*, 11 in Joseph M. Reidy, 'Cline v. American Aggregates Corp. an Ohio Waterloo?' *Capital University Law Review* 13 (1983–1984), 684.

2 Note that these perspectives also constitute drivers for water scarcity; hence, one can expect some overlap in the coming sections.

vital for human survival. However, air is not yet a scarce resource and energy can be generated from readily available resources, preventing scarcity – at least – in the near future.

Approaching water policy and regulation requires an understanding of water resources' physical characteristics, its social contours and its historical and geographical context.[3]

The hydrological cycle is a global system, which affects us all. Any changes in the cycle for reasons of consumption, pollution, climate change or simply nature have a global effect. This unique nature of water is better appreciated from environmental, social and economic perspectives. Regrettably, current uses and abuses of water resources and growing demand put pressures over the availability of quantities necessary to meet basic needs in several regions of the world.

Furthermore, water is often perceived as an asset; consequently, the regulation of water rights – granted to users – may not always be consistent with the physical nature of water resources. In fact, modern policy allocation has changed the structure of water rights and its historical relation to land and the environment. As a result, users perceive water as a resource to be sustainably exploited, a tradable good to be cost-effectively managed 'rather than the basic substance that makes life on earth possible.'[4]

While economists and lawyers have traditionally advocated for secured rights, hydrologists and scientists are conscious of the unpredictable nature of water resources, which disputes the security of such rights. Practitioners from other fields of knowledge, such as economics, argue that water specialists fail to see the larger picture due to their specific knowledge of the subject just 'like the father who refuses to see that his daughter is just a girl.'[5]

2.2.1 *The Physical Characteristics of Water Resources*

Water is a finite and vulnerable resource;[6] 97.5 per cent of which is in the oceans and the remaining 2.5 per cent, is fresh water. From this amount of

---

3   '[I]n order to understand water policy and address current societal needs, […] one must first appreciate the uniqueness of water as revealed in both its physical characteristics and the law's historical approach to water resource issues.' Barton Thompson Jr citing Professor Sax. See Barton H. Jr Thompson, 'Water Law as a Pragmatic Exercise: Professor Joseph Sax's Water Scholarship,' *Ecology Law Quarterly* 25 (1998–1999), 367.

4   Philippe Cullet, 'Water Law in a Globalised World: the Need for a New Conceptual Framework,' *Journal of Environmental Law* 23, no. 2 (2011), 6.

5   Hubert H.G. Savenije, 'Why water is not an ordinary economic good, or why the girl is special,' *Physics and Chemistry of the Earth* 27 (2002), 741.

6   *Dublin Statement on Water and Sustainable Development*, Dublin 31 January, 1992.

THE SPECIAL NATURE OF WATER RESOURCES   19

water, only 1.2 per cent is surface fresh water, 30.1 per cent is groundwater and 68.7 per cent is, currently, frozen in ice caps and glaciers.[7]

Water quantities remain invariable in nature, albeit unevenly distributed in a geographical context.[8] Its finite nature relies mainly on the fact that, in some regions, it cannot be replenished at the same rate at which it is withdrawn.[9]

Physically, water is a system, elusive and bulky. The hydrological cycle constitutes an indivisible system that involves complex processes of rainfall, run-off, infiltration, recharge, seepage, re-infiltration and moisture recycling. These processes are all interconnected and interdependently related to one direction of flow: downstream.[10] Any use of water affects subsequent demands, because it affects the entire cycle.[11]

In contrast to the static nature of land, forests and oil, water is physically elusive and, unless captured and stored, it is in constant state of flux.[12] Water bulkiness greatly affects its transportability.[13]

Finally, water has no substitutes. Indeed, there is no other possible natural resource to which users could turn to when water is not available. This characteristic will be addressed later in this chapter; for now, it suffices to stress that what makes water special is not each characteristic independently considered, but rather the combination of all of them and the aggregate effect that each of them has on its sustainability.

---

7   United States Geological Survey, 'Distribution of Earth's Water,' http://water.usgs.gov/edu/earthwherewater.html, accessed May 5, 2016.

8   'There is precisely the same amount of [water] on the planet as there was in the age of the dinosaurs, and the world's population of more than 6.7 billion people has to share the same quantity as the 300 million global inhabitants of Roman times.' In Geoffrey Lean, 'Water scarcity "now bigger threat than financial crisis,"' *The Independent, 15 March 2009.*

9   World Water Assessment Programme, 'The United Nations World Water Development Report 2: Water a Shared Responsibility,' Paris – New York: United Nations, 2006, 116; Meena Palaniappan and Peter H. Gleick, 'Peak Water,' in *The World's Water 2008–2009: The Biennial Report on Freshwater Resources*, ed. Peter H. Gleick, et al., (Washington: Pacific Institute for Studies in Development, Environment and Security, 2009), 1.

10   Savenije, 'Why water is not an ordinary economic good, or why the girl is special,' 742.

11   'Use of soil moisture diminishes the availability of groundwater; use of groundwater diminishes the availability of surface water etc. Thus any use of water affects the entire water cycle.' In Pieter Van der Zaag and Huber H.G. Savenije, 'Water as an economic good: the value of pricing and the failure of markets,' *Value of Water* Research Report Series no. 19 (2006), 9.

12   Savenije, 'Why water is not an ordinary economic good, or why the girl is special,' 142.

13   *Ibid.* Note that the cost of transportation would exceed the actual value of water, in contrast to most commodities which reflect the costs of production and transportation in the final price.

20   CHAPTER 2

In this context, human consumption and land use interfere with the water cycle, because they affect surface and ground water. Climate change is also affecting water's temporal availability due to evaporation of ocean and fresh waters. These effects are drivers of water variability, which in turn trigger physical and economic redistribution among competing users.

As water does not recognize national territories, it moves according to its natural flow. This means that upstream interferences affect downstream flows both at the national and international levels. The reverse, however, is also possible, downstream users may affect upstream users. Indeed, projects associated with water resources such as dams, mining, irrigation undertaken by downstream users could create historic rights or 'prescriptive rights gained with time,' foreclosing future water demand for upstream users.[14] Current use of water resources for projects in riparian States – upstream or downstream – could create expectations of future quantities of water allocation, not acknowledged by other riparian. As such, reduced downstream availability of water resources can clearly create tensions among competing users, which can in turn cause conflicts between States when transboundary interference is involved.

Addressing problems of water variability and allocation requires an understanding of the most important water demands and their interaction. Looking at water resources from three perspectives, namely environmental, economic and social, may assist such an understanding. Since all three are interconnected, their discussion may involve some unavoidable overlap.

2.2.2   *The Environmental Perspective*

Humans, as well as animals, plants and other microorganisms are part of complex and dynamic units, called ecosystems.[15] The hydrological cycle integrates

---

14   Salman analyses the case of the Baardhere Dam and Water Infrastructure Project in Somalia, involving the use of water of the Juba River of which Ethiopia is an upstream riparian. In this case the World Bank was requested by Somalia to notify Ethiopia of its intentions to develop the project. In response, Ethiopia exposed their future plans of hydroelectricity and irrigation expansions using waters of the Juba River, and expressed concerns for the harm that Somalia's project may cause to their rights over such waters. Although the conclusion of the World Bank and its independent experts was that the project would not foreclose Ethiopia's future water demand, the project was cancelled due to the political situation in Somalia. See Salman M.A. Salman, 'Downstream Riparians Can Also Harm Upstream Riparians: The Concept of Foreclosure of Future Uses,' *Water International* 35, no. 4 (2010), 359–62.

15   The Millennium Ecosystems Assessment Programme defines Ecosystem as follows: 'An ecosystem is a dynamic complex of plant, animal, and microorganism communities and the non-living environment interacting as a functional unit. Humans are an integral part

THE SPECIAL NATURE OF WATER RESOURCES

all the components of ecosystems, such as land, air, forests and livelihoods, all of which, require water in appropriate quantities. Interference in the water cycle, mainly by human action, has an effect on other natural resources, ecosystems and their services. Water quality is therefore essential to the wellbeing of ecosystems and has an impact on the occurrence of droughts, floods, and food and energy production.[16]

There is an inescapable interconnection between the economic, social and environmental perspectives to water resources. Economic and human development require energy, industrial production, and irrigation, all of which, demand large quantities of water resources. This large demand for water involves, in turn, diversion and storage, potentially affecting watershed repletion.[17] Finally, while consumptive uses of water affect availability, non-consumptive uses are likely to affect water quality,[18] creating additional demand for environmental flows.[19]

The Congo Basin's forests, for instance, generate 75 to 95 per cent of rainfall in the region and about 17 per cent of West Africa's rainfall.[20] However, as many river basins in Africa and Asia, it is largely affected by pollution of wastewater discharges and mining.[21] Indeed developing countries are particularly

---

of ecosystems. Ecosystems vary enormously in size; a temporary pond in a tree hollow and an ocean basin can both be ecosystems'. See Millennium Ecosystem Assessment, 'MA Conceptual Framework,' in *Ecosystems and Human Well-being: Current State and Trends, Volume 1: Findings of the Condition and Trends Working Group of the Millennium Ecosystem Assessment*, ed. Rashid Hassan, Robert Scholes, and Neville Ash (Washington, Covelo, London: Island Press, 2003), Box 1.1: Key Definitions, 27.

16   *Ibid.*

17   See Ronald C. Griffin, *Water Resources Economics. The Analysis of Scarcity, Policies and Projects* (Cambridge, Mass.: MIT Press, 2006), Ch. 2.

18   Consumptive use of water, consist of water withdrawals from available sources, which will not return to the water cycle, such use can be found for instance in irrigation and food production. Non-consumptive uses of water, on the other hand, constitute the use of water that can be returned to the water cycle, weather treated or not, e.g. hydro-electricity generation, cooling systems, recreational uses of water and mining.

19   Sandra L. Postel, 'Securing water for people, crops, and ecosystems: New mindset and new priorities,' *Natural Resources Forum* 27, no. 2 (2003), 90–91.

20   Dimple Roy, Jane Barr, and Henry David Venema, 'Ecosystems Approaches in Integrated Water Resources Management (IWRM). A Review of Transboundary River Basins,' IISD and UNEP-DHI Centre for Water and Environment, August 2011, 17.

21   The United Nations World Water Development Report 3 (WWDR3) briefly identifies two main types of polluted water: (1) Black water, which contains the greatest level of pollution, usually with microbes; it is, therefore, unsuitable for human or ecological consumption; and (2) Grey water, which contains lower levels of contamination than black water

vulnerable to ecosystems degradation, due to the lack of appropriate control and monitoring mechanisms. The shrinking of the Aral Sea in Central Asia, as well as the depletion of fish stocks and catchment degradation in Lake Victoria in Africa, constitute striking examples of depletion of ecosystems due to over-consumption and diversion of water resources.[22]

Finally, climate change constitutes a powerful driver of water stress.[23] The World Development Report 2011 asserts that the impact of climate change on climate variability, food production, and energy generation remains to be fully observed.[24] Lack of reliability in rainfall is likely to affect social and economic dynamics within States, affecting their ability to sustain those Millennium Development Goals that have been achieved.[25]

In relation to international investment and water for the protection of the environment, two issues should be considered: first, as sustainability of ecosystem services and biodiversity require fresh water resources to survive and

---

and could be reused; it is generated from domestic activities e.g. laundry, bathing and other washing. See World Water Assessment Programme, 'The United Nations World Water Development Report 3: Water in a Changing World,' Paris – London: United Nations, 2009, 162.

22   World Water Assessment Programme, 'The United Nations World Water Development Report 3,' 128. See also UNEP, 'GEO: Year Book 2003,' in *GEO: Global Environment Outlook* (Washington: United Nations, 2003), available at http://www.unep.org/yearbook/2003/, accessed May 7, 2016. For the case of Lake Victoria, see World Water Assessment Programme, 'The United Nations World Water Development Report 2,' Box 5.1, 163.

23   On the effects of Climate Change see for instance World Water Assessment Programme, 'The United Nations World Water Development Report 3,' Chapter 5; World Bank, 'World Development Report 2011: Conflict, Security, and Development,' Washington: World Bank, 2011; William R. Sutton, Jitendra P. Srivastava, and James E. Neumann, 'Looking beyond the Horizon: How Climate Change Impacts and Adaptation Responses will reshape Agriculture in Eastern Europe and Central Asia,' Washington D.C: World Bank, 2013, available at http://documents.worldbank.org/curated/en/2013/03/17473996/looking-beyond-horizon-climate-change-impacts-adaptation-responses-reshape-agriculture-eastern-europe-central-asia, accessed 7 May, 2016; Bryson C. Bates *et al.*, 'Climate Change and Water. IPCC Technical Paper IV,' Geneva: Intergovernmental Panel on Climate Change, 2008, available at http://ipcc.ch/pdf/technical-papers/climate-change-water-en.pdf, accessed May 7, 2016; Scientific United Nations Educational, Cultural Organization, 'The United Nations World Water Development Report (WWDR4),' Paris: UNESCO – United Nations. 2012.

24   World Bank, 'World Development Report 2011: Conflict, Security, and Development,' 35.

25   Claudia W. Sadoff and Mike Muller, 'Perspectives on water and climate change adaptation. Better water resources management – Greater resilience today, more effective adaptation tomorrow,' Stockholm: Global Water Partnership, 2009, 4.

THE SPECIAL NATURE OF WATER RESOURCES

restore from pollution and degradation, water demand for environmental protection competes with other uses of water resources.[26] In the past, this demand was taken for granted and not accounted for in the allocation of water resources; now it is known that the environment requires water. Second, potential reallocation of water for pollution abatement, ecosystems protection and/or climate change adaptability could affect users' current water entitlements, leading to potential claims of expropriation of water rights.[27]

The protection of the environment, in a broad sense, is of great importance within the field of international economic law, and subject to intense scrutiny by Non-Governmental Organisations (NGOs) and citizens alike.

2.2.3 *The Economic Perspective*

It is increasingly difficult to challenge that water has an economic value that needs to be accounted for, when allocating water resources.

The fourth 'Dublin principle' states that water has an economic value in all its competing uses. Yet, while the principle recognises the right of all humans to access clean water and sanitation at an affordable price, it acknowledges the importance of achieving 'efficient and equitable use' through managing water as an economic good. In doing so, States may provide incentives to avoid wasteful use and induce the adoption of conservation measures.[28]

---

26   The WHO estimates that eight litres of water are required to dilute one litre of 'grey water.' See Stuart Orr, Anton Cartwright, and Dave Tickner, 'Understanding water risks: A primer on the consequences of water scarcity for government and business,' World Wildlife Fund, 2009, 20.

27   See Howard Mann, 'The Right of States to Regulate and International Investment Law,' Geneva: IISD, 2002; Howard Mann, 'Who Owns "Your" Water? Reclaiming Water as a Public Good under International Trade and Investment Law,' Geneva: IISD, 2003; Miguel Solanes and Andrei Jouravlev, 'Revisiting Privatization, Foreign Investment, International Arbitration and Water,' Santiago, Chile: United Nations, 2007; Hugo Muñoz, 'La administración del agua y la inversión extranjera directa ¿Cómo se relacionan?' in *Estudios en homenaje al Dr Rafael González Ballar*, ed. Universidad de Costa Rica (San Jose: Isolma S.A., 2009).

28   Principle No. 4 – *Water has an economic value in all its competing uses and should be recognized as an economic good*: 'Within this principle, it is vital to recognize first the basic right of all human beings to have access to clean water and sanitation at an affordable price. Past failure to recognize the economic value of water has led to wasteful and environmentally damaging uses of the resource. Managing water as an economic good is an important way of achieving efficient and equitable use, and of encouraging conservation and protection of water resources.' *Dublin Statement on Water and Sustainable Development*, Dublin 31 January, 1992.

There is disagreement as to the manner in which this principle should be interpreted.[29] Some experts argue that under the fourth principle, the market will naturally allocate a price to water, based on the value given by each user.[30] Therefore, under competition, water would be priced to its highest economic value, possibly limiting access to water to those unable to pay the market price.[31] The second school of thought does not strictly incorporate the element of financial interaction in its interpretation.[32] In other words, it does not consider water's economic value as based solely on price. It suggests to take into account uses and users that are unable to afford a price, such as ecosystems, cultural and recreational uses, the production of food for personal consumption, etc. This view follows the idea that each of the Dublin principles should be interpreted in light of the others.[33]

Foreign investment is often driven to regions where water is abundant and cheap, and where governments have not yet addressed the real value of water. When this calculation is finally made and a regulatory framework for water resources is put in place, it is likely that foreign as well as national investors see their interests affected by such regulatory changes. This problem could be exacerbated by the lack of substitutes for water.

Indeed, one of the most important characteristics of water, from an economic perspective, is the lack of substitutes. If the price of water were to reflect its real value, its price elasticity demand would be close to zero (inelastic).[34] The ultimate backstop of water would still be water from a different source, such as oceans, but this solution still involves high desalination and transport costs.[35]

---

29 Van der Zaag and Savenije, 'Water as an economic good: the value of pricing and the failure of markets.' 7.

30 *Ibid.*

31 See Green, referring to the neo-classical interpretation of the fourth Dublin statement: Kenneth C. Green, 'If Only Life Were That Simple; Optimism and Pessimism in Economics,' *Physics and Chemistry of the Earth* 25, no. 3 (2000), 205–06.

32 Van der Zaag and Savenije, 'Water as an economic good: the value of pricing and the failure of markets,' 7.

33 Green, 'If Only Life Were That Simple; Optimism and Pessimism in Economics,' 206.

34 The notion of cross-price elasticity demand is relevant to explain the responsiveness of demand toward one good when the price of another good is changed. See Robert S. Pindyck and Daniel L. Rubinfeld, *Microeconomics*, 6th ed. (New Delhi: Prentice Hall of India, 2006), 34.

35 Palaniappan and Gleick, 'Peak Water,' 8–9. It is worth noting that while desalination technologies are rapidly developing, they still imply high costs of operation and for the environment.

THE SPECIAL NATURE OF WATER RESOURCES   25

Economic sectors with intensive consumption of water such as agriculture, which amounts to 70 per cent of water demand,[36] have been often criticised for being wasteful and inefficient.[37] However, addressing this problem through the use of water from non-consumptive uses is also problematic. Water uses are often difficult to harmonise, due to seasonal or geographical incompatibilities. Hydropower generation could transfer water either for agricultural irrigation or human consumption.[38] Still, hydropower demands larger volumes of water during the winter season, when energy demand is high, making its use unlikely for agricultural purposes because crops are typically consumptive of water in the spring and summer seasons.[39] National authorities are, therefore, confronted with numerous trade-offs, as they are called to prioritise and allocate water resources in case of scarcity and, in line with economic and social development policies.

2.2.4   *The Social Perspective – The Human Right to Water*

Social perspectives on water focus mainly on the problem of access to water for human consumption, such as supply of drinking water and sanitation. However, there are many more social uses of water resources, such as cultural and recreational, as well as the empowerment of indigenous and women's rights through water management.[40] These aspects are all interlinked and raise concerns about increasing stress over water resources.[41]

Access to safe drinking water and sanitation are essential to human development. But as several reports highlight the negative effects of the water crisis

---

36   Kerry Turner *et al.*, 'Economic valuation of water resources in agriculture: From the sectoral to a functional perspective of natural resource management,' Rome: Food and Agriculture Organization of the United Nations (FAO), 2004, 3.

37   Agriculture 'is often criticized for high wastage and inefficient use of water at the point of consumption (i.e. at farm level) encouraged by subsidized low charges for water use or low energy tariffs for pumping. It is often claimed that the charges made for irrigation water, fail to signal the scarcity of the resource to farmers.' *Ibid.*

38   Palaniappan and Gleick, 'Peak Water,' 6.

39   See for instance, the conflicts of water availability schedules in Central Asia in Victor A. Dukhovny and Vadim I. Sokolov, *Integrated Water Resources Management: Experience and Lessons Learned from Central Asia – towards the Fourth World Water Forum*, (Tashkent: GWP – CACENA, 2005), 18.

40   World Water Assessment Programme, 'The United Nations World Water Development Report 3,' 38, 51.

41   *Ibid.*, 36–39.

emphasize water inequality[42] and multidimensional poverty, among others.[43] There are still 780 million people lacking access to safe drinking water and 2.5 billion live without improved sanitation, as forecasted by the Millennium Development Goals status report.[44]

The International Covenant on Social, Economic and Cultural Rights recognised the right to quality of life and fulfilment of basic human needs.[45] The right to water was first addressed in 2002 by the Committee on Economic Social and Cultural Rights, which embedded the human right to water in Articles 11 and 12 of the Covenant.[46] In 2010 the General Assembly of the UN expressly

---

42   Note for instance that residents of poor areas in developing countries, such as Accra and Manila, paid more for water supply than residents in London and New York. See UNDP, 'Human Development Report 2006. Beyond scarcity: Power, poverty and the global water crisis,' New York: United Nations, 2006, 1, 52.

43   UNDP, 'Human Development Report 2010. 20th Anniversary Edition. The Real Wealth of Nations: Pathways to Human Development,' New York: United Nations, 2010, 96. The notion of multidimensional poverty is explained in the HDR in terms of The Multidimensional Poverty Index (MPI), which identifies 'multiple deprivations at the individual level in health, education and standard of living.' In this case standard of living is estimated by thresholds of basic access to services, such electricity, clean drinking water, adequate sanitation, clean cooking fuel. It also refer to accessibility to basic goods, such having a home with a dirt-free floor, owning a car, a truck or similar motorized vehicle, and owning at most one of these assets: bicycle, motorcycle, radio, refrigerator, telephone. See *ibid.*, 221.

44   WHO, 'Progress on Drinking Water and Sanitation. 2012 Update,' Geneva: WHO, 2012, 4–5, available at http://www.unicef.org/publications/index_69025.html, accessed May 7, 2016. See also WHO/UNICEF Joint Monitoring Programme for Water Supply and Sanitation (JMP), 'Progress on Sanitation and Drinking Water. 2010 Update,' Geneva: WHO/UNICEF, 2010, 6–7; and United Nations, 'The Millennium Development Goals: Report 2010,' New York: United Nations, 2010, 58, 61.

45   See Article 11 (Right to an Adequate Standard of Living) and Article 12 (Right to Health) of the International Covenant on Economic, Social and Cultural Rights, General Assembly Resolution 2200A (XXI) of 16 December 1966 (ratification and accession), entry into force 3 January 1976.

46   See UN Committee on Economic, Social and Cultural Rights, *General Comment No. 15: The Right to Water (Articles 11 and 12 of the Covenant)*, 20 January 2003, E/C.12/2002/11, paras 1–3. See also: UN Human Rights Council, *Report of the Independent Expert on the Issue of Human Rights Obligations related to Access to Safe Drinking Water and Sanitation, Catarina de Albuquerque, Addendum,* 1 July 2010, A/HRC/15/31/Add.1; UN Human Rights Council, *Human rights and access to safe drinking water and sanitation,* 6 October A/HRC/ RES/15/9; UN Human Rights Council, *Human rights and access to safe drinking water and sanitation,* 24 September, 2010, A/HRC/15/L.14,.

THE SPECIAL NATURE OF WATER RESOURCES   27

recognised the human right to water and sanitation, acknowledging that it is an important vehicle to realise the other human rights.[47]

The realisation of the right to water requires the procurement, by national governments, of private and public investment, as well as aid funding.[48] However, the recent past has shown a tense relationship between foreign investors and host States, adopting regulatory measures related to water supply and sanitation.

2.3   The Global Water Crisis: Pressures over Water Resources

Several regions of the world are under the pressure of water scarcity or water stress.[49] International organisations have been assessing the effects of water scarcity on humans and its link to energy, food and climate change.[50] Poor governance of water resources could be as harmful as the physical scarcity of water.

---

47   UN General Assembly, *The human right to water and sanitation: resolution / adopted by the General Assembly*, 3 August 2010, A/RES/64/292.

48   Human Rights Council, *Report of the independent expert on the issue of human rights obligations related to access to safe drinking water and sanitation, Catarina de Albuquerque*, 29 June, 2010, A/HRC/15/31.

49   This work adopts the notions of water stress and water scarcity based on the amounts of water resources available proposed by the Human Development Report in 2006. The HDR 2006 notes that the quantity of water, considered adequate, to meet industry, agriculture, energy and environmental requirements is 1700 cubic metres per person. Water available below that threshold is considered to be a situation of water stress. On the other hand, availability of water under 1000 cubic metres is regarded as water scarcity, and below 500 cubic metres, extreme water scarcity. See UNDP, 'Human Development Report 2006. Beyond scarcity: Power, poverty and the global water crisis,' 135. There is, however, another approach to water scarcity which does not only consider physical availability of water resources, this aspect was addressed by the HDR 2006:
'Water scarcity can be physical, economic or institutional, and – like water itself – it can fluctuate over time and space. Scarcity is ultimately a function of supply and demand. But both sides of the supply – demand equation are shaped by political choices and public policies.' *Ibid.*, 134.

50   Orr, Cartwright, and Tickner, 'Understanding water risks: A primer on the consequences of water scarcity for government and business'; World Economic Forum, *Global Risks 2011: An initiative of the Risk Response Network*, 6th ed. (Geneva: World Economic Forum, 2011); World Water Assessment Programme, 'The United Nations World Water Development Report 3'; World Water Assessment Programme, 'The United Nations World Water Development Report 2.'

While it is still soon to assert that there is a mechanism of global water governance in place, there is persuasive evidence of emerging mechanisms promoting coordinated and coherent management of water resources.[51] However, the process has proven challenging, due to disagreements amongst the international community striving for a coordinated regime of global water governance.[52]

The WWDR4 highlights the synergies and trade offs arising from the relationship between water, energy and food. The production of agricultural goods, involves energy in a substantial part of the production chain, while water is involved in the whole chain. It is also expected that urbanization and climate change will put pressure on the production of food.[53] There is an inextricable link between water crisis and energy and food security; lack of coordination – or at least communication – among stakeholders could lead to serious consequences, such as political instability and social unrest.[54]

Notably, the water crisis is not only driven by scarcity. Hazards such as flooding, pollution and extreme weather variability, which may be caused by climate change, are also significant drivers of crisis. The effects of these hazards are more visible in developing countries, where the lack of proper risk assessment and management capacity is evident.[55]

Economic integration through trade and mutual investment protection involves sophisticated legal frameworks. Economic growth however, is not without risks; as stated by the UN Secretary General '[a]s global economy grows, so will its thirst.'[56] Extreme energy price volatility, global governance failures, and technology failure, could be added to environmental and societal challenges, discussed in previous sections.[57]

---

51   Claudia Pahl-Wostl, Joyeeta Gupta, and Daniel Petry, 'Governance and the Global Water System: A Theoretical Exploration,' *Global Governance* 14 (2008), 421.

52   Ken Conca, *Governing water: Contentious transnational politics and global institution building* (Cambridge: MIT Press, 2005), 6.

53   World Water Assessment Programme, 'The United Nations World Water Development Report 2014: Water and Energy,' Paris: UNESCO, 2014, 54.

54   World Water Assessment Programme, 'The United Nations World Water Development Report 3,' xx.

55   *Ibid.*, 211.

56   Ban Ki-Moon, Secretary-General, United Nations, as cited in: World Economic Forum Water Initiative, 'The Bubble Is Close to Bursting: A Forecast of the Main Economic and Geopolitical Water Issues Likely to Arise in the World during the Next Two Decades. Draft for Discussion at the World Economic Forum Annual Meeting 2009,' World Economic Forum, 2009, 5.

57   World Economic Forum, *Global Risks 2011*, Figure 1: Global Risks Landscape 2011: Perception data from the World Economic Forum's Global Risks Survey.

THE SPECIAL NATURE OF WATER RESOURCES   29

Water is a powerful vehicle which can potentially interconnect drivers of scarcity and the materialisation of risks.[58] This relationship illustrates the unlikely balance between: the inherent unpredictability of water, the attainment of human security and the need for economic and legal stability.

The water crisis in the global context is a long-term challenge that high and middle-income countries may eventually face. For low-income countries, on the other hand, the water crisis is a silent reality, which already affects mostly the poor.[59]

2.4   Pressures on Water Resources and the Problem of Water Supply

When discussing access to water resources and governance, an important distinction ought to be made. The provision of water supply and services depends, not only on reliable sources of water, but also on large-scale infrastructure to provide drinking water and sanitation.

The global water crisis is the effect not only of increasing demand but also of ineffective governance. Demand for water is not only attributable to demographic growth and human consumption and pollution. Indeed, economic and social activities such as cultural practices, globalization and trade have multiplying effects over the demand for water resources. Climate change constitutes an additional driver exacerbating water's already variable nature.[60]

2.4.1   *Drivers of Water Stress*

Water stress results from an imbalance between water use and renewal of the water cycle.[61] Both quantity and quality of water resources are affected by water stress for reasons of over exploitation and pollution, respectively. The main drivers of water stress, namely demographic, economic and social, also constitute the means to achieve human and economic development. The question

---

58   *Ibid.,* 45.

59   Kristen Lewis, ed. *Water governance for poverty reduction: Key issues and the UNDP response to millenium development goals* (New York: Water Governance Programme, Bureau for Development Policy, UNDP, 2004), 79.

　　　The WWDR3 confirms that poor people are already facing a drinking water crisis: two in every three people lack access to safe drinking water and lives on two dollars a day, one in three lives on one dollar a day, and 385 million people live on less than one dollar a day. See World Water Assessment Programme, 'The United Nations World Water Development Report 3,' 84.

60   *Ibid.*, 68.

61   For a notion of water stress see *supra* note 49.

30   CHAPTER 2

that arises is whether this type of socio-economic development is sustainable in the long run.

It is predicted that in the next 25 years, the population in Latin America and the Caribbean will increase by 50 per cent, while doubling in Africa and Asia.[62] The production of food to meet the demand created by demographic growth and extended life expectancy should increase by 60 per cent.[63] Economic globalisation and trade, such as fashion, IT and food, affect young consumers' habits. Yet, the production of goods and services requires energy, raw materials and labour, all linked to consumption and pollution of water (human and corporations' footprints).[64] Biofuels and 'virtual water'[65] may have an effect on food security, as both activities compete for the use of land, water, and fuel for transportation.[66]

Finally, from a social point of view poverty alleviation and education are linked to an adequate management of water resources. People in poor regions

---

62   James Winpenny, 'Financing Water For All,' Report of the World Panel on Financing Water Infrastructure (Camdessus Report), 2003, 5.

63   World Water Assessment Programme, 'The United Nations World Water Development Report 2014: Water and Energy,' Paris: UNESCO, 2014, 54.

64   See Winpenny, 'Financing Water For All,' 32–36.
       'Footprints' are defined as the measure of human demand on earth's ecosystems.

65   Water-abundant countries have a comparative advantage to produce and trade water-intensive goods. Water embedded in traded goods such as crops has been termed 'virtual water,' which may assist in alleviating water shortages. See Orr, Cartwright and Tickner, 'Understanding water risks: A primer on the consequences of water scarcity for government and business,' 18.
       On the issue of virtual water there are additional concerns: 'It is no longer just the crops that are commodities: rather, it is the land and water for agriculture themselves that are increasingly becoming commoditised, increasingly subject to globalized rights of access.' See Carin Smaller and Howard Mann, 'A Thirst for Distant Lands: Foreign investment in agricultural land and water,' IISD, 7.

66   The High Level Conference on World Food Security, cautiously addressed the link between biofuel production and food crisis, advising further research in order to assess such relationship. The main concern is that the production of biofuels is consistent with the goals of sustainable development. See the Declaration of the High-Level Conference on World Food Security: *The Challenges of Climate Change and Bioenergy*, ed. FAO, WFP, and IFAD (Rome June 5 2008), article 7(f).
       On the other hand, the World Economic Forum warns that the production of biofuels posts high risks for water resources with the potential to 'consume between 20–100% of the total quantity of water now used worldwide for agriculture'; such a situation according to the Forum constitutes an unsustainable trade-off. See World Economic Forum, *Global Risks 2011*, 31.

THE SPECIAL NATURE OF WATER RESOURCES   31

use and often misuse natural resources in an attempt to survive in the short run. Understandably, populations with imminent needs do not pay attention to environmental sustainability and the needs of future generations. Therefore, depletion of inland aquifers and inadequate sanitation services contribute to an accelerated pollution of water resources.

All drivers of water stress are intimately related to investment. Foreign investment is particularly responsive to increased demands for goods and services, due to its capacity to achieve large operations in different States. Yet, foreign investors are also more vulnerable, when social and political conditions change and new legal frameworks are created to regulate economic sectors.

2.4.2   *Drinking Water Supply and Access to Water*

It is important to discuss drinking water supply in the context of this Chapter. High profile investment treaty disputes have arisen out of water supply and services projects. The relationship between water services and investment protection illustrates people's feeling of entitlement towards water resources and the great sensitivities and scrutiny this relationship causes. A detailed analysis of water supply and its regulation is outside the scope of this work and its analysis is limited to the use of water resources for human consumption in relation to other uses of water resources.

The issue of drinking water supply is intimately related to the social perspective of water resources, discussed in Section 2.2.4. Water supply and services have been at the core of the 'human right to water' debates, influencing the manner in which, consumers, governments and corporations, perceive the provision of water services.[67]

---

67   In March 2012 the WHO reported that the MDG's target to reduce by half the amount of people without access to safe drinking water had been met: 'The report, *Progress on Drinking Water and Sanitation 2012*, by the WHO/UNICEF Joint Monitoring Programme for Water Supply and Sanitation, says at the end of 2010 89% of the world's population, or 6.1 billion people, used improved drinking water sources. This is one per cent more than the 88% MDG target. The report estimates that by 2015 92% of the global population will have access to improved drinking water.' See WHO, Media Centre, 'Millennium Development Goal drinking water target met,' March 6, 2012, Geneva – New York, available at: http://www.who.int/mediacentre/news/releases/2012/drinking_water_20120306/en/, accessed May 7, 2016.

In contrast, the goal of providing sanitation to the world's population is behind target. As of 2012, 2.5 billion people still lack access to improved sanitation. See WHO, Media Centre, 'Millennium Development Goal drinking water target met,' March 6, 2012, Geneva – New York, available at http://www.who.int/mediacentre/news/releases/2012/drinking_water_20120306/en/, accessed May 7, 2016.

32   CHAPTER 2

Water supply and sanitation constitute an integral component of water resources management and their provision is part of the overall allocation of
water resources. Water demand for human consumption amounts to ten per
cent of the total demand for water,[68] and its supply has priority over other
demands.[69]

The realisation of the right to water through the provision of water services
supply requires the commitment of long-term investment from public and
private sources.[70] Yet, challenges to the financing of drinking water and sanitation are not only faced by developing countries. Developed countries face
challenges linked to rehabilitation, maintenance and compliance with increasingly strict health and environmental regulations of existing infrastructure.[71]

Private sector participation, with 11 per cent of total capital investment in
water supply and services provision,[72] has not always been successful. Furthermore, there have been instances where disagreements between operators and
host States turned into international disputes. Bechtel in Bolivia,[73] Biwater

---

68   In contrast, agriculture demands 70 per cent and industry and energy, together, 20 per
      cent of the total demand. See World Water Assessment Programme, 'The United Nations
      World Water Development Report 3,' 99.

69   UN Committee on Economic, Social and Cultural Rights, *General Comment No. 15: The
      Right to Water (Articles 11 and 12 of the Covenant)*, 20 January 2003, E/C.12/2002/11, para 6;
      United Nations, 'Conference on Environment & Development, Agenda 21,' Rio de Janeiro,
      Brazil, June 1992, 18.6; United Nations, 'Report of the World Summit on Sustainable Devel-
      opment,' Johannesburg, 2002, para 26, (c). Water resources for human consumption could
      be affected under the Eminent Domain, when water is needed for municipal purposes
      See Article § 11.033 of the 2005 Texas Water Code, Chapter 11, sub-chapter A General Provi-
      sions. The Peruvian Water Act (Ley N° 29338 of 31 de marzo de 2009) pursuant to Article
      35 states the order of priority for uses of water resources: First human consumption (Uso
      Primario-Articles 36–38), which is basic use of water from any source, by mechanical
      means which does not require a licence and is limited to the satisfaction of basic human
      needs; Second: water services supply (uso poblacional-Article 39) and Third: productive
      use (uso productivo- Article 42). The Mexican Water Act, last amendment published on
      8 June 2012 (Ley Nacional de Aguas) gives priority to domestic use and public use (Article
      13 BIS 4, 14 BIS 5 XXII).

70   Winpenny, 'Financing Water For All,' 3.

71   The OECD reports that France and the United Kingdom (UK) may require 20 per cent
      increase in water expenditure, as a share of their gross domestic product (GDP). OECD,
      'Managing Water for All: An OECD Perspective on Pricing and Financing. Key Messages
      for Policy Makers,' Paris: OECD, 2009, 7.

72   David Lloyd Owen, *Pinsent Masons Water Yearbook 2007–2008* (London: Pinsent Masons,
      2007), 27.

73   See *Aguas del Tunari, S.A. v. Republic of Bolivia*, ICSID Case No. ARB/02/3.

THE SPECIAL NATURE OF WATER RESOURCES 33

Gauff in Tanzania,[74] and Azurix, Vivendi and others in Argentina[75] are examples of water supply projects that failed due to a combination of political, social and economic variables, which in the context of foreign investment are exacerbated by the negative perception that the population already has towards the idea of transnational corporations providing national public services.[76] There is a connection between the failure of water services projects, the unique nature of water and consumers' entitlement to meet basic human needs. This connection is linked to the social aspect of water resources, which resists approaching water as an economic good, because it is essential for human life:

> people think of water resources as public property. They feel entitled to water. They have an opinion about it. Because they drink it and know that life isn't possible without it, they can get emotional about water.[77]

The OECD reports that during the 1990s, five international companies were granted 53 per cent of the relevant contracts for water-related projects in developing countries.[78] In contrast, by 2000 the number dropped to 23 per cent.[79] New forms of private participation in water supply and services projects, through less engaging forms of public private partnerships, seek to eliminate political and regulatory risks.[80] Following this trend investment in

---

74 See *Biwater Gauff (Tanzania) Ltd v United Republic of Tanzania*, ICSID Case No. ARB/05/22.

75 See *Compañía de Aguas del Aconquija S.A. and Vivendi Universal S.A. v. Argentine Republic*, ICSID Case No. ARB/97/3.

76 See Mann, 'Who Owns "Your" Water? Reclaiming Water as a Public Good under International Trade and Investment Law,' 3. See also in relation to privatisation processes in water services: Susan Spronk and Carlos Crespo, 'Water, National Sovereignty and Social Resistance: Bilateral Investment Treaties and the Struggles against Multinational Water Companies in Cochabamba and El Alto, Bolivia,' *Law, Social Justice & Global Development* 1 (2008); Maria Sánchez-Moreno and Tracy MacFarland Higgins, 'No Recourse: Transnational corporations and the Protection of economic, social, and cultural rights in Bolivia,' *Fordham International Law Journal* 27, no. 5 (2004); Timothy O'Neill, 'Water and Freedom: The Privatization of Water and its Implications for Democracy and Human Rights in the Developing World,' *Colorado Journal of International Environmental Law and Policy* 17 (2006).

77 See Griffin, *Water Resources Economics*, Ch. 2, 2.

78 OECD, 'Managing Water for All: An OECD Perspective on Pricing and Financing. Key Messages for Policy Makers,' 11.

79 *Ibid.*

80 Marin points out that numerous public-private partnerships increasingly avoid private ownership of the infrastructure, which implies less risk for the private operator. See

divestures and concessions have shifted to shorter concession agreements and lower levels of investment and involvement, such as lease and management contracts.[81,82]

This short account of the problems that arose out of foreign investment involvement in water supply are relevant in the context of international investment and water resources management. Valuable lessons could be drawn from the relationship between international investment and water supply and services regulation. Chapter 3 discusses the main differences between water resources management and water services regulation.

2.5   Conclusions

The drivers for water stress are likely to exacerbate competition for the resource in the near future. The measures necessary to prevent and to settle water conflicts are still under study and far from being identified and tested. In this vein, it is important to consider that legal issues related to water are not always dealt with by water and environmental lawyers. Water resources are central to most human and economic activities, and are therefore potentially subject of disputes outside the realm of water law. It is likely that trade and investment dispute resolution mechanisms may be confronted with disputes over water resources.

Philippe Marin, 'Public-Private Partnerships for Urban Water Utilities A Review of Experiences in Developing Countries,' Washington: World Bank, 2009, 8.

81   OECD, 'Managing Water for All: An OECD Perspective on Pricing and Financing. Key Messages for Policy Makers,' 11.

82   The terms for private involvement, public-private partnership involvement and public involvement in the provision of water services and sewerage are diverse and sometimes allow for different meanings. For the sake of clarity it is useful to address some of these terms. From high to low degrees of private involvement in the provision of water services (drinking water supply and sewerage): divesture, followed by concession, lease contracts, *affermage* and management, franchising and O&M contracts. Public-private partnerships from high to low involvement can be found under: build operate and transfer (BOT), built own operate transfer (BOOT), build own operate (BOO), among the most common ones, as well as joint venture, services, corporatisation and performance contracts. Finally public involvement is undertaken under cooperative and municipal or provincial authorities. See Jeffrey Delmon, 'Understanding Options for Public-Private Partnerships in Infrastructure Sorting out the forest from the trees: BOT, DBFO, DCMF, concession, lease...,' Washington: Finance Economics & Urban Department Finance and Guarantees Unit – World Bank, 2010, 12.

CHAPTER 3

The Governance of Water Resources

3.1 Introduction

The development of water law, as an autonomous area of law, is fairly recent. Yet in this short period water law experts have reached important synergies with other disciplines such as geography, climatology, hydrology and political sciences. These disciplines are critical for understanding the behaviour of the water cycle as well as the close relationship that water has to humans.

Conversely, despite the great potential for cross-fertilization and mutual supportiveness, an effective relationship between water law and other areas of law has not been so clearly established. However, there are also latent conflicts that could arise out of overlaps of regulatory activity between water law and other areas of law, such as international trade and international investment law. This interaction has been extensively discussed in the academic literature.[1]

---

1 See for instance the work of: Joseph Cumming and Robert Froehlich, 'NAFTA Chapter XI and Canada's Environmental Sovereignty: Investment Flows, Article 1110 and Alberta's Water Act,' Toronto: University of Toronto, 2007; Matthias Finger and Geremy Allouche, *Water Privatisation* (London: Spon Press, 2002); Céline Levesque, 'Investment and Water Resources: Limits to NAFTA,' in *Sustainable Development in World Investment Law*, ed. Marie-Claire Cordonier-Segger, Markus Gehring, and Andrew Newcombe (Alphen aan den Rijn, The Netherlands: Kluwer Law International, 2011); Andrew Lang, 'The GATS and Regulatory Autonomy: A Case Study of the Social Regulation of the Water Industry,' *Journal of International Economic Law* 7, no. 4 (2004); Howard Mann, 'Who Owns "Your" Water? Reclaiming Water as a Public Good under International Trade and Investment Law,' Geneva: IISD, 2003; Howard Mann, 'International Economic Law: Water for Money's Sake,' Ottawa: IISD, 2004; Howard Mann, 'Implications of International Trade and Investment Agreements for Water and Water Services: Some Responses from Other Sources of International Law,' *Transnational Dispute Management* 5 (2006); Fabrizio Marrella, 'On the changing structure of international investment law: The human right to water and ICSID arbitration,' *International Community Law Review* 12 (2010); Timothy O'Neill, 'Water and Freedom: The Privatization of Water and its Implications for Democracy and Human Rights in the Developing World,' *Colorado Journal of International Environmental Law and Policy* 17, no. 2 (2006); Stuart Orr, Anton Cartwright, and Dave Tickner, 'Understanding water risks: A primer on the consequences of water scarcity for government and business,' World Wildlife Fund, 2009; Miguel Solanes, 'Privatization, Foreign Investment, Arbitration and Water: A Time to Revisit. Summary of the main issues raised by Michael Hantke-Domas, Howard Mann

---

© KONINKLIJKE BRILL NV, LEIDEN, 2017 | DOI 10.1163/9789004335301_004

The special nature of water, discussed in Chapter 2, plays a pivotal role in the way States design their ownership and allocation frameworks, which contrast with systems of allocation and ownership regulating other natural resources. This chapter provides a general overview of the governance of water resources, at the national as well as the international levels. These legal frameworks are relevant to international investment law because they often constitute the 'regulatory measure,' which could be challenged by foreign investors should they negatively affect their property rights and interests.

It is important to note that the regulation of water supply and sanitation is discussed separately from the broader discussion on water resources management, due to the differences in purpose and scope.

There is increasing awareness among water professionals of the potential effects resulting from the interaction between international investment obligations and the regulation and management of water resources and water services. States hosting foreign investment may seek to pre-empt the risk of international responsibility, such as payment of compensation and reputational

---

and Jorge Barraguirre,' available: http://www.palermo.edu/Archivos_content/derecho/pdf/Revisiting-privatization-foreign-investment.pdf; Miguel Solanes, 'Water Services and International Investment Agreements,' in *Global Change: Impacts on Water and Food Security*, ed. Claudia Ringler, Asit K. Biswas, and Sarah Cline (Berlin – Heidelberg: Springer, 2010); Miguel Solanes and Andrei Jouravlev, 'Revisiting Privatization, Foreign Investment, International Arbitration and Water,' Santiago, Chile: United Nations, 2007; Paul Stanton Kibel, 'Grasp on Water: A Natural Resource that Eludes NAFTA's Notion of Investment,' *Ecology Law Quaterly* 34, no. 2 (2007); Paul Stanton Kibel and Jon Schutz, 'Two Rivers Meet: At the Confluence of Cross-Border Water and Foreign Investment Law,' in *Sustainable Development in World Investment Law*, ed. Marie-Claire Cordonier-Segger, Markus Gehring, and Andrew Newcombe (Alphen aan den Rijn, The Netherlands: Kluwer Law International, 2011); The International Federation of Private Water Operators (AquaFed), 'Bilateral Investment Treaties and the Right to Water: The case of the provision of public water supply and sanitation services,' AquaFed, 2009; Jorge E. Viñuales, 'Access to Water in Foreign Investment Disputes,' *The Georgetown International Environmental Law Review* 21 (2009); Jorge E. Viñuales, 'Iced Freshwater Resources: A Legal Exploration,' *Yearbook of International Environmental Law* 20, no. 1 (2011); Jorge E. Viñuales, *Foreign Investment and the Environment in International Law* (Cambridge: Cambridge University Press, 2012); Jeffory S. Wade, 'Privatization and the Future of Water Services,' *Florida Journal of International Law* 20 (2008); Hugo Muñoz, 'La administración del agua y la inversión extranjera directa ¿Cómo se relacionan?' in *Estudios en homenaje al Dr Rafael González Ballar*, ed. Universidad de Costa Rica (San Jose: Isolma S.A., 2009); Attila Tanzi, 'On Balancing Foreign Investment Interests With Public Interests in Recent Arbitration Case Law in the Public Utilities Sector,' *The law and practice of international courts and tribunals: A Practioners' Journal* 11, no. 1 (2012).

THE GOVERNANCE OF WATER RESOURCES

pressures. In so doing, States may stall the adoption of environmental regulation, including water resources management. This kind of regulatory disincentive could result in 'regulatory chill,' which may occur *ex ante* or *ex post* investment.

From an *ex ante* perspective, UNCTAD points out that capital importing States which are competing to attract foreign investment may have incentives to lower their social and environmental standards.[2] In the case of *ex post* investments, it has been suggested that the broad obligations contained in International Investment Agreements (IIAs) could deter the adoption or amendment of domestic regulations, favouring investment protection.[3] In both cases, governments' ability to adapt to actual or imminent challenges around water resources may be diminished.

3.2 Water Governance: Ownership, Management and Regulation

The analysis of water resources governance requires a two-fold consideration. First, water governance at the international level, and second, water governance at the local or national level; which will be further analysed in this chapter.

It is useful to note that this work uses the term 'regulation' broadly, referring to laws, decrees, administrative acts and any other decision adopted by States, including parliaments, ministries, national and local authorities.

3.2.1 *Global Water Governance*

There is increasing consensus on the need to address and prevent the effects of a potential water crisis, in connection to food and energy crises at the global level.[4] This means that allocation and reallocation of water resources, to meet new and larger demands for water, requires coordination between

---

2 UNCTAD, 'International Investment Agreements: Key Issues Volume II,' Geneva: United Nations, 2004, 73. This phenomenon has also been referred to as a 'race to the bottom' among capital importing countries.

3 Mann, 'The Right of States to Regulate and International Investment Law,' 8.

4 UNDP, 'Human Development Report 2010. 20th Anniversary Edition. The Real Wealth of Nations: Pathways to Human Development,' New York: United Nations, 2010; World Economic Forum, *Global Risks 2011: An initiative of the Risk Response Network*, 6th ed. (Geneva: World Economic Forum, 2011); World Water Assessment Programme, 'The United Nations World Water Development Report 3: Water in a Changing World,' Paris – London: United Nations, 2009; Patricia Wouters, Sergei Vinogradov, and Bjoern-Oliver Magsig, 'Water Security, Hydrosolidarity, and International Law: A River Runs Through It,' *Yearbook of International Environmental Law* 19 (2010).

governments, in line with national policies. In this context, the top-down approach to water governance influences the actions taken by national governments in regulating water resources, and so does the decisions of regional and international tribunals.

The inquiry in the context of this work is whether investment tribunals, assessing governmental measures affecting investors' water entitlements, would take into account emerging, albeit non-binding, principles of water governance, influencing management practices.

The Global Water Partnership (GWP) defines water governance, as:

> [a] range of political, social, economic and administrative systems that are in place to develop and manage water resources, and the delivery of water services, at different levels of society.[5]

In this order of ideas, one should also consider that governments are often subjected to pressure groups representing competing demands; these could be environmental groups, human rights activists or industry.[6]

Over the last fifty years, international institutions as well as governmental and non-governmental organisations (NGOs), have promoted the need for an integrated approach to water resources management. These institutions also recognise the disadvantages of a fragmented institutional approach to the management of water resources. Thus, the focus has been to overcome these disadvantages and achieve sustainability of water resources and services.[7] This section introduces some international instruments adopted by the international community in the area of water management and the protection of the environment.

---

5   Peter Rogers and Alan W. Hall, 'Effective Water Governance,' Stockholm: Global Water Partnership Technical Committee (TEC), 2003, 7.

6   *Ibid.*

7   For a general discussion on fairness and legitimacy of global or international governance and institutions, and the discussion on the legitimacy of this regime, see primarily Thomas M. Franck, *Fairness in International Law and Institutions* (Oxford: Oxford University Press, 1995); Daniel Bodansky, 'The Legitimacy of International Governance: A Coming Challenge for International Environmental Law?' *American Journal of International Law* 93 (1999); Joseph Dellapenna and Joyeeta Gupta, 'Toward Global Law on Water,' *Global Governance* 14, (2008).

   For another critic on the effectiveness of governance of water at the international level, referred to by the author as expert networks, see Ken Conca, *Governing water: Contentious transnational politics and global institution building* (Cambridge: MIT Press, 2005).

THE GOVERNANCE OF WATER RESOURCES

3.2.1.1   UN and other International Conferences

The United Nations Conference on the Human Environment, held in Stockholm in 1972, declared water as representative of a natural ecosystem that must be 'safeguarded for the benefit of present and future generations through careful planning or management.'[8]

The UN Conference on Water held in 1977 in Mar del Plata, Argentina, recognised water as a right for the first time. It declared that all people, no matter their stage of development, have a right to access drinking water. The Conference also promoted greater awareness on the problems of pollution, natural hazards, policy planning and cooperation at the national, as well as, international levels.[9]

The International Drinking Water Supply and Sanitation Decade 1981–1990, launched by the UN, and the Global Consultation on Safe Water and Sanitation, was organised by the UNDP in New Delhi, India in 1990, focused on water supply and sanitation. The New Delhi meeting coined the phrase: 'some for all rather than more for some.' The statement also included guiding principles for the protection of the environment 'through integrated management of water resources.'[10]

In 1992, the International Conference on Water and the Environment held in Dublin, Ireland, adopted the 'Dublin Statement.'[11] The Statement proposes four general guiding principles for the management of water resources:

(i)   fresh water is a finite and vulnerable resource, essential to sustain life, development and the environment;

---

8   United Nations Conference on the Human Environment, 'Report of the United Nations Conference on the Human Environment, Stockholm, 5–16 June, 1972,' New York: United Nations, 1973, Principle 2.

9   United Nations, 'Report of the United Nations Water Conference: Mar del Plata, 14–25 March 1977,' New York, Sales No. E.77.II.A.12 and corrigendum, 1977.

10   See UN General Assembly, *Proclamation of the International Drinking Water Supply and Sanitation Decade: resolution / adopted by the General Assembly*, 10 November 1980, Resolution 35/18. See also UNDP, 'Global consultation on safe water and sanitation for the 1990s: 10–14 September 1990, New Delhi, India,' New York: UNDP, 1990, Guiding Principles and Principle 1.

11   *Dublin Statement on Water and Sustainable Development*, Dublin 31 January, 1992. In this meeting 'The Conference participants call for fundamental new approaches to the assessment, development and management of freshwater resources, which can only be brought about through political commitment and involvement from the highest levels of government to the smallest communities.'

(ii) water development and management should be based on a participatory approach, involving users, planners and policy-makers at all levels;

(iii) women play a central part in the provision, management and safeguarding of water; and

(iv) water has an economic value in all its competing uses and should be recognised as an economic good.[12]

The 'Dublin Statement' informed the recommendations addressing the quality of water supply embedded in 'Agenda 21.'[13] Agenda 21 was adopted in 1992 at the UN Conference on Environment and Development (UNCED) in Brazil.[14]

The Conference, through 'Agenda 21,' promoted greater cooperation among governments with a view to adopt the principles of Integrated Water Resources Management (IWRM).[15] States were encouraged to enhance their IWRM programmes, through specific actions, such as the assessment of: (i) quantities of water resources, (ii) natural disasters, risk assessment and the environment and society, (iii) the interrelation between freshwater bodies, on the surface and underground, and (iv) the conservation of water resources by means of adoption of water-efficient-use programmes.[16]

The International Conference on Freshwaters held in Bonn, Germany in 2001,[17] recognised that water is key to sustainable development, within its

---

12   *Dublin Statement on Water and Sustainable Development,* Dublin 31 January, 1992.

13   Chapter 18 entitles 'Protection of the Quality and Supply of Freshwater Resources: Application of Integrated Approaches to the Development, Management and Use of Water Resources.'

14   UNCED, 'United Nations Conference on Environment and Development: Rio de Janeiro, 3–14 June 1992: item 9 of the provisional agenda: adoption of agreements on environment and development: Agenda 21,' New York, 1992. Subsection Basis for Action of CH 18, Agenda 21 states:

       'The fragmentation of responsibilities for water resources development among sectoral agencies is proving, however, to be an even greater impediment to promoting integrated water management than had been anticipated. Effective implementation and coordination mechanisms are required.'

       See Agenda 21, para. 18.6.

15   By 2000 '(i) To have designed and initiated coasted and targeted national action programmes, and have put in place appropriate institutional structures and legal instruments; (ii) To have established efficient water-use programmes to attain sustainable resource utilization patterns.' By 2025 '(i) To have achieved subsectoral targets of all freshwater programme areas.' See *Ibid.,* para. 18.11.

16   *Ibid.,* para. 18.12.

17   International Conference on Freshwater, 'Bonn Recomendations for Action,' Bonn, 3–7 December, 2001.

THE GOVERNANCE OF WATER RESOURCES   41

economic, social and environmental dimensions. The Conference focused on the impact of implementation of IWRM principles, in light of sustainable development, the needs of poor people, and the promotion of decentralisation.[18] Importantly, the Conference also addressed the issue of risk management and flexible decision-making process to cope with variability and climate change:

> [d]ecision-making mechanisms under uncertainty should ensure flexibility to respond to both rapid onset disasters and long term changes to water resources. Risk management should be an integral part of water resources management. This should include establishing close coordination beyond the water sector.[19]

The 2002 World Summit on Sustainable Development, held in Johannesburg, South Africa, advocated for more accountable and effective international institutions.[20] The Summit proposed several actions to tackle the effects of climate change, climate variability and disaster prevention.

In 2012 UN Water, a UN inter-agency coordination mechanism for freshwater issues, presented through the United Nations Environment Programme (UNEP), the status of implementation of the IWRM principles, launched at the UN Rio+20 Summit. The report was positive regarding the results observed from the implementation of IWRM principles. Eighty per cent of countries have embarked in the adoption of the IWRM principles[21] and 133 countries were responsive to the survey launched by UN Water showing different levels of implementation.[22]

These conferences have largely shaped the management of water resources. They recognise the importance of resilience and adaptation to water variability and the increasing effects of climate change. Overall, the extent to which such declarations and conferences have shaped regulatory frameworks at the

---

18   *Ibid.* See especially Actions in the Field of Governance.

19   *Ibid.*, Actions in the Field of Governance, point 9.

20   United Nations, 'Report of the World Summit on Sustainable Development Johannesburg, South Africa, 26 August–4 September, 2002,' A/CONF.199/20, Johannesburg, 2002, 4, para. 31.

21   UNEP, 'Status Report on the Application of Integrated Approaches to Water Resources Management,' Nairobi, Kenya: UNEP, GWP, SIWI, UNDP, UNEP-DHI Centre for Water and Environment, 2012, vi, 76.

22   See *Ibid.* 6–7. Chapter 6 addresses the status of implementation of IWRM principles in the context of broader discussion of property rights under international investment law. This discussion is relevant in the context of investment arbitration as it assesses the likelihood of changes in legislation that could affect current water rights, especially of foreign investors. See Chapter 6, Section 6.2.1.

42 CHAPTER 3

national level remains to be evaluated within each national legal system, on a case-by-case basis.

3.2.1.2 World Water Forums and Congresses

A different policy-making process for water governance takes place every three years through the World Water Forum.[23] While each forum focuses on specific themes, they all promote multi-stakeholder participation and discussion, through the organisation of thematic meetings, related to water management, water services, global and local governance, economic regulation of water supply and sanitation, access to water for the poorest and financing, amongst others.

These forums serve as a platform of interaction between governments, international and regional organisations, civil society and NGOs. As intergovernmental conferences, they shape global policy, showing that management policies and strategies do not only emerge from the work of local governments and international institutions, but also from the work of various stakeholders, NGO's and/or 'expert networks,' such as the GWP, World Water Council and Worldwide Fund for Nature, among others.[24]

Similarly, the World Water Congress is organised every three years under the auspices of the International Water Resources Association (IWRA). This non-governmental and educational organization seeks to provide a global interdisciplinary forum, bridging different regions of the world to exchange information and experiences. It also provides a platform for discussion among water professionals, academics and individuals, with a view to expand the understanding of water issues across disciplines.

Intergovernmental and non-governmental conferences have positively influenced the adoption of integrated management policies, showing their relevance in the development of a global community framework for water governance.[25]

---

23 The first Forum took place in Morocco in 1997, followed by the Netherlands 2000, Japan 2003, Mexico 2006, Turkey 2009, France 2012, and Korea 2015.

24 As referred to by Conca in his analysis of global networks and water governance. See Conca, *Governing water: Contentious transnational politics and global institution building*.

25 See Dellapenna and Gupta, 'Toward Global Law on Water,' 6. On the assessment of global water conferences and water initiatives. See: Robert G. Varady and Matthew Iles-Shih, 'Global Water Initiatives: What Do the Experts Think? Report on a Survey of Leading Figures in the World of Water,' in *Workshop on Impacts of Megaconferences on Global Water Development and Management* (Sponsored by Third World Centre for Water Management (Mexico) with support from the Sasakawa Peace Foundation (USA and Japan), January 29–30, 2005); Peter H. Gleick and Jon Lane, 'Large International Water Meetings: Time for

THE GOVERNANCE OF WATER RESOURCES

3.2.1.3 International Treaty Negotiation

Notwithstanding, the adoption of numerous international declarations, governments have often been reluctant to legally bind themselves to the international obligation to cooperate and adopt harmonised rules for the protection of fresh water resources. One possible reason may be governments' reluctance to give up part of their sovereign control over their natural resources. One such example is the *United Nations Convention on the Law of the Non-Navigational Uses of International Watercourses* (UN Watercourses Convention), adopted in 1997 and in force only since 2014.[26] It has also been suggested that an 'epistemic community' among experts in the area of fresh water resources may be still at an early stage.[27]

This section focuses on two global international agreements, the UN Watercourses Convention and the United Nations Economic Commission for Europe of 1992 (UNECE) *Convention on the Protection and Use of Transboundary Watercourses and International Lakes*, (UNECE Convention). These international agreements are potentially relevant in investment treaty arbitration, as their implementation in the domestic legal systems of host States, shape the

---

    a Reappraisal,' *Water International* 30, no. 3 (2005); Asit K. Biswas and Cecilia Tortajada, *Impacts of Megaconferences on the Water Sector* (Berlin: Springer, 2009).

26   This issue is further discussed in Chapter 4 addressing the exercise of sovereignty in the context of the police power of States.

27   Dellapena and Gupta comparing water governance communities with other environmental communities such as climate change, note that: 'Water lawyers are not yet integrated into the nascent epistemic community on water management, and as such there is little integration of policy ideas between these communities.' Dellapenna and Gupta, 'Toward Global Law on Water,' 450.

    Note for instance that despite the fact that water is admittedly one of the most important vehicles of the effects of climate change, it has been difficult to include it within the negotiations on adaptation to climate change. See for instance the speech of Pasquale Steduto:

    'Let me be very clear. There is no development without water. There is no food security without water. There is most likely also no energy security without water. Water is the primary medium through which climate change influences the Earth's ecosystems and therefore people's livelihoods and well-being. If water is not further recognized in adaptation strategies and plans, we are making a big mistake.'

    Pasquale Steduto, Chair, UN-Water and Service Chief, FAO Global Water Partnership, 'Water evaporates from the climate change negotiating text,' Press Release, November 3, 2009. In addition, the GWP asserts:

    '[T]he latest iteration of the negotiating text on adaptation, the so-called Non-Paper 31, has deleted any clear references to water and its management as a vital consideration for climate change adaptation.'

national laws related to the use, allocation and entitlements of water resources. These aspects will be further discussed in Chapters 6 to 9.

Prior to the analysis of the Conventions, it is important to refer to the 1966 Rules on the Uses of the Water of International Rivers (Helsinki Rules), relating to navigational and non-navigational uses of rivers. These rules were drafted by the International Law Association, which codified principles that originated in State practice with a view to clarify the equitable use and management of shared international watercourses.[28]

The UN Watercourses Convention is the result of the work of the International Law Commission. It largely reflects rules of customary international law; among the substantive provisions it is important to mention the obligation of 'reasonable and equitable utilization' (Article 5), the obligation 'not to cause significant harm' (Article 7), and the 'protection and preservation of ecosystems' (Article 20). The Convention includes procedural rules, such as the requirement of information and notification of planned measures (Articles 11–19).[29] Notably, Article 10(1) establishes no priority whatsoever to the use of international watercourses,[30] unless an agreement or a rule of custom states the contrary. However, should conflict between uses arise, paragraph 2 accords special regard to the requirements of vital human needs.

The interpretation of the term of 'vital human need,' firstly used by the UN Watercourses Convention, requires a determination of the 'minimum individual water requirement.' The term 'vital human needs' does not only refer to a minimum amount of drinking water to sustain life, the term includes the minimum amount required to produce food to sustain life. Another important clarification, as stated in the commentary, considers that the provision of Article 10 makes reference to conflict between uses of a watercourse and not a dispute between watercourse States.[31]

28　See International Law Association, 'Report of the Fifty-second Conference,' London: International Law Association, 1967.

29　36 ILM 700 (1997); G.A. Res. 51/229, U.N. GAOR, 51st Sess., 99th mtg., UN Doc A/RES/51/229 (1997) (UN Watercourses Convention). See also Salman M.A. Salman, 'Entry into Force of the UN Watercourses Convention: Why Should It Matter?' *International Journal of Water Resources Development* (2014).

30　*Ibid.* UN Watercourses Convention, Article 10.

31　See International Law Commission, 'Draft articles on the law of non-navigational uses of international watercourses and commentaries thereto and resolution on transboundary confined groundwater,' in *Yearbook of the International Law Commission 1994* (New York – Geneva: United Nations, 1994) Vol. II, Part Two, 110. See also the UN

THE GOVERNANCE OF WATER RESOURCES 45

The UNECE Convention includes 56 countries located within the European Union (EU) zone, and outside the EU such as the areas of the Caucasus, Central Asia and North America.[32] The Convention is open for accession by UN members and other organisations outside the UNECE region since early 2016. Like the UN Watercourses Convention, the UNECE Convention has the purpose to ensure quantity, quality and sustainability of transboundary water resources. It sets out the obligation for its members to adopt mechanisms necessary to pursue joint objectives to secure water-quality (Article 9). In contrast, the UN Watercourses Convention merely establishes an obligation to enter into consultations for the adoption of mechanisms to attain water-quality standardisation (Article 21.3).[33]

These international instruments set the relevant general rules of international and customary law, which could serve as additional elements of analysis when solving investment treaty disputes. They could bring light to the rationale behind amendments to domestic laws and the factual background to the adoption of regulatory measures in specific cases.

3.2.2 *Water Resources Management: The National Law Dimension*

The integrated approach to water management, promoted in several international conferences, informs the regulatory framework for the allocation and eventual reallocation of water resources. In the international investment law context, these norms may assist to assess the extent to which regulatory flexibility may be invoked by host States, and in turn, the level of deference that investment tribunals may confer to the exercise of regulatory prerogatives of States. Ultimately, the purpose of the arbitral tribunal – in the context of this work – is to identify a legitimate regulation from an indirect expropriation.

Traditional regulation of water resources continuously evolves in response to the increase and diversified water demand. The special characteristics of water resources justify differences in regulation over land and other natural resources, subject to some sort of property rights or entitlements.

Watercourses Convention Online Users' Guide, available at http://www.unwater-coursesconvention.org, accessed May 26, 2016.

32   1936 UNTS 269; 31 ILM 1312 (1992).

33   For a detailed comparison between these Conventions see: Attila Tanzi, 'UN Economic Commission for Europe Water Convention,' in *The UN Watercourses Convention in Force: Strengthening international law for transboundary water management*, ed. Flavia Rocha Loures and Alistair Rieu-Clarke (Oxon, Routledge: 2013).

3.2.2.1 Towards an Integrated Water Management Approach

Under the umbrella of international declarations and action plans, States are encouraged to bring together their water resources management strategies. IWRM seems to be the preferred, albeit not the only, approach to water management. IWRM is defined as:

> [a] process which promotes the co-ordinated development and management of water, land and related resources, in order to maximize the resultant economic and social welfare in an equitable manner without compromising the sustainability of vital ecosystems.[34]

This concept incorporates the three perspectives on water resources, discussed in Chapter 2, environmental, economic and social.[35] Besides these aspects, each national legal system ought to consider its cultural realities when implementing some common principles.[36]

As the International Conference on Freshwaters recommended, the implementation of water management principles should take place at the 'lowest appropriate level.' Indeed, community organisations, local governments and stakeholders groups are all capable to manage some level of decision-making.[37] Bottom-up participation in decision-making has the advantage of informing national water policies and regulation by taking into account the needs of large and small consumers from different sectors and geographical points.

While this is a positive step in terms of democratic legitimacy, it may also lead to disagreements among stakeholders, for example between central and regional governments, economic sectors and communities of users. After all, there are key interests at stake that seek to influence the process of water allocation, potentially destabilising the overall balanced apportion of water resources. Furthermore, non-obvious uses, such as protection of in-stream flows and environmental uses are integrated inadequately or not integrated at all.[38]

These challenges, however, rarely stay in the local sphere; they often have repercussions in the relations between States and foreign investors. Projects associated to extractive industries and to the provision of water services,

---

34 Global Water Partnership Technical Advisory Committee (TAC), 'Integrated Water Resources Management,' Stockholm: Global Water Partnership, 2000, 22.

35 See Chapter 2, Sections 2.2.2, 2.2.3 and 2.2.4.

36 Salman M.A. Salman and Daniel D. Bradlow, *Regulatory Frameworks for Water Resources Management: A Comparative Study* (Washington: The World Bank, 2006), 11.

37 International Conference on Freshwater, 'Bonn Recomendations for Action,' Actions in the Field of Governance, Point 11.

38 The World Bank, 'Water Resources Management,' Washington: The World Bank, 1993, 43–44.

THE GOVERNANCE OF WATER RESOURCES

illustrate the conflicts that could arise from deficient planning in water alloca-tion, as it will be further discussed in Chapter 6.

Adaptability is a fundamental element of IWRM, as prioritisation and al-location of water rights involve continuous risk assessment and is dictated by the variability of the hydrological cycle. It follows that if adaptability requires adjustment of water uses, it may affect the security and stability of water entitlements.

There are, however, new drivers of water scarcity. Climate change may jus-tify further the need for adaptability and flexibility in the regulation of water resources.

3.2.2.2   Concerns around Hydrological Variability and Climate Change: New Challenges

As discussed earlier, institutional and legal water frameworks historically relied on the assumption of limited variability and some consistency of the water cycle.[39] This assumption informed the allocation of water entitlements within national water regimes, as well as international agreements.

However, additional pressures over water are likely to challenge traditional approaches, revealing a growing need for prediction and reaction mechanisms. It is widely acknowledged that water resources constitute a vehicle of the im-pacts of climate change, such as water hazards. It follows that climate change is expected to have considerable impact on renewal and reliability.[40] The effects of climate change over previous historical patterns are likely to exac-erbate competition among water users in the coming years,[41] turning past wa-ter entitlements and mechanisms no longer viable.[42] In the past, water policy

---

39   According to Zbigniew W. Kundzewicz et al., 'Freshwater resources and their manage-ment,' in *Climate Change 2007: Impacts, Adaptation and Vulnerability. Contribution of Working Group II to the Fourth Assessment Report of the Intergovernmental Panel on Climate Change*, ed. M.L. Parry et al., (Cambridge: Cambridge University Press, 2007) 173–210, 196.

40   Martin Beniston, Markus Stoffel, and Margot Hill, 'Impacts of Climatic Change on Water and Natural Hazards in the Alps: Can Current Water Governance Cope with Future Chal-lenges? Examples from the European "Acqwa" Project,' *ENVSCI Environmental Science and Policy* 14, no. 7 (2011), 738–39. See also Jessica Troell and Greta Swanson, 'Adaptive Wa-ter Governance and the Principles of International Water Law,' in *Transboundary Water Governance: Adaptation to Climate Change*, ed. Juan Carlos Sanchez and Joshua Roberts (Gland: International Union for Conservation of Nature, 2014).

41   See Denis A. Hughes and S.J.L. Mallory, 'The importance of operating rules and assess-ments of beneficial use in water resource allocation policy and management,' *Water Poli-cy* 11 (2009), 732.

42   Claudia W. Sadoff and Mike Muller, 'Perspectives on water and climate change adapta-tion. Better water resources management – Greater resilience today, more effective adap-tation tomorrow,' Stockholm: Global Water Partnership, 2009, 3–4, 11.

instruments developed over long periods of time; currently States may be in need of new and enhanced mechanisms which allow flexibility and institutional learning.[43] For developing States this is an even greater challenge, as they need to tackle current regulatory vulnerability, while attempting to anticipate severe climate change effects.[44]

In the context of energy and climate change, for instance, the promotion of renewable energy generation through subsidies and other incentives may require regulatory space to revise, adjust and adapt newly created legal schemes. However, market conditions and energy costs are not always predictable, and States could be ill prepared to adapt such schemes without affecting investors' expectations. Currently, there are a number of renewable energy related disputes against Spain, Italy and Czech Republic to be decided under the Energy Charter Treaty (ECT).[45]

3.2.3 *Ownership, Control and Allocation of Water Resources*

A discussion of adaptive management and regulation of water resources would not be complete without reference to the ownership and allocation of water resources. A combination between the physical characteristics of water and its historical context, determines the way in which water is owned and regulated.[46]

Water ownership and property rights over water are understood as two different concepts. Ownership, on one hand, constitutes property – narrowly understood – over water resources, generally held by the State or under stewardship of the State. Allocation of water permits through concessions and licences, on the other, constitute entitlements which allow the enjoyment of the resource under certain conditions and for certain purpose. In the context of international investment law, water permits (or water rights) are likely to fall

---

43 Jessica Troell and Greta Swanson, 'Adaptive Water Governance and the Principles of International Water Law,' in *Transboundary Water Governance: Adaptation to Climate Change*, ed. Juan Carlos Sanchez and Joshua Roberts (Gland: Switzerland, 2014), 31.

44 Alejandro Camacho, 'Adapting Governance to Climate Change: Managing Uncertainty Through a Learning Infrastructure,' *Emory Law Journal* 59 (2009), 17.

45 For an extensive account of the renewable energy disputes, its background and critique, see Daniel Behn and Ole Kristian Fauchald, 'Governments under Cross-Fire? Renewable Energy and International Economic Tribunals,' *Manchester Journal of International Economic Law* 12, no. 2 (2015).

46 Philippe Cullet, 'Water Law in a Globalised World: the Need for a New Conceptual Framework,' *Journal of Environmental Law* 23, no. 2 (2011), 6.

THE GOVERNANCE OF WATER RESOURCES   49

under the 'definition of investment,' thereby protected by the provisions of the relevant investment agreement.[47]

Most societies have embraced the basic premise, within their water laws, that water should not be subject to ownership by any individual.[48] The mechanisms to allocate water rights to different users vary amongst different national legal systems.[49]

The development of property systems in water and in land has followed two different paths. Although they might have shared a similar origin within an open-access regime or common property regime, property over land soon moved towards individual and private property systems.[50] Water remained within the realm of open-access or was nationalised by governments to be managed for the common good. Rarely do water resources become subject to private or individual ownership.

i)   Common *versus* Public Good

The distinction between 'common property' (*res commune*) and 'open-access' (*res nullius*) regimes is relevant from an institutional perspective, as it assists in understanding the evolution of water ownership, allocation and (non) exclusion.[51]

---

47   See for instance, the *obiter dictum* by the arbitral tribunal in *Bayview Irrigation District et al., v. United Mexican States*, ICSID Case No. ARB(AF)/05/1, Award of 19 June, 2007, discussed in Chapter 6, Section 6.3.3.

48   Philippe Cullet, 'Water Law in a Globalised World: the Need for a New Conceptual Framework,' 6.

49   For a comparison of national legal systems and allocation of water rights, see Salman and Bradlow, *Regulatory Frameworks for Water Resources Management: A Comparative Study*; Sarah M. Hendry, *Frameworks for Water Law Reform* (Cambridge: Cambridge University Press, 2014); Dante Augusto Caponera, *Principles of Water Law and Administration: National and International* (Rotterdam: A.A. Balkema, 1992); and Stephen Hodgson, 'Modern Water Rights. Theory and Practice,' Rome: Development Law Service FAO Legal Office, Food and Agriculture Organization of the United Nations, 2006.

50   The late Professor Elinor Ostrom clarified the difference between open-access regimes and common property regimes in her article 'Private and Common Property Rights,' in *Encyclopedia of Law and Economics: Civil Law and Economics*, ed. Gerrit De Geets and Bouckaert Boudewijn (Gent: Cheltenham, Edward Elgar, 2000), 335–36.

51   Note that from an economic perspective, the term 'institution' encompasses more than the organisation constituted by government, regulatory agency, etc. In this case institution means 'the rules of the game,' which consider formal and informal constrains and their enforcement rules. 'Institutions are the humanly devised constrains that structure human interaction.' Douglas North, 'Economic Performance Through Time,' *American Economic Review* 84, no. 3 (1994), 360.

The concept of 'common property' implies some way of exclusion for the benefit of the members of the community and some rules of enjoyment and use. 'Open-access' is a system of non-property, non-exclusion and no rules.[52] The term 'open-access' is akin to the concept of 'public goods,' which are generally non-rival, and non-exclusive, such as the open seas and the atmosphere.[53]

The terms, 'open access' and 'common property' however, have been often used indistinctively over the years to describe resources that had no-owners (*res nullius*), such as the fisheries in the high seas:[54]

> [t]he problems of managing fisheries in territorial waters and those on the high seas have similarities – they are fugitive resources – but they are very different in actual and potential institutional regulation.[55]

'Common-pool' regimes share with 'open access' the difficulty of physical and institutional exclusion of beneficiaries. As a result, beneficiaries may over exploit the resource, lacking incentives to invest in monitoring and protection. 'Common-pool' and 'private goods' regimes share the characteristic that one user's consumption affects quantities available to other users.[56]

---

52 Legal academics such as Caponera use the term public ownership of water resources, not to be confused with a common property regime used by Ostrom above. On public ownership and its comparison with private ownership of water resources, see Dante A. Caponera, 'Possible contents of and reasons for water law,' in *Principles of water law and administration: national and international*, ed. Dante A. Caponera and Marcella Nanni (Routledger – Taylor & Francis, 2007), 138.

53 Ostrom adds that open access regimes are less discussed in the literature. Some open-access regimes are the result of 'conscious public policies' which aim to guarantee access to all citizens 'to the use of a resource within a political jurisdiction. The concept of *jus publicum* applies to their formal status, but effectively these resources are open access.' See Ostrom, 'Private and Common Property Rights,' 336.

54 In this vein, several academics argue that Hardin referred to an *open access* regime in his seminal work: *The Tragedy of the Commons*, rather than a common property regime. See for instance: Ostrom, 'Private and Common Property Rights,' 335–36; Lee Anne Fennell, 'Ostrom's Law: Property Rights in the Commons,' *International Journal of the Commons* 5, no. 1 (2011), 12. Hardin's work describes the problem of open pastures where farmers could bring their cattle to graze. According to Hardin, each farmer would have incentives to bring as much cattle as possible to graze, imposing the costs of overgrazing to other farmers also using the common land. Ultimately, such costs would result in the pastures being overexploited and consequently damaged.

55 S.V. Ciriacy-Wantrup and Richard C. Bishop, '"Common Property" as a Concept in Natural Resources Policy,' *Natural Resources Journal* 15 (1975), 715.

56 Ostrom, 'Private and Common Property Rights,' 337–38. See also Harold Demsetz, 'Toward a Theory of Property Rights,' *The American Economic Review* 57, no. 2 (1967).

THE GOVERNANCE OF WATER RESOURCES 51

There is no automatic relationship between 'common-pool' and 'common property' regimes, despite some similar characteristics.[57] 'Common-pool' resources such as rivers, lakes or basins may be owned or stewarded by the State, where several users share the resources. The problem of overuse and the lack of control to access the resource have been solved, in practice, through mechanisms of allocation of water rights, with narrower scope of enjoyment, use and alienability than, for instance, individual property of land.[58]

From a different perspective, Richard Epstein explains that water pertains to the community as a whole, where – by default – everyone is entitled to it, and no one can be deprived of it:

> [the term *res commune* is used to] establish a background legal environment for water rights that is the exact opposite of what it is for land [...] the paradigmatic act of acquiring ownership of land (reducing it to private possession) now constitutes the quintessential violation of the communal rights to water.[59]

There seems to be an overall acknowledgment, among legal scholars, of water as *res commune* (within the broader notion of 'common-pool'), whose nature does not allow for ownership. Under such a view, a portion of water is, thus, used and restored to the flow for the use of the rest of the community: a term that has been referred to as 'negative community.'[60] The notion of 'commons' remains useful to distinguish the implications of the regulation of water from the regulation of land.[61]

ii)   Toward Individual Property Systems: Land and Water

Property rights are one of the main drivers of economic development.[62] The shift from common property systems towards individual property systems in relation to land, responds to the need of full internalization of costs and benefits for the use of land. These costs involve actual investments to exclude, monitor and protect from competitors, as well as the implied costs of land pollution

---

57   Ostrom, 'Private and Common Property Rights,' 338.

58   Epstein provides a discussion on the development of water rights, in comparison with land rights. See Richard A. Epstein, 'The Historical Variation in Water Rights,' in *The Evolution of Markets for Water: Theory and Practice in Australia*, ed. Jeff Bennett (Cheltenham: Edward Elgar, 2005), 25–26. See also Ostrom, 'Private and Common Property Rights,' 336–37.

59   *Ibid.*, 25.

60   Anthony Scott and Georgina Coustalin, 'The Evolution of Water Rights,' *Natural Resources Journal* 35 (1995), 836. See also Epstein, 'The Historical Variation in Water Rights,' 28.

61   Epstein, 'The Historical Variation in Water Rights,' 25.

62   Ostrom, 'Private and Common Property Rights,' 334.

and depletion.[63] However, communities only identify these externalities over long periods of time, and often without full rationalisation of the effects of land ownership on the attainment of economic development.[64]

In contrast to the ownership of land, water not only remains away from the concept of individual property systems, there is recently a tendency to remove past traditional systems of ownership, such as riparian and prior appropriation rights and to return them to the control and management of the State.

Historically, appropriation systems and control mechanisms responded to a community context, geographical location, and cultural values among others: 'in general, regions that were water rich had little need to develop rules, while water-poor regions had great need to do so.'[65] Indeed, regions facing water scarcity were more likely to develop legal regimes with defined private property rights.[66] This provided those who grab the resources first, with the right to keep it, 'first in time, first in right.'[67]

While water scarcity triggered the development of a system of prior appropriation in the Western part of the US;[68] water abundance gave rise to a riparian system within the common law of England.[69] Under the riparian system the landowner had a right to the water bordering his land. Other legal systems, such as the Spanish one, adopted customary rules developed by the Moors. These traditions were later exported from Spain to its colonies in South

---

63   This need of full internalization would make sense, when its benefits outweighs its costs. See Demsetz, 'Toward a Theory of Property Rights,' 350; Robert C. Ellickson, 'Property in Land,' *Yale Law Journal* 102 (1992–1993).

64   'I do not mean to assert or to deny that the adjustments in property rights which take place need be the result of a conscious endeavor to cope with new externality problems. These adjustments have arisen in western societies largely as a result of gradual changes in social mores and in common law precedents.' See Demsetz, 'Toward a Theory of Property Rights,' 350.

65   Dellapenna and Gupta, 'Toward Global Law on Water,' 439.

66   Dellapenna explains this situation more specifically, when referring to the evolution of water allocation in the United States: '[a]s a result, concern over water law evolved to the west of Kansas City in the direction of well-defined private property rights – appropriative rights or dual systems that at least avoid the worst of the tragedy of the commons.' See Joseph W. Dellapenna, 'United States: The Allocation of Surface Waters,' in *The Evolution of the Law and Politics of Water*, ed. Joseph W. Dellapenna and Joyeeta Gupta (Springer, 2009), 191.

67   Salman M.A. Salman and Daniel D. Bradlow, *Regulatory Frameworks for Water Resources Management: A Comparative Study* (Washington: The World Bank, 2006), 143.

68   Dan A. Tarlock, 'National water law: the foundations of sustainable water use,' *Journal of Water Law* 15 no. 3–4 (2004), 121.

69   Epstein, 'The Historical Variation in Water Rights,' 7. For the development and evolution of water rights see Scott and Coustalin, 'The Evolution of Water Rights.'

THE GOVERNANCE OF WATER RESOURCES

America and North America.[70] Australia received the common law tradition from England of riparian water law,[71] which ill fitted Australia's geography and availability of water.[72]

It follows that changes to the current legal frameworks would not come without cost. The Western US 'prior appropriation' system has been difficult to adjust to new and more efficient water demands.[73] Likewise, within the framework of foreign investment and its protection, the adjustment and reallocation of water rights should be a matter of balance between the assurances offered to investors prior to the establishment in the host State and the legitimate pursuit of common interests.

iii) Hydrological Distinctions and Ownership

Inadequate knowledge of the hydrological cycle in the past gave rise to misunderstandings of the water sources that integrated a single system. In other words, the unity of the hydrological cycle was not understood in its whole dimension. The Ohio Supreme Court, following the English rule of absolute ownership of the resources under the soil (groundwater), considered:

> the existence, origin, movement and course of such waters, and the causes which govern and direct their movements, are so secret, occult and concealed, that an attempt to administer any set of legal rules in respect to them would be involved in hopeless uncertainty, and would be, therefore, practically impossible.[74]

The ownership of groundwater was historically attached to the land, '*a caelo usque ad centrum*' – 'the owner of the land owns everything located above and below his land, including groundwater.'[75]

---

70   Tarlock, 'National water law: the foundations of sustainable water use,' 121.

71   Hodgson, 'Modern water rights. Theory and practice,' 9. See also Scott and Coustalin, 'The Evolution of Water Rights,' 902.

72   Janice Gray, 'Legal approaches to the ownership, management and regulation of water from riparian rights to commodification,' *Transforming Cultures* 1, no. 2 (2006), 72.

73   Steven J. Shupe, Gary D. Weatherford, and Elizabeth Checchio. 'Western Water Rights: The Era of Reallocation,' *Natural Resources Journal* 29, no. 2 (1989); Dan A. Tarlock, *Law of Water Rights and Resources* (New York: C. Boardman, 1988).

74   *Frazier v. Brown*, 12 Ohio St. 294, 311 (Ohio 1861). See also Juliane R. Bourquin and A. Matthews, 'Modern approach to groundwater allocation disputes: Cline v. American Aggregates Corporation,' *Journal of Energy Law Policy* 7, no. 2 (1986), 361.

75   Caponera, 'Possible contents of and reasons for water law,' 138. Salman and Bradlow, *Regulatory Frameworks for Water Resources Management: A Comparative Study*, 145.

54   CHAPTER 3

Currently, it is widely acknowledged that groundwater is connected to surface water. Article 2 of the UN Watercourses Convention defines 'watercourse' as a 'system of surface and groundwaters'.[76] Groundwater withdrawals impose a burden on both the river (surface water) and groundwater systems,[77] affecting many more types of uses than was previously thought. As a result, an increasing number of legal systems have shifted groundwater under the ownership and control of the State.[78] As discussed in the previous Section 'grandfather rights' and prior uses,[79] often deter the introduction of such modifications, as they may be deemed expropriatory.[80]

3.2.4   *Water Rights and Entitlements: A Fragile Right*

States allocate water resources in a number of ways; let us consider three of them, which can be observed alternatively or in combination: (i) a *free use* regime, of rainwater, springs, ponds, flows within the boundaries of their private property (excessive use and conflicts with other neighbouring users, should be avoided),[81] (ii) a *declaration/registration* regime, which requires water users to register their use of water (this regime applies to measured uses of water in shallow wells and irrigation of limited areas),[82] and (iii) a *permit system,* which is the most widely used regime for the regulation of water resources. The definition of a permit, in a broad sense, encompasses several types of

---

76   International Law Commission, 'Draft articles on the law of non-navigational uses of international watercourses and commentaries thereto and resolution on transboundary confined groundwater,' 90; Savenije, 'Why water is not an ordinary economic good, or why the girl is special,' 9. Principle No. 1 of the *Dublin Statement* recognizes that management of water resources should be undertaken under the 'whole catchment area and groundwater aquifer', see *Dublin Statement on Water and Sustainable Development,* Dublin 31 January, 1992. In the same vein the definition of Integrated Water Resources Management, adopts the holistic approach to the management of water, land and related resources, see Technical Advisory Committee (TAC), 'Integrated Water Resources Management,' 22.

77   Epstein, when addressing the treatment of groundwater, makes reference to the externalities that increasing consumption by some users impose on other uses, justifying as Demsetz before, the shift from one system of property rights to another, in this case from private ownership to public ownership. See Epstein, 'The Historical Variation in Water Rights,' 30–31.

78   Salman and Bradlow, *Regulatory Frameworks for Water Resources Management: A Comparative Study,* 145. See also, e.g. Ley de Aguas No. 276 de la República de Costa Rica, Article 4. (Water Act, No. 276, Republic of Costa Rica, Article 4).

79   See for instance Morocco Water Law Article 6; Arizona Groundwater Code.

80   Hendry, *Frameworks for Water Law Reform,* 38.

81   Caponera, 'Possible contents of and reasons for water law,' 139–40.

82   *Ibid.*

administrative acts allowing users the enjoyment of, mostly, fixed quantities of water specified within the conditions provided in the authorisation, lease, licence or other administrative instrument.[83]

Termination of water rights is expressly provided in domestic laws. Some causes for termination range from expiration of the permit; harm through the use of water resources; excessive extraction; different use than that stated in the permit; and reallocation without permission of the administrative authority.

Water permits and permits to extract oil, gas, minerals, land or forests, share some similar characteristics; however, there are important differences that require careful consideration. Water is not present in fixed quantities in catchments and basins; it flows through the hydrological cycle, affected by atmospheric and other physical conditions. In contrast, oil, forest reserves, minerals and land can be found in wells and reservoirs; few sources of water share a similar storage system. Land, forests and minerals are reliable sources due to their rather static nature; fossil fuels are volatile in price, but predictable in terms of availability. It follows that the legal regime for each type of natural resource requires different levels of regulatory flexibility, reflecting their own intrinsic characteristics.

Indeed while more general regimes seek to secure, exclusive, individual entitlements, for reasons of public interest and interrelated common use, water rights regimes cannot always guarantee complete enjoyment of property rights.[84] As discussed, the Western US is one example of a property-based system requiring improved regulatory flexibility, but it is a good illustration of the challenges that regulatory adaptability faces.[85]

---

83   *Ibid.*

84   Tarlock, 'National water law: the foundations of sustainable water use,' 121–22. See also Caponera, 'Possible contents of and reasons for water law,' 145; Hodgson, 'Modern water rights. Theory and practice.'

85   Neuman inquired: 'Water users who hold vested water rights in arid regions hold valid property rights, even though they are considerably different than ownership rights to a piece of land. How, indeed, could those rights be made more "flexible?" .... Yet to truly incorporate adaptive management, there needs to be some "give" at the individual level as well. One way to achieve this goal is to "regulate" for it.' See Janet Neuman, 'Adaptive Management: How Water Law Needs to Change,' *Environmental Law Reporter* 31 (2001), 11436. In this vein, Ross agreed that water property rights are of a fragile nature, see Shelley Ross Saxer, 'The Fluid Nature of Property Rights in Water,' *Pepperdine University School of Law. Legal Studies Research Paper Series* Paper Number 2010/13 (2010), 3.

The question that follows is whether water entitlements deserve less protection than other property rights.[86] In other words, should governments enjoy more deference for regulatory interference with water entitlements?

Those who hold an affirmative answer, also consider that the level of compensation, in case of takings or expropriation of water rights should be limited:[87]

> [c]ompensation requirements should be narrowly drawn to avoid over deterrence of regulatory change. Courts should require takings claimants to prove that they have been the victims of a change in the principles governing use or ownership of their property.[88]

Other views argue that in case of termination of permits, due to environmental protection, courts should consider the extent of the deprivation suffered by the holder; as these types of cases represent incremental risks that the water-rights holders are already subject to.[89] A more conservative opinion asserts that compensation should be paid, when termination of the water permit is not attributable to any action of the holder. Under this rationale the holder should be protected against losses of the capital invested.[90]

At least three situations should be differentiated: (i) termination of water rights; (ii) reallocation of water rights; and (iii) restriction of water usage within a given permit. In this context, considering the positions referred to above, adjudicators may inquire whether any of the three situations constitutes expropriation or whether it is a legitimate regulation. Even in a case of expropriation, some domestic legal systems do not stipulate payment of compensation for cancelation of water permits, as will be discussed in Chapter 7.

---

86 Joseph Sax, 'The Constitution, Property Rights and the Future of Water Law,' *University of Colorado Law Review* 61 (1990), 260. Joseph L. Sax, 'Takings and the Police Power,' *Yale Law Journal* 74, no. 36 (1964); For Thompson citing Professor Sax, see Barton H. Jr Thompson, 'Water Law as a Pragmatic Exercise: Professor Joseph Sax's Water Scholarship,' *Ecology Law Quarterly* 25 (1998), 369.

87 See Sax, 'The Constitution, Property Rights and the Future of Water Law,' 259.

88 Holly Doremus, 'Takings and Transitions,' *Journal of Land Use* 19, no. 1 (2003), 45.

89 Tarlock, 'National water law: the foundations of sustainable water use,' 125.

90 Caponera, 'Possible contents of and reasons for water law,' 143. See also Callies and Chipcase, addressing several American court decisions, where courts order the payment of compensation upon the determination of water property rights. David L. Callies and Calvert G. Chipchase, 'Water Regulation, Land Use and the Environment,' *University of Hawai'i Law Review* 30 (2007), 73–74.

3.3 The Regulation of Water Supply

This chapter would not be complete without addressing the regulation of water supply and services, in connection with the special nature of drinking water supply and access to water, discussed in Chapter 2.[91]

Since water providers also require water permits regulating the use over quantity and quality, part of the regulation of water supply falls under the scope of water resources management. Regulatory mechanisms for water supply involve specific institutional arrangements, such as the separation of water sector policymakers from regulatory bodies of water supply and service provision.[92] It would therefore be 'misleading to discuss resources management and services delivery in the same institutional context.'[93]

The activity of water supply is integrated in the planning and management of water resources. Yet, once extracted and introduced in the network of distribution, it moves into a different sphere or regulatory activity. The challenges surrounding water supply and services are less about availability and more about the management and operation of infrastructure and the price at which these services would be supplied.

The distribution of water services shares the natural monopolistic nature of other network industries such as telecommunications and electricity.[94] Economic regulation of monopolistic infrastructure, in general, aims to resemble a competitive market in long-run equilibrium, in order to set an optimal price for the provision of services. In so doing, it allows the provider to cover his production costs and receive a reasonable return for the investment.[95] There are several methodologies for price regulation in the area of water supply and sanitation, but their analysis is outside the scope of this book.[96] It suffices to

---

91 See Section 2.4.2.

92 For some examples in the Latin American context see: Roberto Lentini, 'Servicios de Agua Potable y Saneamiento: Lecciones de Experiencias Relevantes,' Santiago: CEPAL and Ministerio Federal de Cooperacion Economica y Desarrollo, 2011, 7.

93 World Water Assessment Programme, 'The United Nations World Water Development Report 3,' 51.

94 See Eija M. Vinnary, 'The Economic Regulation of publicly owned water utilities: The case of Finland,' *Utilities Policy* 14, no. 3 (2006), 159. Yet, this may depend on the various structures in place.

95 Alfred E. Kahn, *The Economics of Regulation. Principles and Institutions* (London: Massachusetts Institute of Technology, 1988), 63. See also Michael Klein, 'Economic Regulation of Water Companies,' Washington: World Bank, 1996, 3.

96 Christopher Decker, *Modern Economic Regulation: An Introduction to Theory and Practice* (Cambridge University Press, 2015), 378–83. See also Public-Private Infrastructure

58   CHAPTER 3

stress that they are largely based on the cost and risks associated with capital investments.

In some cases the materialisation of risks was the cause of the failure of a number of projects in developing countries. The end of some of these projects and the exit of foreign companies from the host States, gave rise to a new discourse against the privatisation of water supply. The notions of 'full recovery'[97] and 'water as economic good' were contested; as some scholars argued, given its strategic importance, water supply should be under the responsibility of public institutions.[98]

These are the scenarios under which several investment disputes took place. The next section discusses some high profile water services-related investment disputes. The purpose is to illustrate the high political and sensitive nature of the water sector, which so far has mainly been revealed in the water supply and services sector. The lessons learned from the regulation of water as a public utility may be relevant in the context of water resources management.[99]

Advisory Facility and World Bank, 'Approaches to private participation in water services: A toolkit' Washington, DC: International Bank for Reconstruction and Development and World Bank, 2006, 115–16. See also David Hall and Emanuele Lobina, 'Water as a Public Service,' Public Services International, 2006, 35–36.

[97] The TAC provides the following account of 'full recovery': '[t]he recovery of full cost should be the goal for all water uses unless there are compelling reasons for not doing so. While, in principle, the full cost needs to be estimated and made known for purposes of rational allocation and management decisions, it need not necessarily be charged to the users.' See Technical Advisory Committee (TAC), 'Integrated Water Resources Management,' 20.

[98] 'The financial focus needs to be switched from providing incentives and subsidies for multinational operators, to identifying the financial needs of local public sector water providers, and ways in which they can be supported.' Hall and Lobina, 'Water as a Public Service,' 63. See also Stefan M.M. Kuks, 'The privatisation debate on water services in the Netherlands: public performance of the water sector and the implications of market forces,' *Water Policy* 8 (2006); Maude Barlow and Tony Clarke, *Blue Gold The Battle Against Corporate Theft of the World's Water* (London: Earthscan Publications Ltd, 2003); Christopher McCrudden, *Regulation and Deregulation. Policy and Practice in the Utilities and Financial Services Industries* (Oxford: Clarendon Press, 1999), 276; Sergio Navajas, 'El Servicio de Agua Potable y Desagues Cloacales en Buenos Aires,' in *La Regulación de la Competencia y de los Servicios Públicos. Teoria y Experiencia Argentina Reciente* (Buenos Aires: Fundación de Investigaciones Economicas Latinoamericanas, 1999) and Anthony Ogus, *Regulation. Legal Form and Economic Theory* (Oxford: Clarendon Press, 1994), 46–54.

[99] Besides the three cases discussed in this section there is number of investment disputes in the area of water supply and sanitation: *Azurix Corp. v. Argentine Republic*, ICSID Case No. ARB/01/12; *Suez Sociedad General de Aguas de Barcelona S.A. and Vivendi Universal S.A. v. Argentine Republic*, ICSID Case No. ARB/03/19; *Suez Societad General de Aguas de Barcelona S.A. and Interagua Servicios Integrales de Agua S.A. v. Argentine Republic*, ICSID

THE GOVERNANCE OF WATER RESOURCES

3.3.1 *Investment Treaty Arbitration and the Supply of Water Services*
3.3.1.1 Aguas del Tunari S.A. v. Bolivia[100]

The process of liberalisation of water supply and sanitation in Bolivia is well known due to the civil unrest that gave rise to the so-called Cochabamba 'water war.' Cochabamba had a long-term problem of droughts and access to reliable sources of water for human consumption, agriculture and other uses. Although the central and local governments had agreed on the need of a large infrastructure project to secure the delivery of water to the city of Cochabamba, they held different views on how to achieve this objective in the short term.

The Misicuni project had been promised to Cochabamba by a large number of Governments throughout the years. Thus it had been long awaited by the citizens of Cochabamba and was strongly advocated by the local government. The central Government proposed an alternative project – Corani – which would source water from hydroelectric generation to serve the city of Cochabamba. Corani was part of the central government's privatisation programme, hence highly contested by a number of interest groups.

Finally, the Misicuni project was put forward and the central government proceeded with the bidding process which concluded with the negotiation of a forty-year concession contract with Bechtel and Abengoa, as the main shareholders of Aguas del Tunari S.A.[101] The disproportionate increase in tariffs at a very early stage of the project and the continuous problem of water scarcity caused social unrest, resulting in violent events in early 2000. Water consumers, irrigators and several local organisations organised strikes and demonstrations, condemning the privatisation process until the final expulsion of the company and the cancellation of the concession contract.

The foreign investor brought an investment claim against the government of Bolivia before the International Centre for the Settlement of Investment Disputes (ICSID), claiming USD50 million in compensation under the

---

Case No. ARB/03/17; *Saur International v. Argentine Republic*, ICSID Case No. ARB/04/4; *Société Française d'Etudes et de Conseil (SOFRECO) v. Republic of Chad*, EDF Rules; *Mattioli Joint Venture v. The Ministry of Water and Energy representing the Federal Democratic Republic of Ethiopia*, Ad-Hoc arbitration, administered by PCA.

100 *Aguas del Tunari S.A. v. Bolivia*, ICSID Case No. ARB/02/3.

101 For a background of the privatization process of water services in the city of Cochabamba, see William Finnegan, 'Letter from Bolivia. Leasing the Rain: The Race to Control Water Turns Violent,' 46–47; The Democracy Center, 'Water Revolt: The World Bank Letters,' June 2002, available at http://democracyctr.org/bolivia/investigations/bolivia-investigations-the-water-revolt/bechtel-vs-bolivia-role-of-the-world-bank/water-revolt-the-world-bank-letters/, accessed May 28, 2016.

Bolivia – Netherlands Bilateral Investment Treaty BIT.[102] The proceedings were settled between the parties for a token payment of two Bolivianos (about USD 0.30).[103] The settlement has been attributed to the active lobby of NGOs and civil society, advocating for the right to water at affordable prices.

The Aguas del Tunari case illustrates how internal struggles in the governance systems of host States, as well as people's strong feelings of entitlement, may result in loss for all the parties involved. The citizens of Cochabamba do not yet have access to water from Misicuni.[104]

3.3.1.2 Biwater Gauff (Tanzania) Limited v. United Republic of Tanzania[105]

City Water Services Limited[106] signed a number of contracts for the provision of water services in the city of Dar es Salaam. The difficulties in meeting its contractual obligations, such as billing and tariffs collection, became apparent shortly after the concession contracts started operating. The Tanzanian government denied requests to modify the contractual provisions and adopted several measures to recover the control of the service, including: (i) the cancellation of the contract; (ii) the occupation of City Water's facilities; (iii) the takeover of the management of the company; and (iv) the deportation of senior managers. These actions triggered several claims under the BIT between the United Kingdom and Tanzania.[107]

The arbitral tribunal concluded that the investor had performed poor management of the utility from the bidding process and failed to meet its contractual obligations. However, it found that Tanzania had breached its

---

102   The Democracy Center On-Line, 'Bechtel VS. Bolivia: The People Win!!,' 2006, http://www .democracyctr.org/newsletter/vol69.htm, accessed May 28, 2016.

103   Susan Spronk and Carlos Crespo, 'Water, Sovereignty and Social: Investment Treaties and the Struggles against Multinational Water Companies in Cochabamba and El Alto, Bolivia,' *Law, Social Justice & Global Development* (LGD) 1 (2008), 8.

104   Over ten years later the Misicuni Project has not yet been concluded. In this regard, OOSKA News reports that Bolivia still needs USD 32.5 million to complete the project. The contract with the CHM Consortium was cancelled and was later taken over by Misicuni Company, resulting in a 120 days suspension of the works. See OOSKA News, 'Bolivia Needs Another $32.5 Million to Complete Misicuni Project,' March 21, 2014, accessed May 28, 2016, http://www.ooskanews.com/story/2014/03/bolivia-needs -another-325-million-complete-misicuni-project_159851.

105   *Biwater Gauff (Tanzania) Ltd v. United Republic of Tanzania*, ICSID Case No. ARB/05/22.

106   Biwater (UK) and Gauff (Germany) incorporated as BGT for the tender and later incorporated under Tanzanian laws as City Water Services Limited to provide the service in partnership with Dar es Salaam Water and Sewerage Authority (DAWASA).

107   *Biwater Gauff (Tanzania) Ltd v. United Republic of Tanzania*, ICSID Case No. ARB/05/22, Award of July 24, 2008.

THE GOVERNANCE OF WATER RESOURCES

BIT obligations under the standards of expropriation,[108] fair and equitable treatment,[109] and full protection and security.[110] Yet it did not grant any compensation to the investor, since the economic value of the utility was 'nil' at the time of the investment claim.[111]

Biwater is one of the first cases in which an arbitral tribunal allowed *amicus curiae* submissions. The submissions requested the tribunal to consider social concerns such as human rights, access to water and sustainable development.[112] However, none of the issues raised in the *amicus curiae* submissions were specifically addressed by the tribunal in the substantive part of the Award.

Like in *Aguas del Tunari*, the duty of legal, political and social due diligence should not be underestimated, when investment projects are linked to infrastructure intended to provided basic public services such as water and sanitation.

3.3.1.3 Compañía de Aguas del Aconquija S.A. and Vivendi Universal S.A. v. Argentine Republic[113]

Vivendi Universal from France[114] and Aguas de Aconquija from Argentina (CAA) signed a thirty-year concession agreement for the provision of water services to the Province of Tucumán. The newly elected Government of Tucumán expressed its discontent with the tariff increases and exhorted the company to reduce tariffs and to modify the concession agreement, seeking a significant tariff reduction. The investor alleged that such reductions were politically motivated and accused the government of Tucumán of going so far as encouraging consumers not to pay their water bills. After a period of unsuccessful re-negotiations, the concession was terminated and, as per provisions of the

---

108   *Biwater Gauff v. Tanzania,* paras. 451–520.

109   *Ibid.*, paras. 586–675. The tribunal did not uphold all Biwater's claims with regard to the Fair and Equitable Treatment standard.

110   *Ibid.,* paras. 724–31.

111   The tribunal concluded that by the time of the wrongful acts adopted by Tanzania the value of the assets was already zero and that termination of the contract was inevitable in any event *Biwater Gauff v. Tanzania,* para. 799. See also Andrea K. Bjorklund, 'ICSID Tribunal Finds Tanzania to Have Violated Bilateral Investment Treaty but Declines to Award Any Damages,' *The American Society of International Law* (ASIL) 12, no. 17 (2008).

112   Five organisations presented amicus submissions: Lawyers' Environmental Action Team; the Legal and Human Rights Centre; the Tanzania Gender Networking Programme; the Centre for International Environmental Law; and the International Institute for Sustainable Development.

113   *Compañía de Aguas del Aconquija S.A. and Vivendi Universal S.A. v. Argentine Republic,* ICSID Case ARB/97/3.

114   Formerly the French Compagnie Général des Eaux.

62 CHAPTER 3

Agreement, CAA was required to continue providing the services for ten additional months.[115]

The situation was exacerbated by two events of turbidity of water, which led the Ministry of Health to warn citizens of Tucumán of health issues, such as cholera, typhoid and hepatitis.[116] The arbitrators concluded that the incidents of turbidity presented no risk for human health, as shown by tests undertaken by the regulatory authority.[117]

The arbitral tribunal found that Argentina had breached the fair and equitable treatment and expropriation standards, awarding USD105 million compensation in favour of the claimants.[118]

In response to Argentina's allegations of public interest, the tribunal contended that it is the effect of the measure and not the intent of the government the determining factor for the violation of the expropriation standard.[119] The role of the Government of Tucumán in the evolution of the conflict played an important role in the decision of the tribunal.[120]

3.4   Conclusions

Water governance is informed by international, national and local policy, and seems to be in constant evolution. The principles of water management are

---

115   Pursuant to article 15.11 of the Concession Agreement in the event of termination of the agreement, an 18-month extension will apply unless the Province finds an adequate replacement for the provider. See the investor's claims summarised by the tribunal: *Compañía de Aguas del Aconquija S.A. and Vivendi Universal S.A. v. Argentine Republic*, ICSID Case No. ARB/97/3, Award of 20 August, 2007, paras. 5.3.19–5.3.23

116   *Ibid.*, paras. 4.13.11–4.13.13.

117   *Ibid.*

118   This was the second request for arbitration presented by Vivendi Universal, as the first Award was partially annulled in 2002.

119 · *Aguas del Aconquija S.A. and Vivendi Universal S.A. v. Argentine Republic*, Award of 20 August, 2007, para. 7.5.20. See also *Compañia del Desarrollo de Santa Elena S.A. v. Republic of Costa Rica*, ICSID Case No. ARB/96/1, Award of 17 February, 2000 and Rectification of Award of June 8, 2000; and *Técnicas Medioambientales Tecmed v. United Mexican States*, ICSID Case No. ARB(AF)/00/2, Award of 29 May, 2003, para. 116.

120   The tribunal quotes the working paper of a World Bank expert, who served as Argentina's witness during the arbitration proceedings: 'Instead of coming out and explaining the reasons for the changes, the Tucumán Government added its voice to the protests. In truth, a veritable chorus was formed, where legislators, journalists, politicians and leaders from civil society competed to be perceived as the most virulent.' See *Vivendi v. Argentina*, Award of 20 August, 2007, para. 7.4.20.

THE GOVERNANCE OF WATER RESOURCES

yet to be fully implemented by national governments, which means that harmonising competing demands by way of management could negatively affect water entitlements of some users to meet the needs of others, with potential expropriatory implications for foreign investors.

However, not only regulatory adaption to new environmental challenges is foreseeable in the coming years. Less developed countries, which may have achieved certain levels of economic development, are also expected to adopt more sophisticated mechanisms of water management in the near future.

An aspect that remains unchanged is the stance that most States have toward water resources ownership. The character of water ownership must have a close relationship with the allocation and use of water. The extent, to which legal water frameworks are flexible, could have direct correlation to the level of protection of water rights. The manner in which rights may be constructed in order to assess their level of protection will be discussed in detail in Chapter 7.

In the aftermath of the termination of the water concessions in Cochabamba, Dar es Salaam, Tucumán, and several other cities which faced challenges to their water provision, the academic literature has focused mainly on the human right to water and its interplay with investment treaty arbitration.[121] Arbitral tribunals have not yet determined how the right to water may be realised in an investment arbitration context; even more so in a context of no water scarcity or competition, where systems of infrastructure governance and price regulation are at the core of the dispute. In some cases States may invoke their regulatory prerogatives to protect the human health and the public interest; but they should be prepared to defend the legitimacy of such regulatory prerogatives.

---

121 Marrella makes reference to several States proposing constitutional amendments, on the human right to water, such as Bolivia, Argentina, Ecuador, etc. See Marrella, 'On the changing structure of international investment law: The human right to water and ICSID arbitration,' 339; William Schreiber, 'Realizing the Right to Water in International Investment Law: An Interdisciplinary Approach to BIT Obligations,' *Natural Resources Journal* 48, no. 1 (2008). See also Juan Pablo Bohoslavsky's presentation on 'Tratados de protección de las inversiones e implicaciones para la formulación de políticas publicas' in the workshop: 'Tratados internacionales de protección a la inversión y regulación de servicios públicos,' Buenos Aires: ECLAC, November 2010; Heather L. Bray, 'ICSID and the Right to Water: An Ingredient in the Stone Soup,' *ICSID Review* 29, no. 2 (2014); and Bree Farrugia, 'The Human Right to Water: Defences to Investment Treaty Violations,' *Arbitration International* 31, no. 2 (2015).

CHAPTER 4

Revisiting the Doctrine of the Police Power of States

4.1 Introduction

Sovereignty constitutes the quintessential element of a States' political independence and territorial integrity. A significant part of a State's sovereignty is its legitimate authority to adopt measures that could potentially affect the interests and expectations of individuals. The police power doctrine encompasses this aspect of a State's sovereignty and provides a justification for a State's regulatory measures with a presumption of legality so long as that measure connects in some way to the achievement of public welfare.

According to this view, the police power of States to regulate the environment, health and security, among others, within its territory is not contested under international law, just as the exercise of eminent domain or expropriation is not *per se* unlawful under both domestic and international law, under certain conditions. However, regulatory activity could become expropriatory, when its effects go beyond the legitimate exercise of the police power; either by depriving substantially the economic value of the property or by disguising ulterior purposes, different from the public interest. It follows that limiting the regulatory activity of host States might have been the very purpose of a first generation of international investment agreements (IIAs). In addition, it has also been alleged that contracting States to IIAs negotiated broad provisions, so as to protect a wider group of investors against a broad range of possible State measures. Perhaps one could also argue that arbitral tribunals may have interpreted these provisions in such a way that the decisions were somewhat beneficial to investors. Indeed, the alleged broad interpretation of the expropriation standard raised concern among some developed States who had to defend themselves in early investment-related arbitrations.

As a result of these early arbitrations under the dispute settlement provisions in IIAs, several States began to question the legitimacy of not only the agreements they had themselves negotiated but also the impartiality of the arbitral tribunals authorised under such agreements. States began to perceive that their obligations under IIAs had the potential to have a chilling effect on

© KONINKLIJKE BRILL NV, LEIDEN, 2017 | DOI 10.1163/9789004335301_005

the ability of a State to regulate in the public interest.[1] Relatively recent investment treaty negotiations suggest that States are seeking to secure the exercise of their police power by contracting out certain specific economic sectors from the scope of the treaty or providing specific guidance on the interpretation of certain provisions such as expropriation. To this end States have adopted IIAs with weaker rights for foreign investors and greater scope for States' regulatory discretion. The negotiation of IIAs seems to have shifted from an era of home State capital-exporting centric negotiations to an era of host State regulatory centric focus. However, there is still an important number of first generation IIAs in force, which have not been renegotiated or denounced by either party. This means that there are still potential disputes that will be decided under these – arguably – broad treaty provisions.

As some investment experts argue, investment treaty arbitration has also experienced a progressive development in the quest to balance investor's rights and States' regulatory prerogatives, due to the evolution of the work of arbitral tribunals and the interaction amongst its members.[2]

This work seeks to identify the extent to which investment tribunals could incorporate the special nature of water resources in the assessment of regulatory or legislative measures over water resources, which have been claimed to be expropriatory by foreign investors. On the one hand, changes in the regulatory regime governing the management of water resources could negatively

---

1 See for instance Jonathan Bonnitcha, *Substantive Protection under Investment Treaties, A Legal and Economic Analysis* (Cambridge: Cambridge University Press, 2014); Lorenzo Cotula, 'Do Investment Treaty Unduly Constrain Regulatory Space?' *Questions of International Law* 9 (2014), http://pubs.iied.org/X00128.htm; J. Pedro Martinez-Fraga and C. Ryan Reetz, *Public Purpose in International Law: Rethinking Regulatory Sovereignty in the Global Era* (Cambridge: Cambridge University Press, 2014); William Schreiber, 'Realizing the Right to Water in International Investment Law: An Interdisciplinary Approach to BIT Obligations,' *Natural Resources Journal* 48, no. 1 (2008); Howard Mann, 'Implications of International Trade and Investment Agreements for Water and Water Services: Some Responses from Other Sources of International Law,' *Transnational Dispute Management* 5 (2006); Gus Van Harten, 'Five Justifications for Investment Treaties: A Critical Discussion,' *Trade, law and development Trade, Law and Development* 2, no. 1 (2010); Lorenzo Cotula, 'Stabilization Clauses and the Evolution of Environmental Standards in Foreign Investment Contracts,' *Yearbook of International Environmental Law* 17 (2006); Joseph Cumming and Robert Froehlich, 'NAFTA Chapter XI and Canada's Environmental Sovereignty: Investment Flows, Article 1110 and Alberta's Water Act,' Toronto: University of Toronto, 2007.

2 Charles N. Brower and Stephan W. Schill, 'Is Arbitration a Threat or a Boon to the Legitimacy of International Investment Law?' *Chicago Journal of International Law* 9, no. 2 (2009), 471–98.

affect the overall investment project by rendering it useless and thus *de facto* expropriated. On the other hand, as investment tribunals have argued, there cannot be a legitimate expectation that the existing regulatory regime will not be reformed 'to respond to changing circumstances in the public interest.'[3] It would therefore be unreasonable to expect that a highly variable and unpredictable resource, such as water, should remain subject to static rules, hindering adaption and resilience in times of scarcity and climate variability.

This chapter proposes revisiting the doctrine of the police power of States. In the context of international investment law the police power doctrine could be considered as the most important analytical framework for understanding the legitimate exercise of regulatory prerogatives as challenged by foreign investors. If interpreted expansively, the police power doctrine could immunise States from any regulatory or legislative changes that might run afoul of a foreign investors' rights under international law. If adjudicators were to take this approach, there would be the risk that the utility of the international investment regime in protecting foreign investor rights would be rendered impotent. However, the opposite can also occur. If the police power is interpreted narrowly by adjudicators, there is the risk that foreign investor rights, as protected by international law, will trump any uses of the prerogative of the State to limit the exercise of individual liberties (such as those of foreign investors) through regulatory changes.

The proposed revisit to the doctrine of the police powers in this chapter focuses on its scope and assesses its legitimacy in the context of international legal obligations. This aspect of the police power constitutes the analytical framework through which this book looks at the management of water resources.

The conception of the police power gives rise to questions originating specifically in the area of investment treaty arbitration, where the applicable law is typically an IIA and the rules of procedure are stipulated by the contracting parties in the IIA . Under this legal framework, investment tribunals are called to assess whether the action of the host State, in this case a water-related regulatory measure, conforms to the standard of investment protection provided for in the IIA. It thus follows that such an analysis would require that adjudicators evaluate the water laws of the host State to the extent that they may violate a standard of protection under an IIA.

---

3   *Electrabel S.A. v. The Republic of Hungary,* ICSID Case No. ARB/07/19, Award on Jurisdiction, Applicable Law and Liability of 30 November, 2012, para. 7.77. See also *International Thunderbird Gaming Corporation v. The United Mexican States,* UNCITRAL rules, Award of 26 January, 2006; *Charanne (the Netherlands) and Construction Investments (Luxembourg) v. Spain,* Arbitration No.: 062/2012, Final Award of 21 January, 2016. (unofficial translation by Mena Chambers).

Revisiting the doctrine of the police power requires a discussion of its foundations, namely the sovereignty of States. This discussion is followed by the analysis of the jurisprudence of the United States (US), whose practice has arguably shaped the doctrine as it interacts with the law of international investment today.

4.2 The Sovereignty of States: A Foundation for the Police Power

Despite being a relatively old concept, sovereignty still provides a strong basis for the scope of international law and its relationship with the idea of the State. In regard to sovereignty and international law, it has been noted that there is a constant interaction between present and past, and 'the "brave new world" of international dispute settlement turns out to have a great deal of the old world in to it too.'[4]

In the last forty years there has been significant theoretical discussion about the weakening of the sovereignty of States with a rise in the number of international legal obligations that States have opted to be bound by. Particularly, this discourse came on the heels of the negotiations that gave birth to the United Nations (UN) General Assembly's resolutions on the Permanent Sovereignty over Natural Resources (PSNR)[5] and the New International Economic Order (NIEO),[6] which generated resentment between capital importing and capital exporting States; and focused on newly independent States asserting their sovereignty as a means of reducing the influence of their previous colonial occupiers. As the influence of the PSNR and NIEO waned in the 1980s and 1990s, States found themselves in a new era of globalisation that abandoned the desire for absolute sovereignty in exchange for the prospect of increased prosperity that economic integration might garner.[7] While economic integration

---

4   James Crawford, 'Continuity and Discontinuity in International Dispute Settlement: An Inaugural Lecture,' *Journal of International Dispute Settlement* 1, no. 1 (2010), 4. In this context, he expressed that public international law is seeded and nourished by old practices of public international law, referring specifically to the dispute settlement regime. Judge Crawford contends that international law develops 'through processes of accumulation and accretion' and, in comparison, domestic law develops by displacement of present over past uses. *Ibid.*, 23.

5   Resolution 1803(XVII) of 14 December, 1962.

6   Resolution 3201(S-VI) of 1 May, 1974.

7   The Association of Southeast Asian Nations ASEAN (1967), Acuerdo de Cartagena (1969), Caribbean Community CARICOM (1973), MERCOSUR (1991), The Marrakech 'WTO' Agreement (1994), North American Free Trade Agreement NAFTA (1994), Common Market for Eastern

68   CHAPTER 4

agreements become more commonplace in this period, other areas of international governance (such as international environmental governance) found States less willing to give up their sovereignty. This confirms perceptions towards States' inherent power over their own natural resources and their respective environmental agendas.[8] This is not to say that all negotiations in the area of trade and investment have succeeded; in fact, many have failed due to the lack of consensus.[9]

4.2.1   *The Use of Sovereignty in* ex ante *Treaty Negotiations and* ex post *Treaty-Breach Justification*

Sovereignty is often perceived as a hurdle to further cooperation and integration, but also as a gatekeeper preventing the adoption of overly onerous international obligations.[10]

States may adopt two types of approaches towards international law obligations. Under the first approach, negotiating parties may invoke sovereignty as an *ex ante* preventive strategy to avoid State responsibility. In other words,

---

and Southern Africa COMESA (1994), Agreement on the European Economic Area (1994), and the close to 3500 IIAs that have been signed by the end of 2015. See UNCTAD, 'Towards a New Generation of International Investment Policies: UNCTAD's Fresh Approach to Multilateral Investment Policy – Making,' Geneva: United Nations, 2013, 4.

8   There are roughly 500 Multilateral Environmental Agreements, according to the United Nations Environment Programme, see http://www.unep.org/delc/EnvironmentalGovernance/tabid/54638/Default.aspx, accessed May 1, 2016. For instance, in 2011 climate change negotiations lost three important players at its meeting in Durban, South Africa, when Canada, Japan and Russia pulled out of the Kyoto protocol (December 2011). The 1997 Convention on the Law of Non-Navigational Uses of International Watercourses (UN Watercourses Convention), only entered into force on 31 July 2015, when the 35th signatory State ratified the Convention. The International Convention for the Regulation of Whaling has been subject to several reservations and notifications of withdrawal since it was signed in 1946. Norway, Iceland, Japan and Canada have presented substantial oppositions to the provisions of this Convention. See https://iwc.int/members, accessed May 1, 2016.

9   OECD Multilateral Agreement on Investment (MAI), ceased negotiations in December 2008, see http://www.oecd.org/daf/mai/intro.htm, accessed May 1, 2016; International Trade Organisation, negotiated in the Havana Conference in 1947, was never ratified by its members, most notably the United States, see http://www.wto.org/english/thewto_e/whatis_e/tif_e/fact4_e.htm, accessed May 1, 2016. The WTO Doha Round started negotiations in 2001, has proved a difficult challenge. Currently the Transatlantic Trade and Investment Partnership (TTIP) between the United States and European Union is still going through lengthy negotiations.

10   José E. Álvarez, 'The Return of the State,' *Minnesota Journal of International Law* 20, no. 2 (2011), 225.

States might prefer to refrain from entering into international agreements that are perceived as a hindrance to the exercise of their sovereign powers. By the second approach, sovereignty may be invoked as a means to justify an *ex post* measure that breaches the State's obligation under international agreements. Note, however, that the reasons why sovereign States choose one or another strategy cannot be explained from a purely legal perspective. On the contrary, such situations may be better explained through the lens of political science and international relations. Notwithstanding, given the narrow scope of this work, we will consider the two scenarios from a legal perspective.

The first scenario – *ex ante* prevention of State responsibility – could be illustrated within the sphere of water resources management and transboundary shared water resources. As discussed in Chapters 2 and 3, the unique nature of water justifies its global governance, albeit without ignoring local and basin-level decision-making. However, significant efforts to develop global water governance have proved challenging; the prominent example is the Convention on the Law of the Non-Navigational Uses of International Watercourses (UN Watercourses Convention) of 1997.[11] During the negotiations of this Convention, the parties strived to reach consensus on the scope of the right of upstream States to 'reasonably and equitably' use international waters within their territory. This played out, in contrast, as the right invoked by downstream States not to be 'harmed' by upstream riparian States.[12] Sovereignty played an important role in the negotiators' positions, for example China, Turkey and the Czech Republic, expressly pointed out their concerns with regard to the limitations of their sovereign rights as an effect of adopting several provisions of the UN Watercourses Convention:

> [t]erritorial sovereignty is a basic principle of international law. A watercourse State enjoys indisputable territorial sovereignty over those parts of international watercourses that flow through its territory. It is incomprehensible and regrettable that the draft Convention does not affirm this principle.[13]

---

11 For a discussion on the ratification and enter into force of the Convention see Chapter 3. For a discussion on the adoption process and its obstacles see Salman M.A. Salman, 'The United Nations Watercourses Convention Ten Years Later: Why Has its Entry into Force Proven Difficult?' *Water international.* 32, no. 1 (2007); Alistair Rieu-Clarke and Flavia Rocha Loures, 'Still not in Force: Should States Support the 1997 UN Watercourses Convention?' *Review of European Community & International Environmental Law* 18, no. 2 (2009).

12 These principles are discussed in Chapter 3, Section 3.2.1.3.

13 Statement of the representative of China, 'Official Records of the United Nations Conference on the Convention on the Law of the Non-Navigational Uses of International

In the context of the UN Watercourses Convention negotiations, State sovereignty, as a recognised principle of international law, became an obstacle to the achievement of global protection and sustainable use of fresh water resources. In other words, the use of State sovereignty in the *ex ante* scenario allows States to restrict the scope and type of international obligations they will agree to be bound by. This example is telling of the sensitivity involved in the management of water resources at the local and national levels, which may hinder overarching sustainability goals at the international level.[14]

The second scenario – *ex post* State-breach justification – could be observed in the ambit of economic integration through trade and investment agreements. There were close to 3500 IIAs signed by 2015.[15] Virtually all these treaties incorporate obligations under which the contracting States agree to protect foreign investors and provide a secure and predictable business environment. Capital exporting States proposed strong standards of investment protection in order to guarantee adequate investment conditions for their nationals. These early IIAs, as promoted by capital exporting States through model agreements, were 'highly investor-protective.'[16] While capital exporting States were the drivers of these models, capital importing States have also signed IIAs with strong investment protections among themselves in recent years[17]

It is granted that the negotiation of past economic integration agreements proved challenging – comparable to the *ex ante* scenario. For example, the global trading system operated on an *ad hoc* basis for nearly fifty years under the provisions of the GATT 1947 until the WTO Agreement was adopted in 1994. Yet, since then, almost every State has negotiated – or is currently

---

Watercourses,' A/51/PV.99, New York: United Nations, General Assembly, May 12, 1997, 6. See also the Statements of Turkey, *Ibid.*, 5 and Rwanda, *Ibid.*, 12.

14   In the context of the local management of water, States enjoy ample margin of discretion in the manner they allocate and regulate water resources. Such recognition is one of the main attributes of State sovereignty.

15   UNCTAD, 'World Investment Report 2015. Reforming International Investment Governance,' Geneva: UNCTAD, 2015, 106.

16   José E. Álvarez, 'A BIT on Custom,' *New York University Journal of International Law and Politics* 42, no. 1 (2009), 13.

17   These agreements, referred to as South-South investment treaties, may have incorporated the provisions of capital exporting States model agreements. For instance the Cuba – Cambodia BIT has adopted an investor-protective model and China has negotiated IIAs similar to the US model BIT. Álvarez compares the expansive definition of protected investment contained in the Cuba-Cambodia BIT of 2001. See *ibid.*, 13. See also the Cambodia -Cuba (2001).

negotiating – accession to the WTO. Likewise, virtually every State is now party to at least one IIA or FTA.

Recently the legitimacy of the international investment regime has been put to test, as both developed and developing States have expressed concerns about its fairness. Venezuela, Ecuador, Argentina and Bolivia have criticised the regime after being subject to a number of investment arbitration disputes that resulted in awards costing the State hundreds of millions of US Dollars.[18] Russia has threatened to retaliate against States who attempt to freeze its assets abroad as a result of enforcement proceedings arising out of the USD 50 billion award won by shareholders in the oil company Yukos.[19] The US and Canada, for instance, have also been subject to a number of claims for breaches of their international obligations under the NAFTA Chapter 11.[20] Further, Germany, Spain and Australia have recently become subject to claims under IIAS.[21] Such a situation appears to have put in perspective the need for revisiting the regulatory prerogatives of States and the risks that IIAs pose for the sovereign autonomy of developing and developed States alike.[22]

---

18   By 2011, Argentina's Award liabilities reached close to USD 430 million (plus interest), see Luke Eric Peterson, 'Argentina by the numbers: Where Things Stand with Investment Treaty Claims arising out of the Argentine Financial Crisis,' *IA Reporter*, 1 February 2011, accessed May 1, 2016. www.iareporter.com/articles/20110201_9. In October 2012, Occidental Petroleum Corporation was awarded USD 1.77 billion (without interest), in the case followed against the Government of Ecuador, see Tai-Heng Cheng and Lucas Bento, 'ICSID's Largest Award in History: An Overview of Occidental Petroleum Corporation v the Republic of Ecuador,' *Investment Arbitration Blog*, 19 December 2015, accessed May 1, 2016. http://kluwerarbitrationblog.com/blog/2012/12/19/icsids-largest-award-in-history-an-overview-of-occidental-petroleum-corporation-v-the-republic-of-ecuador/.

19   Neil Buckley, 'Russia's Yukos threats signal a lurch away from international law,' *Financial Times*, 5 August 2015, accessed May 2, 2016. http://www.ft.com/cms/s/0/61bafiec-3b6f-11e5-bbd1-b37bc06f590c.html#axzz3rGRoMfui. See *Yukos Universal Limited (Isle of Man) v. The Russian Federation*, PCA Case No. AA 227 under the UNCITRAL Rules, Final Award of 18 July, 2014. However, the awards have been set aside by the Hague District Court.

20   See for instance: *Chemtura Corporation v. Government of Canada,* UNCITRAL, Award of 2 August, 2010; *AbitibiBowater Inc. v. Government of Canada* (NAFTA); *Methanex Corp. v. United States of America,* UNCITRAL, Award of 3 August 2005, *Glamis Gold Ltd v. United States of America,* UNCITRAL; *Sun Belt v. Her Majesty the Queen* (*Government of Canada*), UNCITRAL; *Ethyl Corporation v. the Government of Canada,* UNCITRAL.

21   *Vattenfall AB, et al. v. Federal Republic of Germany*, ICSID Case No. ARB/12/12 (nuclear phase-out); *Charanne* (*the Netherlands*) *and Construction Investments* (*Luxembourg*) *v. Spain*, SCC Arbitration No.: 062/2012 (renewable energy); *Philip Morris Asia Limited v. The Commonwealth of Australia*, UNCITRAL, PCA Case No. 2012-12 (tobacco regulations).

22   See José E. Álvarez, 'The Return of the State'; José E. Álvarez, 'A BIT on Custom.'

A State's failure to comply with both economic integration and environmental governance agreements is often shielded behind the right to exercise internal sovereignty. However, what sovereignty means, in this context, is often unclear and – as a pendulum – seems to shift overtime. Past nationalistic conceptions of sovereignty, adopted during the negotiations on the PSNR, shifted toward more nuanced approaches in order to further economic integration. Yet, recent waves of nationalisation in Latin America show a shift back to a more protective conception of sovereignty.

4.2.2 *Several Meanings of Sovereignty*

Sovereignty has been described as an 'illegitimate offspring,' subject to several meanings, some of which may be even 'destructive of human values.'[23] There are difficulties in approaching the meaning of sovereignty under a single discipline of knowledge, for sovereignty belongs to the realm of law as much as it belongs to the realms of politics and international relations.[24]

The origin of sovereignty may be found in law, politics and power simultaneously, as has been long proposed by Kelsen and Schmitt. These somewhat opposing views, induce competing approaches that are both objective (Kelsen) and subjective (Schmidt) in terms of what is the law to which a State is bound. In practice, however, it has been suggested that they can both exist simultaneously as States exercise of sovereign power often oscillates between both law and fact:[25]

> [i]n general, law and politics have similarities and differences. They are similar in that they are broadly concerned with the problem of power. The definition of politics should probably be partly included in the

---

23   Louis Henkin, 'That "S" Word: Sovereignty, and Globalization, and Human Rights, Et Cetera,' *Fordham Law Review* 68, no. 1 (1999), 1. For discussions on the positive and negative meaning of sovereignty, see Martti Koskenniemi, 'What Use for Sovereignty Today?' *Asian Journal of International Law* I (2011).

24   There appears to be new attempts to approach the principle of sovereignty – as well as other several notions – from an interdisciplinary perspective. See for example, Winston Nagan and Craig Hammer, 'The Changing Character of Sovereignty in International Law and International Relations,' *Columbia Journal of Transnational Law* 43, no. 1 (2004), 2; Antony Anghie, *Imperialism, Sovereignty, and the Making of International Law* (Cambridge – New York: Cambridge University Press, 2005); Martti Koskenniemi, *The Gentle Civilizer of Nations: The Rise and Fall of International Law, 1870–1960* (Cambridge – New York: Cambridge University Press, 2002).

25   See Martti Koskenniemi, *From Apology to Utopia* (New York: Cambridge University Press, 2005).

REVISITING THE DOCTRINE OF THE POLICE POWER OF STATES

definition of law because it certainly seems that all law is politics but not all politics is law.[26]

This theoretical background becomes useful for addressing different meanings of sovereignty, serving the needs and values of States.[27] These needs and values are all contextual, as they have spatial, temporal and cultural components. Indeed, looking at the exercise of sovereignty in different circumstances may assist in identifying not only the meaning that the State is giving to it in the context of the measure, but also how such conceptions reflect on the police power of the State.

Academics have attempted to split the concept of sovereignty into different meanings. Three Weberian 'ideal types': (i) 'the prince' where the supreme power of the State requires no justification, (ii) 'the protector' as the power justifying the ability to protect the State's citizens from internal and external threats and (iii) 'the citizen' as holder of rights and obligations granted by a larger, perhaps international, community.[28] The aim is not to answer what sovereignty is, but how in fact it works in shaping international legal analysis and discourse.[29] In the context of investment treaty arbitration this language may

---

26   Nagan and Hammer, 'The Changing Character of Sovereignty in International Law and International Relations,' 146, fn.21.

27   The Treaty of Westphalia of 1648 brought the notion of sovereignty in line with that of territory and independence to regulate internal affairs. See Douglas Howland and Luise White, 'The state of sovereignty territories, laws, populations,' *Indiana University Press*, accessed May 1, 2016. http://public.eblib.com/EBLPublic/PublicView.do?ptiID=437616. With regard to the influential effect of the Westphalia Treaty in current international law, Gross asserts that Westphalia constitutes a milestone in the separation of international law from religion. See Leo Gross, 'The Peace of Westphalia, 1648–1948,' *American Journal of International Law* 42, no. 1 (1948), 26.

28   See Alison Von Rosenvigne, 'Creating a working vocabulary of sovereignty language at the International Court of Justice,' *Comparative Research in Law & Political Economy, Network. CLPE Research Paper* 05/2010, 6, no. 2 (2010), 3.

       See *Legality of the Threat or Use of Nuclear Weapons, Advisory Opinion, I.C.J. Reports 1996*, p. 226; Fisheries Jurisdiction (Spain v. Canada), Jurisdiction of the Court, Judgment, I.C.J. Reports 1998, p. 432; *Legal Consequences of the Construction of a Wall in the Occupied Palestinian Territory, Advisory Opinion, I.C.J. Reports 2004*, p. 136; *Gabčíkovo-Nagymaros Project (Hungary/Slovakia), Judgment, I.C.J. Reports 1997*, p. 7 ; *Application of the Convention on the Prevention and Punishment of the Crime of Genocide (Bosnia and Herzegovina v. Serbia and Montenegro), Judgment, I.C.J. Reports 2007*, p. 43. (in Von Rosenvigne)

29   See Alison Von Rosenvigne, 'Creating a working vocabulary of sovereignty language at the International Court of Justice,' 1–3.

74   CHAPTER 4

be a useful tool to analyse ways in which States, investors and arbitrators approach the exercise of sovereign power.

Host States could be playing a 'protective' role when adopting measures deemed to pursue welfare objectives. Sovereignty from this perspective involves the limitation of individuals' liberties in order to protect the interest of a much larger portion of society or promoting the public interest through positive action. Such prerogatives can be found in the doctrines of the police power and eminent domain, respectively.

The foreign investor's perspective, of the same measure, may be perceived as a unilateral act of the State, exercising its supreme power as the 'prince.' This approach inherently involves the Hobbesian model of protection and obedience: a conception of the State where the power of the 'prince' can never be contested. Past and present concerns over political and regulatory risk may be illustrated under this perspective. Investors as well as States, for instance, assess these risks before embarking on the negotiation of concession agreements and IIAs, which may incorporate standards of treatment and stabilisation clauses.[30]

Arbitral tribunals may delineate the boundaries – and meaning – of sovereignty, when assessing the exercise of regulatory prerogatives. This approach looks at State sovereignty as the 'citizen,' under which a sovereign State functions as a member of a larger international community with rights and obligations. This view is compatible with the approach adopted by the Permanent Court of International Justice (PCIJ) in the *SS Wimbledon* case of 1923:

> [t]he Court declines to see, in the conclusion of any treaty by which a State undertakes to perform or refrain from performing a particular act, an abandonment of its sovereignty ... the right of entering into international engagements is an attribute of State sovereignty.[31]

---

30 Prosper Weil identifies two types of stabilisation clauses: (i) stabilisation clauses *per se*, limiting the legislative risk, whereby States may modify the contract by a legislative action; and (ii) Clauses *D'intagibilite*, which seek to limit the exercise of the public authority of the State. See Prosper Weil, 'Les Clauses de Stabilisation ou D'intangibilité Insérées dans les Accords de Développement Economiques,' in *Mélanges offerts à Charles Rousseau: La Communauté Internationale*, ed. Mélanges Rousseau (Charles) (Paris: Editions A. Pedone, 1974). See also A.Z. El Chiati, 'Protection of investment in the context of petroleum agreements,' in *Recueil des Cours* Vol. 204 (The Hague: The Hague Academy of International Law, 1987).

31 *S.S. Wimbledon (U.K. v. Germany), 1923 P.C.I.J. (ser. A) No. 1 (Aug. 17)*, para. 35. On this case see also Ian Brownlie, *Principles of Public International Law*, 7th ed. (Oxford: Oxford University Press, 2008), 290; Koskenniemi, 'What Use for Sovereignty Today?'; José E. Álvarez,

The act of limiting a State's own sovereign prerogatives is precisely an exercise of sovereignty.[32] The subjective right of the State remains, but its effectiveness is limited by its own action.

A number of investment disputes that originated during the Argentinean financial crisis could serve to illustrate the appraisal of the State's sovereignty as the 'citizen.' Some arbitral tribunals assessed Argentina's critical situation as grave enough to invoke the protection of the 'essential security interests' clause in the applicable BIT:[33]

> [t]hese interests such as "ensuring internal security in the face of a severe economic crisis with social, political and public order implications" may well raise for such a party, notably for a developing country like Argentina, issues of public order and essential security interest objectively capable of being covered under Art. XI [...] Moreover, in the Tribunal's view, this objective assessment must contain a significant margin of appreciation for the State applying the particular measure: a time of grave crisis is not the time for nice judgments, particularly when examined by others with the disadvantage of hindsight.[34]

However, not all arbitral tribunals afforded Argentina the same level of deference for the adoption of emergency measures. A number of them understood that the State – as a citizen – was prevented, under the provisions of the BIT, from exercising internal sovereignty.[35] These awards highlight the great degree of discretion enjoyed by arbitral tribunals in the assessment of the exercise of sovereign powers. Furthermore, they raise questions as to whether the prerogatives reserved to sovereign States could be questioned to the extent that some tribunals did.

If there are indeed new understandings of sovereignty, the question that follows is what might they bring to contemporary practice?[36]

'The Return of the State'; Jan Klabbers, 'Clinching the Concept of Sovereignty: Wimbledon Redux,' *Austrian Review of International and European Law* 3, no. 3 (1998).

32   See the case *Nationality Decrees Issued in Tunis and Morocco (French Zone) on November 8th, 1921, Advisory Opinion,* [1922] *P.C.I.J. 3,* 23–24.

33   Article XI of the United States – Argentina BIT (1991).

34   *Continental Casualty Company v. Argentine Republic,* ICSID Case No. ARB/03/9, Award of 5 September, 2008, para. 181.

35   See for instance *Sempra Energy International v. Argentine Republic,* ICSID Case No. ARB/02/16, Award of 28 September, 2007 and *CMS Gas Transmission Company v. Argentina,* ICSID Case No. ARB/01/8, Award of 12 May, 2005.

36   See Martti Koskenniemi, 'What Use for Sovereignty Today?.'

Despite the high degree of global governance and transnational harmonisation and cooperation, communities still share ties made of values and common concerns. These values and common concerns evolve internally within the boundaries of States, often adopted under a democratic process, which gives rise to a new meaning of sovereignty:

> [a] vocabulary for articulating alternative preferences and for carrying out (strategic) manoeuvres in order to limit the powers of global executive classes and expert groups. This would mean, inevitably, highlighting the importance of the vocabulary of political sovereignty as the expression of local values and preferences as well as traditions of self-rule, autonomy, and continuous political contestation.[37]

In the last ten years, States have shown a tendency to shift from a *laissez-faire* model to a regulatory one, driven by environmental, social and economic concerns.[38] Perhaps a new meaning of sovereignty is emerging, that of the 'mediator of local values.' The protection of these values often requires the restriction of the enjoyment of individual liberties, through the exercise of the police power.

However, some academics warn that as civil society and local communities have been empowered to actively participate in decision-making processes, a new dynamic has been created between governmental decision-making and interest groups, whose policy preferences might deviate from those preferred by governments.[39] Combined, these shifting patterns in governmental decision-making may have the effect of constraining the way in which some States manage the structure of their international obligations. One way of grasping these patterns may be through the reflexion of the manner in which States regulate, and one of the most prominent examples is the doctrine of the police power.

4.3 The Police Power

The doctrine of the police power in the context of international investment law has been long analysed by scholars and practitioners alike. Invoked in early investment treaty arbitration cases, arising from the NAFTA, the doctrine is now well established and almost always incorporated in the analysis of claims

---

37 *Ibid.*, 68.

38 Michael Reisman, 'The Evolving International Standard and Sovereignty,' *Faculty Scholarship Series. Paper 960.* (2007), 464.

39 *Ibid.*

of *de facto* or regulatory expropriation. In this and the following chapters the doctrine of the police power will be assessed by: (i) tracing its origins, (ii) examining how it is assessed by arbitral tribunals and (iii) considering the relevance of the police power in specific investment cases, some linked to water resources management.

There are important reasons to adopt the police power as an analytical framework. It constitutes the corollary – within the internal sovereignty of States – for the exercise of regulatory prerogatives and the protection of public welfare objectives such as health, safety and the environment. It is essential to the internal functioning of States, and it cannot be derogated from, with the limitation that the use of the power does not operate in a disguised manner, so as to serve its own interests. Against this backdrop, the police power will be looked at in regard to how this doctrine can inform the analysis of indirect expropriation in the context of water-related investment disputes.

The origin of the term 'police' can be traced back to ancient Greece. The term polis means cities and government. The social contract theories that flourished during the 1600s and 1700s underlined the idea of authority, protection and order. The sovereign of Hobbes (Leviathan) does not recognise control over himself because he is the law. However, the government under the Lockean model, which is underpinned by the consent of the majority, introduces a sovereign that is beholden to itself through a separation of powers with the authority to watch over each other.[40] Interestingly, Locke's federal arrangement grants the executive branch of government with a *doctrine of prerogative* that can be used to regulate in the absence of the law or even against the law; 'the power of doing public good without a rule,' also referred to as 'the preservation of human life.'[41] Such a prerogative has been compared with the modern notion of 'eminent domain.'[42] It follows that abuse of power by the executive branch is not only possible but also likely; and therefore needs additional safeguards in case such a prerogative is exceeded.

---

40 See Alex Tuckness, 'Locke's Political Philosophy,' ed. Edward N. Zalta, *The Stanford Encyclopedia of Philosophy*, accessed May 1, 2016. http://plato.stanford.edu/entries/locke-political/.

41 'Locke's understanding of separation of powers is complicated by the doctrine of prerogative. Prerogative is the right of the executive to act without explicit authorization for a law, or even contrary to the law, in order to better fulfil the laws that seek the preservation of human life.' (*Two Treatises* 1.159–67). *Ibid.*, Section 6.

42 Steven Smith, 'Locke, The American Regime and the Current State of Political Philosophy,' *Lectures on Political Philosophy (Open Yale Courses)*, accessed May 3, 2016. http://oyc.yale.edu/political-science/plsc-114/lecture-17.

78 CHAPTER 4

This brief reference to the social contract, illustrated by the work of Hobbes and Locke, attempts to draw a line of similarity across two opposite stands of the nature of humankind and the origin of governments. It suggests that there is a common acceptance of an overarching power to organise the functioning of societies, which provides a basic justification for the police power of States.

The development of the notion of the police power, as invoked by host States in the context of investment treaty arbitration, appears to find parallels with the constitutional jurisprudence developed by the US Supreme Court. As it will be discussed in the next sections, the influence of US constitutional law and jurisprudence has been of significant importance for the development of the definition and interpretation of indirect expropriation in newly negotiated IIAs. One can suggest numerous parallels between current conflicts arising from regulatory activity in international investment law, and the two spheres of government in the US, namely the States of the Union and the Federation.

4.3.1 The Police Power in the United States

The term 'police power' was coined by the US Supreme Court,[43] and its definition is the result of the then evolving relationship between the States and the Federation's powers on the basis of residual sovereignty.[44] This relationship is comparable with current interaction between the host State's prerogative to regulate and obligations owed to a broader international community of economic integration, under IIAs.

Two notions are of special interest from those addressed by the framers of the US Constitution. The first notion refers to 'division of sovereignty' between the Federation and the States (of the Union), under which the Federation was empowered to regulate general matters of interest to the Union. States' residual sovereignty to regulate over matters related to their citizens; 'constitutes the origin of the police power and eminent domain.'[45]

The second notion, inherited from Blackstone, is the *doctrine of vested rights*,[46] which is recognised in the US Constitution, but was later overridden,

---

43   *Brown v. Maryland – 25 US 419 (1827), March 12 1827.*

44   As Denny asserts the term was not articulated until after the notion was developed: 'The term is nowhere found in our Constitution, and it first appears in our jurisprudence slightly less than one hundred years ago. It found no place in Bouvier's Law Dictionary until 1883, and the United States Digest did not contain it until 1879.' See Collins Denny, 'The Growth and Development of the Police Power of the State,' *Michigan Law Review* 20, no. 2 (1921), 173.

45   *Ibid.*

46   Blackstone on the absolute rights of individuals: 'For the principal aim of society is to protect individuals in the enjoyment of those absolute rights, which were vested in them

REVISITING THE DOCTRINE OF THE POLICE POWER OF STATES   79

or at least, balanced against the general principle of public interest.[47] In Freund's view it was never the purpose of the framers of the US Constitution to subject the police power to the control of the Federation. If anything, State legislation was restricted in order to avoid 'invasions of vested rights by retroactive statutes.'[48] Other authors agree by asserting that 'no society, certainly no democracy, could thrive on the pristine simplicity of such a foundation [of vested rights].'[49]

These two notions have been interpreted and applied by the US Supreme Court, reflecting the changing needs of a given context and time. Through this implied policy making, one could argue that US constitutional jurisprudence has defined the contours of the police power, and has influenced its appraisal under investment treaty arbitration. Let us consider a few cases relevant to understand the origin of the police power in the US tradition.

In *Dartmouth College v. Woodward*,[50] where public education was the interest under protection, the US Supreme Court acknowledged the notion of the police power without explicitly referring to the term. By upholding its previous judgment in *Fletcher v. Peck*[51] (on the protection of vested rights), the US Supreme Court stated:

by the immutable laws of nature, but which could not be preserved in peace without that mutual assistance and intercourse which is gained by the institution of friendly and social communities.' See William Blackstone, *Commentaries on the Laws of England*, Vol. 1 – Books I & II. Chapter I (1893), available at: http://oll.libertyfund.org/index. php?option=com_content&task=view&id=1415&Itemid=262, accessed May 3, 2016. In the context of the US Jurisprudence, see Justice Marshall's Opinion in *Fletcher v. Peck, 10 U.S. (6 Cranch) 87, (U.S. 1810)*, 136.

47   On this guarantee, it is useful to refer to the Fourteen Amendment of the US Constitution, an extended commentary can be found at: http://www.gpo.gov/fdsys/pkg/GPO-CONAN-1992/pdf/GPO-CONAN-1992-10-15.pdf, accessed May 26, 2016.

48   Ernst Freund, *The police power public policy and constitutional rights* (Chicago: Callaghan & Company, 1904), 65.

49   Wallace Mendelson, 'New Light on Fletcher v. Peck and Gibbons v. Ogden,' *The Yale Law Journal* 58, no. 4 (1949), 572.

50   *Dartmouth College v. Woodward, 4 Wheat. 518, 629 (U.S. 1819)*.

51   *Fletcher v. Peck* shows a strong conviction in favour of the principle of vested rights that the US Supreme Court under the presidency of Chief Justice Marshall held. In Marshall's opinion:

'Conveyances have been made, those conveyances have vested legal State, and, if those States may be seized by the sovereign authority, still that they originally vested is a fact, and cannot cease to be a fact. When, then, a law is in its nature a contract, when absolute rights have vested under that contract, a repeal of the law cannot divest those rights; and the act of annulling them, if legitimate, is rendered so by a power applicable to the case of

> [t]he framers of the Constitution did not intend to restrain the States in the regulation of their civil institutions adopted for internal government, and that the instrument they have given us is not to be so construed is admitted.[52]

In *Gibbons v. Ogden,* Justice Marshall acknowledged that: '[the] power of the State to regulate its police, its domestic trade and to govern its own citizens may enable it to legislate on this subject to a considerable extent.'[53] Nonetheless, he made clear that State legislation could not override the commerce clause and powers vested on Congress.[54]

Years later, in *Charles River Bridge v. Warren Bridge,*[55] Justice Taney adopted an interpretation of the police power which was deferent to the States' legislature, against the position of more Federalist justices. He brought to an end an implied monopoly of the railroad under the premise that such would forestall economic development. Justice Taney expressed:

> we must not forget that the community also have rights, and that the happiness and wellbeing of every citizen depends on their faithful preservation... We cannot deal thus with the rights reserved to the States, and, by legal intendments and mere technical reasoning, take away from them any portion of that power over their own internal police and improvement, which is so necessary to their wellbeing and prosperity.[56]

Similarly to investment arbitrators today, the US Supreme Court went through various tests to ascertain when a regulation was to be considered the exercise

---

every individual in the community. It may well be doubted whether the nature of society and of government does not prescribe some limits to the legislative power; and, if any be prescribed, where are they to be found if the property of an individual, fairly and honestly acquired, may be seized without compensation?'

Fletcher v. Peck, 10 U.S. (6 Cranch) 87, (U.S. 1810), 136.

52 *Dartmouth College v. Woodward, 4 Wheat. 518, 629 (U.S. 1819).* See also Mendelson, 'New Light on Fletcher v. Peck and Gibbons v. Ogden,' 567–68.

53 In this case the Court turned down an injunction of Court Chancery of New York, banning Gibbons to navigate on New York state waters. See *Gibbons v. Ogden 22 U.S. (9 Wheat.) 1(U.S. 1824).*

54 *Gibbons v. Ogden 22 U.S. (9 Wheat.) 1(U.S. 1824).*

55 *Charles River Bridge v. Warren Bridge, 36 U.S. 420 (1837).*

56 *Ibid. at 36.* Some commentators argue that Tanney's views were aimed at protecting the regulatory prerogatives of the States. See Mendelson, 'New Light on Fletcher v. Peck and Gibbons v. Ogden,' 573, note 24.

of the police power and not an expropriation (or takings under US constitutional law).

In *Mugler v. Kansas,* an 1880 legislature repealed a previously enacted law that allowed the production of spirits only to producers that held a permit. The new legislation banned all production of alcohol, affecting those already producing under previously issued permits. Even though the value of the plaintiff's brewery was substantially diminished, the US Supreme Court considered that:

> [a] prohibition simply upon the use of property for purposes that are declared, by valid legislation, to be injurious to the health, morals, or safety of the community cannot in any just sense be deemed a taking or an appropriation of property for the public benefit.[57]

Conversely, in the 1922 *Pennsylvania Coal Co. v. Mahon* case, the Pennsylvania legislature forbade the removal of coal that could cause damage to the surface, so as to protect home constructions and other structures (also known as the Kohler Act). In practice, this law was preventing mining in urban areas. However, most surface owners had acquired their property with express notice that coal miners would not be liable for damaged caused to surface property. The US Supreme Court decided, on appeal, that the mining company's contract and property rights were under the protection of the US Constitution:

> [t]he general rule at least is, that while property may be regulated to a certain extent, if regulation goes too far it will be recognized as a taking. [...] We are in danger of forgetting that a strong public desire to improve the public condition is not enough to warrant achieving the desire by a shorter cut than the constitutional way of paying for the change.[58]

There must be a diminution in the value of the property affected, and such has to be sizable 'before the Court would be interested.' This test, diminution in value, is essential to determine when a regulation has become a taking.[59]

The 'diminution of value' test advanced by Justice Holmes in *Pennsylvania Coal* was further developed in 1978 in *Penn Central Transportation v.*

---

57 *Mugler v. Kansas 123 U.S. 623 (1887).*

58 *Pennsylvania Coal Co. V. Mahon, 260 U.S. 393 (1922) 260 U.S. 393, Decision of December 11, 1922.*

59 William A. Fischel, *Regulatory Takings: Law, Economics and Politics* (Cambridge: Harvard University Press, 1995), 15.

82   CHAPTER 4

New York.[60] The Penn Central Transportation Company was the owner of the historic Grand Central Terminal, which had been designated as a landmark of the city of New York by the Landmark Preservation Commission. As a result, the Company could not transform or destroy the exterior of the building without the approval of the Commission. When Penn Central sought to sell its rights to build structures above its terminal, the Commission stopped the sale, stating that it would constitute a breach of State's regulations. Penn Central sued the Commission, alleging its property had been taken without compensation; but it lost the case in first instance. On appeal, the New York Supreme Court of Appeals ruled in favour of the city. The US Supreme Court confirmed the judgement, applying a test to determine when a regulation would in fact constitute a taking: (i) the character of the governmental measure, (ii) interference with investment-backed expectations and (iii) extent of the diminution of value.[61]

This brief overview of the US tradition intends to provide an illustration of the parallels between the development of the police power in US jurisprudence and what has become the appraisal of the police power in international investment law. It also assists in understanding the underlying issues that preceded its current shape. The development of the doctrine of the residual powers of the States in relation to the Commerce Clause, in the context of the US Constitutional provisions, could be compared with the recognition of the police power of host States in the area of International Investment Law. Even more significant is the adoption of the Penn Central three-fold test by the second generation of IIAs to determine the existence of an indirect expropriation, which will be further discussed below.[62]

4.3.2   *Scope of the Police Power*
The development of the notions of the police power and vested rights has been to various degrees influenced by the political ideology of the members of the US Supreme Court and the needs and preferences of society at different points in time. There are two aspects which could be reflected upon in the context of the current international investment regime and the appraisal of regulation

---

60   *Penn Central Transportation Co v. New York City, 366 N.E. 2d 1271 (NY 1977), affirmed 438 U.S. 104 (1978).*

61   The test of *Penn Central* has been criticised by Fischel as vague, because its elements of analysis – in his view – do not give enough information to predict a decision. Moreover, according to Fischel, the Court did not state the weight that each criterion should be given by a court. See Fischel, *Regulatory Takings: Law, Economics and Politics*, 50–51.

62   The inspiration drawn from the test adopted in *Penn Central v. New York* will be addressed in Chapter 5 and further developed in Chapters 8 and 9.

versus expropriation. First, the protection of vested rights appears to lessen proportionally to the growing deference given to the exercise of police power of States. Second, the police power was not applied as an open-ended carve-out to regulatory activity; it had a scope of application to certain, but not all regulatory measures by the States of the Union.

The US Constitutional jurisprudence and the work of renowned academics, identify three major spheres of activity under the scope of the police power. They were classified according to their level of development: (i) a *conceded* sphere affecting safety, order and morals, under the type of restrictive legislation which appears to broaden as activities increase, (ii) a *debatable* sphere, linked to the generation and distribution of wealth, for which regulatory activity in relation to investors is still incipient, although with exceptions, and (iii) an *exempt* sphere, developing under the principle of individual liberty, linked to moral, intellectual and political movements.[63] The conceded sphere (safety, order and morals) continues to be restricted to the protection of such values and maintains this narrow scope.[64]

Interestingly, these spheres of public interest have not changed greatly over the past hundred years; notably one important addition is the protection of the environment. It is of course true that the elements of the *conceded* sphere are broad and virtually every regulatory measure may fall under such categories. The police power could also be narrowly linked to regulations of negative obligation or obligations of omission. As Professor Freund expresses:

> [u]nder the police power, rights of property are impaired not because they become useful or necessary to the public, or because some public advantage can be gained by disregarding them, but because their free exercise is believed to be detrimental to public interests; it may be said that the State takes property by eminent domain because it is useful to the public, and under the police power because it is harmful.[65]

Regulations put in place under the scope of the police power have exponentially grown in number as well as in complexity. Professor Sax applies a broader approach than that of Freund, asserting that, while there is no definition of

---

63 Freund, *The police power public policy and constitutional rights*, 11.

64 In Freund's words: 'It is a power so vital to the community that it is often conceded to local authorities of limited powers. It is the police power in this narrower sense of the term, which the Supreme Court of the United States concedes on principle to the States, even where its exercise affects interstate and foreign commerce.' See *Ibid.,* 7.

65 *Ibid.,* 546–47.

police power, the notion generally relates to the 'prohibitions which are valid and which may be invoked without payment of compensation.'[66] Furthermore, Sax confirms that the use of the notion of the police power is commonly employed to protect safety, health and morals, but notes nonetheless that such scope was not intended to be exclusive to those narrow uses.[67]

The exercise of the police power is not always expressed in the form of negative obligations, such as prohibitions and bans. It is also expressed in the form of positive obligations, such as the imposition of taxes.

The police power is common to most legal systems. It may be known with different names, but it generally refers to the State's prerogative to regulate or the regulatory freedom of the State.

Scholars familiar with the civil law tradition identify the police power within the regulatory prerogatives of the executive branch. Some civil law traditions find the sources of the police power in the faculties of the administration to clarify the limits of individual rights as guaranteed by the normative system. The regulatory prerogative of States is often linked to the discretionary competences of governmental agencies, rooted in the normative system of the State, which imposes on society some negative obligations.[68]

Other Latin American scholars consider that the police power has been distributed across the regulatory activities of the State, acting within the sphere of its own prerogatives, as provided in the law. Under this view, at the core of the police power seems to be the justification for the limitation of individual liberties. This 'old' doctrine is opposed by some scholars, who argue that it

---

66   Joseph L. Sax, 'Takings and the Police Power,' *Yale Law Journal* 74, no. 36 (1964), 36–37.

67   *Ibid.*

68   'Polícia administrativa é a atividade administrativa, exercitada sob previsão legal, com fundamento numa supremacia geral da Administração, e que tem por objeto ou reconhecer os confins dos direitos, através de um processo, meramente interpretativo, quando é derivada de uma competência vinculada, ou delinear os contornos dos direitos, assegurados no sistema normativo, quando resultante de uma competência discricionária, a fim de adequá-los aos demais valores albergados no mesmo sistema, impondo aos administrados uma obrigação de não fazer.' See Clóvis Beznos, Poder de polícia (São Paulo-Brazil: Revista dos Tribunais 1979), 76. (Police power is the administrative activity, exercised under the law and supported by the supremacy of the General Administration. It aims to delimit the rights of individuals, through a process merely interpretative of a broader mandate that outlines the contours of the rights of individuals, in order to adapt them to other values embedded in the same legal system, through an obligation of not-to-do.) [Author's translation].

should be derogated altogether – becoming the exception – in order to give a place to the protection of individual freedoms, as the doctrinal rule.[69]

4.3.3 *The Police Power as 'Limitation' of Individual Freedoms*

As a corollary of the excessive exercise of internal sovereignty of States, the police power can become an instrument of abuse of power or discrimination. It therefore, requires scrutiny so that constitutional guarantees of freedom remain protected to a reasonable extent. Due process, non-discrimination and proportionality constitute important elements of scrutiny of the legitimate exercise of the police power.

While this doctrine pursues the protection of the public interest, generally by means of limiting individual freedoms, of both natural and legal persons, it is not clear whether it constitutes a rule or an exception.

Several administrative law jurisdictions would examine the following: (i) whether the authority has the mandate to adopt the regulatory measure under scrutiny, (ii) whether the authority adopting the measure acts in representation of the State (a question of attribution), (iii) whether the purpose of such regulation has been adopted to fulfil a public purpose, and (iv) whether the goal of the regulation has been achieved in a proportional manner. Further, and for the purpose of the impact of the exercise of the police power in international law, two additional elements appear to be relevant: (i) whether there could be a disguised aim behind the adoption of the regulatory measure, which suggests an undue exercise of the police power and (ii) whether the host State has provided assurances as regards the stability of the regulatory environment, which gives investors legitimate expectations.

One may recall early conflicts in the US between the Federation and the States of the Union, which dealt with cases where disguised actions of protectionism sought to enhance the economic interests of particular States of the Union, as well as the development of an incipient industry, under the veil of public interest regulation. The assessment of the legitimacy and transparency of the exercise of the police power in regard to safety or health measures, for instance, addressed the following questions:

> [d]oes a danger exist if so is it of sufficient magnitude? does it concern the public? does the proposed measure tend to remove it? is the restraint or requirement in proportion to the danger? is it possible to secure the

---

69   Agustín Gordillo, *Tratado de Derecho Administrativo 'La Defensa del Usuario y del Administrado,'* Tomo 2 (Buenos Aires: Fundación de Derecho Administrativo, 2006), Capítulo 5.

object sought without impairing essential rights and principles? does the choice of a particular measure show that some other interest than safety or health was the actual motive of legislation?[70]

Further parallels can be drawn with the development of the European Union's (EU) single market economic integration.[71] Likewise, the WTO has provided for general exceptions (Article XX) to the obligations under the GATT 1994. The assessment of governmental measures, however, is undertaken under strict rules in order to determine whether the measure adopted by the State does not actually constitute a disguised restriction to trade.[72]

Similarly, when the exercise of police powers negatively affects foreign investors' property rights under an IIA, the question arises as to what is the degree of deprivation of the investment. Some arbitral tribunals have considered whether the regulatory measure adopted was proportionate to the aims sought by the governmental measure.[73] In other cases, arbitral tribunals have adopted a broad definition of expropriation, which covers regulatory activity undertaken through the exercise of the police power, even when the effects of the measure do not reach a substantial level of deprivation or are non-discriminatory.

Chapter 5 addresses the police power in the context of investment treaty arbitration law, considering current debates on indirect expropriation through the lens of the exercise of the police power.

---

70   Freund, *The police power public policy and constitutional rights*, 133.

71   The European Communities, customs union and economic integration is briefly referred to in this work, only as an example of States' measures adopted disguisedly to protect national interests, and internal industry competitiveness. See for instance *Commission of the European Communities v. Federal Republic of Germany*, Judgement of 27 September 1988 (Charging of fees for inspections carried out during intra-Community transport of live animals), Case 18/87; *Rewe-Zentral AG v. Bundesmonopolverwaltung für Branntwein (Cassis de Dijon)*, Judgement of 20 February 1979 (Measures having an effect equivalent to quantitative restrictions – Reference for a preliminary ruling: Hessisches Finanzgericht – Germany), Case 120/78.

72   Article XX (General Exceptions) of the General Agreement on Tariffs and Trade 1994 (GATT 1994):

        'Subject to the requirement that such measures are not applied in a manner which would constitute a means of arbitrary or unjustifiable discrimination between countries where the same conditions prevail, or a disguised restriction on international trade, nothing in this Agreement shall be construed to prevent the adoption or enforcement by any contracting party of measures ...'

73   See for instance *Técnicas Medioambientales Tecmed, S.A. v. United Mexican States*, ICSID Case No. ARB(AF)/00/2, Award of 29 May, 2003, para. 122.

4.4   Conclusions

An important number of investment treaty arbitration cases discuss the application of the police power, especially in the context of indirect expropriation. However, the assessment undertaken by these tribunals has not always reached consistent conclusions. Indeed, arbitrators have not always applied the same criteria to assess the legitimacy of the police power, as well as the pursuit of the public purpose. There have been instances in which arbitral tribunals, while not contesting the police power of States, have focused only on the effects the regulatory measure had on the investors' property rights and interests, finding a breach of the expropriation standard. Yet, there have also been instances in which arbitrators showed deference to the regulatory prerogative of the host State and considered whether it can be balanced against the substantial effects the measure might have had on the protected investment.

Scholars have reflected on the criteria used by arbitrators when deciding claims of indirect expropriation. There is agreement among them with regard to the relevant elements of analysis that may determine the existence of indirect expropriation.[74] However, there is opposition that argues that this test is not part of the framework of investment arbitration.[75] Chapters 7 to 9 address this debate and discuss a possible framework of analysis linked to potential claims of expropriation of rights and entitlements relating to water resources.

---

74   See August Reinisch, 'Legality of Expropriations,' in *Standards of Investment Protection*, ed. August Reinisch (Oxford: Oxford University Press, 2008); August Reinisch, 'Expropriation,' in *Oxford Handbook of International Investment Law*, ed. Peter Muchlinski, Federico Ortino, and Christoph Schreuer (Oxford: Oxford University Press, 2008); Brigitte Stern, 'In Search of the Frontiers of Indirect Expropriation,' in *Contemporary Issues in International Arbitration and Mediation*, ed. Arthur W. Rovine (Brill, The Netherlands: Martinus Nijhoff Publishers, 2007). See also the analysis of Article 1110 of NAFTA in the issue of expropriation versus regulation in the Separate Opinion of Dr Brian Schwartz in the Partial Award of 12 November, 2000 in *S.D. Myers Inc. v. The Government of Canada*.

75   Kenneth J. Vandevelde, *Bilateral Investment Treaties. History, Policy, and Interpretation* (Oxford: Oxford University Press, 2010).

CHAPTER 5

Indirect Expropriation and International Investment Law

5.1 Introduction

International Investment Agreements (IIAS) have been regulating the relations between foreign investors and host States for over sixty years.[1] IIA dispute settlement provisions have been instrumental in the shift from diplomatic protection through inter-State dispute settlement to investor-State dispute settlement, mainly by means of arbitration.

The promotion and protection of foreign investment aims to cover a wide range of economic activities, taking place in each of the contracting parties to an IIA. Hence the standards of protection of such investments tend to be – at least in the first generation of IIAs – open-ended and rather broad. The standards of investment protection typically provide for: (i) national treatment, (ii) most-favoured nation treatment, (iii) fair and equitable treatment; (iv) full protection and security; and (vi) no expropriation without compensation.[2]

The enforcement of standards of protection under IIAs has implications for the regulatory freedom of the contracting parties, in this case, States hosting foreign investments. In developed, as well as in developing States, exercise of

---

1 UNCTAD, 'World Investment Report 2015: Reforming International Investment Governance,' New York – Geneva: United Nations, 2015, 125. The term IIAs includes generally Bilateral Investment Treaties (BITs), Preferential Trade and Investment Agreements, such as Free Trade Agreements (FTAS) or other cooperation agreements. Up to 2011, UNCTAD included International Taxation Agreements (ITAs) in the group of IIAS.

2 These standards are perhaps the most discussed in the literature, but they are not all of them. There is extensive literature on the standards of protection, among which some of the most influential ones have been written by Rudolph Dolzer and Christoph Schreuer, *Principles of International Investment Law*, 2nd ed. (Oxford: Oxford University Press, 2012); August Reinisch, *Standards of Investment Protection* (Oxford: Oxford University Press, 2008); M. Sornarajah, *The International Law of Foreign Investment*, 3rd ed. (Cambridge: Cambridge University Press, 2010); Andrew Newcombe and Lluís Paradell, *Law and Practice of Investment Treaties: Standards of Treatment* (Alphen aan den Rijn, The Netherlands, Kluwer Law International and Wolters Kluwer, 2009); Surya P. Subedi, *International Investment Law: Reconciling Policy and Principle* (Oxford – Portland: Hart, 2008). See on the Fair and Equitable Treatment Standard Peter Muchlinski, '"Caveat Investor"? The Relevance of the Conduct of the Investor under the Fair and Equitable Treatment Standard,' *International and Comparative Law Quarterly* 55 (2005).

© KONINKLIJKE BRILL NV, LEIDEN, 2017 | DOI 10.1163/9789004335301_006

INDIRECT EXPROPRIATION AND INTERNATIONAL INVESTMENT LAW 89

their police power has been challenged before arbitral tribunals, who in turn, have taken it upon themselves to interpret the vague and broad standards of protection.

This chapter focuses on the standard of expropriation. It explores it further in close connection with the analysis of the police power of States. The definition of expropriation in the context of IIAs is slowly changing, as States adopt new stances toward their police power and the scope of its application in the context of international investment law. IIAs negotiated in the 1980s and 1990s, many of which are still in force, provide vague definitions of indirect expropriation, which typically include terminology that aims to cover a broad variety of governmental measures that could have a confiscatory effect over foreign investors' assets.[3] The provisions of IIAs generally cover expropriation and any other *measure tantamount or equivalent* to expropriation or measures having a *similar or equivalent effect* to expropriation.

5.2 Early Negotiations on the Protection of Investors and Alien Property

Negotiation of commercial and peace treaties, including provisions for the protection of private property and payment of compensation, started during the eighteenth and nineteenth centuries primarily between the US and Europe, and some Latin American States.[4] For example, the Jay Treaty famously set out provisions on security for the peaceful enjoyment and protection of property.[5] Similar obligations were set out in Treaties of Friendship, Commerce and Navigation (FCN) as well as in Treaties of Friendship, Commerce and Consular Rights, which focused on trade and often included investment provisions.[6]

---

3 Brigitte Stern, 'In Search of the Frontiers of Indirect Expropriation,' in *Contemporary Issues in International Arbitration and Mediation*, ed. Arthur W. Rovine (Brill, The Netherlands: Martinus Nijhoff Publishers, 2007), 30.

4 Robert R. Wilson, 'Property-Protection Provisions in United States Commercial Treaties,' *American Journal of International Law* 45, no. 1 (1951), 91–93. See for instance the Treaty of Friendship Commerce and Navigation between the United States and Argentina, proclaimed in 1855, in which Articles XII and XIII provided for the protection of property, yet on the basis of non-discriminatory and full protection principles. Available at http://avalon.law.yale.edu/19th_century/argen02.asp, accessed June 2, 2016.

5 *Ibid.*, 91. The Jay Treaty between United States and Great Britain guaranteed several years of peace between the signatory parties and an end to the American Revolution.

6 For instance the Treaty of Friendship, Commerce and Consular Rights between the United States and Germany, signed on December 8, 1923, US Treaty Series 725, promoting cultural, spiritual, economic and commercial aspirations of their citizens. Article 1 provides:

Most FCN treaty provisions, before 1923, included references to access to courts, embargoes and detentions, protection and security of property, as well as expropriation and compensation.[7] FCN treaties, signed after 1945, noticeably contained provisions related to the obligation to pay compensation for takings of property.[8] The standard of compensation in these instruments resemble the Hull Formula of prompt, adequate and effective compensation.

The negotiation and conclusion of commerce-based treaties in the post-War period was, in many cases, a reaction against the perceived shift in customary international law, resulting from the United Nations (UN) General Assembly resolutions calling for the New International Economic Order (NIEO).[9] Bilateral treaty negotiations parallel to the discussions over the NIEO, shortly before and after 1974, were regarded as a period of 'rationalization undertaken by the

---

'The nationals of each high contracting party shall receive within the territories of the other, upon submitting to conditions imposed upon its nationals, the most constant protection and security for their persons and property, and shall enjoy in this respect that degree of protection that is required by international law. Their property shall not be taken without due process of law and without payment of just compensation.'

The Treaty of Friendship, Commerce, and Consular Rights between the United States and El Salvador, signed on 22 February 1926, US Treaty Series N. 827. Article 1 provides that persons and their property shall enjoy constant protection and security at all times, in accordance with international law. The taken of property, should only be undertaken upon payment of just compensation and in observance of due process of law. In contrast, the Treaty of Commerce and Navigation between the United States of America and the Turkish Republic, signed on 1 October 1929, US Treaty Series N. 813, which contains mainly trade provisions and the most-favoured-nation treatment standard. See also Stephan Schill, *The multilateralization of international investment law* (Cambridge: Cambridge University Press, 2009), 29–30, and Newcombe and Paradell, *Law and Practice of Investment Treaties: Standards of Treatment*, 41–42.

7 Wilson referring to the treaties of commerce negotiated and signed by the United States. See Robert R. Wilson, 'Property-Protection Provisions in United States Commercial Treaties,' 92.

8 In reference to the treaties of commerce negotiated and signed by the United States in the period between 1945 and 1956: Robert R. Wilson, 'A Decade of New Commercial Treaties,' *American Journal of International Law* 50, no. 4 (1956), 930. Note, for instance, the Treaty of Friendship, Commerce and Navigation between the United States and Japan of 1953, in which the parties agree to refrain from taking of property, except for a public purpose and upon payment of prompt and just compensation (Article VI-3). Available at http://www.marad.dot.gov/documents/FCN_japan.pdf, accessed June 2, 2016.

9 Eventually, the discussion over the treatment of aliens and the protection of their assets was taken to a new forum, the UN General Assembly. After several years of negotiations the General Assembly adopted Resolution 1803 on the Permanent Sovereignty over Natural Resources and later Resolution 3201 on the NIEO.

INDIRECT EXPROPRIATION AND INTERNATIONAL INVESTMENT LAW   91

State.'[10] During this period of NIEO negotiations, the collective position adopted by developing States in their international economic relations, differed from the stances adopted individually at the national level in the attempt to attract foreign investment.[11]

The second half of the twentieth century shows the adoption of more specific rules with regard to expropriation for public purpose and the payment of compensation. While the prerogative of states to regulate does not appear to be clearly articulated in FCN treaties, it was at the heart of the Permanent Sovereignty over Natural Resources (PSNR) and NIEO discussions. However, there does not seem to be significant cross-fertilization between the conclusion of FCNs and later IIAs on the one hand, and the Resolutions adopted by the UN General Assembly (*i.e.* PSNR and NIEO Resolutions) on the other hand.

5.3   The Protection of Property

Expropriation has been the most important standard of protection in both customary international law and treaty law for a long time.[12] In the past, the protection of foreign investments was equivalent to protection against direct expropriation without compensation.[13] However, today there are few instances of direct expropriation and it is more common for regulatory, creeping and indirect expropriations to take place.[14]

Expropriation is not illegal *per se*. The right to expropriate has been widely recognised in public international law under the principle of internal sovereignty, whereby a State derives an ability to legitimately exercise its discretionary power over nationals and aliens equally.[15] The 1959 International Law Commission (ILC) Report on the Responsibility of the State for Injuries Caused in its Territory to the Person or Property of Aliens – Measures Affecting Acquired Rights, stated:

---

10   M. Sornarajah, *The International Law of Foreign Investment*, 23.

11   *Ibid.*

12   Christoph Schreuer, 'Introduction: Interrelationship of Standards,' in *Standards of Protection*, ed. August Reinisch (Oxford: Oxford University Press, 2008), 1.

13   *Ibid.*

14   *Ibid.*

15   International Law Commission, 'Documents of the eleventh session including the report of the Commission to the General Assembly,' in *Yearbook of the International Law Commission 1959 – Volume II* (New York: United Nations, 1959), 11.

> [i]n fact, save in the exceptional circumstances [...] an act of expropriation, pure and simple, constitutes a lawful act of the State and, consequently, does not per se give rise to any international responsibility whatever.[16]

The ILC Report identifies that State responsibility may arise when expropriatory measures are adopted inconsistently with the international standards guiding the exercise of the right to expropriate. In such cases, the omission to observe such standards constitutes an arbitrary exercise of the right of States to expropriate. The ILC identifies the following elements of analysis, which are useful to determine whether an expropriation could be arbitrary: (i) the motives and purpose of the expropriation, (ii) the method or procedure adopted, (iii) discrimination between nationals and aliens, and (iv) the payment of compensation.[17]

These elements of analysis inform the test of lawful expropriation,[18] which today has been incorporated in most IIAs: (i) public purpose, (ii) non-discrimination, (iii) due process of law, and (iv) payment of compensation.

Some IIAs may omit some criteria, while others add additional requirements seeking to meet their particular needs. There have also been modifications to some of these requirements, through renegotiation of new IIAs, in the face of new challenges and situations, which were not foreseen by the parties in the original negotiations.

One of these situations is the issue of regulatory measures that have an effect, substantial or not, permanent or temporary, on the property of foreign investors. In this case, a transfer of ownership from the investor in favour of the State, its institutions or third parties, does not take place. Instead, substantial deprivation or dispossession of the investment's value may have an effect equal to expropriation, rendering the investment useless.

Parties to IIAs might find themselves at odds with situations in which a host State adopts a regulatory measure that somehow diminishes the value of a foreigner's investment. Certainly, such acts almost always raise a claim of expropriation of investment rights and interests. However, when the transfer

---

16 *Ibid.*

17 *Ibid.*, 8, 14.

18 *Ibid.* The ILC report identifies 'wrongful' from 'arbitrary' expropriation. The former consist of non-compliance with an international obligation and breach of commitments, hence they are intrinsically against International Law. Arbitrary acts on the other hand, arise from the legal exercise of prerogatives; yet such act of omission may be contrary to international law, this concept is linked to the concept of abuse of rights. *Ibid.*, 7.

of ownership was not an attribute of such governmental measures, the determination of whether an expropriation had occurred is less clear.

Regulatory measures taken by host States can, at this point, be examined in parallel to the evolution of the US Constitutional jurisprudence in the context of the police power doctrine and the takings clause, as discussed in the previous chapter. In such cases, a methodology to identify regulation from expropriation was needed, whereby almost all types of regulatory measures taken by the State would not amount to an expropriation and would thus be consistent with Constitutional obligations.

The report of the ILC on Expropriation expressly considers such difficulty:

> [the] distinction between a State's acts of expropriation founded on the right of 'eminent domain' and those which fall within the exercise of its police power – a distinction which originally stems from differences in grounds and purposes and also has a bearing on the question of compensation – is daily becoming more difficult to make, because of the evolution which the conception of the State's social functions has undergone in both those areas.[19]

Such distinction has also been long discussed in the field of international investment law, as it is important to clarify the rights and obligations of investors *vis-à-vis* those of host States.

The next sections discuss direct and indirect expropriation as a way of introduction to the more contentious issue of distinguishing indirect expropriation from legitimate regulation, linked to the exercise of the police power of States.

5.4   Direct Expropriation

The Institut de Droit International in 1952 defined nationalisation as:

> The transfer to the State by legislative act and in the public interest, of property or private rights of a designated character, with a view to their exploitation or control by the State, as to their direction to a new objective by the State.[20]

---

19   *Ibid.*, 12.

20   44 *Annuaire de l'Institutde Droit International* (*II*) 279 et seq. (1952), 283, See also Kenneth S. Carlston, 'Concession Agreements and Nationalization,' *The American Journal of*

This definition was further developed by Francioni with a view to include indirect expropriations with a strong regulatory component. He suggested to incorporate a number of relevant elements to the definition above: (i) the compulsory nature of the transfer, (ii) the general and impersonal character of the legislative act, and (iii) the transfer of control or management to public bodies or private individuals/entities designated by the State.[21]

Likewise, the definition of expropriation generally considers the same elements, except for the character of singularity and the issue of compensation.[22] In a direct expropriation, the measure by the government is undertaken by individual administrative acts, for a public purpose and is aimed at specific property rights. Nationalisation, on the other hand, concerns the transfer of an entire segment of the economy or an important part thereof. On certain occasions, the nationalisation measure may affect individual investments, such as in the extractive industries,[23] or large banks.[24]

There is, however, a key element that differentiates nationalisation from expropriation. There are strong political implications in the case of nationalisation, the intention of the State to intervene and implement new planning in a whole sector of the economy.[25]

International Law 52, no. 2 (1958); Newcombe and Paradell, *Law and Practice of Investment Treaties: Standards of Treatment.*

21   Francesco Francioni, 'Compensation for Nationalisation of Foreign Property: The Borderland between Law and Equity,' *The International and Comparative Law Quarterly* 24, no. 2 (1975), 257.

22   See for instance, the Report on Expropriation prepared by the Special Rapporteur Garcia Amador in 1959 which stated:

'therefore, except in the matter of compensation, where important distinctions can be noted, the two juridical institutions [nationalisation and expropriation] are, at least from the point of view of international law, substantially the same.'

International Law Commission, 'Documents of the eleventh session including the report of the Commission to the General Assembly,' 13.

23   Decreto Supremo (supreme decree) 493 and 494 of 1 May 2010 and 'Bolivia revierte a su dominio fundidora Vinto Antimonio,' Agencia Boliviana de Información, 2 May 2010. See http://www.unctad.org/en/docs/webdiaeia20105_en.pdf, accessed June 3, 2016.

24   Decree No. 56, June 7, 2010. The *Kyrgyz Republic* nationalised one of the State's largest banks, the foreign-controlled Asia Universal Bank. UNCTAD, 'World Investment Report 2011: Non-Equity Modes of International Production and Development,' Geneva: United Nations, 2011, 98.

25   Francioni, 'Compensation for Nationalisation of Foreign Property: The Borderland between Law and Equity,' 258, fn. 10.

Nationalisation was common during the first half of the last century, which was characterised for being sector-wide or industry-wide.[26] At the beginning of the 1900s, Mexico undertook large-scale nationalisations of land and natural resources in the aftermath of the Mexican agrarian revolution. Central and Eastern European States adopted similar measures after the First World War.[27]

Expropriation, on the other hand, is generally directed at a single investor or applied to one specific property.[28] Governmental measures resulting in nationalisations or direct expropriation are increasingly rare.[29] The unfavourable publicity of such a drastic action would negatively affect the investment climate in the host State, for this reason direct seizure of property is not considered as a wise undertaking.[30]

Categorising a measure as direct expropriation is generally not a difficult task.[31] Investment arbitral tribunals, which are called to decide on a measure that directly expropriates an investment, need not enter into further consideration as to whether an expropriation has occurred (that is, in contradistinction to a legitimate regulation).

---

26 Meg N. Kinnear, Andrea K. Bjorklund, and John F.G. Hannaford, *Investment Disputes under NAFTA. An Annotated Guide to NAFTA Chapter 11* (Alphen aan den Rijn, The Netherlands: Kluwer Law International, 2006), 1110–13.

27 UNCTAD, 'International Investment Agreements: Key Issues Volume I,' Geneva: United Nations, 2004, 6.

28 Kinnear, Bjorklund, and Hannaford, *Investment Disputes under NAFTA. An Annotated Guide to NAFTA Chapter 11*, 1110–13.

29 Note however, that some Latin American governments have started a trend of nationalisations: In 2006, President Evo Morales nationalised oil fields in Bolivia. In 2007, President Hugo Chavez also nationalised oil fields in Faja de Orinoco, operated by American, Norwegian, French and British investors. ('Estamos recuperando la propiedad y la gestión de estas áreas estratégicas') 'We are recovering the ownership and control of these strategic sectors,' he asserted (own translation). See BBC News, 'Chavez Nacionaliza Campos Petroleros,' BBC World.com, 27 February 2007, accessed June 3, 2016, http://news.bbc.co.uk/hi/spanish/business/newsid_6399000/6399481.stm.

30 Christoph Schreuer, 'The Concept of Expropriation under the ECT and other Investment Protection Treaties,' in *Innvestment Arbitration and the Energy Charter Treaty*, ed. Clarisse Ribeiro (Huntington, New York: JurisNet, 2006), 109.

31 See *Suez, Sociedad General de Aguas de Barcelona, S.A. and Vivendi Universal, S.A. v. Argentine Republic*, ICSID Case No. ARB/03/19 and *AWG Group Ltd. v. Argentina*, UNCITRAL, Decision on Liability of 30 July, 2010, para. 132; and *Marvin Roy Feldman Karpa v. United Mexican States*, ICSID Case No. ARB(AF)/99/1, Award of 16 December, 2002, para. 100. Both tribunals stated that recognising a direct expropriation is not difficult, comparing the task with identifying an indirect expropriation.

96   CHAPTER 5

In such cases, tribunals will generally assess the illegality of the expropriation by examining whether the requirements established under the IIA have been met. Claims of direct expropriation may become contentious over the issue of compensation.[32]

In *Santa Elena,* the issue of direct expropriation was discussed in the context of the creation of a natural reserve to protect the environment. In 1978, Costa Rica issued an expropriation decree for Santa Elena, proposing a compensation of approximately USD 1,900,000.[33] The Claimant, while not objecting to the expropriatory measure, did contest the price of the property,[34] and claimed approximately USD 40,337,750 as fair market value of the property.[35] In this case, the right of the Respondent to expropriate the property was not in dispute, neither was the size of the property.[36] The tribunal limited its review to the issue of compensation and its calculation, rather than the motives for the expropriation:

> [w]hile an expropriation or taking for environmental reasons may be classified as a taking for a public purpose, and thus may be legitimate, the fact that the Property was taken for this reason does not affect either the nature or the measure of the compensation to be paid for the taking. That is, *the purpose of protecting the environment for which the Property was taken does not alter the legal character of the taking for which adequate compensation must be paid.* The international source of the obligation to protect the environment makes no difference.[37]

---

32   See for example *Compañía del Desarrollo de Santa Elena, S.A. v. The Republic of Costa Rica,* ICSID Case No. ARB/96/1; *and Libyan American Oil Company (Liamco) v. the Government of the Libyan Arab Republic,* Ad Hoc Tribunal (Draft Convention on Arbitral Procedure, ILC 1958), Award of 12 April, 1977; where the sole arbitrator considered the case of nationalisation of concessions for the exploration and exploitation of oil fields in Libya. In this case the arbitrator concluded that *restitutio in integrum* was impossible, and expressed that the investor was entitled to indemnification for what was considered a lawful nationalisation of assets.

33   The sum resulted from an appraisal of the property conducted by one of the government's agencies. Less than one month earlier the Government approved the Decree (14 April 1978). See *Compañía del Desarrollo de Santa Elena, S.A. v. The Republic of Costa Rica,* ICSID Case No. ARB/96/1, Final Award of 17 February, 2000, para. 17.

34   The Claimant advised for approximately USD 6,400,000. This amount was the result of an appraisal of the property by Santa Elena and conducted by the Chief Appraiser of Banco de Costa Rica in February 1978, three months prior to the expropriatory Decree. *Ibid,* para.19.

35   *Ibid.,* para. 38.

36   *Ibid.,* para. 55.

37   *Ibid.,* para. 71 [emphasis added].

The tribunal worked on the basis of a decree of direct expropriation, which otherwise seemed to comply with all the other conditions of lawful expropriation under international law. Similar measures may be taken under nationalisation and the exercise of regulatory prerogatives, often with similar outcomes. If anything, the tribunal would have undertaken further scrutiny of the public purpose related to the governmental measure.

5.5   Indirect Expropriation

Indirect expropriation is interchangeably referred to as 'regulatory, constructive, consequential, disguised, de facto or creeping expropriation.'[38] It has been subject of extensive discussion among scholars and practitioners; first due to its increasing occurrence, and second, due to the difficulties to distinguish it from other non-compensable regulatory measures. Wälde referred to the ever-increasing taking of property via regulatory measures as 'regulatory risk' in addition to the effects of 'political risk.'[39]

An indirect expropriation does not necessarily involve a physical taking of property or transfer of ownership, but may still result in the effective loss of management, use or control, or a significant depreciation of the value, of the assets of a foreign investor.[40] There are several difficulties in asserting an accurate definition of indirect expropriation, especially when it comes to differentiating it from 'non-compensable regulation.'[41] Therefore, the 'fuzzy' character of indirect expropriation contributes to the lack of consensus regarding the conditions necessary to distinguish an act of indirect expropriation from a regulation.

---

38   Michael Reisman and Robert D. Sloane, 'Indirect Expropriation and its Valuation in the BIT Generation,' *British Yearbook of International Law* (2004), 119. With regard to the issue of creeping expropriation, it should be briefly noted that:

'[b]ecause of their gradual and cumulative nature, creeping expropriations also render it problematic, perhaps even arbitrary, to identify a single interference (or failure to act where a duty requires it) as the 'moment of expropriation.'

See *ibid.*, 125.

39   Thomas Wälde and Stephen Dow, 'Treaties and Regulatory Risk in Infrastructure Investment. The Effectiveness of International Law Disciplines Versus Sanctions by Global Markets in Reducing the Political and Regulatory Risk for Private Infrastructure Investment,' *Journal of World Trade* 34, no. 2 (2000); Abba Kolo and Thomas Wälde, 'Environmental Regulation, Investment Protection and "Regulatory Taking" in International Law,' *International and Comparative Law Quarterly* 50, no. 4 (2001).

40   UNCTAD, 'International Investment Agreements: Key Issues Volume I,' 235.

41   OECD Directorate for Financial and Enterprise Affairs, '"Indirect Expropriation" and the "Right to Regulate" in International Investment Law,' Paris: OECD, 2004, 3.

There have been important developments in the definition of indirect expropriation in the past years, originating in the US Model BIT 2004, whose Annex B provisions are to be used as a means of interpreting Article 6 (Expropriation). However, the question remains as to how general measures seeking to protect public health, safety and the environment may be identified from those 'rare' circumstances in which, the measure is in fact, a disguised act of expropriation.

The US Model BIT 2004 and IIAs adopting similar provisions are currently a point of departure for appraising claims of indirect expropriation. The focal point of this work is the analysis of the exercise of the police power by host States and the assessment of its legitimacy, as a basis to determine whether an indirect expropriation has taken place. As Professor Stern has observed, the definitions of expropriation in FTAs and BITs are diverse and cover different terminology, adding further complications to the pursuit of consistency in arbitral practice:[42]

> [i]n light of these various expressions, it is particularly difficult to determine whether or not either the measure or the effect must be rigorously equivalent to an expropriation, or if the degree of similarity can be more or less important.[43]

Some scholars associate the nature of the industry to the occurrence of indirect expropriation.[44] In this vein, water management measures could be particularly sensitive to claims of indirect expropriation, due to the essential importance of water resources and its lack of substitutes, as discussed in Chapters 2 and 3.

Indirect expropriation is linked to several types of regulatory acts and/or omissions that are attributable to governments and which have an effect on the property rights of foreign investors, both material and immaterial. Arguably, while this conception of indirect expropriation makes a formal distinction from direct expropriation, it still does not provide an objective and concrete definition of indirect expropriation.[45]

---

42   Stern, 'In Search of the Frontiers of Indirect Expropriation.'

43   Stern, 'In Search of the Frontiers of Indirect Expropriation,' 34.

44   Kolo and Wälde, 'Environmental Regulation, Investment Protection and "Regulatory Taking" in International Law,' 847.

45   See Gorge C. Christie, 'What Constitutes a Taking of Property under International Law,' *The British Yearbook of International Law* 38 (1962); Burns H. Weston, '"Constructive Takings" under International Law: A Modest Foray into the Problem of "Creeping

INDIRECT EXPROPRIATION AND INTERNATIONAL INVESTMENT LAW   99

In 1922 the Permanent Court of Arbitration, in the *Norwegian Shipowners' Claims,* was first confronted with the assessment of an indirect expropriation – in the context of rights under contracts. The tribunal disagreed with the respondent's arguments, the US, that international law did not protect contractual rights, and concluded that the series of measures adopted by the US, affecting the rights of the Norwegian shipbuilders, constituted an indirect expropriation.[46]

To date UNCTAD reports that between 1994 and 2015, there have been 317 cases involving claims of indirect expropriation brought by foreign investors against host States, under the provisions of IIAs.[47]

Earlier investment treaty tribunals stated that a series of actions and omissions by the host State constituted 'constructive expropriation' of contractual rights, unless the respondents could show through 'persuasive evidence *sufficient justification for these events.*'[48] In *Pope & Talbot* the tribunal set a high threshold *of interference* to conclude that an indirect expropriation had occurred.[49] In *Metalclad* as some commentators have argued, the

---

Expropiation,"' *Virginia Journal of International Law* 16, no. 1 (1975); Dolzer Rudolf, 'Indirect Expropriations: New Developments?' *New York University Environmental Law Journal* 11 (2002); Stern, 'In Search of the Frontiers of Indirect Expropriation'; Anne Hoffmann, 'Indirect Expropriation,' in *Standards of Investment Protection*, ed. August Reinisch (Oxford; New York: Oxford University Press, 2008). In *Suez & Vivendi v. Argentina* the tribunal proposed the following definition of indirect expropriation: 'In case of an indirect expropriation, sometimes referred to as a "regulatory taking," host States invoke their legislative and regulatory powers to enact measures that *reduce the benefits* investors derive from their investments but without actually changing or *cancelling investors' legal title to their assets or diminishing their control over them* [Emphasis added and footnote omitted].'

    See Suez, Sociedad General de Aguas de Barcelona S.A., and Vivendi Universal S.A. v. Argentina, ICSID Case No. ARB/03/19; *AWG Group Ltd. v. Argentina,* UNCITRAL, Decision on Liability of 30 July, 2010, para. 132.

46   *Norwegian Shipowners' Claims (Norway) v. United States of America*, Permanent Court of Arbitration, Award of the Tribunal of October 13, 1922, 11–18.

47   See UNCTAD, 'Investment Dispute Settlement Navigator,' available at http://investment-policyhub.unctad.org/ISDS/FilterByBreaches, accessed June 3, 2016.

48   See *Biloune and Marine Drive Complex Ltd v. Ghana Investments Centre and the Governments of Ghana,* UNCITRAL, Award on Jurisdiction and Liability of 27 October, 1989, 95 ILR 183, 209 [emphasis added].

49   *Pope & Talbot Inc. v. The Government of Canada,* UNCITRAL, Interim Award of 26 June, 2000.

tribunal focused on *the effects* of the governmental measure.[50,51] Other commentators argue that this tribunal, in fact, suggested a list of regulatory measures with an expropriatory effect, rather than a comprehensive definition of indirect expropriation.[52]

The tribunal in *Tecmed* addressed some elements of analysis which complement a more comprehensive definition of indirect expropriation:

> [...] if due to the actions of the Respondent, *the assets involved have lost their value or economic use for their holder and the extent of the loss.* This determination is important because it is one of the main elements to distinguish, from the point of view of an international tribunal, between a regulatory measure, which is an ordinary *expression of the exercise of the State's police power that entails a decrease in assets or rights, and a de facto expropriation that deprives those assets and rights of any real substance.*[53]

In *Impregilo* the tribunal adopted a similar approach to indirect expropriation as the tribunal in *tecmed*. Both tribunals recognised that the exercise of the host State's police power could 'seriously' affect the investor's economic interest, without constituting indirect expropriation. However, host States' actions could also restrict the use of property to the point of rendering it useless.[54]

There is no doubt about the impact that a regulatory measure may have on the 'owner's ability to use and enjoy his property.'[55] However, some scholars question whether the effect of the measure is the only and exclusively relevant

---

50 See for instance Dolzer, 'Indirect Expropriations: New Developments?' 72; Suzy H. Nikièma, 'Best practices indirect expropriation,' (Winnipeg, Man.: International Institute for Sustainable Development, 2012), 13; Miguel Solanes and Andrei Jouravlev, 'Revisiting Privatization, Foreign Investment, International Arbitration and Water,' Serie Recursos Naturales e Infrastructura 129 (2007), 60.

51 *Metalclad Corp. v. Mexico*, Arb (AF)/97/1, 5 ICSID Reports, 209, para. 103. See also *Southern Pacific Properties (Middle East) Ltd v. Arab Republic of Egypt (S.P.P. v Egypt)*, ICSID Case No ARB/84/3, Award of 20 May, 1992, at para. 163–64, 172; *Compañía de Aguas del Aconquija S.A. and Vivendi Universal v. Argentine Republic,* ICSID Case No. ARB/97/3, Award of 20 August, 2007, para. 7.5.20-21.

52 Jan Paulsson as cited in Kinnear, Bjorklund, and Hannaford, *Investment Disputes under NAFTA. An Annotated Guide to NAFTA Chapter 11*, 1110–21. In the view of Bjorklund et al., such an interpretation by Paulsson and Douglas does not consider that *Metalclad* concentrates on the adverse effects of the measure over the interest of the investor.

53 *Técnicas Medioambientales Tecmed, S.A. v. United Mexican States,* ICSID Case No. ARB(AF)/00/2, Award of 29 May, 2003, para. 115 [emphasis added].

54 *Impregilo S.p.A. v. Argentine Republic,* ICSID Case No. ARB/07/17, Award of June 21, 2011, para. 270.

55 Dolzer, 'Indirect Expropriations: New Developments?' 79.

INDIRECT EXPROPRIATION AND INTERNATIONAL INVESTMENT LAW 101

criterion to be considered when assessing an indirect expropriation claim.[56] For instance, Stern identifies two possible approaches to distinguish indirect expropriation from legitimate regulation. While both approaches assess the level of interference with the property rights of the investor, one considers that indirect expropriation entails a lesser interference with the investment than that required under direct expropriation. The second approach raises the threshold to find indirect expropriation, since the effect of the governmental measure should be equivalent to a direct expropriation.[57]

Should the level of interference with the investment be the sole test guiding the determination of indirect expropriation, investment tribunals adopting the first approach may be less deferential to the exercise of a States' regulatory prerogatives. In *Metalclad* the tribunal concluded that expropriation under NAFTA constitutes 'interference [...] in whole *or in significant part*' of the use of property.[58] Since a significant part is not a whole, this definition appears to follow Stern's first approach. However, the *Metalclad* tribunal largely considered the principle of due process, in addition to the level of interference to reach its decision.[59]

In contrast, also under the provisions of the NAFTA, the tribunal in *Pope & Talbot* stated that the word 'tantamount' used in Article 1110 of the NAFTA simply means equivalent; hence it cannot encompass more (than a direct expropriation). In this case, the tribunal may be setting a higher threshold for a finding of indirect expropriation, and for this reason the tribunal may also be more deferential to the governmental measure.

The main concern has been and continues to be that the protections granted in IIAs may trump the regulatory activity of States in areas such as environmental protection, health and safety, public interest, etc. As one scholar expressed:

> [t]he effect of the Award is to open the door to 'tantamount to expropriation claim' on many environmental regulations (or other national regulations intended to protect human health), including some adopted pursuant to international treaty obligations (such as the 1992 Convention on Biological Diversity or the 1971 Wetlands Convention).[60]

---

56 *Ibid.* See the opinion of the Arbitral Tribunal in *Chemtura Corporation v. Canada*, UNCITRAL, Award of 2 August, 2010, para. 248.

57 See Stern, 'In Search of the Frontiers of Indirect Expropriation,' 39.

58 *Metalclad Corp. v. Mexico*, Arb (AF)/97/1, 5 ICSID Reports, 209, para. 103.

59 See Veijo Heiskanen, 'The Contribution of the Iran-United States Claims Tribunal to the Development of the Doctrine of Indirect Expropriation,' *International law FORUM du droit international* 5, no. 3 (2003), 186.

60 Sands' comment on the award in *Metalclad v. Mexico*. See Philippe Sands, 'Litigating Environmental Disputes: Courts, Tribunals and the Progressive Development of International

The exercise of the police power of States has become central to the analysis of indirect expropriation. While its exercise by host States is not contested under public international law, there is still the possibility that regulatory measures can constitute an indirect expropriation under several IIAs still in force. The next chapters further discuss and develop the dividing line between regulation and indirect expropriation, using water resources management as a case study of the exercise of the police power of States.

5.6 The Police Power Doctrine in the context of IIAs

5.6.1 Earlier IIAs and Comparable Provisions in Other International Agreements

International instruments in the past have generally addressed the regulatory prerogatives of States within the scope of the provisions on expropriation, as they relate to the protection of aliens' property rights. While some instruments have recognised the police power doctrine, some others have sought to extend the protection against its exercise.

Interestingly the first instrument to be mentioned is not one linked to economic integration, it is rather a human rights protection agreement. Article 1 The *European Convention on Human Rights* provides:

> [e]very natural or legal person is entitled to the peaceful enjoyment of his possessions. No one shall be deprived of his possessions except in the public interest and subject to the conditions provided for by law and by the general principles of international law. The preceding provisions shall not, however, in any way impair the right of a State to enforce such laws as it deems necessary to control the use of property in accordance with the general interest or to secure the payment of taxes or other contributions or penalties.[61]

The first part of Protocol 1 recognises the right of States to expropriate property in the public interest and – while not expressly provided for – upon payment of compensation. These obligations may derive from the provisions of national

---

Environmental Law,' Paris: Global Forum VII on International Investment, 27–28 March, (2008), 10.

61 ETS 5; 213 UNTS 221 (Convention for the Protection of Human Rights and Fundamental Freedoms (Paris: 1950)), as amended by Protocol No. 11 (Paris: 1952).

law and customary international law. The second paragraph of Article 1 further recognises the police power of States to regulate and limit the enjoyment of private property subject to the public interest. This prerogative, however, is not conditioned on the payment of compensation.[62]

Within the framework of customary international law, the ILC also recognised that the police power of States may potentially interfere with the property of aliens, without raising international responsibility:

> [t]he possibility of the State incurring international responsibility is remote; and it is equally so when the State destroys property belonging to aliens for reasons of *public safety or health*, provided that the circumstances are ones in which the notion of *force majeure* or state of necessity is recognized by international law. In international jurisprudence *exemption from responsibility has also been based on the 'police power' of the State.*[63]

The *Harvard Draft Convention* on the developments of international law, entrusted to Sohn and Baxter,[64] addressed the exercise of the police power of the State, under the scope of uncompensated takings. Article 10 (5) of the *Harvard Draft Convention* refers to uncompensated takings, or deprivation of the use and enjoyment of aliens' property, as those actions of the government, which – among others – seek to maintain the public order, health and morals or are 'incidental of the normal operation of the laws of the State.'[65] In all these cases the actions shall not be considered wrongful.[66] In sum, such actions are otherwise justified by circumstances universally recognised as legitimate and necessary.[67]

Measures adopted by the State must also observe certain conditions: (i) non-discrimination, (ii) non-denial of justice or adverse judgment, (iii) no

---

62   Protocol 1, Article 1, Third Rule.

63   International Law Commission, *Yearbook of the International Law Commission – Volume II*, (United Nations, 1959), para. 43 [emphasis added].

64   In 1969, Harvard Law School undertook the project of revising the *Draft Convention on Responsibility of States for Damage Done in Their Territory to the Person or Property of Foreigners* prepared in 1929 by Professor Borchard.

65   Louis B. Sohn and R.R. Baxter, 'Responsibility of States for Injuries to the Economic Interests of Aliens,' *American Society of International Law* 55 (1961), 553–54.

66   *Ibid.*

67   *Ibid.*

104   CHAPTER 5

departure from the principles of justice as recognised by civilised nations, and (iv) should not be an abuse of power or covert act of deprivation.[68]

Article 3 of the 1967 *OECD Draft Convention on the Protection of Property* covers direct and indirect deprivation of property, which may be lawfully undertaken upon compliance of the well-known requirements set out under international law.[69] The State's right to regulate in the public interest, is otherwise recognised whenever the regulatory measure does not amount to a disguised act of expropriation.[70] However, an assessment of indirect deprivation requires interference to be determined, considering the duration and extent of the measure.[71] The extent of the measure is therefore qualified by the loss of title or the loss of substance.[72]

The *Restatement Third of the Foreign Relations Law of the United States* expressly recognises the State's right to regulate, under the police power doctrine:

> [a] State is not responsible for loss of property or for other economic disadvantage resulting from bona fide general taxation, regulation, forfeiture for crime, or other action of the kind that is commonly accepted as within the police power of States, if it is not discriminatory [...].[73]

Likewise, the *Draft Multilateral Agreement on Investment* contemplates the exercise of the police power of States. Article 3 (right to regulate) states that contracting parties may adopt measures deemed appropriate to protect health, safety and the environment, in accordance with the Agreement.[74]

In connection with this provision, the interpretative note to Article 5 on expropriation states:[75]

---

68   See *ibid.*

69   See Section 5.3 above. Note that a provision adds a condition that no undertakings should have been given by the State in relation to the property. OECD Draft Convention on Foreign Property, 12 October 1967. See text with notes and comments to Article 3, available at http://www.oecd.org/investment/internationalinvestmentagreements/39286571.pdf, accessed 5 June, 2016.

70   OECD Draft Convention on Foreign Property, 12 October 1967. See notes and comments to Article 3.

71   See Annotation to Article 3 A(1)(a) and A(1)(b). *Ibid.*

72   OECD Draft Convention on Foreign Property, 12 October 1967. See Notes and comments to Article 3.

73   See American Law Institute, 'Restatement of the Law Third, the Foreign Relations of the United States,' Vol. 1, 1987, Section 712, Comment: g.

74   OECD, 'The Multilateral Agreement on Investment (Report by the Chairman to the Negotiating Group),' DAFFE/MAI(98)17, 4 May, 1998.

75   Proposed by the Chairman in the package on Labour and Environment.

INDIRECT EXPROPRIATION AND INTERNATIONAL INVESTMENT LAW   105

[t]his Article [...] does not establish a new requirement that Parties pay compensation for losses which an investor or investment may incur through regulation, revenue raising and other normal activity in the public interest undertaken by governments. It is understood that default by a sovereign State subject to rescheduling arrangements undertaken in accordance with international law and practices is not expropriation within the meaning of this Article.[76]

It seems paradoxical, in the context of capital exporting/capital importing State negotiations that efforts to recognise the States' prerogative to regulate are mostly included in multilateral agreements as opposed to bilateral ones. For instance, the failure of the MAI negotiations, which was partly attributed to the – allegedly – disadvantageous position of capital importing states in the negotiations, contain provisions that were not contemplated in BITs; and yet, would have possibly contributed to increased host State's regulatory freedom and more consistent arbitral awards.

5.6.2   *The Beginning of a New Generation of IIAs*

In the last eight to ten years there has been a shift in the approach towards a more balanced negotiation of IIAs with important developments for the definition and scope of indirect expropriation. Governments have sought to formulate more specific provisions seeking to restore their regulatory freedom. Notably the 2004 and 2012 US Model BIT, the Dominican Republic-Central American Free Trade Agreement (DR-CAFTA), the Canada Model – Foreign Investment Promotion and Protection Agreement (FIPA) 2004 and the negotiations under the EU-Canada Comprehensive Economic and Trade Agreement (CETA), among several others, have adopted similar frameworks to clarify and restrict the expansive interpretation of the standard of indirect expropriation, in connection with the exercise of regulatory prerogatives.[77]

---

76   Article 5, fn. 5, available at http://www1.oecd.org/daf/mai/pdf/ng/ng9817e.pdf, accessed June 5, 2016. See the comments on this and the abovementioned provisions in: OECD Directorate for Financial and Enterprise Affairs, '"Indirect Expropriation" and the "Right to Regulate" in International Investment Law.'

77   UNCTAD reported in 2010: '[M]any recent treaties, whether new, renegotiated or revised, suggest that governments, developed and developing countries alike, are increasingly seeking to formulate agreements more precisely, by clarifying the scope of treaties or the meaning of specific obligations, in order to preserve States' right to regulate.' UNCTAD, 'World Investment Report 2010: Investing in a low-carbon economy,' New York: United Nations, 2010, xxvi, 87. See for instance 2004 and 2012 US Model Bilateral Investment Treaty; Foreign Investment Promotion and Protection Agreement, 2004 Canada (FIPA), available at http://www.italaw.com/documents/Canadian2004-FIPA-model-en.pdf, last visited October 1,

Most IIAS of this new generation have included interpretative Annexes to the provisions on expropriation under a 'shared understanding' of the meaning of indirect expropriation, so as to provide extensive guidance in the interpretation of claims of expropriation. Some IIAS have introduced such guidance in the substantive part of the agreement, as part of the standard of expropriation.[78] Finally, some IIAS incorporate the interpretative provisions on the determination of indirect expropriation in a protocol to the agreement, which constitutes an integral part of the agreement's text.[79]

There are two types of interpretative provisions, expected to assist the distinction between indirect expropriation and legitimate regulation, embedded in annexes, protocols and exchange of letters between the contracting parties.[80]

The first type of interpretative provisions, addresses the exercise of the police power *latu sensu*,[81] which covers a broad sphere of regulatory action not specified in those provisions. This test is inspired by the one adopted by the US Supreme Court in *Penn Central*.[82] Newer IIAS stipulate a case-by-case analysis, considering generally the following elements of assessment:

> [t]he determination of whether an action or series of actions by a Party, in a specific fact situation, constitutes an indirect expropriation, requires a case-by-case, fact-based inquiry that considers, among other factors: (i) the economic impact of the government action, although the fact that an action or series of actions by a Party has an adverse effect on the

---

2015; Dominican Republic-Central America Free Trade Agreement, 2004 (DR-CAFTA), available at: http://www.ustr.gov/trade-agreements/free-trade-agreements/cafta-dr-dominican-republic-central-america-fta, last visited 1 April 2016; ASEAN Comprehensive Investment Agreement, 2012. Available at http://www.thaifta.com/trade/ascorner/asean_doc2.pdf, last visited 1 April 2016; Common Market for an Eastern and Southern African Investment Agreement, Common Investment Area 2007 (COMESA); United States – Korea Free Trade Agreement 2012; Canada-Benin Bilateral Investment Treaty 2014; Canada – Latvia Bilateral Investment Treaty 2011; Trans-Pacific Partnership 2016.

78   See China – Uzbekistan BIT (2011), Article 6; China – Tanzania BIT (2013), Article x; Canada – Kuwait BIT (2014), Article 10.

79   See the Agreement between the Government of Japan, the Government of the Republic of Korea and the Government of the People's Republic of China for the Promotion, Facilitation and Protection of Investment (2012).

80   See exchange of letters in the Comprehensive Economic Cooperation Agreement between the Republic of India and the Republic of Singapore (2005), Article 6.5.

81   This work refers to the exercise of the police power '*latu sensu*' as the broad sphere of regulatory activity undertaken by host States, which is to be assessed on a case-by-case basis. This sphere of regulatory activity should be distinguished from the narrow sphere of regulatory activity aimed to protect the public welfare objectives, for example public health, safety, and the environment, referred in this work as police power '*strictu sensu.*'

82   See Chapter 4.

INDIRECT EXPROPRIATION AND INTERNATIONAL INVESTMENT LAW

economic value of an investment, standing alone, does not establish that an indirect expropriation has occurred; (ii) the extent to which the government action interferes with distinct, reasonable investment-backed expectations; and (iii) the character of the government action.[83]

Notably the US-Korea FTA, while in line with previous US FTAS as well as the 2004 and 2012 US Model BITs, elaborates further the stipulations of its interpretative provisions: (i) the economic impact of the governmental action, even if adverse to the investor, should not be considered in isolation, (ii) investment backed expectations should be reasonable (*i.e.* investors are expected to appreciate the particular dynamics of the sector they are entering into) and (iii) the governmental action should be characterized in regard to the level of burden that investors are expected to endure for the public interest; this analysis should be construed on a case-by-case basis (which seemingly incorporates a principle of proportionality into the test).[84] Another notable example is CETA – not yet in force – which includes the element of duration of the measure, following the approach of the Iran-United States Claims Tribunal (IUSCT) in *Tippets*.[85]

The second type of interpretative provisions addresses the exercise of the police power *strictu sensu*. It covers a restrictive sphere of governmental action with the aim of protecting specific public welfare objectives.[86] The wording of such provisions is similar to the following:

> [e]xcept in rare circumstances, non-discriminatory regulatory actions by a Party that are designed and applied to protect legitimate public welfare objectives, such as public health, safety, and the environment, do not constitute indirect expropriations.[87]

Under the second approach there is a restricted sphere of governmental action (police power *strictu sensu*), which would rarely constitute an indirect expropriation.

---

83   2004 US Model BIT, Annex B (4)(a).

84   United States – Korea Free Trade Agreement (2007), Annex 11-B (3)(a)(ii) footnote 18 and (3)(a)(iii).

85   CETA was signed on 30 October 2016, after seven years of negotiations.

86   See *supra* note 81.

87   2004 US Model BIT, Article 6: Expropriation, Annex B (b). Likewise, the DR-CAFTA has adopted in Annex 10-C (4)(b) the same provision regarding the exceptional character of regulatory measures applied over investors' property rights.

Some IIAs clarify that such 'rare circumstances' may be associated to 'extremely severe or disproportionate' circumstances.[88] Or that 'rare circumstances' may constitute a breach of the principle of good faith.[89] In most cases, the burden of proof will lie with the claimant, to show that the exercise of the police power *strictu sensu* does not respond to specific public welfare objectives (rare circumstance), for the manner in which the measure was adopted by the host State.

It is important to determine the conceptual nature of this interpretative provision. The provision affords to *bona fide,* non-discriminatory regulations, adopted under specific objectives a presumption of legality. Some argue that it constitutes a formal carve-out under international law, rather than an exception to responsibility for breach of international obligations.[90] This is an important conceptual difference, which has implications for the allocation of the burden proof. It is also important because it sets, at least in principle, the dividing line between compensable indirect expropriation and legitimate regulation.

Exception provisions in the context of expropriation in IIAs are almost identical to the general exceptions set out in Article XX of the General Agreement of Tariffs and Trade (GATT 1994) and Article XIV of the General Agreement on Trade in Services (GATS). These involve a breach of treaty obligations, which can be justified under strict conditions.

This WTO-type exception can be found in some IIAs such as the India-Singapore Comprehensive Economic Cooperation Agreement:

---

88   See US – Korea FTA, Annex 11-B (b).

89   'Except in rare circumstances, such as when a measure or series of measures is so severe in the light of its purpose that it cannot be reasonably viewed as having been adopted and applied in good faith, non-discriminatory measures of a Party that are designed and applied to protect legitimate public welfare objectives, such as health, safety and the environment, do not constitute indirect expropriation.'
See Canada – Peru BIT (2006), Annex B.13(1).

90   *Spence International Investments, LLC, Bob F. Spence, Joseph M. Holsten, Brenda K. Copher, Ronald E. Copher, Brette E. Berkowitz, Trevor B. Berkowitz, Aaron C. Berkowitz and Glen Gremillion v. Costa Rica,* ICSID Case No. UNCT/13/2, Submission of the United States of America of 17 April, 2015, para. 31; See also Jorge E. Viñuales, 'Foreign Investment and the Environment in International Law: The Current State of Play,' in *Research Handbook on Environment and Investment Law,* ed. Kate Miles (Cheltenham: Edward Elgar, forthcoming 2016), Chapter 2. Available at http://papers.ssrn.com/sol3/papers.cfm?abstract_id=2661970, accessed May 25, 2016. This aspect, of whether such provisions constitute carve-outs will be further discussed in Chapter 9.

INDIRECT EXPROPRIATION AND INTERNATIONAL INVESTMENT LAW   109

1. Subject to the requirement that such measures are not applied in a manner which would constitute a means of arbitrary or unjustifiable discrimination against the other Party or its investors where like conditions prevail, or a disguised restriction on investments of investors of a Party in the territory of the other Party, nothing in this chapter shall be construed to prevent the adoption or enforcement by a Party of measures: (a) necessary to protect public morals or to maintain public order; (b) necessary to protect human, animal or plant life or health; (c) necessary to secure compliance with laws or regulations which are not inconsistent with the provisions of this chapter including those relating to: [...] (iii) safety; [...] (e) relating to the conservation of exhaustible natural resources if such measures are made effective in conjunction with restrictions on domestic production or consumption.[91]

While an analysis of the interpretation and application of these types of provisions is outside the scope of this work, it is worth noting that WTO Panels and the Appellate Body have regularly interpreted general exceptions in a restrictive manner. Nonetheless, it remains to be seen whether investment tribunals will follow the reasoning of the WTO dispute settlement system or whether they will draw their own – perhaps more expansive – interpretation. Whatever the case may be, in the context of claims of indirect expropriation, it seems that measures adopted to address public welfare goals are now harder to challenge. First, the high threshold for the determination of whether a measure constitutes indirect expropriation has been formally set under these new generation of IIAs. Second, if the measure is otherwise found expropriatory, the respondent State may still invoke the application of a general exception provisions, when available under the agreement.

5.7   The Police Power Doctrine in the Context of Investment Treaty Arbitration

The broad provisions contained in the first generation of IIAs, many of which are still in force, left significant discretion to adjudicators, to interpret standards of protection according to factual and contextual specificities of the

---

91   See Chapter 6 (Investment), 6.11 (General Exceptions) of the Comprehensive Economic Cooperation Agreement between the Republic of India and the Republic of Singapore (2005). See also Article 10 (General Exceptions) of the Agreement between Canada and the Republic of Peru for the Promotion and Protection of Investments (2006). Available at http://www.treaty-accord.gc.ca/text-texte.aspx?id=105078&lang=eng, accessed June 1, 2016.

case. Such discretionality however, raised concern among governments and investors due to the potential for inconsistent decisions, with an obvious effect on the predictability of the investment arbitration regime.

By 1 January 2016 about 696 investment-treaty disputes were initiated. The highest number of investment disputes – 70 in one year – was recorded in 2015.[92] Interpretation of IIAs provisions is therefore, essential to the development of investment treaty arbitration because it has an effect on the consistency and predictability of the investment regime as a whole.[93]

As regards to the interpretation of expropriation provisions, Lowe highlighted the difficulties that still exist in distinguishing 'lawful regulation from unlawful expropriation' after the clarifications and interpretative provisions incorporated in the new generation of BITs, referred to in the previous sections.[94] Paulsson, on the other hand, argues:

> there is no magical formula, susceptible to mechanical application, that will guarantee that the same case will be decided the same way irrespective of how it is presented and irrespective of who decides it. Nor is it possible to guarantee that a particular analysis will endure over time; the law evolves, and so do patterns of economic activity and public regulation.[95]

---

92   UNCTAD, 'International Investment Agreement Navigator.'

93   There is vast academic production on investment treaty interpretation under the Vienna Convention on the Law of Treaties; thus, an in depth analysis of interpretative issues is beyond the scope of this work. For authoritative writings in the area of treaty interpretation, see Campbell McLachlan, 'The principle of systemic integration and Article 31(3) (C) of the Vienna Convention,' *International and Comparative Law Quarterly* 54, no. 2 (2005); Diane A. Desierto, 'Conflict of Treaties, Interpretation, and Decision-Making on Human Rights and Investment During Economic Crises,' *Transnational Dispute Management* 1 (2013); William W. Burke-White and Andreas Von Staden, 'Investment Protection in Extraordinary Times: The Interpretation and Application of Non-Precluded Measures Provisions in Bilateral Investment Treaties,' *University of Pennsylvania Law School Public Law and Legal Theory Research Paper Series*, no. 07–14 (2007); Bruno Simma and Theodore Kill, 'Harmonizing Investment Protection and International Human Rights: First Steps Towards Methodology,' in *International Investment Law for the 21st Century Essays in Honour of Christoph Schreuer*, ed. Ursula Kriebaum Christina Binder, August Reinisch, and Stephan Wittich (Oxford – New York: Oxford University Press, 2009); J. Romesh Weeramantry, *Treaty Interpretation in Investment Arbitration* (Oxford: Oxford University Press, 2012).

94   Vaughan Lowe, 'Changing Dimensions of International Investment Law,' *Oxford Legal Studies* no. 4/2007 (2007), 76.

95   Jan Paulsson, 'Indirect expropriation: is the right to regulate at risk?' in *Making the Most of International Investment Agreements: A Common Agenda* (Paris: OECD, 2005), 1.

The awards rendered by arbitral tribunals deciding claims of indirect expropriation have been important to assess the legitimate exercise of the police power, and to determine the existence of indirect expropriation. Such an assessment is relevant, in the context of this work, since the regulation and management of water resources may have important implications to the security of water permits and the overall stability of the investment operation. Therefore, while the hydrological cycle becomes more *unpredictable*, it is *predictable* that legal rights over water resources may become *insecure*. Note that the notion of predictability, in this case, plays a relevant role in the framework of analysis that will be discussed in the next chapters, as it is linked to the issue of legitimate expectations. The relationship between the exercise of States' police power and the determination of indirect expropriation is discussed below.

In *Chemtura*, a dispute decided under the NAFTA, the tribunal recognised the validity of the police power doctrine as a defence for the decision of the Canadian government to phase out the chemical lindane for agricultural applications. The tribunal stated that regardless of the deprivation suffered by the investor – which was not substantial – it did not make a finding of expropriation, since Canada had lawfully exercised its police power by seeking to protect public health and the environment.[96] The tribunal spelled out a set of conditions to distinguish the exercise of regulatory prerogatives from indirect expropriation, concluding that, even in the event of a substantial deprivation of the investment, there would be still no expropriation because:

> [i]rrespective of the existence of a contractual deprivation, the Tribunal considers in any event that the measures challenged by the Claimant constituted a valid exercise of the Respondent's police powers. As discussed in detail in connection with Article 1105 of NAFTA, the PMRA took measures within its mandate, in a non-discriminatory manner, motivated by the increasing awareness of the dangers presented by lindane for human health and the environment. A measure adopted under such circumstances is a valid exercise of the State's police power and, as a result does not constitute an expropriation.[97]

In *Methanex,* the exercise of the police power was not expressly articulated, but the tribunal provided a powerful statement, which is often invoked:

---

96   *Chemtura Corporation v. Canada*, UNCITRAL, Award of 2 August, 2010, paras. 265–67.

97   *Ibid.*, para. 266.

[...] as a matter of general international law, a non-discriminatory regulation for a public purpose, which is enacted in accordance with due process and, which affects, inter alios, a foreign investor or investment is not deemed expropriatory and compensable unless specific commitments had been given by the regulating government to the then putative foreign investor contemplating investment that the government would refrain from such regulation.[98]

In *Saluka,* the tribunal asserted that the police power doctrine is now part of customary international law.[99] Yet, the tribunal also acknowledged the challenges in determining what regulations are permissible, thus not raising the obligation to compensate. In view of the tribunal, such a dividing line between regulation and deprivation of property was yet to be drawn:[100]

[i]t thus inevitably falls to the adjudicator to determine whether particular conduct by a state 'crosses the line' that separates valid regulatory activity from expropriation. Faced with the question of when, how and at what point an otherwise valid regulation becomes, in fact and effect, an unlawful expropriation, international tribunals must consider the circumstances in which the question arises.[101]

The tribunal in *Pope & Talbot* adopted a more cautious approach to the analysis of the police powers doctrine.[102] In addressing the argument put forward by Canada that every regulation that is non-discriminatory falls outside the scope of Article 1110 of the NAFTA, the tribunal cautioned that regulations even falling within the State's police power could amount to creeping expropriation. Therefore, 'a blanket exception for regulatory measures would create a gaping

---

98   *Methanex Corp. v. United States of America*, UNCITRAL, Final Award of 3 August, 2005, Part IV – Chapter D – Page 4, para. 7.

99   *Saluka Investments BV (The Netherlands) v. Czech Republic*, UNCITRAL, Partial Award of 17 March, 2006, para. 262. The tribunal echoed the approach adopted in *Methanex Corp. v. USA*, Final Award, para. 410. See also *Too v. Greater Modesto Insurance Associates, 23 Iran U.S. Cl. Trib. Rep. 378*, para. 26; *S.D. Myers, Inc. v. Canada, 40 ILM 1408*, para. 281; *Lauder (USA) v. Czech Republic*, Final Award of 3 September, 2002, para. 198; *Tecnicas Medioambientales Tecmed S.A. v. United Mexican States*, ICSID Case No. ARB(AF)/00/2, Award of 29 May, 2003, para. 119.

100 *Saluka Investments BV (The Netherlands) v. Czech Republic,* Partial Award, para. 363.

101 *Ibid.*, para. 264.

102 *Pope & Talbot v. Canada*, Interim Award of 26 June, 2000, para 99.

INDIRECT EXPROPRIATION AND INTERNATIONAL INVESTMENT LAW   113

loophole in international protections against expropriation.'[103] In a footnote to this paragraph, however, the tribunal clarifies that this would not mean to express that every 'regulatory restraint' can be compared to expropriation, apparently emphasising the element relating to the degree of interference with the property.[104] Based on these assertions, the tribunal proceeded to determine whether the level of interference in the case at hand was significant.

A comparison between *Chemtura* and *Pope & Talbot*, show these two cases at two ends of the spectrum. *Chemtura*, on one hand relies on the legitimacy of the police power, irrespective of the level of deprivation suffered by the investor, to make a determination of the existence of indirect expropriation. *Pope & Talbot*, on the other hand, based its analysis on the level of deprivation of the property of the investor, setting a high threshold to determine the existence of indirect expropriation.

The elements of analysis used by the tribunal in *Chemtura* may serve as a starting point to define an analytical framework that assesses the legitimate exercise of the police power.

5.8   Conclusions

Not only has there been an important expansion of new FTAs with investment chapters, responding to a shift from BIT negotiation to regional economic integration, the last five years has also been an 'era of exit and revision' of IIAs.[105] The decisions of arbitral tribunals have influenced the adjustment of the provisions contained in the first generation of IIAs. As a result of enlightening, but also sometimes controversial awards, States have sought: (i) clearer and more precise treaty provisions, (ii) consistency with States' public policy, right to regulate, and economic agenda, (iii) balance between investors and states' interests, and (iv) adjustment of IIAs to new developments, such as the interpretation adopted by arbitral tribunals.[106] Regulatory freedom has been at the forefront of the legitimacy debate in investor-State arbitration.[107]

From this perspective, one could argue that the investment arbitration regime has contributed significantly to the development of international

---

103   *Ibid.* para 99.

104   This additional element is also referred to in the 'Restatement of the Law Third Foreign Relations Law of the United States,' para. 712 comment (g) and fn. 6.

105   UNCTAD, 'World Investment Report 2015,' 121.

106   UNCTAD, 'World Investment Report 2010,' 85.

107   *Ibid.*, 87.

114　　　　　　　　　　　　　　　　　　　　　　　　　　　　　　　　CHAPTER 5

investment law overall.[108] There is now a much deeper understanding regarding the interpretation and content of standards of protection; scholars and practitioners agree, for instance, on the high threshold required to prove a claim of indirect expropriation. Substantial deprivation is an element particularly challenging to show for claimants invoking the breach of this standard.[109]

The notion of the police power constitutes a useful analytical framework for assessing measures linked to management of water resources. Such measures may fall under the exercise of the police power *strictu sensu* and *latu sensu*, deserving different levels of arbitral deference. In some cases, water-related disputes may be framed under a broader framework of analysis, such as the environment and public health. The arbitral tribunal in *Methanex*, for example, adopted such a broader approach in assessing the ban adopted by the government of California on MTBE, in order to protect groundwater resources. The exercise of the police power, in that case, was not further scrutinised by the tribunal and the claim of expropriation was dismissed.

The legitimacy of the exercise of the police power may be subject to an examination of the measure under standards of proportionality and non-discrimination – among others – in order to avoid its abuse by host States.

The next chapters analyse the exercise of States' police power in the context of water resources management and regulation. Chapter 6 identifies possible governmental measures, which could affect the stability of water rights (permits, concessions and licences), raising potential claims of expropriation. Chapters 7, 8 and 9, in turn, suggest a framework of analysis to address such claims of expropriation, in the light of current developments in relation to this standard of protection.

108　UNCTAD, 'World Investment Report 2009: Transnational Corporations, Agricultural Production and Development,' Geneva: United Nations, 2009, 32.

109　See on this issue Meg Kinnear, 'The Continuing Development of the Fair and Equitable Treatment Standard,' in *Investment Treaty Law: Current Issues III*, ed. Andrea K. Bjorklund, Ian A. Laird, and Sergey Ripinsky (London: British Institute of International and Comparative Law: 2009), 237–38; Lucy Reed and Daina Bray, 'Fair and Equitable Treatment: Fairly and Equitably Applied in Lieu of Unlawful Indirect Expropriation?' in *Contemporary Issues in International Arbitration and Mediation: The Fordham Papers 2007*, ed. Arthur W. Rovine (Leiden – Boston: Martinus Nijhoff Publishers, 2008), 14.

CHAPTER 6

Water Management and Indirect Expropriation

6.1 Introduction

The exercise of the police power, if broadly understood, covers a wide range of regulatory activity. Analysed in this fashion, the police power *latu sensu* may cover wealth redistribution, economic development and social policy; in sum, all aspects of government's regulatory activity. The traditional sphere of the police power, *strictu sensu*, covers a much more constrained range of regulatory activity. It seeks to impose restraint on the behaviour of individuals and is limited to a number of welfare objectives: 'do not pollute,' 'do not pose risks on public health', 'do not endanger safety,' and 'do not offend public morals.' The regulation and management of water resources might fall within both the exercise of police power *latu sensu* and *strictu sensu*.

Water as a resource is an input for virtually any investment operation, and for this reason water-related disputes may be brought within the context of wider investment claims.[1] When water resources management measures trigger investment claims, arbitral tribunals may not often address them individually. In *Methanex,*[2] the tribunal did not enter into detailed analysis in relation to the pertinence of the water-related measure, adopted by the government of California. Similarly, in *Vattenfall I,*[3] which was settled, it is not clear whether the respondent, Germany, would have framed its defence mainly focusing on the protection of the quality of water resources to justify its measure. It remains to be seen whether the tribunal in *PacRim*[4] will consider the underlying water quality problem, potentially caused by the mining project, as claimed by the respondent, El Salvador.

In the area of water resources management, regulatory action and political motivation are often intertwined. Timing and context play a role in the manner in which governments adopt regulatory measures; and community

---

1 See for instance the classification of investment claims prepared by UNCTAD, which links each claim to primary, secondary or tertiary economic activity, following the International Standard Classification of all Economic Activities. 'Investment Dispute Settlement Navigator,' available at: http://investmentpolicyhub.unctad.org/ISDS/FilterByEconomicSector, accessed June 3, 2016.

2 *Methanex Corp. v. United States of America*, UNCITRAL.

3 *Vattenfall AB, Vattenfall Europe AG, Vattenfall Europe Generation AG v. Federal Republic of Germany*, ICSID Case No. ARB/09/6.

4 *Pac Rim Cayman LLC v. Republic of El Salvador*, ICSID Case No. ARB/09/12.

© KONINKLIJKE BRILL NV, LEIDEN, 2017 | DOI 10.1163/9789004335301_007

preferences and ideological stances often influence and shape governmental measures. Water resources in general and water services, in particular, constitute a good example of the pressure that interest groups may exert over governmental decisions. Water-related measures could result from unforeseen and abrupt changes in the circumstances of the host State or those of the foreign investor. For instance in the so-called 'Cochabamba water war' the rise in tariffs and subsequent users' reaction may not have been completely unforeseeable from either the government or the foreign investors' perspective. However, it is unlikely that the government could have prevented the rapid escalation of events and the outcome that followed these events.[5]

Regulatory measures resulting from slow or evolutionary changes may provide governments time to devise policy responses, in consultation with different stakeholders. For instance, the measures adopted by the government of California towards the protection of groundwater resources, which resulted in a ban of the fuel additive MTBE, appear to have been adopted after consultations with major stakeholders. Furthermore, there could be situations arising from governmental policy, which rule out any possible negotiation between State and investors. The phase-out of nuclear power plants in Germany and the plain packaging policy on tobacco products adopted by Australia, illustrate this situation.

It seems increasingly unreasonable to expect that legal frameworks remain static. Increased hydrological variability affects water availability and the stability of water permits, posing new commercial risks on investor's expectations. However, should foreign investors reasonably expect changes in the regulatory environment? If so, does the economic sector in which they operate become relevant in determining such expectations?

Under these circumstances, foreign investors may be confronted with great uncertainty when operating in highly sensitive or heavily regulated sectors. The question that follows is how the burden of risk of unexpected events and the cost of legislative responses may be allocated between host States and investors.

As discussed in Chapter 5, several IIAs negotiated post-2000 include specific provisions in relation to regulatory measures aiming to achieve public welfare objectives. Interpretative provisions in many of these agreements suggest that investors may bear the risk of regulatory measures adopted under State's police power, particularly the police power *strictu sensu*. The exercise of the police power *latu sensu* is, under these IIAs, subject to a higher degree of scrutiny, and requires context-based analysis.

---

5 *Aguas del Tunari, S.A. v. Republic of Bolivia*, ICSID Case No. ARB/02/3 has been discussed in Chapter 3.

WATER MANAGEMENT AND INDIRECT EXPROPRIATION 117

If the police power is indeed central to the determination of whether a measure constitutes indirect expropriation, as suggested here, the manner in which host States adopt regulatory measures plays a significant role in ascertaining the legitimacy of its exercise. Indeed, the anatomy of water-related measures is relevant to the examination of the nature of the regulation that gave rise to the governmental measure.

Therefore, for the purpose of discussing a framework of analysis to assess claims of indirect expropriation in the context of water-related disputes, it is important to identify governmental measures that could potentially trigger an investment dispute. This chapter considers three salient investment cases, which provide relevant examples of the interaction between water resources management and investment treaty arbitration.

6.2 Governmental Measures Associated to Water Resources Management: Measures over Quantity and over Quality

It is difficult to anticipate the wide range of water-related measures that host States could adopt. The economic sectors (e.g. mining, farming, energy, manufacturing) in which water-related measures could be undertaken by States to manage water resources are quite broad. This section suggests two categories of water measures: (i) measures related to water quantity, and (ii) measures related to water quality.

The taxonomy and foundations of such measures require careful consideration. Differing types of water measures do not originate exclusively in the domestic sphere; sometimes, regulatory measures may be the result of the implementation of international obligations arising out of transboundary watercourses agreements negotiated among riparian States. Some of these international agreements may cover environmental, human rights and other social aspects linked to both water quantity and quality.

The implementation of such obligations, at the domestic level, could affect the enjoyment of water rights (e.g. licences, permits or concessions) for nationals and foreign investors alike.[6] Enforcement of the provisions of the UN Watercourses Convention, for instance, could require the amendment or the adoption of new domestic legislation to comply with obligations of 'reasonable utilisation,' 'no harm' and 'protection of ecosystems.' Indeed, under some

---

6 Note, however, that the remedies available to nationals and foreign investors would often follow different paths.

scenarios, host States may consider it necessary to revisit and modify prior water uses, thereby affecting historic water rights.[7]

Whether regulatory measures are the result of treaty implementation, or the result of the exercise of the internal sovereignty of the host State, they could conflict with States' obligations to protect foreign investment under IIAs.

Assessing water related measures as the central component of an investment dispute may provide arbitrators with an improved perspective on the exercise of the police power. This approach might require arbitral tribunals to adopt a holistic perspective on the nature of water property rights. This means an analysis – when appropriate – of the domestic laws regulating water resources individually (constitutional provisions and water-related laws), as part of the whole legal framework (mining laws, energy laws, human rights laws and other legislation that might affect the quantity and quality of water resources) and in relation to one another. As a result, the characterisation of a water right would reflect its nature, scope and the appropriate level of investment protection.

6.2.1   *Regulatory Measures Linked to Quantity of Water Resources*
States may adopt regulatory measures linked to water quantity – allocation and reallocation of water resources – at two levels: (i) implementation of international agreements – in fields other than international investment law – and (ii) the adoption of domestic legislation.

Chapter 3 describes the efforts in the area of domestic water law to implement the principles of Integrated Water Resource Management (IWRM), which

---

7   See also the Great Lakes Water Quality Agreement between the United States and Canada, discussed in Section 6.2.2. The Agreement on the Nile River Basin Cooperative Framework (not yet into force) creates a legal and institutional framework for the 'use, development, protection, conservation and management of the Nile River Basin and its resources' (Article 1). The Framework Agreement under the influence of the UN Watercourses Convention will facilitate harmonisation of national laws among its members. See Musa Mohammed Abseno, 'Nile River Basin,' in *The UN Watercourses Convention in Force: Strengthening international law for transboundary water management*, ed. Flavia Rocha Loures and Alistair Rieu-Clarke (Oxon: Routledge: 2013), 151. The United Nations Economic Commission for Europe (UNECE) Convention on the Protection and Use of Transboundary Watercourses and International Lakes, which is currently open to membership by States outside the UNECE region, sets out the obligation for its members to adopt mechanisms necessary to pursue joint objectives regarding water-quality (Article 9). In contrast, the UN Watercourses Convention merely establishes an obligation to enter into consultations for the adoption of such mechanisms of water-quality standardisation (Article 21.3). See Chapter 3, Section 3.2.1.3.

WATER MANAGEMENT AND INDIRECT EXPROPRIATION

take into consideration the all-encompassing nature of water resources. The 'Status Report on the Application of Integrated Approaches to Water Resources Management'[8] (Water Management Report) states that nearly 80 per cent of the surveyed countries are implementing IWRM principles.[9] Yet, globally only 33 per cent of the countries surveyed are at an advanced stage of implementation of new water laws and regulations.[10] This suggests that most issues around water entitlements, hydrological assessment, allocation and reallocation have been resolved through consensus and democratic process.

The Water Management Report also shows that approximately 67 per cent of the countries surveyed have not completed implementation, perhaps because they have not been able to reach an agreement on the IWRM process. This could be explained by the fact that in some cases the implementation of IWRM principles requires reallocation of water entitlements, or substantial changes in water legislation, risking potential claims of expropriation of vested rights, which could include water permits. Indeed, most legal systems protect vested rights, which may complicate reallocation of water resources planned through new policies and laws.[11]

---

8   The United Nations Commission on Sustainable Development directed a global survey with the participation of 133 countries in order to assess the progress towards sustainable management of water resources, using integrated approaches. The surveyed countries were classified under the Human Development Index (HDI), which is a composite index that measures health, knowledge, and income. Countries are categorized in four HDI bands: 'Low', 'Medium', 'High' and 'Very High.' See UNEP, 'Status Report on the Application of Integrated Approaches to Water Resources Management,' Nairobi, Kenya: UNEP, GWP, SIWI, UNDP, UNEP-DHI Centre for Water and Environment, 2012, 6.

9   See Chapter 3, Section 3.2.1.1, for an account of the adoption of Agenda 21 and the commitments agreed by States towards the protection of water resources.

10   UNEP, 'Status Report on the Application of Integrated Approaches to Water Resources Management,' 12, Figure 2.2. Note that the status of implementation of main water laws is full in 71 per cent of the very high HDI countries, and 20, 16, and 13 per cent in high, medium and low HDI countries, respectively.

11   The report states that Mexico, for instance, has made comments on the difficulties in adopting water legislation and policy due to vested rights. The Water Act (Ley de Aguas Nacionales) transitory provisions (Ninth), recognises vested rights that were granted before the adoption of the new law. Some other have found difficult to implement policies and laws due to lack of consensus among stakeholders. *Ibid.*, 15, Box 2.2.

    The Texas Water Code protects vested rights in water: '§ 11.001. Vested Rights Not Affected. (a) Nothing in this code affects vested private rights to the use of water, except to the extent that provisions of Subchapter G of this chapter might affect these rights, and (b) This code does not recognise any riparian right in the owner of any land the title to

One could reasonably expect more States, especially medium and low Human Development Index (HDI) States, to incorporate water management improvements in water policies and laws in the coming years. It is therefore possible that changes in water legislation may trigger investment disputes, should investors' water rights be affected by new regulations.

Potential conflicts could also arise from the adoption of new regulations affecting the apportionment of water resources previously granted to foreign investors under licences or contracts. One such potential conflict could arise from reallocation of water resources in large-scale agricultural projects.[12] African countries have been granting large extensions of farmland in concession to foreign investors to grow crops, which are subsequently exported. Ethiopia for instance, has granted 3,619,509 hectares as of January 2011.[13] While in most cases the crops are rain-fed, there exist large extensions of land that are irrigated with water from rivers or lakes. Notably, most water consuming crops, such as sugarcane, cotton, rice and fruit, are produced for export, and foreign investors have incentives to build infrastructure and use technology that will

---

which passed out of the State of Texas after July 1, 1895.' Yet, these could be affected under the Eminent Domain of the State, when water is needed for municipal purposes (Article § 11.033). See the 2005 Texas Water Code, Chapter 11, Subchapter A General Provisions.

The Peruvian Water Act (Ley de Recursos Hídricos No 29338–2009) also recognises that water is under the dominion of the State and expressly prohibits the private property of water resources. Yet, it recognises and protects vested rights through the Principle of Legal Certainty; (Article 36) gives priority to human consumption (uso primario), water services supply (Article 39: uso poblacional) and productive use (Article 42: uso productivo), where Article 43 of the Act lists agriculture, fisheries, energy, health, industry, mining, etc. The Act does not express any preference among these water users. Pursuant to Article 73 the water authority can terminate a water licence due, among others, an official declaration of water scarcity. Compensation is not expressly provided for. In addition, Reglamento de la Ley N 29338 Ley de Recursos Hídricos (Complementary Act to the application of the Water Act) exceptionally allows to grant new water licences for water services supply (uso poblacional) when it is proven that there are no other water sources available, under the condition to pay due compensation to other users, whose rights may have been affected by this measure. (Article 128.2).

12   On the concept of 'virtual water', see Chapter 2, Section 2.4.1, footnote 65. In some instances the concept of virtual water could be linked to the phenomena of 'land grabs' and/or 'water grabs.' On these issues see the work of Carin Smaller and Howard Mann, 'A Thirst for Distant Lands: Foreign investment in agricultural land and water', IISD, 2009; John A. Allan et al., eds., *Handbook of Land and Water Grabs in Africa: Foreign Direct Investment and Food and Water Security* (Abingdon, New York: Routledge International, 2013).

13   The Oakland Institute, 'Understanding Land Investment Deals in Africa. Country Report: Ethiopia,' The Oakland Institute, 2011, 18.

WATER MANAGEMENT AND INDIRECT EXPROPRIATION 121

increase crop-growing efficiency.[14] This increasing demand for water, added to Ethiopia's dams project for electricity generation and irrigation, may put additional pressure on water quantities.

Another element that plays an important role in forecasting potential water investment disputes, in the area of irrigation, is the consideration that adequate water management can only be reached through monitoring and measurement of water resources.[15] The Water Management Report states that less than ten per cent of high, medium and low HDI States have a fully implemented water monitoring and information management system.[16] In this regard, overcoming deficiencies in information and monitoring of water resources could be used to implement more efficient and fair water uses; again potentially affecting existing water entitlements.

As governments negotiate and sign new IIAS, they should also be aware of the scope of protection their water laws provide to investors' interests and property rights. This aspect will be further discussed in Chapter 7, addressing the nature of entitlements over water resources.

Water allocation systems such as licensing, riparian (land-based), or prior appropriation, do not provide the same scope of protection to water entitlements under domestic law. In the context of international investment law, regulatory measures affecting quantities of water previously allocated to users; for instance to protect environmental flows, may also enjoy different levels of protection, considering whether the exercise of the police power is *strictu* or *lato sensu*.

There may be situations in which governments are confronted with the need to prioritise water uses. Due to: (i) water scarcity, or (ii) specific public policy objectives (in absence of scarcity). In the latter, governments could pursue policy objectives, seeking to develop a specific sector of the economy or benefit specific interest groups. For instance, the discovery of new mineral or oil deposits could be prioritised over other downstream projects, such as

---

14   Oakland Institute reports:

'Saudi Star spokesperson, [...] told OI that water will be their biggest issue, and numerous plans are being established (including the construction of 30 km of cement-lined canals and another dam on the Alwero River) to ensure that there is adequate water for their rice production[...]'

Ibid., 46.

15   Monitoring and measurement includes information on water quality, quantity, aquatic ecosystems, water use and early warning systems, as expressed in the report UNEP, 'Status Report on the Application of Integrated Approaches to Water Resources Management,' 31, Figure 4.4.

16   *Ibid.*

farming. This appears to be the case in the controversial hydro and irrigation Majes Siguas II Project in Peru. This project illustrates potential disputes that could arise between communities and foreign investors, and between communities and governments; who as part of an economic development agenda may prioritise infrastructure projects over community's interests.[17]

The examples of Ethiopia and Peru suggest that in certain instances governments are willing to attract investment; yet, they are not always able to provide a secure environment to foreign investors. The mismatch between the expectations of investors and, the sometimes contradicting communities' expectations and government promises, may create mistrust between investor and communities. This is because governments do not always integrate community concerns when promoting infrastructure projects.[18] Further, new governments often bring changes in policy, empowering communities' change of attitude towards foreign investors.[19]

As discussed above, when a situation of water scarcity arises, governmental measures adopted to solve competing uses could fall within the scope of the police power *strictu sensu,* if and when such measures seek to protect safety, public health and the environment. The 2014 Emergency Regulation adopted by the State of California, introduces restrictions on water suppliers to adopt a 25 per cent reduction in potable urban usage. The regulation does not

---

17   For many years the Peruvian government has been developing a hydro and irrigation project, Majes Siguas II. This project involves the construction of three dams for electricity generation, which would also feed water resources for irrigation downstream. On the one hand, this project confronted the communities of Arequipa – beneficiary of the project – and Cusco – opposing the project – over water resources. See La Republica, 'Proyecto Majes Siguas II ya no represará aguas del Apurímac', *La Republica*, August 14, 2012, accessed May 25, 2016. http://www.larepublica.pe/13-08-2012/ proyecto-majes-siguas-ii-ya-no-represara-aguas-del-apurimac. In addition, one of the three dams, Tucurani was licensed to Tucarani Generation Company S.A. by the former president Valentin Paniagua (2001). There exists concern that the operation of Tucarani may negatively impact the operation of two other dams and irrigation of Majes Siguas II. Elizabeth Huanca, Region Sur, 'Tarucani sí afectará inversión en Majes II', *La Republica*, May 23, 2013, accessed May 25, 2016. http://www.larepublica.pe/23-05-2013/ tarucani-si-afectara-inversion-en-majes-ii.

18   See Chapter 4 Section 4.2.2, on the discussion of the meanings of sovereignty. States may be exercising its sovereign power under a role of the 'mediator of local values.'

19   See for instance *Methanex v. the United States* where the protection of groundwater resources was at stake; *TECMED v. Mexico* where the host State alleged the need to prevent environmental pollution due to the proximity of a land fill; *Vivendi v. Argentina* where the new local government and the citizens of Tucumán disagreed with the conditions of water services provided by the investor.

affect commercial, industrial and institutional uses, other than implementing efficiency measures.[20] The regulation also includes end-user requirements for the promotion of water conservation, with the exception that some uses may be necessary to address health and safety needs.

As discussed above, governments may have specific public policy objectives. The adoption of water measures, affecting investor's rights could, nonetheless, fall within the broader sphere of police power, *latu sensu*. Some of these regulatory measures may seek to protect public health or to provide ecosystem services in the long run by preserving water quantities for human consumption and environmental flows. The question that follows is whether long-term goals seeking to preserve water resources, with no immediate need to address health or environmental concerns, should be deemed an exercise of the police power *strictu* or *latu sensu*.

It is reasonable to expect that investment tribunals may be more deferential to regulatory measures dealing with water scarcity, for two reasons. First, due to the interpretative provisions, adopted in new IIAs, assisting the determination of indirect expropriation.[21] Second, investment treaty arbitration is increasingly seen as having a public nature, which could lead some arbitral tribunals to adopt more deferential decisions towards the provision of water supply and services, as well as towards the management of water resources.[22]

Generally, changes in water quantity could affect water quality and vice versa, since measures seeking to protect water quality may be adopted through reallocation of water quantities.

6.2.2 *Regulatory Measures Linked to the Quality of Water Resources*
Water quality measures and pollution controls are likely to occur at some stage of the life of investments associated to the exploitation of natural resources, such as mining and other extractive industries. As States continue to develop, environmental legislation and pollution controls become more sophisticated and costly to implement. Furthermore, public awareness and stakeholder

---

20 Adopted text of Emergency Regulation (2014): Article 22.5. Drought Emergency Water Conservation, Sec 863.

21 See Chapter 5.

22 See for instance the argument advanced by Anthea Roberts with regard to increasing discussion over the public nature of investor-State arbitration. According to Roberts there is much debate as to the adoption of more deferential standards of review towards States' regulatory activity. Anthea Roberts, 'The Next Battleground: Standards of Review in Investment Treaty Arbitration,' *International Council for Commercial Arbitration Congress Series* 16 (2011), 175–80.

participation increase scrutiny over corporate behaviour, putting pressure on governments and investors to engage in environmental sustainability.

In *Bear Creek Mining Co* – pending – Peru issued Decree 083 declaring Bear Creek's investment of public necessity and approved the Santa Ana mining concession. Indigenous communities began protests and organised strikes due to concerns over pollution of water resources and the proximity of mining pits to their lands. Ultimately, the Government repealed Decree 083, allegedly responding to popular pressure, and decried the investor's inability or unwillingness to listen to local communities and consider their concerns.[23] The investor alleges that the protests were organised by interests groups, Frente de Defensa, advocating against mining projects. They add that the repeal of Decree No. 083 was motivated by a political calculation between the protesters and the President of Peru.[24]

Water quality-related measures are not strange to investment treaty arbitration. In *Vattenfall I* governmental measures sought to prevent water quality diminution, due to temperature changes in a local river.[25] In *PacRim* and *Bear Creek,* it is alleged that governments sought to prevent water pollution.[26] In *Methanex,* the government prevented depletion of fresh groundwater reserves.[27] In *Lucchetti* the governmental measure sought to protect wetlands.[28] Finally, in *Lone Pine Resources* an Act to limit oil and gas activities revoked exploration licences located in St Lawrence River.[29]

---

23   *Bear Creek Mining Corporation v. Republic of Peru,* ICSID Case No. ARB/14/21, Respondent's Counter-Memorial on the Merits and Memorial on Jurisdiction of 6 October, 2015, para 68–69.

24   *Bear Creek Mining Corporation v. Republic of Peru,* ICSID Case No. ARB/14/21, Claimant's Memorial on the Merits of 29 May, 2015, paras 75–76.

25   See *Vattenfall AB, Vattenfall Europe AG, Vattenfall Europe Generation AG v. Federal Republic of Germany.*

26   *Bear Creek Mining Corporation v. Republic of Peru*; *Pac Rim Cayman LLC v. Republic of El Salvador.* In this case the Government of El Salvador refused to grant new mining licences in favour of the investor, who previously undertook the exploration of mineral reserves in 'El Dorado.' See *Pac Rim Cayman LLC v. Republic of El Salvador,* Notice of Arbitration of 30 April, 2009, para. 9. The reason for the El Salvatorian Government refusal to grant additional mining licences appears to be the intention to protect water resources. See Katie Zaunbrecher, 'Pac Rim Cayman v. Republic of El Salvador: Confronting Free Trade's Chilling Effect on Environmental Progress in Latin America,' *Houston Journal of International Law* 33, no. 2 (2011), 497.

27   *Methanex Corp. v. United States of America.*

28   *Empresas Lucchetti, S.A. and Lucchetti Peru, S.A. v. Republic of Peru,* ICSID Case No. ARB/03/4.

29   *Lone Pine Resources Inc. v. The Government of Canada,* ICSID Case No. UNCT/15/2.

Water-protective measures may be adopted through amendments to existing water, environmental, mining and energy legislation. For instance, the 'Water trigger Bill,' which amends the Environment Protection and Biodiversity Conservation Act 1999, adopted by the Federal Senate of Australia, requires additional Commonwealth approval for: 'an action involving coal seam gas development or large coal mining development that has, will have, or is likely to have a significant impact on a water resource.'[30]

California's ban on the sale and use of the gasoline additive 'MTBE,' provided:

> [t]he Legislature hereby finds and declares that the purpose of this act is to provide the public and the Legislature with a thorough and objective evaluation of the human health and environmental risks and benefits, if any, of the use of methyl tertiary-butyl ether (MTBE), as compared to ethyl tertiary- butyl ether (ETBE), tertiary amyl methyl ether (TAME) and ethanol, in gasoline, and to ensure that the air, *water quality*, and soil impacts of the use of MTBE are fully mitigated.[31]

Likewise, governments could modify requirements with regard to levels of pollution. These modifications may be implemented in water or environmental laws, as well as in specific permits granted to investors, as will be discussed in the next sections.

At the domestic level, it is foreseeable that regulatory frameworks dealing with issues of pollution control will not remain static. This is particularly the case in countries where environmental standards have not reached an optimum level, due to ineffective policy and law implementation. International agreements may include water quality standards, which often require implementation in domestic legal systems. The Great Lakes Water Quality Agreement between the US and Canada aims at restoring and maintaining 'the chemical, physical, and biological integrity of the Waters of the Great Lakes.'[32]

---

30   See Andrew Poulos, 'Australia: Senate passes Economic Protection and Biodiversity Conservation "water trigger" Bill,' *Mondaq*, June 24, 2013, accessed May 27, 2016. http://www.mondaq.com/australia/x/246634/Environmental+Law/Senate+passes+Economic+Protection+and+Biodiversity+Conservation+water+trigger+Bill.

31   See Section 2 of the California Senate Bill 521, 1997 [emphasis added].
      See also *Methanex Corp. v. United States of America*, Final Award of 3 August, 2005, Part II – Chapter D – Page 3, para. 9. Challenge to the Bill was later withdrawn by Methanex.

32   Article 2(1) of the *Protocol Amending the Agreement of Great Lakes Water Quality of 1978 as amended on October 16, 1983 and on November 18, 1987. Between Canada and the United States.*

In order to do so, the parties agree to implement 'measures that are sufficiently protective to achieve the purpose of [the] Agreement.'[33]

Implementation of international obligations by host States, may have a restrictive or onerous effect on existing investment operations. In such cases, investors and States could renegotiate the economic equilibrium of the investment, so as to avoid potential disputes.

As discussed above, water-quality regulation could fall within the scope of environmental and health measures, under the police power *strictu sensu*. Yet, given the highly political component of water measures, environmental or health reasons do not warrant good faith or proportionality of the governmental measure. The question remains as to whether arbitral tribunals could focus their review on the specific aspects of the water resources measure within a dispute and decide accordingly.

6.3 Water Resources and International Investment Law

This section introduces a brief discussion of three investment arbitration cases which, directly or indirectly, dealt with water-related measures. These cases illustrate potential conflicts arising from the regulation of water resources in the context of international investment law (distinct from disputes relating to the provision of water services). These cases cover three spheres relating to the nature of water and its interaction with investors, water users and governments, namely water as a good, competition over water resources, and environmental and health concerns.

6.3.1 *Sun Belt Inc. v Canada*

As alleged by the claimant, towards the end of 1980 the Government of British Columbia adopted an initiative for the export of fresh water. The initiative attracted investors to apply or expand existing licences to export bulk water via marine vessels. Sun Belt's Canadian partner applied for an extension of its water export licence, which was apparently delayed by British Columbia. In the meantime, in 1991 Sun Belt was awarded an international contract to export bulk water to Goleta Water District in California. However, the government of British Columbia imposed a moratorium on new and expanded export licences, discriminating all competitors in favour of Western Canada Water Enterprises Ltd, a Canadian prospective exporter.

In October 1999, Sun Belt filed a Notice of Arbitration against Canada, under NAFTA, seeking to reverse a national ban imposed on the export of fresh

---

33   *Ibid.*, Article 2(3).

WATER MANAGEMENT AND INDIRECT EXPROPRIATION

water by marine tankers from the Great Lakes. It also requested the restoration of the fresh water export licensing arrangements. The investor claimed initial temporary loss of business and opportunity costs for USD 468 million, with the further claim that these costs could rise up to USD 1.5 billion.[34] The dispute was settled between the parties, and the conditions of the settlement and possible compensation remain unknown.[35]

Trade in fresh water has and continues to be a sensitive issue among water-rich and water-deprived States. Academics and practitioners have long discussed the merits and demerits of treating water resources as a commodity. Furthermore, there is no general consensus on the point at which water becomes a tradable good: is it when it is still in a watershed or when it has been put in a pipeline or water-tanker?[36]

In 1993, the governments of Canada, Mexico and the United States issued a Joint Statement with the purpose to correct potential false interpretations regarding water resources:

> [t]he NAFTA creates no rights to the natural water resources of any Party to the Agreement. Unless water, in any form, has entered into commerce and become a good or product, it is not covered by the provisions of any trade agreement, including the NAFTA. And nothing in the NAFTA would oblige any NAFTA Party to either exploit its water for commercial use, or to begin exporting water in any form. Water in its natural state in lakes, rivers, reservoirs, aquifers, water basins and the like is not a good or product, is not traded, and therefore is not and has never been subject to the terms of any trade agreement.[37]

Recent negotiations on the Comprehensive Economic and Trade Agreement between the European Union (EU) and Canada (CETA) have echoed the Statement adopted under NAFTA.[38]

---

34 *Sun Belt Inc. v. Her Majesty the Queen,* Notice of Claim and Demand for Arbitration, 12 October 1999, 4.

35 For an analysis of this case in the context of the relationship between Canadian domestic law and the NAFTA, see Joseph Cumming and Robert Froehlich, 'NAFTA Chapter XI and Canada's Environmental Sovereignty: Investment Flows, Article 1110 and Alberta's Water Act,' Toronto: University of Toronto, 2007.

36 Valerie Hughes and Gabrielle Marceau, 'WTO and Trade in Natural Resources,' in *International Law and Freshwater: The Multiple Challenges*, ed. Laurence Boisson de Chazournes, Christina Leb, and Mara Tignino, (Cheltenham: Elgar, 2013), 267.

37 1983 Canada, Mexico and the United States Joint Statement.

38 Article 1.9 (Rights and obligations relating water) states: The Parties recognise that water in its natural state, including water in lakes, rivers, reservoirs, aquifers and water basins, is

128   CHAPTER 6

6.3.2 *Vattenfall AB, Vattenfall Europe AG, Vattenfall Europe Generation AG v. Federal Republic of Germany*

In 2007, the city of Hamburg agreed on a provisional licence in favour of Vattenfall to meet future energy demand through the development of a coal-fired power plant situated at the banks of Elbe River. The negotiation was undertaken despite the opposition of environmental and political groups who argued that the project was larger than what was needed to meet the demand for energy in Hamburg.[39] In 2008, when the final approval for the project was due, the city of Hamburg issued a new permit, including additional restrictions on the use of water for the project in order to avoid negative impacts on the volume of water, temperature and oxygen content.[40] The claimant observed that, under German law, without the water permit the company would not be entitled to the immission control permit for the construction of the plant. Such modifications led Vattenfall to initiate an investment dispute against Germany for €1.4 billion in compensation.[41] In 2010 the parties reached an agreement to settle the dispute, and Germany issued new water permits, in line with the original ones, since the project was not possible without access to water resources.[42]

Aguas del Tunari S.A. in Bolivia, Tecmed in Mexico and Bear Creek Mining in Peru constitute examples that inadequate channels of communication between governments, citizens and investors could have detrimental effects on the development of the project. Social pressure (or disguised political pressure) could ultimately bring an investment project to an end. It is worth noting that social pressure invoked as a defence in the context of investment arbitration should be addressed with caution. In *Tecmed,* the tribunal rejected the defence of social pressure invoked by the defendant, on the basis that such defence did not have the connotations of a serious crisis or emergency, nor the project seriously compromised the ecological balance of the site.[43]

It will remain unknown whether justifications that Germany could have invoked in defence of its measures, could have convinced the tribunal. Ultimately, only States are in the position to assess the strength of their arguments and likelihood of success, before settling an investment dispute.

---

  not a good or a product. [...].

39   See Nathalie Bernasconi, 'Background Paper on Vattenfall v. Germany Arbitration,' Winnipeg: IISD: 2009, 1.

40   *Vattenfall v. Germany*, Request for Arbitration of 30 March, 2009, paras 37–40.

41   *Ibid.*

42   *Ibid.*, Award of 11 March, 2011, p. 17 (Article 2: Conditions).

43   *Técnicas Medioambientales Tecmed, S.A. v. United Mexican States*, ICSID Case No. ARB (AF)/00/2, Award of 29 May, 2003, paras. 147–48.

WATER MANAGEMENT AND INDIRECT EXPROPRIATION   129

6.3.3   *Bayview Irrigation District et al. v. United Mexican States*[44]

This case is of significant relevance in terms of the special nature of water resources. The dispute arose, under NAFTA, out of a claim initiated by irrigators in the State of Texas (US) against Mexico for alleged diminution of their water rights. The permits had been granted by the State of Texas, presumably in accordance with the allocation of water resources as provided in the Treaty for the 'Utilization of the Waters of the Colorado and Tijuana Rivers and of the Rio Grande/Rio Bravo,' signed on 3 February 1944 between Mexico and the US. The question addressed by the tribunal, in deciding its jurisdiction, was whether the claimants had an investment in the territory of Mexico. The tribunal recognised the existence of an investment in the form of water rights, granted in Texas, since the claimants' farms and irrigation rights were situated in the US. Further, the tribunal concluded that the claimants were not investors in Mexico.[45] As a result the dispute did not fall within the scope of NAFTA Chapter 11, which prompted the Tribunal to dismiss the case due to lack of jurisdiction.

The arbitral tribunal, however, articulated an important *obiter dictum* with regard to the ownership of water resources:

> [o]ne owns the water in a bottle of mineral water, as one owns a can of paint. If another person takes it without permission, that is theft of one's property. But the holder of a right granted by the State of Texas to take a certain amount of water from the Rio Bravo / Rio Grande does not 'own,' does not 'possess property rights in,' a particular volume of water as it descends through Mexican streams and rivers towards the Rio Bravo / Rio Grande and finds its way into the right-holders irrigation pipes.[46]

Further the tribunal made an important distinction between ownership over water resources and 'water rights.' The latter are created by the State and granted to the user; a definition of the former depends on the domestic laws of each State. The tribunal, in that case, analysed Mexican domestic law, concluding that under the Mexican Constitution 'the ownership of waters within the boundaries of the national territory originally belongs to the Nation.'[47]

Finally, the tribunal dismissed imaginative interpretations proposed by the claimants in relation to the apportionment of the waters of the Rio Bravo / Rio

---

44   *Bayview Irrigation District et al. v. United Mexican States,* ICSID Case No. ARB (AF)/05/1, Award of 19 June, 2007.

45   *Ibid.,* 112–13.

46   *Ibid.,* para. 116.

47   See *ibid.,* paras. 117–18.

Grande under the 1944 Treaty between Mexico and the US. The tribunal gave due regard to the ordinary meaning of the Treaty provisions, which apportion the water as it arrives in the international watercourse between Mexico and the US. The tribunal was clear that a dispute arising out of an improper diversion of the waters in the River should be decided under the dispute settlement procedures of the 1944 Treaty.

6.4 Addressing Claims of Expropriation Arising from Water Management and Regulation

It is likely, as experience shows, that investors' claims over measures affecting their water rights or permits, are going to be assessed in the context of whether they constitute an expropriation of such rights.

Before introducing this framework, two aspects should be considered: (i) the first aspect relates to the type of water entitlement and its relationship to the overall investment, and (ii) the second relates to the manner in which the investment claim is presented to the arbitral tribunal.

(i) Water in relation to the overall investment: In most types of investment projects including, among others, commercial farming, industry, electricity generation and mining, the extraction of water resources often does not constitute the main investment. However, no operation could develop without a permit or a right to use water. In other investment projects, water is the product or object that is being traded, such is the provision of water services, bottled water, commercial irrigation and – to some extent – hydroelectric projects. Therefore one could suggest that under the first type of projects, water permits constitute one element of the whole investment, whereas under the second type of projects, water permits constitute the investment as such. The above is relevant when assessing the economic impact of the measure on the overall investment, as will be further discussed in the next chapters.

On one hand, a regulatory measure could constitute a direct expropriation when it revokes or cancels water entitlements. On the other hand, authorities may not affect the water entitlement directly by reducing water allocation, but could modify standards of water quality by restricting pollution or imposing higher standards of water quality. This type of measure would still have an impact on water quantity.

(ii) The investment claim and the scope of the decision: The manner in which arbitral proceedings are framed by the arbitral tribunal – in its terms of reference – largely depends on the parties' strategy. Consequently, the decision awarded by arbitral tribunals, is essentially shaped by the legal arguments and

WATER MANAGEMENT AND INDIRECT EXPROPRIATION

evidence provided by the claimant and the defences raised by the respondent. Even when the core of the dispute concerns the use and management of water resources, the anatomy of the governmental measure will be largely analysed by arbitral tribunals. The consistency, transparency and due process of the measure, could in the end overweigh the claim of public interest. As a way of example, one could look at the decisions in *Tecmed*, *Metalclad*, and *Methanex*.

With these two considerations in mind, the next three chapters focus on the analysis of indirect expropriation claims, arising from water-related measures. Such analysis proposes the following methodology, which will be further elaborated in Chapters 7 to 9.

The First stage relates to the jurisdictional phase of the proceedings and addresses two inquiries in turn. The first line of inquiry considers whether there is a property right related to water resources, which is subject to expropriation, and what the nature of such a right is.[48] The second inquiry considers whether such property right in water – if it exists – constitutes an investment protected under the IIA.

The Second stage addresses the merits of the case. On the basis of the practice of various arbitral tribunals, it adopts a 'quantitative' approach to determine the level of economic deprivation suffered by the investor.[49] The level of economic deprivation from a 'quantitative' perspective focuses primarily on the effects of the measure over the investment. The analysis of economic deprivation is accompanied by the tests of control and duration. This work further submits that the analysis should not conclude there, as that would mean to adopt a *sole effects* approach. It is, therefore, important to continue with the analysis of the 'quality' of the governmental measure.

The Third stage, also related to the merits, follows the previous 'quantitative' determination. It adopts a 'qualitative' approach, which seeks to ascertain the legitimacy of the regulatory measure; in other words the legitimacy of the exercise of the police power. In order to dismiss a possible disguised act of

---

48   The existence of property rights (ownership, permits, licences or other), and the determination of whether these rights are considered an investment under the meaning of the IIA, constitute a necessary analysis by arbitral tribunals. This analysis should be undertaken prior to addressing each of the specific investor's claims, in this case the claim of indirect expropriation.

49   The terms 'quantitative' and 'qualitative' analysis have been proposed by Professor Brigitte Stern, and they are borrowed, under this framework to address claims of indirect expropriation. See Brigitte Stern, 'In Search of the Frontiers of Indirect Expropriation,' in *Contemporary Issues in International Arbitration and Mediation*, ed. Arthur W. Rovine (Brill, The Netherlands: Martinus Nijhoff Publishers, 2007).

132   CHAPTER 6

expropriation, this approach considers whether the measure conforms to standards of good faith and proportionality.

6.5   Conclusion

Potential water-resource conflicts could arise in different economic sectors, such as mining and energy projects that could cause water pollution, effecting small-scale farming and other livelihoods. Relatively new investment projects over large extensions of land in Africa, for irrigation and farming, have the potential of displacing indigenous communities competing for water resources, as one commentator suggests:

> early movers are seeking to lock in access to water for agriculture with investments in States perceived to have a surplus of water today. Countries where water resources are traditionally scarce, started to invest in agricultural lands, with leased periods of 50 to 90 years, and extension up to 1 million hectares.[50]

As discussed in Chapters 2 and 3, developing countries are advised to achieve certain levels of economic and human development prior to undertaking measures towards the protection of the environment, and prior to adopting more sophisticated water management mechanisms. The implementation of water management principles could trigger new legislation to normalise water uses, potentially affecting previously granted water entitlements.

On one hand, it is reasonable to acknowledge that increasing resilience and adaptation are at the forefront of water resources management, especially in the face of hydrological variability and climate change. On the other hand, foreign investment requires stable and secure legal environments that may not always be available in times of water stress.

---

50   Smaller and Mann, 'A Thirst for Distant Lands: Foreign Investment in Agricultural Land and Water,' 5–6.

CHAPTER 7

The Nature of Property Rights over Water Resources

The Role of Domestic Law

7.1 Introduction

There is more than one notion of property that comes to mind when we talk about *property rights* in general and specifically in relation to water. Ownership is perhaps the most prominent notion relating to *property rights*, which often encompasses the idea of absolute dominion over the object, as once described by Blackstone. A more nuanced notion is often depicted as a bundle of rights. This metaphor conveys the idea that property does not involve a sole owner in isolation of other individuals and things, 'but multiple parties tied together in relationships that are social as well as legal.'[1] This notion better describes individuals and communities' relation with water resources. These relations are particularly important when defining *property rights* in water because each stick of the bundle of rights granted to water users will shape the manner in which their property rights are construed. This point may well be illustrated in the words of Sax:

> [t]he roots of private property in water have simply never been deep enough to vest in water users a compensable right to diminish lakes and rivers or to destroy the marine life within them. Water is not like a pocket watch or a piece of furniture, which an owner may destroy with impunity. The rights of use in water, however long standing, should never be confused with more personal, more fully owned, property.[2]

The limits of *property rights* or interests in water resources will depend largely on the allocation system adopted by each national or regional jurisdiction. Allocation of water resources in jurisdictions where water is scarce or abundant, such as the Western regions of the US and England, respectively, was introduced and discussed in Chapter 3. Modern systems of water rights are granted through the issuance of permits and licenses. Under such systems,

---

1   Jane B. Baron, 'Rescuing the Bundle-of-Rights Metaphor in Property Law,' *University of Cincinnati Law Review* 82, no. 1 (2013), 58.

2   Joseph Sax, 'The Limits of Private Rights in Public Waters,' *Environmental Law* 19 (1989), 482.

© KONINKLIJKE BRILL NV, LEIDEN, 2017 | DOI 10.1163/9789004335301_008

quantity is generally allocated by considering the purpose for which the permit has been requested.

In the context of international investment law, water rights in the form of permits, licences and concessions will often fall within the definition of investment, provided in IIAs; it is unlikely that investors, as well as other individuals, acquire some kind of water appropriation right. However, in a State with less developed allocation mechanisms, riparian systems may provide more extensive rights to foreign investors. This is, for instance, the case of foreign investment in large-scale or commercial farming, where intensive water use in large expanses of farmland could affect downstream users.[3]

One of the first considerations in an investment dispute originating under a claim of expropriation, be it direct or indirect, is whether those allegedly affected rights exist and thus, whether they can be subject to expropriation:

> [i]nvestments disputes are about investments, investments are about property, and property is about specific rights over things cognisable by the municipal law of the host state.[4]

Only following a determination of the nature and scope of water rights under the domestic law of the host State can one examine a claim of indirect expropriation under the standards of international law.

This chapter discusses the role of municipal or domestic law in the construction of *property rights* in water resources within a legal system. In so doing, it aims to contribute to the debate on the relationship between international and municipal law, especially in regard to the role and applicability of municipal law in solving investment disputes. More importantly, however, it seeks to ascertain whether the construction of such rights, as a bundle shaped by constitutional principles and national laws, evokes the special nature of water resources. If the answer is affirmative, one could then argue that the extent of protection of the investment, as defined under IIAs, may be bound by the nature and limits of the water right.

---

3 Commercial farming investment often takes place in riparian jurisdictions, such as Ethiopia, Zambia, Cameroon and Mozambique. Such investment may be potentially conflictive as the high demand for water resources involving large farmland may affect other downstream users. See Makane Moïse Mbengue and Susanna Waltman, 'Farmland Investments and Water Rights: The Legal Regimes at Stake,' Geneva: IISD, May 2015, 20–23.

4 Zachary Douglas, 'The Hybrid Foundations of Investment Treaty Arbitration,' *The British Yearbook of international Law* 74 (2003), 197.

THE NATURE OF PROPERTY RIGHTS OVER WATER RESOURCES 135

The role of domestic law in the construction of property rights in water has implications in the definition of investment for the purpose of IIA protection. It is likely that water rights, either in the form of licences, permits or concessions, fall within the definition of investment under most IIAs. In such cases, the protection provided under the applicable IIA should not transcend the special nature of water resources as recognised under domestic law.

7.2 Constructing Domestic Property Rights in International Investment Law: A Legal Fiction?

Judge Higgins is often cited in reference to her remarks about the importance of understanding the notion of property in the context of expropriation under international law. How can we assess the loss of property rights, 'unless we really understand what property is?' She asks, and further observes:

> [s]till less can we decide whether a particular deprivation is permissible, and if so on what grounds, and indeed whether it is a deprivation that does or does not entitle the former owner to compensation, unless we have some sense of the social function of property and what it is that judges and arbitrators are doing when they make these decisions.[5]

It is common ground, at least in principle, that property rights are not acquired under international law.[6] In order to determine the existence and scope of property rights, two approaches are required. First, one must look into the municipal law of the host State where the investor claims to have an investment subject to protection.[7] Second, domestic law may also be addressed as facts,

---

5 Rosalyn Higgins, 'The Taking of Property by the State. Recent Developments in International Law,' *Recueil des Cours (The Hague Academy of International Law)* T. 176 (1982), 268.

6 Yet, this does not preclude that some patrimonial rights may be conferred by international treaty, as has been stated in decisions of the International Court of Justice. See International Law Commission, *Yearbook of the International Law Commission – Volume II*, (United Nations, 1959), 3.

7 Zachary Douglas offers a comprehensive analysis of the relationship between property rights and the municipal law of the host State in the context of an investment dispute. In this vein, the following notion is important to note: 'Rule 4. The law applicable to an issue relating to the existence or scope of property rights comprising the investment is the municipal law of the host state, including its rules of private international law.' See Zachary Douglas, *The International Law of Investment Claims* (Cambridge: Cambridge University Press, 2009), 52. See also Monique Sasson, *Substantive Law in Investment Treaty Arbitration: The Unsettled Relationship between*

136   CHAPTER 7

providing evidence of State practice and of compliance with international obligations.[8]

The first approach to municipal law – ascertaining property rights within domestic law – highlights the interaction between international and municipal law. International law, as the applicable rule to solve the dispute, requires incorporating the provisions of national law as a precondition to apply the international standard. In the second approach, 'the provisions of internal law are relevant facts in determining the international standard.'[9]

This theoretical distinction however is not always clear in practice. International tribunals have often approached domestic law as facts, largely because they sought to defer to the sovereignty of the State whose national laws may have breached an international obligation. In so doing, arbitral tribunals need not pronounce on whether the internal laws of the States are effective, fair or adequate. The Permanent Court of International Justice (PCIJ) in *Certain German Interests over Polish Upper Silesia*, was confronted with such a question:

> [i]t might be asked whether a difficulty does not arise from the fact that the Court would have to deal with the Polish law of July 14th, 1920. This, however, does not appear to be the case. From the standpoint of International Law and of the Court which is its organ, municipal laws are merely facts which express the will and constitute the activities of States, in the same manner as do legal decisions or administrative measures.[10]

However, the PCIJ was also confronted with a more substantial consideration of municipal law. The Polish government, in its defence, had argued that the affected property belonged to the German Government and not to private

---

     International Law and Municipal Law, (Alphen aan den Rijn, The Netherlands: Kluwer Law International, 2010); Hege Elisabeth Kjos, *Applicable Law in Investor-State Arbitration. The Interplay between National and International Law* (Oxford: Oxford University Press, 2013) and Ivar Alvik, 'The Hybrid Nature of Investment Treaty Arbitration – Straddling the National/International Divide,' in *The New International Law: An Anthology*, ed. Christoffer C. Eriksen and Marius Emberland (Leiden: Martinus Nijhoff Publishers, 2010).

8   See for instance, *India – Patent Protection for Pharmaceutical and Agricultural Chemical Products (India- Patents (US))*, Appellate Body Report WT/DS50/AB/R, adopted on 16 January 1998, paras. 65–66 and 68.

9   James Crawford, *The International Law Commission's Articles on State Responsibility* (Cambridge: Cambridge University Press, 2002), 89.

10   *Certain German Interests in Polish Upper Silesia* (Germany v. Poland), August 25, 1925 P.C.I.J. (ser. A) No. 7, 19.

THE NATURE OF PROPERTY RIGHTS OVER WATER RESOURCES   137

entities; this aspect would have been the determinant for a finding of expropriation under the Treaty of Versailles.[11] The Court had to determine whether two German companies held property rights over movable and immovable property linked to the Chorzow Factory. The PCIJ asserted that as a preliminary matter it would determine the existence of property rights by looking at German municipal law, which was the legal framework under which the Chorzow Factory was transferred to the owners:

> [i]t must be observed that the Court, in the exercise of the jurisdiction granted by Article 23 of the Geneva Convention, will not examine, save as an incidental or preliminary point, the possible existence of rights under German municipal law.[12]

The issue of domestic law as a matter of fact was again considered by the International Tribunal for the Law of the Sea (ITLOS) in the *M/V SAIGA* case.[13] The tribunal stated that the relevant question was whether the SAIGA ship had the nationality of Saint Vincent and the Grenadines at the time of the arrest.[14] ITLOS applied Article 91 of the United Nations Convention on the Law of the Sea, which provides that every State would set the conditions for the grant of nationality to ships, their registration and the right to fly a flag.[15] The tribunal further stated that these are matters regulated by national law and are thus under the sovereignty of each State, hence the nationality of the ship was a question of fact 'to be considered like other facts in the dispute before it.'[16]

The approach of the ITLOS tribunal appears to be more cautious in deferring to the sovereignty of the State by referring the issue as a factual matter. Yet, the tribunal undertook a somewhat substantial construction of domestic law to ascertain the nationality of the SAIGA.

In *China – Auto Parts*, the US, the EU and Canada claimed that Decree 125 and other legal provisions adopted by China were in breach of its obligations under the GATT 1994 and other covered agreements. In order to determine a possible breach, the WTO Panel proceeded to the construction of Article 2(2)

---

11   *Ibid.*

12   *Ibid.*, 42.

13   *The M/V 'SAIGA' (No.2) Case – Saint Vincent and The Grenadines v Guinea,* International Tribunal for the Law of the Sea, Judgement of 1 July 1999.

14   *Ibid.*, para. 62.

15   Article 91 of the United Nations Convention on the Law of the Sea.

16   *The M/V 'SAIGA' (No.2) Case – Saint Vincent and The Grenadines v Guinea,* International Tribunal for the Law of the Sea, Judgement of 1 July 1999, para. 66.

and the overall structure of China's Decree 125.[17] The Panel had to make an objective assessment of the matter and the facts within the scope of its terms of reference. As the Panel stated:

> [a]lthough we are mindful that the measures are part of the domestic law of China, we will be required to determine the meaning of particular provisions of the measures if interpretations of such provisions are contested by the parties. Our examination in such cases will be for the sole purpose of determining the conformity of the measures with relevant obligations under the WTO covered agreements [...][18]

On appeal, the WTO Appellate Body revised the construction of China's Municipal Law undertaken by the Panel with the following caveat:

> [w]e recognize that there may be instances in which a panel's assessment of municipal law will go beyond the text of an instrument on its face, in which case further examination may be required, and may involve factual elements. With respect to such elements, the Appellate Body will not lightly interfere with a panel's finding on appeal.[19]

In contrast to the *M/V SAIGA* case, the WTO Panel did not have to determine the existence of legal entitlements and nationality. Chinese law, in that case, constituted evidence of compliance with the WTO covered agreements.

Some experts warn of the fallacy of looking at domestic law as facts; a decision concerning the existence of property rights, which constitute an investment must, as Douglas observes:

> be decided in accordance with the municipal law of the host state for this is not a dispute about evidence (facts) but a dispute about legal entitlements.[20]

---

17   *China – Measures Affecting Imports of Automobile Parts,* Panel Report WT/DS339/R, WT/DS340/R, WT/DS342/R, adopted on 12 January 2009.

18   *Ibid.,* para. 7.2.

19   One should note that pursuant to Article 17 (6) of the Dispute Settlement Understanding, the Appellate Body's mandate is limited to issues of law discussed in the panel report, such as the legal interpretations developed by the panel. *China – Measures Affecting Imports of Automobile Parts,* WT/DS339/AB/R, WT/DS/340/AB/R, WT/DS342/AB/R, Panel Report, adopted 12 January 2009, para. 225 [Footnotes omitted].

20   Douglas, *The International Law of Investment Claims,* 70.

THE NATURE OF PROPERTY RIGHTS OVER WATER RESOURCES

A legal construction of property rights, in application of domestic law, is significant to the determination of the scope of the legal entitlement, as it allows for a comprehensive analysis of all legal rules that shape the property under analysis.[21]

Investment treaty arbitration provides prominent examples of the relevance of domestic law in the assessment of international obligations. In *Suez* for instance, the tribunal was called to decide on a claim of expropriation relating to contractual rights. It asserted that comparable to a case of expropriation of physical assets, where one must understand the nature of such rights, 'one must look at the domestic law under which the rights were created.'[22]

It can be claimed that the examples provided above in relation to the ITLOS and the PCIJ could be viewed as approaching the application of domestic law as a matter of *legal fiction,* with a cautious and preliminary approach to domestic law. Yet, even when a tribunal explicitly approaches domestic law as facts, it is bound to consider all the evidence, laws and regulations that will shape the nature of such legal entitlements.

It is outside the scope of this work to provide a full account of this theoretical issue. The construction of property rights is however pivotal to the determination of the nature of water rights and arguably the scope of its protection.

---

21   *Ibid.,* 69–72. Douglas notes that it is one thing to analyse domestic law within the context of assessing a breach of the investment treaty, in which case the governmental measure constitutes a fact, because the analysis takes place in the plane of international law. It is a different thing, that the rules of international law – under which the claim of expropriation is addressed – provide a *renvoi* to domestic law, in order to determine the scope of property rights.

22   *Suez, Sociedad General de Aguas de Barcelona S.A., and Vivendi Universal S.A. v. Argentina,* ICSID Case No. ARB/03/19; *AWG Group Ltd. v. Argentina,* UNCITRAL, Decision on Liability of 30 July, 2010, para. 151. See also *Bayview Irrigation District et al. v. United Mexican States,* ICSID Case No. ARB (AF)/05/1, Award of 19 June, 2007, analysing the nature of ownership over water resources. See also *EnCana v. Ecuador,* where the tribunal addressed a claim of VAT returns, which the claimant alleged to be entitled to under Ecuadorian law. 'Unlike many BITs there is no express reference to the law of the host State. However for there to have been an expropriation of an investment or return (in a situation involving legal rights or claims as distinct from the seizure of physical assets) the rights affected must exist under the law which creates them, in this case, the law of Ecuador.' See *En Cana Corporation v. Republic of Ecuador,* London Court of Arbitration (UNCITRAL rules), Award of 3 February, 2006, para. 184.

140   CHAPTER 7

7.3   A Construction of Property Rights in Water

The determination of the nature and scope of water rights requires the arbitral
tribunal to analyse the nature and historical background of water resources
and the way in which they shape the expectations and preferences of users
in a particular State. Such analysis may involve an understanding of: (i) why
under most legal systems water resources are not subject to private ownership,
(ii) why water resource-entitlements differ from other resource-entitlements
(such as land or oil) and (iii) why the use and management of water resources
requires a holistic approach.

These aspects are somewhat embedded in most domestic legal systems, and
reflect social, economic and physical realities pertaining to the nature of water
resources in each State. Chapter 6 makes reference to a number of domestic
water laws, as they provide an indication of the extent to which water rights
are protected under domestic law and the order of prioritisation in cases of
water scarcity or instances in which competition arises.[23]

It is important to provide a general overview of the relevant provisions en-
visaged in most domestic water laws. There is, however, an inextricable challenge in drawing detailed commonalities across domestic water legal systems.
Likewise, emerging international principles of water management are increasingly embraced by water regulators and management bodies, such as the Dublin Principles and IWRM, as discussed in Chapter 3; some of these emerging
principles have been adopted and implemented under some domestic legal
systems, as discussed in Chapter 6.

Property rights scholars argue that the construction of property rights,
while delimiting the scope of protection subject to the application of domestic
law, also harmonizes such protection *vis-à-vis* other members of society.[24] In
so doing, countries embed societal values which involve limitations on the enjoyment of certain types of property. These values should not be overlooked.[25]

The construction of water rights under domestic law is underpinned by the
sovereignty and police power of the host State, as well as an array of institutional and legal mechanisms. These elements are not easily transposed onto the international investment regime due to the latter's broad approach to protected
rights and interests. In *Pope and Talbot* the tribunal found that access to the

---

23   See Chapter 6, Sections 6.2.1 and 6.2.2, as well as footnote 8.

24   Amnon Lehavi and Amir N. Licht, 'BITS and Pieces of Property,' *The Yale Journal of Inter-
      national Law* 36, no. 1 (2011), 133–34.

25   Richard Barnes, *Property rights and natural resources: Studies in international law no. 19*
      (Oxford, Portland: Hart Publishing, 2009), 27.

THE NATURE OF PROPERTY RIGHTS OVER WATER RESOURCES   141

US market was a *property interest* thus protected under Article 1110 of NAFTA.[26] The tribunal, however, did not offer a clear analysis as to how market access falls within the scope of Article 1139 or whether such *property interest* exists under Canadian domestic law. On this point some scholars observe:

> [i]n this sense, Investors aspire to be shielded by a kind of property *lex specialis* that would bind not only the host government but also other private actors that may have rival contentions to rights in these assets.[27]

Water experts often question the extent of investment protection under the definition of investment against the significant limitations of private rights acquired under domestic law. To what extent could such limitations at the domestic level, be relevant for assessing potential breaches under an IIA's standards of protection?

In most domestic water systems, the right to exclude other users from sources of water is subject to limitations.[28] The US Supreme Court made this point clear in a case in which the government of Mississippi had affected the riparian rights of the owner of a water dam:

> [r]ights, property or otherwise, which are absolute against all the world are certainly rare, and water rights are not among them. Whatever rights may be as between equals such as riparian owners, they are not the measure of riparian rights on a navigable stream relative to the function of the Government in improving navigation. Where these interests conflict, they are not to be reconciled as between equals, but the private interest must give way to a superior right, or perhaps it would be more accurate to say that, as against the Government, such private interest is not a right at all.[29]

Most domestic legal systems have priority mechanisms in place which define rights in relation to other property holders, either for reasons of public

---

26   *Pope & Talbot v. Canada*, Interim Award of 26 June, 2000, para 96. See further reference to the definition of investment in Section 7.4 below.

27   Lehavi and Licht, 'BITs and Pieces of Property,' 130.

28   Stanton Kibel asserts, in his analysis of the definition of investment under Article 1139 NAFTA, that under domestic law private rights acquired to use water are subject to significant limitations. The question that follows is to what extent such limitations, apposite at the domestic level, are relevant under NAFTA's definition of investment. See Paul Stanton Kibel, 'Grasp on Water: A Natural Resource that Eludes NAFTA's Notion of Investment,' *Ecology Law Quaterly* 34, no. 2 (2007), 107.

29   *United States v. Willow River Power* Co., 324 U.S. 499 (1945), 510.

interest or competition among users.[30] Therefore, a preliminary conclusion suggests that under domestic law, property rights relating to different natural resources and other assets subject to appropriation enjoy different levels of protection. The decision of the US Supreme Court highlights important limitations to the enjoyment of the different sticks of the bundle of rights, under which this type of property might have been otherwise 'good against the world.'[31] Note however that under international investment law, the level of protection of such property rights might differ, in accordance with the provisions of each IIA.

A decision of the German Constitutional Court also illustrates this point. An amendment to the Federal Water Resources Act, required all prospective users that would be likely to alter the quantity and quality of groundwater, to apply for a permit, which was limited in time and purpose. The amendment potentially affected the owner of a gravel pit who had been using the groundwater flowing under his property for extracting gravel. Eventually the permit was rejected, affecting the gravel extraction activity. The Federal Court of Justice referred the question to the German Constitutional Court; it asked whether the Water Resources Act, as amended, was compatible with the right to property protected under the Constitution, and whether it was consistent with the Civil Code. The Constitutional Court expressed that the Civil Code was not the exclusive body of law providing for the scope and limits to property:

> [t]he totality of regulations over property that exist at particular points in time determine the concrete right the property owner enjoys. If these regulations divest the property owner of a certain control over his or her property, then this control is not included in the right to property.[32]

In this case the Court concluded that the Water Resources Act did not expropriate the property of the plaintiff.

---

30 It has been argued that property does not entail rights to the holder, but also obligations towards society. See for instance Gregory S. Alexander, *The Global Debate over Constitutional Property: Lessons for American Takings Jurisprudence* (Chicago: University of Chicago Press, 2006) and Amnon Lehavi, 'Mixing Property,' *Seton Hall Law Review* 38, no. 1 (2007).

31 Zachary Douglas, 'Property, Investment and the Scope of Investment Protection Obligations,' in *The Foundations of International Investment Law*, ed. Joost Pauwelyn, Jorge E. Viñuales, and Zachary Douglas (Oxford, Oxford University Press, 2013).

32 Groundwater Case, 58 BVerfGE 300 (1981) (German Federal Constitutional Court), as commented and translated in Donald P. Kommers and Russell A. Miller, *The Constitutional Jurisprudence of the Federal Republic of Germany*, 3rd ed. (Duke University Press, 2012), 642.

THE NATURE OF PROPERTY RIGHTS OVER WATER RESOURCES

7.3.1 *Reconciling the Bundle (Web) of Property Rights in Water*

Arbitral tribunals are primarily bound to undertake the construction of property rights over water resources to ascertain a claim of expropriation. In practice, however, host States are called to present their defence through evidence of the whole legal framework pertaining to the water right under analysis. This is because a host State has a deeper knowledge and understanding of the intertwined relationships of its domestic water law in relation to the overall legal system.[33] In this context, arbitral tribunals are required to adopt a holistic approach to the legal rules pertaining directly or indirectly to the construction of a water entitlement in order to reconcile this convoluted web of interrelated interests.

Depending on the domestic legal tradition, different water rights may allow for more or less sticks within the bundle of property rights.[34] After all, it is reasonable that unpredictable natural resources such as water, give rise to precarious property entitlements.

Each entitlement involves complicated relations at both horizontal and vertical levels.

7.3.1.1 Horizontal Interrelations in Domestic Laws

The arrangement of norms of the same hierarchy pertains to the enjoyment of different sticks of the bundle of water rights in their interrelation to other stick-holders' rights, for instance land, forest, or downstream users. Domestic laws regulating each stick resemble a web of sticks rather than a bundle of individual sticks.[35] In such a scenario, water laws are connected to other laws of the same hierarchy, including the laws of land, environmental protection, forestry, and indigenous rights (unless they have a higher hierarchy, in which case the relationship will become vertical). It is only reasonable to expect that this intertwined web of legislation confers certain expectations to other water users, who would, as a result, acquire some sort of interest *vis-à-vis* the investor's entitlement to use water resources or to discharge water resources.

---

33   See for instance Schill *et al.* on the analysis of deference in International Investment Law. Stephan W. Schill, and Vladislav Djanic, 'International Investment Law and Community Interests' Society of International Economic Law (SIEL), Fifth Biennial Global Conference, Online Proceedings, Working Paper No 2016/01 (2016). Available at SSRN: http://ssrn.com/abstract=2799500, last visited 1 July 2016, 19.

34   A brief reference to the concept of the bundle of rights in property law has been made in Chapter 1, Section 1.4.3 footnote 38.

35   Zellmer and Harder use the metaphor of a web rights trying to depict the real interlinks between different right holders and the enjoyment of intertwined property rights. Sandi Zellmer and Jessica Harder, 'Unbundling Property in Water,' *College of Law, Faculty Publications* (2007), available at http://digitalcommons.unl.edu/lawfacpub/11/.

For instance, there is a relationship between pollution permits for mining (with an effect over water quantity and/or water quality) and downstream farmers. Even when downstream farmers lack formal water entitlement to set volumes of water or to receive it in a certain quality, there will be potential for conflict if the resource upstream does not comply with certain standards of quality or if such standards need improvement for water quality and quantity purposes.

Some domestic legal systems, such as the Alberta Water Act, do not provide for the payment of compensation in cases of withdrawal or cancellation of water rights.[36] As a matter of legal construction this legal provision seems to play a double role in the sphere of international treaty arbitration: (i) it is applicable domestic law in its role of defining the scope of property rights in water, and (ii) it is also factual evidence of a possible breach of an IIA.

A final consideration likely to be discussed in an investment dispute is whether water entitlements constitute a physical asset or an intangible right to use water resources conferred to investors by host States. This issue has been analysed in cases of prior appropriation rights in the context of US takings jurisprudence. Leshy explains that the argument is often invoked in cases of takings or expropriation claims against governmental measures affecting water rights because physical occupation would be deemed a *per se* taking under US jurisprudence.[37]

The implications of water permits as physical assets – in investment arbitration – is that regulatory measures modifying quantity or quality of the water entitlement, at the point of extraction, could be claimed to constitute a direct expropriation if considered physical occupation.[38] From a property rights perspective, as discussed in Chapter 3, a water entitlement 'does not give ownership of the molecules of water,' but the right to use a certain amount of water.[39] For this reason, an approach to water entitlements that considers water as a physical asset would be fundamentally misleading.

---

36 s 55(2), Water Act RSA 2000 c. W-3 (Alberta Canada).

37 A prominent case on physical takings is *Loretto v. Teleprompter Manhattan CATV Corp., 458 U.S. 419, 421–22 (1982)*. Arbitral tribunals in investment arbitration cases have adopted a similar view in their analysis of expropriation through physical occupation. Grant asserts that US Courts have found, in the past, that reduction of water entitlements constitute *per se* physical taking. Yet, they have been widely criticised. See Douglas L. Grant, 'ESA Reductions in Reclamation of Water Contract Deliveries: A Fifth Amendment Taking of Property?' *Environmental Law* 36, no. 4 (2006).

38 See for instance *Burlington Resources Inc. v. Republic of Ecuador*, ICSID Case No. ARB/08/5, Decision on Liability of 14 December, 2012.

39 John D. Leshy, 'A Conversation About Takings and Water Rights,' *Texas Law Review* 83, no. 7 (2009).

THE NATURE OF PROPERTY RIGHTS OVER WATER RESOURCES   145

7.3.1.2   Vertical Interrelations in Domestic Laws

Vertical normative constructs look at primary and secondary rules to shape property rights. National constitutions are generally the first and most important legal source; through them States have consistently avoided private ownership of water resources.[40] As some academics observe:

> [t]he public good nature of water...has had a decisive influence on the legal status of water. In Roman Law, and, subsequently, in English and American common law, and to an extent in Civil Law systems, flowing waters are treated as common to everyone (*res communis omnium*), and are not capable of being owned.[41]

Almost all States have adopted legal arrangements that are predominantly based on State ownership or stewardship over water resources.[42] The English system, for instance, does not recognise ownership over flowing water;[43] its use is therefore under the stewardship of the government.[44] The US has complex systems of water allocation, depending on the region.[45]

---

40 Stanton Kibel, 'Grasp on Water: A Natural Resource that Eludes NAFTA's Notion of Investment,' 134.

41 *Ibid.*, 104 (Haneman, as quoted by Stanton).

42 For instance Brazil's Constitution 1988 (as amended 2004) recognises ownership of water resources by the States (Article 26) and the Union (Article 20). Likewise, the Mexican Constitution recognises that water resources belong to the Nation (Article 27.5 Constitution of Mexico 1917, amended 2004); Kazakhstan's Constitution claims the ownership of water resources and other natural resources in favour of the State (Article 6). These examples are drawn from the work of Salman and Bradlow, see Salman M.A. Salman and Daniel D. Bradlow, *Regulatory Frameworks for Water Resources Management: A Comparative Study* (Washington: The World Bank, 2006), 24, 68 and 76.

43 Jane Ball, 'The Boundaries of Property Rights in English Law,' *Electronic Journal of Comparative Law: Report to the XVIIth International Congress of Comparative Law* 10, no. 3 (2006), 19.

44 Stephen Hodgson, 'Modern water rights. Theory and practice,' Rome: Development Law Service FAO Legal Office, Food and Agriculture Organization of the United Nations, 2006, 22. Also relevant is the German system of water permits which does not have constitutional provisions regarding the ownership of water resources. However, Article 89 of the German Constitution provides federal ownership over inland waterways. The use of water requires a permit or licence under the Federal Water Act. See Salman and Bradlow, *Regulatory Frameworks for Water Resources Management*, 61–63.

45 The literature regarding the American system of water rights and ownership is extensive, and it concentrates in two main traditions: the prior appropriation doctrine, used in the west part of the country, and riparian doctrine, used in the east of the country.

146   CHAPTER 7

Currently, domestic water laws are moving towards systems of permits and licences and they seem to favour higher levels of flexibility in the management of the resource.[46] It follows that the need for more flexibility to tackle hydrological variability, for example, may have an impact on the security and predictability of water rights.[47] But are the implications under domestic and international law comparable?

The *Restatement of the Law, Second: Foreign Relations Law of the United States,* for example, states that even when property rights are to be conferred in conformity with the domestic law of the host State, this arrangement 'may not violate international standards of justice.'[48]

In turn, some domestic laws reflect international obligations acquired through treaty implementation. In this vein, one could argue that international agreements, as implemented in domestic law are relevant in the construction of property rights. The 1944 Treaty between the US and Mexico for the utilization of water on the Colorado and Tijuana Rivers and the Rio Grande is illustrative. Article 3 provides an order of preferences to serve as a guide for the joint use of international waters: (i) domestic and municipal uses, (ii) agriculture and stock-raising, (iii) electric power, (iv) other industrial uses, etc.[49] It may be argued that certain uses could be prioritised in case of competition among users due to water scarcity. However, the question may be more complex because of the extent to which domestic courts would treat previously granted water entitlements in the light of international agreements. Such discussion is however outside the scope of this work.

Furthermore arbitral tribunals have favoured the analysis of the physical characteristics of water resources and the resulting intangible nature of the water rights (see also discussion in Section 4.3.1.1). In *Bayview Irrigation District* the tribunal addressed the issue of water rights in some detail. In constructing the rights alleged by the claimants the tribunal took into consideration

---

An account of these two common law systems can be analysed in Hodgson, 'Modern water rights. Theory and practice,' 11–14.

46   Chapter 3 discusses the increasing need for a flexible approach to the management of water resources.

47   See Zellmer and Harder, 'Unbundling Property in Water,' 687–88.

48   American Law Institute, *Restatement of the Law, Second: Foreign Relations Law of the United States. As adopted and promulgated by the American Law Institute at Washington D.C. in May 26 1962* (St. Paul, Minn. : American Law Institute Publishers, 1965), paras. 185, 555–56.

49   Treaty between the United States of America and Mexico Respecting Utilization of Waters of the Colorado and Tijuana Rivers and of the Rio Grande, U.S.-Mex., Feb. 3, 1944, 59 Stat. 1219.

THE NATURE OF PROPERTY RIGHTS OVER WATER RESOURCES 147

the Mexican Constitution, which does not recognise property rights in water (ownership).[50] It also considered that Mexican Law does not guarantee the existence of permanence of the water, subject to concession.[51] Interestingly, the tribunal also considered the 1944 Treaty in shaping the alleged rights claimed by the irrigators:[52]

> there is an evident and inescapable conceptual difficulty in positing the existence of property rights in water up-river in Mexico in a context where the entitlement of each Claimant depends upon the apportionment of a certain volume of water, [...] which can be determined only by reference to the volume of water that actually reached the main channel of the Rio Bravo / Rio Grande.
> [...] the holder of a right granted by the State of Texas to take a certain amount of water from the Rio Bravo/Rio Grande does not 'own,' does not 'possess property rights in,' a particular volume of water [...].[53]

In relation to international obligations arising out of decisions rendered by international tribunals, the question remains as to their effect in the construction of property rights under domestic law. To illustrate this issue, let us consider a hypothetical example. What if the Pulp Mills case between Argentina and Uruguay had come to a different outcome?

If the ICJ in the Pulp Mills case had granted Argentina's request to dismantle the Orion (Botnia) Mill due to breaches of procedural obligations,[54] the decision of the Court could have interfered with investment rights of the Finish investor in charge of the project. Under the Finland – Uruguay BIT, such an interference could have triggered an investment treaty dispute between the investor and Uruguay.[55]

If the ICJ's hypothetical decision had applied retroactively, the following questions may have arisen: (i) would Uruguay have been able to grant licences and permits for the installation of the mill, (ii) would the investor's property

---

50 See *Bayview Irrigation District et al. v. United Mexican States*, ICSID Case No. ARB (AF)/05/1, Award of 19 June, 2007, para. 118.

51 *Ibid.*

52 *Ibid.*, paras. 120–21.

53 *Ibid.*, paras. 115–16. See also Chapter 6 Section 6.3.3.

54 *Pulp Mills on the River Uruguay (Argentina v. Uruguay)*, *Judgment, I.C.J. Reports 2010*, p. 14, 275.

55 Finland – Uruguay Agreement on the Promotion and Protection of Investments (2002), available at http://investmentpolicyhub.unctad.org/IIA/country/225/treaty/1548.

148   CHAPTER 7

rights under such permits be considered legal, and (iii) would the investor be able to uphold such rights under the BIT?

7.4   The Definition of Investment

The question of whether all assets constitute an investment subject to protection under an IIA does not always have an affirmative answer. Following the determination of whether the domestic laws of the host State confer a property right to the investor (Section 7.3), it remains to be examined whether those property rights constitute an investment under the relevant IIA. This section addresses two issues, namely whether water rights constitute an investment; and if so, whether the investment and its protection are shaped, constrained and bound by its construction under domestic law.

Water entitlements may not be the sole or most obvious purpose of the investment. Depending on the nature of the project, water rights could constitute an autonomous investment or may be part of the operation of the investment as a whole.

Since water entitlements are generally granted in the form of licences, permits or concessions, a water entitlement might be defined as an investment. The Energy Charter Treaty (ECT), which is a sector-specific agreement, includes every kind of asset, present and future, which is related to the economic activity in the energy sector:

> (f) any right conferred by law or contract or by virtue of any licenses and permits granted pursuant to law to undertake any Economic Activity in the Energy Sector.[56]

---

56   See the Energy Charter Treaty's definition of investment, provided for in Article 1 (6) "'Investment" means every kind of asset, owned or controlled directly or indirectly by an Investor and includes: (a) tangible and intangible, and movable and immovable, property and any property rights such as leases, mortgages, liens, and pledges; [...] (d) Intellectual Property; (e) Returns; (*f*) *any right conferred by law or contract or by virtue of any licenses and permits granted pursuant to law to undertake any Economic Activity in the Energy Sector.* A change in the form in which assets are invested does not affect their character as investments and the term "Investment" includes all investments, whether existing at or made after the later of the date of entry into force of this Treaty for the Contracting Party of the Investor making the investment and that for the Contracting Party in the Area of which the investment is made (hereinafter referred to as the "Effective Date") provided that the Treaty shall only apply to matters affecting such investments after the Effective Date. "Investment" refers to any investment associated with an Economic Activity in the

THE NATURE OF PROPERTY RIGHTS OVER WATER RESOURCES 149

DR-CAFTA Article 10.28 on the definition of investment includes 'licenses, authorizations, permits, and similar rights conferred pursuant to domestic law.'[57] Further footnote 10 to letter (g) clarifies:

> [w]hether a particular type of license, authorization, permit, or similar instrument (including a concession, to the extent that it has the nature of such an instrument) has the characteristics of an investment depends on such factors as the nature and extent of the rights that the holder has under the law of the Party. *Among the licenses, authorizations, permits, and similar instruments that do not have the characteristics of an investment are those that do not create any rights protected under domestic law.* For greater certainty, the foregoing is without prejudice to whether any asset associated with the license, authorization, permit, or similar instrument has the characteristics of an investment.[58]

For the purpose of this analysis, it may be useful to compare the whole investment project with a bundle of rights, a bundle of investment rights. This is because the role of each investment right is relevant to the success of the project as a whole.

Water may appear as a modest stick within the bundle of investment rights; it is inexpensive, weakly regulated (especially in developing countries where most extractive industries operate) and often easy to access. However, without water, most projects would become unviable; water has no substitutes in nature, and it is difficult to transport and store in large quantities. In contrast, one could argue that other types of assets required to develop a project might be substitutable in case of shortage.

From a social perspective, water may become an all or nothing investment asset. The presence of social pressure and the absence of political will could significantly undermine negotiations to protect the investment project.[59]

Energy Sector and to investments or classes of investments designated by a Contracting Party in its Area as "Charter efficiency projects" and so notified to the Secretariat' [emphasis added].

57   Dominican Republic – Central America Free Trade Agreement (DR-CAFTA), Chapter 10 (Investment) provides for list of covered investments. See also the Commission's Draft Text of the Transatlantic Trade and Investment Partnership Chapter 11 – Investment: Defines 'investment' as: '(f) an interest arising from: (i) a concession conferred pursuant to domestic law [...] to exploit natural resources.'

58   *Ibid.* [emphasis added]

59   In the area of water services, *Aguas del Tunari S.A. v. Bolivia, Biwater v. Tanzania* and *Compañía de Aguas del Aconquija S.A. and Vivendi Universal S.A. v. Argentine Republic,*

150   CHAPTER 7

Only in a few instances have arbitral tribunals declined jurisdiction on the basis that the interest at issue was not backed by property rights under the domestic law of the respondent State, and therefore, did not constitute an investment under the IIA and Article 25(1) of the ICSID Convention (when applicable).[60]

The discussion on the determination of water entitlements as protected investments under IIAs does not present major difficulties. The notion of investment in the context of water resources is of interest, since water resources are needed for most types of industrial activity, and yet they will not necessarily constitute the sole purpose of the investment. Water resources may be an element of input in the production process or will be subject to pollution as a result of different production processes.[61] Less often water rights might constitute the main purpose of the investment, e.g. when water is provided as a service, bottled for consumption, or exported as a commodity.

A discussion on the relevance of water permits could arise in a case in which the regulatory measure only affects the water entitlements, leaving the rest of the elements of the investment untouched (e.g. mining concessions, electricity generation permits, land leases, etc.).[62] Could such measures be deemed a partial expropriation? In such a case, could the project continue without water resources in the quantity and quality granted under the permits?

Arbitral practice is still incipient on this issue. However, tribunals have provided some guidance when discrete investments have been affected as part of a whole investment project. In *Electrabel* the tribunal deciding a claim of expropriation under the ECT, stated:

---

     constitute good examples. See also the discussion on the social and political problems around water resources in Chapters 3 and 6.

60   See for instance *Emmis International Holding, B.V. Emmis Radio Operating, B.V. Mem Magyar Electronic Media Kereskedelmi Es Szolgáltató Kft. v. The Republic of Hungary,* ICSID Case No. ARB/12/2, Award of 16 April, 2014, and *Accession Mezzanine Capital L.P. and Danubius Kereskedőház Vagyonkezelő Zrt v. The Republic of Hungary,* ICSID Case No. ARB/12/13, Award of 17 April, 2015.

61   In this regard pollution may not be only linked to water quality *per se* (as in *Pacific Rim v. El Salvador*), but also to its temperature (as was the case in *Vattenfall v. Germany*); in general, changes in its original state may affect the normal development of ecosystems and safety for consumption.

62   The complexity of international projects requires a combination of licences, concessions and contracts, among others, in order to put in place the infrastructure necessary to carry out the operation.

THE NATURE OF PROPERTY RIGHTS OVER WATER RESOURCES

[i]n this Tribunal's view, it is clear that both in applying the wording of Article 13(1) ECT and under international law, the test for expropriation is applied to the relevant investment as a whole, even if different parts may separately qualify as investments for jurisdictional purposes.[63]

Each of these pieces of property rights are complementary to the materialisation of the investment as a whole, and thus comparable to a bundle of investment rights, as proposed by the tribunal in *ATA Construction*.[64] However, the bundle formed by each discrete investment should be treated as an indivisible whole. This was the position of the tribunal in *Holiday Inns*:

> it is well known, and it is being particularly shown in the present case, that investment is accomplished by a number of juridical acts of all sorts. It would not be consonant either with economic reality or with the intention of the parties to consider each of these acts in complete isolation from the others. It is particularly important to ascertain which is the act which is the basis of the investment and which entails as measures of execution the other acts which have been concluded in order to carry it out.[65]

In *Joy Mining*[66] the tribunal departed from the approach of *Holiday Inns* and *CSOB*, and concluded that bank guarantees under a contract constituted contingent liabilities that could not be considered an asset under the relevant BIT.[67]

---

63   *Electrabel S.A. v. The Republic of Hungary,* ICSID Case No. ARB/07/19, Award on Jurisdiction, Applicable Law and Liability of 30 November, 2012, para. 6.58.

64   The comparison of the investment with a bundle of rights was adopted for instance in *ATA Construction, Industrial and Trading Company v. Hashemite Kingdom of Jordan,* ICSID Case No. ARB/08/2, Award of 18 May, 2012, para. 96.

65   *Holiday Inns v. Morocco,* ICSID Case No. ARB/72/1, Decision on Jurisdiction of 12 May, 1974. As cited in Pierre Lalive D'Epinay, 'The first "World Bank" arbitration (Holiday Inns v. Morocco): Some legal problems,' *British Yearbook of International Law* 51 (1982), 159. See also *Teskoslovenska Obchodni Banka, A.S. v. The Slovak Republic (CSOB v Slovakia),* ICSID Case No. ARB/97/4, Decision on Jurisdiction of May 24, 1999, para. 72; *Fedax N.V. v. Republic of Venezuela,* Decision on Jurisdiction, 37 I.L.M. 1378, July 11, 1997, para. 24.

66   *Joy Mining Machinery Limited v. The Arab Republic of Egypt,* ICSID Case No. ARB/03/11, Award on Jurisdiction of 6 August, 2004.

67   The tribunal did not disagree with the approach adopted in *CSOB v Slovakia, FEDAX NV v. Venezuela,* and *Salini v. Morocco.* The tribunal did not find that the facts of these cases were comparable to the specific issues dealt with in the case at hand. See *Joy Mining*

In *Enron* the tribunal noted in respect to the complementarity of different sticks of the bundle of investment rights:

> an investment is indeed a complex process including various arrangements, such as contracts, licences and other agreements leading to the materialization of such investment, a process in turn governed by the Treaty. This particular aspect was explained by an ICSID tribunal as 'the general unity of an investment operation' and by one other tribunal considering an investment based on several instruments as constituting 'an indivisible whole'[68]

In a challenge to jurisdiction, for instance, a respondent host State may argue – most likely unsuccessfully – that a water permit or any type of water entitlement does not constitute an investment on its own. The assessment of this argument may take place in two stages of the proceedings: (i) the jurisdictional stage, where the tribunal may weigh the relevance of each stick of the bundle and its complementarity in relation to the other sticks, and (ii) the merits stage at which point the tribunal may decide if one discrete investment stick (a water permit) could negatively affect the overall investment. This last point will be further discussed in the next chapter.

7.5   Conclusions

The construction of property rights of water requires an assessment of the whole domestic legal framework. As discussed earlier, an application and interpretation of domestic law, as a *renvoi* of international law, may more accurately shape the scope of such rights. The determination of property rights, looking at domestic law as facts, is losing support among international investment law academics. A third possibility is that a determination of property rights in domestic law is only possible through application and interpretation of such, but it is a legal fiction.

Machinery Limited v. The Arab Republic of Egypt, ICSID Case No. ARB/03/11, Award on Jurisdiction of 6 August, 2004, paras. 41–63.

68   *Enron Corporation and Ponderosa Assets, L.P. v. Argentine Republic,* ICSID Case No. ARB/01/3, Decision on Jurisdiction of 14 January, 2004, para. 70. See also *Klöckner Industrie-Anlagen GmbH and others v. United Republic of Cameroon and Société Camerounaise des Engrais,* ICSID Case No. ARB/81/2, Award of 21 October, 1983. (ICSID Reports, Vol. 2, p. 3).

THE NATURE OF PROPERTY RIGHTS OVER WATER RESOURCES 153

In undertaking such a construction, arbitral tribunals would be expected to consider the unpredictability and variability of the hydrological cycle, as an essential part of the nature of water resources. Tribunals may also consider that the communal characteristic of water resources, traditionally limits the bundle of rights linked to water licences. These considerations are substantially different from those informing the construction of other property rights, such as those on land.[69]

As to the notion of investment and the jurisdiction of the tribunal, two considerations are of special relevance. First, water entitlements could be seen as standalone investments e.g. licences to extract water resources for the provision of water services. Secondly, in most cases water licences may form part of an overall investment project. In both cases it is likely that they are defined as investments and are therefore protected under IIAs. The notion of the 'unity of economic purpose and functionality' of the investment is important in asserting the jurisdiction of the arbitral tribunal to hear the merits of the case.[70] Therefore, consideration of complementary rights and interests widens the types of investments that could fall within the definition of investment included in the relevant IIA and therefore fall under the jurisdiction of the tribunal.

---

69   See Shelley Ross Saxer, 'The Fluid Nature of Property Rights in Water,' *Pepperdine University School of Law: Legal Studies Research Paper Series* 2010/13 (2010), 3.

70   UNCTAD, 'EXPROPRIATION: A Sequel. UNCTAD Series on Issues in International Investment Agreements II,' New York – Geneva: UNCTAD, 2012, 22–23.

CHAPTER 8

The Impact of Regulatory Measures on Foreign Investments

The 'Quantitative' Approach

8.1 Introduction

As discussed in Chapter 5, an assessment of a claim of direct expropriation does not normally present major complications. The dispute might focus primarily on the quantum of compensation. However, a claim of indirect expropriation involves a preliminary determination, namely whether the investor has suffered any deprivation of the enjoyment of his property:

> [i]n the case of an indirect taking or an act tantamount to expropriation such as by a regulatory taking, however, the threshold examination is an inquiry as to the degree of the interference with the property right. This often dispositive inquiry involves two questions: the severity of the economic impact and the duration of that impact.[1]

This stage pertains to a 'quantitative' analysis (to borrow the term used by Stern)[2] of a claim of indirect expropriation. This analysis which focuses on the effects of a regulatory measure may provide insights as to whether the level of deprivation or interference with the investor's property rights is 'substantial' enough as to amount to an indirect expropriation. The analysis of the effects of the measure over the investment is in practice the most common approach used by investment tribunals, and rarely do they step further afield,

---

1   *Glamis Gold Ltd. v. United States of America,* Award of 8 June, 2009, para. 356.

2   See Brigitte Stern, 'In Search of the Frontiers of Indirect Expropriation,' in *Contemporary Issues in International Arbitration and Mediation*, ed. Arthur W. Rovine (Brill, The Netherlands: Martinus Nijhoff Publishers, 2007), 38.

   In addition, Dalhuisen and Guzman have proposed a similar test to address claims of indirect expropriation under international law. They consider that a regulatory measure that have a *de minimis* effect over the investment, would be considered an expropriation, unless the measure is adopted for a public purpose ('super public purpose') or it is adopted under regular governmental activity. The authors give a close look into the lawfulness of the taking. See H. Jan Dalhuisen and Andrew T. Guzman, 'Expropriatory and Non-Expropriatory Takings Under International Investment Law,' *UC Berkeley Public Law Research Paper No. 2137107* (2012).

© KONINKLIJKE BRILL NV, LEIDEN, 2017 | DOI 10.1163/9789004335301_009

THE IMPACT OF REGULATORY MEASURES ON FOREIGN INVESTMENTS 155

into the analysis of the quality of the measure in determining the existence of an indirect expropriation. The interpretative provisions on expropriation introduced in the new generation of IIAs, as discussed in Chapter 5, do not necessarily clarify the standard applied to the level of deprivation. While there are variations in wording, most of these agreements reflect, with more or less clarifications, the provisions included in the 2004 and 2012 US Model BITs:

> 4. [...] (a) The determination of whether an action or series of actions by a Party, in a specific fact situation, constitutes an indirect expropriation, requires a case-by case, fact-based inquiry that considers, among other factors:
> (i) the economic impact of the government action, although the fact that an action or series of actions by a Party has an adverse effect on the economic value of an investment, standing alone, does not establish that an indirect expropriation has occurred;[3]

As proposed in Chapter 6, the severity of the level of deprivation, as expressed in this provision, does not necessarily allow the conclusion that the deprivation ought to be 'substantial' or 'total.' Article 6 of the 2012 US Model BIT has kept the phrase 'measures equivalent to expropriation,' but does not include the words 'tantamount to expropriation,' in contrast to other agreements such as the NAFTA. It is arguable that in the context of ascertaining indirect expropriation this exclusion – in some treaties – has little impact. As discussed below, investment tribunals continue to apply a criterion to assert deprivation that is close to 'total.'

In the context of water-related measures affecting investment rights, the 'quantitative' approach may be insufficient to reach a conclusion of whether the measure constitutes either an indirect expropriation or a non-compensable regulation. From such a perspective, water-related measures that cancel or diminish previous water entitlements could render the whole investment useless, leading – rather straight forwardly – to conclude that an indirect expropriation took place. Nonetheless, it is important to discuss the assessment of the level of deprivation, as adopted by investment tribunals. The 'quantitative' approach could be associated with three elements, which will be discussed in turn: (i) the economic impact of the measure in question, (ii) the duration of the regulatory measure and (iii) the control over the investment. While the following analysis is structured accordingly, one should

---

3 2012 US Model BIT (Annex B). See also US-Korea FTA (Article 11.6), TPP (Article 9.8), Peru – US FTA (Article 10.7).

156   CHAPTER 8

address the issue of the *sole effects* approach and its inadequacy before turning to the test on the level of deprivation. The *sole effects* approach relates to the 'quantitative' approach, but is less sophisticated and focuses exclusively on the objective effects of the measure in relation to the foreign investment.

8.2 Preliminary Consideration: The Inadequacy of the *Sole Effects* Approach

The *sole effects* approach is adopted:

> if the effect of the measures on the value of the investment is made the sole criterion in assessing the measure's legality and no attention is paid to the nature of the act.[4]

While the *sole effects* approach has not been expressly spelled out in the provisions of IIAs, its application responds to an interpretative approach of the rather broad provisions on expropriation included in IIAs. However, not all investment tribunals have adopted such an interpretative approach: an important and increasing number of investment tribunals defer to the host State's exercise of its police powers. The academic literature has long compared two investment arbitration awards, often identifying the *Methanex* case with the application of the police power doctrine and the *Metalclad* case with the application of the *sole effects* approach.[5] In both cases the claimant invoked a breach of Article 1110 of the NAFTA in relation to environmental regulations with allegedly expropriatory effects. While each investment tribunal focused on the factual circumstances of the case, their departing point, i.e. the reading of the provisions on expropriation applicable to the facts, was quite distinct.

In *Metalclad,* the tribunal began its analysis from the following reading of Article 1110 of the NAFTA:

---

4   Veijo Heiskanen, 'The Contribution of the Iran-United States Claims Tribunal to the Development of the Doctrine of Indirect Expropriation,' *The Journal of the International Law Association: International Law Forum du Droit International* 5, no. 3 (2003), 177.

5   See Rudolf Dolzer, 'Indirect Expropriations: New Developments?' *New York University Environmental Law Journal* 11 (2002); Caroline Henckels, 'Indirect Expropriation and the Right to Regulate: Revisiting Proportionality Analysis and the Standard of Review in Investor-State Arbitration,' *Journal of International Economic Law* 15, no. 1 (2012).

THE IMPACT OF REGULATORY MEASURES ON FOREIGN INVESTMENTS   157

expropriation under NAFTA includes [...] also covert or incidental interference with the use of property which has the effect of depriving the
owner, in whole, or in significant part, of the use of reasonably-to-be-
expected economic benefit of property even if not necessarily to the obvious benefit of the host State.[6]

In *Methanex,* the claimant relied on the definition adopted by the tribunal in
Metalclad.[7] While the tribunal acknowledged that a discriminatory regulation
may constitute an expropriation,[8] it departed from such a definition, stating:

a non-discriminatory regulation for a public purpose, which is enacted
in accordance with due process and, which affects, *inter alios*, a foreign
investor or investment is not deemed expropriatory and compensable
unless specific commitments had been given...[9]

In a similar case applying the approach in *Metalclad*, the tribunal in *Suez and
InterAgua*, noted that its inquiry was: '...directed particularly at the "effects"
of the measure on an investment, rather than at the intent of the government
enacting the measure.'[10]

The Iran – US Claims Tribunal (IUSCT) has a somewhat different mandate,
in relation to expropriation, to that accorded to investment tribunals under
most standard IIAS. The jurisdiction of the IUSCT covers 'expropriations or
other measures affecting property rights.'[11] As observed by some practitioners,
this mandate covers a wider range of other measures, including *de facto* takings, such as physical seizures appropriations of property by governmental

---

6   *Metalclad Corp. v. Mexico*, Arb(AF)/97/1, 5 ICSID Reports, 209, para. 103.

7   *Methanex Corp. v. United States of America,* Final Award of 3 August, 2005, Part IV –
    Chapter D – para. 4.

8   *Ibid.*, Part IV – Chapter D – para. 16.

9   *Ibid.*

10 *Suez, Sociedad General de Aguas de Barcelona S.A., and Vivendi Universal S.A. v. Argen-
    tina,* ICSID Case No. ARB/03/19 and *AWG Group Ltd. v. Argentina*, UNCITRAL, Decision
    on Liability of 30 July, 2010, para. 122; *Biloune v. Ghana,* as cited in Rudolf Dolzer and Felix
    Bloch, 'Indirect Expropriation: Conceptual Realignments?' *International Law Forum du
    Droit International* (2003), 162 (95 I.L.R. 183, 209) and *Fireman's Fund Insurance Company
    v. Mexico,* ICSID Case No. ARB (AF)/02/1, Award of 17 July, 2006, para. 176(f).

11 Article 11 of the US-Iran Claims Settlement Declaration, 19 January 1981, available at
    http://www.iusct.net/General%20Documents/2-Claims%20Settlement%20Declaration.
    pdf. See also Heiskanen, 'The Contribution of the Iran-United States Claims Tribunal to
    the Development of the Doctrine of Indirect Expropriation,' 179.

158   CHAPTER 8

forces and other deprivations, even if temporal.[12] Increasingly, investment tribunals show deference to the regulatory prerogative of the host State, departing from a *sole effects* approach. In other words, tribunals are moving towards a reasonable consideration of both, the effects and purpose of the governmental measure. It is important to note that tribunals have relied on the police power of the State to scrutinise the governmental measure in the past, without leaving aside an assessment of the impact of the measure on the investment.[13]

New provisions on indirect expropriation suggest that contracting States seek more deference towards their regulatory prerogatives by providing less weight to the effects of the governmental measure on the investor's property rights.[14]

8.3 The Level of Deprivation: Economic Impact, Duration and Control over the Investment

8.3.1 *General Approach to the Level of Deprivation*
There seems to be agreement, within the academic literature as well as within the body of arbitral awards, that the impact of the measure ought to be substantial enough to conclude that an indirect expropriation has taken place.

The word 'substantial,' however, does not offer a clear standard in defining the level of interference. Practitioners and academics have used various words including 'serious,' 'significant,' 'severe' and 'fundamental' in describing the

---

12   *Ibid.*, 181. As pointed out by Heiskanen, the IUSCT was consistent in its application of the *sole effects* in cases such as *Tippetts, Abbett, McCarthy, Stratton v. TAMS-AFFA Consulting Engineers of Iran, Award No. 141-7-2 (June 29, 1984), reprinted in 6 IRAN-U.S. CT.R. 225–26; Sedco, Inc., et al. v. National Iranian Oil Co., et al., Award No. ITL 55-129-3 (Oct. 28, 1985), reprinted in 9 IRAN-U.S. CT.R. 248, 276–79; Phelps Dodge Corp., et at. v. Islamic Republic of Iran, Award No. 217-99-2 (Mar. 19, 1986), reprinted in 10 IRAN – U.S. C.T.R. 121, 129–30.*

13   *Chemtura v. Canada*, UNCITRAL, Award of 2 August, 2010, para. 266; *Glamis Gold v. United States*, Award, para. 354; *Saluka Investments B.V. v. Czech Republic*, UNCITRAL, Partial Award of 17 March, 2006, para. 262; *Continental Casualty Company v. Argentina*, ICSID Case No. ARB/03/9, Award of 5 September, 2008, paras. 276–78 *and S.D. Myers, Inc. v. Canada, 40 ILM 1408*. See also Dolzer and Bloch, 'Indirect Expropriation: Conceptual Realignments?' 159–61.

14   See discussion in Chapter 5. See also UNCTAD, 'EXPROPRIATION: A Sequel. UNCTAD Series on Issues in International Investment Agreements II,' New York – Geneva: UNCTAD, 2012.

THE IMPACT OF REGULATORY MEASURES ON FOREIGN INVESTMENTS 159

severity of the measure in question. Yet these words do not always lead to the same conclusion.[15] In fact, it is difficult to imagine what kind of standard could provide meaningful guidance on each of these terms. As cautiously suggested by the tribunal in *Chemtura*, 'it would make little sense to state a percentage or a threshold that would have to be met for the deprivation to be "substantial"'[16] since contextual particularities of each case may require different approaches to the term 'substantial.' Some studies point out that formulations used by arbitral tribunals to describe the level of deprivation suggest that interference with property rights should be 'total' or close to 'total' rather than simply 'significant' or 'substantial.'[17] This analysis resembles the approach taken by the tribunal in *Pope & Talbot*.[18] The tribunal assessed a claim of expropriation under Article 1110 of the NAFTA noting that 'the test is whether that *interference is sufficiently restrictive* to support a conclusion that the property has been "taken" from the owner.'[19] The tribunal qualified 'sufficiently restrictive' by further stating:

> '[t]antamount' means nothing more than equivalent. Something that is equivalent to something else cannot logically encompass more.[20]

---

15 In this regard see for instance the analysis undertaken by the tribunal in *GAMI* of the arbitral award in *Pope & Talbot v. Canada* as regards to the level of deprivation. *GAMI Investments v. Mexico*, UNCITRAL, Final Award of 15 November, 2004, para. 125–28. See also Stifter and Reinisch referring to *Electrabel v. Hungary* on the use of the terms 'substantial' 'devastating,' 'virtual annihilation.' In Lukas Stifter and August Reinisch, 'Expropriation in the Light of the UNCTAD Investment Policy Framework for Sustainable Development,' in *Shifting Paradigms in International Investment Law: More Balanced, Less Isolated, Increasingly Diversified*, ed. Steffen Hindelang and Markus Krajewski (Oxford: Oxford University Press, 2016), 87.

16 *Chemtura Corporation v. Canada*, UNCITRAL, Award of 2 August, 2010, para. 249.

17 The UNCTAD Report refers to Fortier and Drymer's recollection of arbitral awards assessing the level of interference required to make a finding of indirect expropriation. See UNCTAD, 'EXPROPRIATION: A Sequel,' 64.

18 *Pope & Talbot v. Canada*, Interim Award of 26 June, 2000.

19 *Ibid.*, para. 102 [emphasis added].

20 *Ibid.*, para. 104. See also the conclusions of Professor Stern on this issue: Stern, 'In Search of the Frontiers of Indirect Expropriation,' 34. Cases that have followed this line of reasoning and have ruled under a similar approach to *Pope & Talbot* are *CMS Gas Transmition Company v. Argentina*, Award of 12 May, 2005, para. 262; *Occidental Exploration and Production Co. v. Ecuador*, Award of 1 July, 2004, para. 89; *Glamis Gold, Ltd. v. United States of America*, Award of 8 June, 2009, para. 357.

160   CHAPTER 8

Likewise, the tribunals in *Venezuela Holdings* and *Total* adopted an equivalent stance deciding on claims of indirect expropriation. In *Venezuela Holdings,* the tribunal noted:

> deprivation requires either a total loss of the investment's value or a total loss of control by the investor of its investment, both of a permanent nature.[21]

Consequently, one could preliminary conclude that the test of indirect expropriation under NAFTA and other IIAS require that the measure must impact property rights in their entirety. It is important to note that the application of these provisions, included in the NAFTA, the US – Iran Claims Settlement Declaration (Algiers Accord) and other IIAS, constitute *lex specialis.* Therefore, in the context of expropriation, direct or indirect, tribunals should abide by the specific mandate accorded to them by the provisions of each agreement.[22] The decision in *Pope & Talbot* remains a source of inspiration for numerous investment tribunals, under both the NAFTA and other IIAS of the first generation.[23] The tribunal in *Burlington,* for example, analysed the tax laws on oil revenues adopted by Ecuador. The tribunal did not find that the taxes (on windfall profits) applied at 42 per cent substantially deprived the company from expected revenues, nor did it find a substantial deprivation at 99 per cent. The arbitrators considered that despite these levels of taxation, the company was not substantially deprived from its investment because it was still in control of the oil-producing blocks.[24] On the other hand, the tribunal did find that Ecuador's subsequent

---

21   Venezuela Holdings, B.V., *et al.* v. Venezuela, ICSID Case No. ARB/07/27, Award of 9 October, 2014, para. 286; *Total v. Argentina,* ICSID Case No. ARB/04/1, Decision on Liability of 27 December, 2010, paras. 195, 199.

22   See Heiskanen, 'The Contribution of the Iran-United States Claims Tribunal to the Development of the Doctrine of Indirect Expropriation,' 179. Abtahi refereing to *Harza Engineering Company v. Iran,* where the tribunal suggested in an *obiter dictum* that 'unreasonable interference' is sufficient to constitute an expropriation, Robert Abtahi, 'Indirect expropriations in the jurisprudence of the Iran-United States Claims Tribunal,' *Journal of Law and Conflict Resolution* 3, no. 7 (2011), 28. See also Rudolf Dolzer and Margrete Stevens, *Bilateral Investment Treaties* (The Hague: Martinus Nijhoff, 1995).

23   *Occidental Exploration and Production Company v. The Republic of Ecuador,* London Court of Arbitration (UNCITRAL Rules), Case No. UN3467, 1 July 2004, para. 89. Similar approach in *Archer Daniels Midland Company and Tate & Lyle Ingredients Americas, Inc. v. Mexico,* ICSID Case No. ARB (AF)/04/05, Award of 21 November, 2007, para. 240; *Burlington Resources Inc. v. Republic of Ecuador,* ICSID Case No. ARB/08/5, Decision on Liability of 14 December, 2012, para. 396.

24   *Burlington v. Ecuador,* paras. 456–57.

THE IMPACT OF REGULATORY MEASURES ON FOREIGN INVESTMENTS 161

intervention on blocks 7 and 21 amounted to a physical takeover and, therefore, to a direct expropriation.[25] This background provides the basis to analyse possible disputes involving water-related measures. A regulatory measure affecting – in total or in part – a discrete water entitlement could, in theory, form the basis for a finding of expropriation. The claimants in *Venezuela Holdings* argued that Venezuela had expropriated discrete rights by adopting measures such as new or higher taxes and imposing discriminatory export curtailments. Each of these measures, alleged by the claimant, amounted to expropriation under the BIT.[26] The tribunal however agreed with the respondent's argument that a proper determination of expropriation should consider the effect on the investment as a whole. As noted by the tribunal:

> [t]he Tribunal considers that, under international law, a measure which does not have all the features of a formal expropriation may be equivalent to an expropriation if it gives rise to an effective deprivation of the investment as a whole.[27]

There are two elements to this decision, which are worth analysing in the context of investment disputes involving water resources. The first is the unity of investment approach, and the second is the special nature of water, whose absence in partial or in whole may lead to a total deprivation of the value of the investment.[28] This consideration would give rise to a *prima facie* finding of indirect expropriation almost invariably.

8.3.2 *Measures Affecting the Enjoyment of Water Rights*

A tribunal's approach to the construction of water rights and to the definition of investment under a relevant IIA is bound to have an effect on its analysis of the level of deprivation.

A preliminary question requires the following reflection. At which point, if any, should the construction of property rights be taken into consideration by the tribunal when ascertaining indirect expropriation? Is it when determining the level of deprivation (a 'quantitative' approach) or when assessing the legitimacy of the application of the police power (a 'qualitative' approach)? The answer is likely to lie within both stages of analysis, namely 'quantitative' and 'qualitative'; and it is expected to become clearer as the argument is developed.

---

25   *Ibid.,* paras. 123–24, 537.

26   See *Venezuela Holdings v. Venezuela*, para. 283.

27   *Ibid.*, para. 286.

28   See the discussion on the Definition of Investment in Chapter 7, Section 7.4.

162   CHAPTER 8

For the purposes of determining the level of deprivation, the affected water entitlement should be examined as: (i) a discrete property right in order to ascertain its construction under the domestic law of the host State and (ii) a stick in the bundle of investment rights, which is part of the whole operation. The first step serves to shape and determine the complexity that such a property right has acquired by virtue of the domestic legal framework in which it originates. The second step follows arbitral practice. It considers that if a water entitlement were to be assessed in isolation of the rest of the bundle of investment rights (i.e. just the level of deprivation) in relation to the investment as a whole, it might not be appropriately assessed, possibly leading to an equivocal dismissal of the claim of indirect expropriation.

8.3.2.1   Water as a Discrete Property Right

The construction of property rights under the domestic law of the host State is discussed in Chapter 7. It is argued that if such a construction is going to have any relevance in the determination of expropriation, the 'construed' water permit should be a factor in the determination of the level of deprivation of the investment. Otherwise, it would be almost disingenuous to undertake such a construction, concluding that the water right constitutes an investment under the relevant IIA and apply a level of protection that is equivalent to the protection of land rights or other assets. As proposed throughout this work, water property rights are precarious in nature; the challenge is to incorporate such a nature into the analysis of the alleged breaches of an investment treaty dispute.

This issue has important implications for host States and the policies associated to water resources management, which could have a *de facto* expropriatory effect over the whole investment. Put in practical terms, water unavailability could undermine the entire project. *A contrario* argument might suggest that such a situation could arise in the context of the management of any natural resource (such as hydrocarbons, land, forests and timber), which could be affected by a regulatory measure limiting their use. On this point, it is important to note that while other natural resources are present in set quantities on or under the soil, the variability of water resources does not allow for secure predictions.[29]

Amendments to water permits, as opposed to withdrawal or cancellation, by reducing the volumes of water allocation, should not lead to the conclusion that the level of deprivation may not be substantial.[30] This type of measure

---

29   See Chapter 2.

30   It is important to consider, however, that despite the fact that numerous countries have adopted modern water right systems; these are not always implemented due to

THE IMPACT OF REGULATORY MEASURES ON FOREIGN INVESTMENTS   163

may have two types of effects: (i) either a reduction of the investment project's outputs, e.g. less production of beer, or rationing drinking water; or (ii) a rendering of the investment as useless, when the project depends on minimum quantities of water to operate, e.g. cooling turbines. While water permits of a shorter duration may allow flexibility for reallocation purposes to tackle water scarcity, they may provide less incentive for foreign investors to embark on large projects.[31] Large infrastructure projects require permits of long duration, such as hydropower projects which may last between fifty and seventy years.[32]

8.3.2.2   Water as a Stick in the Bundle of Investment Rights

Both water entitlements that allocate water resources, and entitlements allowing discharge of pollutants, are essential to the overall operation of certain types of investments that require water as a critical input for their operation.[33] A situation where a water authority reallocates water resources, either amending or cancelling a water permit, could give rise to a claim of direct expropriation in relation to that entitlement. It could also raise a claim – possibly unsuccessfully – of physical seizure of the water resources under the permit, since the amount of water available to operate the investment would be diminished partially or totally.[34] The latter scenario, which would view water as a physical asset that could be susceptible to a claim of expropriation, could prove to be problematic, from both practical and theoretical perspectives; since a 'physical deprivation' is likely to be deemed a *per se* expropriation. Under this approach, host States would be unable to defend regulatory action affecting directly the water permit. In addition, the approach is also untenable from a theoretical perspective. As discussed in Chapters 3 and 6, it is generally agreed that water becomes an asset only when it is physically subtracted from its hydrological flow. Prior to that moment, a water entitlement only constitutes an expectation of the benefit to use the resource under a given allocation system. This follows from the inherent nature of water resources, whose

---

monitoring and enforcement problems. See Stephen Hodgson, 'Modern Water Rights. Theory and Practice,' Rome: Development Law Service FAO Legal Office, Food and Agriculture Organization of the United Nations, 2006, 61.

31   *Ibid.*, 62.

32   *Ibid.*

33   Allocation of water will generally be related to issues of quantity, while pollutant discharge to the issue of quality. See Chapter 6.

34   See Chapter 6, Section 6.3.1.1, on the discussion of the alleged physical nature of water entitlements.

allocation systems do not entitle the users to specific molecules of water, but rather to an amount (or even share) of water at a given time.

Regardless of the approach adopted to determine the nature of the measure, the assessment leads back to the original inquiry, namely the determination of the level of deprivation, exerted by the regulatory measure. In both cases, assuming that the economic activity cannot be undertaken without the input of water resources, the effect of the measure would render the overall investment useless. The economic value of a water permit or licence to develop an investment may not be significant; yet the importance and role of such a permit or licence is essential to the overall project. For example, in *Khan Resources,* the suspension of a mining and exploration licence deprived the foreign investors of their rights under the Founding and Mineral Agreements.[35]

In *Vattenfall I*, the investor alleged the government of Hamburg blocked the issuance of the water permit, which was essential to issuance of the final construction permit.[36] The claimant alleged:

> [o]n 30 September 2008, the BSU granted the immission control permit and the water use permit. However, both permits were coupled with restrictions. In particular, the restrictions with respect to the water use permit are extremely severe. They clearly deviate from the Moorburg Agreement and from what the Vattenfall Group was entitled to expect.[37]

As the factual scenario in *Vattenfall I* was presented, since the quantities allocated for cooling water were decisive for electricity output, the reduction estimated for Vattenfall's output would have been in the order of 45 per cent of the plant's normal output.[38] Germany and the foreign investor, Vattenfall, eventually settled the case. In relation to a determination of expropriation, the question remains whether the reduction of output capacity imposed on Vattenfall could have amounted to indirect expropriation. However, since this reduction was imposed before the project started operations, the measure might have affected the company's economic equilibrium of the investment in the long run; or as suggested by the investor, the project had become unviable from its inception.

---

35 *Khan Resources Inc., Khan Resources B.V. and Cauc Holding Company Ltd. v. the Government of Mongolia*, PCA Case No. 2011-09, Award on the Merits of 2 March, 2015, paras. 311–12.

36 *Vattenfall AB, Vattenfall Europe AG, Vattenfall Europe Generation AG v. Federal Republic of Germany*, Request for Arbitration of 30 March, 2009, para. 34. For an extended comment on *Vattenfall I v Germany*, see Chapter 6.3.2.

37 *Ibid.,* para. 36.

38 *Ibid.,* para. 40.

THE IMPACT OF REGULATORY MEASURES ON FOREIGN INVESTMENTS   165

There could, however, be a few exceptions to the analysis above. One could look at the water entitlement as an independent investment and assess it on its own merits. In such a case, the question that arises is whether one could argue that a partial expropriation has occurred (partial expropriation will be further discussed below).[39]

This scenario could be illustrated by the type of water rights granted to AbitibiBowater by Canada in 1905. The Province of Newfoundland and Labrador had granted the company a perpetually renewable lease of ninety nine years, for 2000 square miles of surface, timber and water rights in the Exploits River watershed for the operation of paper mills and hydroelectric generation.[40] According to the investor, most of these rights were perpetually renewable and not conditional on the continuous operation of the paper mill.[41] In 2008 the Province issued Bill 75 providing for the withdrawal of several rights relating to the use of timber, water and land, which triggered a claim against Canada for various breaches of the NAFTA.[42] While the claimant admitted that some water rights were conditional to the functioning of the Grand Falls Mill (which was closed in 2009) other land, water and timber rights, were not subject to such conditions.[43] Although, the instant case is one of unlawful direct expropriation, as claimed by AbitibiBowater, the question is still relevant as to the treatment of discrete property rights in natural resources where enjoyment is not conditional to the operation of the main investment.

8.3.3 Partial Expropriations when Water Rights have been Negatively Affected

Cases of partial expropriation are unlikely to occur, presumably due to the preponderance of the unity of investment approach applied by investment tribunals. A partial expropriation in general terms would occur when 'only parts of the overall investment are taken.'[44] Often investors have an extended portfolio

---

39   The issue of partial expropriation is discussed in Section 8.3.3.

40   See *AbitibiBowater Inc., v. Government of Canada*, Notice of Intent to Submit a Claim to Arbitration under Chapter 11 NAFTA of 23 April, 2009, paras. 13–17.

41   *Ibid.*, para. 23.

42   Bill 75 entitles '*An Act to Return to the Crown Certain Rights Relating to Timber and Water Use Vested in Abitibi-Consolidated and to Expropriate Assets and Lands Associated With the Generation of Electricity Enabled by those Water Use Rights,*' 16 December 2008.

43   *AbitibiBowater Inc., v. Canada*, para. 29.

44   Ursula Kriebaum, 'Partial Expropriation,' *The Journal of World Investment & Trade* 8, no. 1 (2007), 72.

of investments within the host State (e.g. provision of water services, provision of electricity, etc.). In such cases, it seems more appropriate to speak of several investments.[45]

As discussed in Chapter 7, an investment is formed by a group of discrete assets, compared to a bundle of investment rights (i.e. licences, permits, contracts, physical assets). All these assets are necessary for the operation of the investment, and therefore should be seen as a whole. In the context of international investment law, this is particularly true. The presence of the investor in the host State has the sole purpose of developing a particular project, for which each of the assets has been acquired to serve one function only.

Three question may be asked to determine if an investment tribunal is confronted with a partial expropriation: (i) whether the investment can be disassembled into discrete rights, (ii) whether the State's measure affects rights which fall within the definition of investment, under the relevant IIA, and (iii) whether the property right could be subject of exploitation independently of the overall investment.[46]

For example, the tribunal in *GAMI* analysed a factual scenario under which a direct expropriation of the national investor's assets (GAM's sugar mills) potentially constitutes an indirect expropriation of the foreign investor's assets (GAMI's shares in GAM), protected under NAFTA.[47] The tribunal was of the view that the governmental measure partially expropriated GAM's sugar mills (i.e. expropriation of two mills out of five would still constitute expropriation), even when the damage was not total or equal to a total expropriation.[48]

Since the sugar mills were not GAMI's property, the tribunal could not rule on the direct expropriation of some mills, but rather on an act tantamount to expropriation of the value of the shares that GAMI had in GAM. In this vein, the

---

45   *Ibid.*

46   *Ibid., 83.*

47   GAMI brought an investment dispute against Mexico under NAFTA Chapter 11 Article 1110 (expropriation) among others. GAMI owned 14.18 per cent of the shares in the Grupo Azucarero Mexico S.A. de CV (GAM), which was subject to an expropriatory measure by the Mexican Government of five sugar mills. Following a challenge against the expropriatory act, GAM recovered three of the mills and did not pursue further actions regarding the two remaining mills, apparently due to their lack of economic value. The questions for the tribunal were whether the investment (shares) of GAMI in GAM was indirectly expropriated and whether the shares owned by GAMI lost all of their value. The tribunal did not find that GAMI's investment was expropriated. *GAMI Investments v. Mexico*, UNCITRAL, Final Award of 15 November, 2004, para. 126.

48   *Ibid.*, paras. 126–27. Note however, that tribunal made such consideration on a hypothetical basis, since it could not assess the case of GAM, which was not a foreign investor.

arbitral tribunal analysed the severity of the impact of the measure in order to determine whether the loss of value of GAMI's shares in GAM constituted indirect expropriation (a 'taking' in the words of the tribunal).[49] The tribunal, however, seemed ready to admit that a partial expropriation of the mills was possible, and hence compensable.[50]

Partial expropriation in the context of water permits seems plausible. Section 8.3.2.2 above discussed the example of the *AbitibiBowater* case, which ultimately resulted in a settlement between the claimant and the government of Canada. The case is relevant, as it illustrates that certain historic water rights may not be conditional to the operation of the investment project, and thus they may be enjoyed as discrete rights.

The systems for allocation of water entitlements thus continue to be important in this case, as not all water permits would be specific as to the volume, duration and conditions of water usage. Most modern water rights systems grant permits for specific uses, and therefore the water entitlement would only grant investors the use of the resource to contribute to the realisation of their investment project. There are also legal systems which allow exploitation of water resources without the abovementioned conditions.[51]

There are States that still hold riparian systems of water allocation. In many African States, where commercial farming is common in the context of foreign investment, water resources are often acquired through the use of land. In such cases, it is arguable that different assets or investment rights may not be conditional to the operation of the investment project, giving rise to potential claims of partial expropriation.

This differentiation is relevant to the analysis of partial expropriations. Specifically, a water permit that is granted with no specific condition of use, holds some autonomy in relation to the whole investment. It follows that an approach to a partial expropriation could be viable. Conversely, a water permit granted with the sole purpose of supplementing the main investment project will have no autonomy in practice because the licence would only allow the use of water for the purpose of the operation of the investment. The discussion over partial expropriation may not be mainstream within the

---

49   The tribunal stated: [t]he Tribunal cannot be indifferent to the true effect on the value of the investment of the allegedly wrongful act. GAMI has neglected to give any weight to the remedies available to GAM. Assessment of their effect on the value of GAMI's investment is a precondition to a finding that it was taken.' See *GAMI Investments v. Mexico*, Final Award, para. 133.

50   *Ibid.*, paras. 116–31.

51   Hodgson, 'Modern water rights. Theory and practice,' 64.

168   CHAPTER 8

analysis of indirect expropriation. It is, however, a useful exercise that links
the nature of a water permit with the definition of investment, and the
overall role of the specific asset – water permit – in the context of the operation of the investment.

8.4 Additional Elements to Assess the Level of Deprivation: Duration and Control

As discussed earlier in this Chapter, the notion of 'substantiality' is used by an
important number of investment tribunals to assess the level of deprivation.
However, it has also been noted that 'equivalent' to or 'tantamount' to (a direct
expropriation), requires a term that is closer to 'total.'

The tests of duration of the governmental measure and control over the investment, may assist an investment tribunal in accurately articulating the economic test of 'substantial' or 'total' deprivation. The notions of duration and
control are indicative of the level of severity of the governmental measure, as
assessed against the specific facts of the case.

The IUSCT noted in *Tippets*:

> while assumption of control over property by a government does not au-
> tomatically and immediately justify a conclusion that the property has
> been taken by the government, thus requiring compensation under in-
> ternational law, such a conclusion is warranted whenever events demon-
> strate that the owner was deprived of fundamental rights of ownership
> and it appears that this deprivation is not merely ephemeral.[52]

In *S.D. Myers*, the tribunal described expropriation as a '*lasting removal* of the
ability of an owner to make use of its economic rights.'[53] In this context, the
tribunal concluded:

> the Interim Order and the Final Order were designed to, and did, curb
> SDMI's initiative, *but only for a time*. CANADA realized no benefit from the

---

52   *Tippetts, Abbett, McCarthy, Stratton v. Government of the Islamic Republic of Iran, Award
      No. 141-7-2, 22 June, 1984*, 225.

53   *S.D. Myers, Inc. v Canada*, First Partial Award of 13 November, 2000, para 283 [emphasis
      added].

THE IMPACT OF REGULATORY MEASURES ON FOREIGN INVESTMENTS 169

measure. The evidence does not support a transfer of property or benefit directly to others. An opportunity was delayed.[54]

The tribunal clarified that in certain circumstances an act of expropriation could be found as a result of a partial and temporary measure.[55]

In the context of water resources management, a measure adopted with the purpose of tackling water scarcity, through reallocation and prioritisation of uses, is likely to be temporary. However, confronted with a permanent measure, a tribunal's inquiry may be directed at whether the measure reduces volumes of water or completely withdraws the water permit or licence. The latter scenario brings two additional complications: first, the withdrawal or cancellation of a licence could be regarded as a direct expropriation; second, for the reasons discussed above, such a cancellation could substantially impact the overall investment, justifying a claim of indirect expropriation.[56]

For example, in the case of *Tidewater,* the claimants – operating in Venezuela since 1958 – submitted that Venezuela's acts had deprived Tidewater Caribe (second claimant) of control of SEMARCA, rendering the shares in SEMARCA worthless.[57] As the company continued operation, the respondent, Venezuela, argued that the Reserve Law neither deprived the investor of control of the company nor did it negatively affect its accounts receivable.[58] The tribunal found, in light of several decisions issued by Venezuelan courts, that in practice the claimants were unable to exercise effective control over SEMARCA because they lacked ownership to pursue legal recourse in Venezuela due to the fact that the 'Venezuelan Courts treated the State as the effective owner of SEMARCA.'[59]

Foreign and national investors face a degree of economic and political risk, often in the form of loss of control over the investment and permanent or temporal deprivation of property rights. The severity of these risks might depend on the region where the investment takes place and the internal political situation of the host State. However, one could argue, in relation to the duration of the deprivation, that such severity might be relative to the size of the project

---

54 *Ibid.*, para. 287 [emphasis added].

55 Ibid., 283.

56 As discussed in previous subsections, the tribunal might approach the water licence as part of the investment unity and in rare situations may also treat the measure as partial expropriation.

57 *Tidewater Inc., Tidewater Investment SRL, Tidewater Caribe, C.A., et al. v. Venezuela,* ICSID Case No. ARB/10/5, Award of 13 March, 2015, paras. 35–36.

58 *Ibid.*, para. 41.

59 *Ibid.*, paras. 111–14.

and wealth of the investor. In other words, investors with large sunk costs may feel more pressure to negotiate with the government of the host State before initiating an investment dispute.

A mere decrease in the control of the investment, as well as a permanent reduction of profitability, may fail to reach the high threshold of expropriation. Where the prospects of profits continue to exist and the value of the investment remains, investment tribunals seem to find difficulties in concluding that an expropriation has occurred. The tribunal in *Burlington* addressed such an issue in some detail:

> while losses in one year may indicate that the investment has become unviable and will not return to profitability, this is not necessarily so and a finding of expropriation would need to assess the future prospects of earning a commercial return. It must be shown that the investment's continuing capacity to generate a return has been virtually extinguished.[60]

Having concluded that no indirect expropriation took place, after the application of Law 42,[61] the tribunal undertook a similar stance in the context of the physical deprivation of Burlington's oil-producing blocks. The tribunal, resorting to the *duration* test, noted:

> at that time, there still appeared to be – in the words of the tribunal in *Sedco v. Iran* – a 'reasonable prospect' that the investor could 'return [to] control' its investment. As long as there was such prospect, Ecuador's occupation could not be deemed to be a permanent measure.[62]

However, one must note that since, ultimately, the blocks were permanently taken over by Ecuador, the tribunal concluded that the claimant's investment was directly expropriated.[63]

---

60   *Burlington Resources Inc. v. Republic of Ecuador*, ICSID Case No. ARB/08/5, Decision on Liability of 14 December, 2012, para. 399. In line with this approach and cited by the tribunal in *Burlington v. Ecuador*, see *Sergei Paushok et al. v. the Government of Mongolia*, UNCITRAL, Award on Jurisdiction and Liability of 28 April, 2011, para. 334; and *Archer Daniels Midland Company and Tate & Lyle Ingredients Americas, Inc. v. Mexico*, ICSID Case No. ARB (AF)/04/05, Award of 21 November, 2007, para. 251.

61   *Burlington Resources Inc. v. Republic of Ecuador*, ICSID Case No. ARB/08/5, Decision on Liability of 14 December, 2012, para. 485.

62   *Ibid.*, para. 532 [footnote omitted]. In this vein see also *Sedco, Inc. v. National Iranian Oil Company and the Islamic Republic of Iran*, Interlocutory Award of 28 October, 1985, 23.

63   *Ibid.*, paras. 536–37.

THE IMPACT OF REGULATORY MEASURES ON FOREIGN INVESTMENTS

Experts point out that investment tribunals are increasingly shifting from an economic test to control and duration tests.[64] Several arbitral tribunals deciding disputes brought against Argentina, during the period of economic emergency, considered tests of control and duration as important elements of interpretation in regard to claims of indirect expropriation.

The 'quantitative' approach to indirect expropriation could lead to a preliminary conclusion that a government's action may reach a substantial deprivation of the investment. Such a determination nonetheless could be confirmed by considering whether the investor retains control over its operations. In *CMS*, the tribunal found persuasive the explanation of the respondent that the investor controlled and managed the daily operation of its business.[65] In *LG&E*, the three tests are orderly applied, presumably in the order of relevance specified by the tribunal:

> although the State adopted severe measures [...] such measures did not deprive the investors of the right to enjoy their investment [...] Further, it cannot be said that Claimants lost control over their shares in the licensees [...] Thus, the effect of the Argentine State's actions has not been permanent on the value of the Claimants' shares.'[66]

Currently, the development of water intensive projects (in terms of both quantity and quality) such as hydropower, commercial farming, mining and fracking are under intense scrutiny by local communities who are often sensitive to or affected by these activities. The amendment of a water permit, by reducing water allocation or imposing higher standards of quality, is likely to severely affect the whole investment. Where the measure has been adopted with the sole purpose to tackle severe water scarcity, the test of duration could play an

---

64   See Reisman on the shift from *Pope & Talbot*'s economic test to *CMS* control test W. Michael Reisman and Rocio Digon, 'Eclipse of Expropriation?' in *Contemporary Issues in International Arbitration and Mediation: The Fordham Papers*, ed. Arthur W Rovine (Leiden: Nijhoff, 2009), 35.

65   *CMS Gas Transmission Company v. Argentina*, ICSID Case No. ARB/01/8, Award of 12 May, 2015, paras. 261–64.

66   *LG&E Energy Corp., LG&E Capital Corp., and LG&E International Inc. v Argentina*, ICSID Case No ARB/02/1, Decision on Liability of 3 October, 2006, paras. 198–200. See also *Enron Corporation and Ponderosa Assets, L.P. v. Argentina*, ICSID Case No. ARB/01/3, Award of 22 May, 2007, paras. 221, 245; *Sempra Energy International v. Argentina*, ICSID Case No. ARB/02/16, Award of 28 September, 2007, paras. 249, 252, 284–85. See also *Tecnicas Medioambientales TECMED S.A. v. The United Mexican States*, ICSID Case No. ARB (AF)/00/2, Award of 29 May, 2003, para. 116.

172   CHAPTER 8

important role in the determination of the level of deprivation. In such cases, once the measure has ceased, negative effects on profitability may be reverted.

8.5   Conclusions

In the context of the analysis of the merits of an investment dispute, the test to determine the level of deprivation focuses on the economic impact of the governmental measure, further qualified by the tests of duration and control. To this end, the comparison of each investment asset with a bundle of investment rights, assists in assessing the function and relative importance of each stick in relation to the overall investment project. The nature of water resources, highlighted throughout this work, is likely to have an important effect on the determination of the level of deprivation.

The case of *Feldman* illustrates an analysis of the protection of investment rights, underpinned (even when not expressly) by the notion of bundle of investment rights. In the context of control over the investment, the tribunal noted:

> ... the regulatory action has not deprived the Claimant of control of his company ... interfered directly in the internal operations ... or displaced the Claimant as the controlling shareholder. The claimant is free to pursue other continuing lines of business activity ... Of course, he was effectively precluded from exporting cigarettes [...] However, this does not amount to Claimant's deprivation of control of his company.[67]

From such a perspective, a preliminary determination of whether a water-related measure has rendered the whole investment useless, may require an inquiry of whether the project: (i) can still be carried out, (ii) can still make profit and (iii) can be undertaken until its conclusion (or the expiration of the other licences). It is certainly difficult to foresee an affirmative answer to these questions considering the lack of substitutes for water resources and the fact that some investments may not be able to function with reduced amounts of water resources. In such cases, it is reasonable to argue that the test of duration may take precedence over a test of control.

---

67   *Feldman v. Mexico,* ICSID Case No. ARB (AF)/99/1, Award 16 December, 2002, para. 152. See also *Methanex Corp. v. United States of America,* Final Award of 3 August, 2005, Part IV – Chapter D – Page 7, para. 16. The tribunal examined a claim of expropriation, arising out of tax provisions, which affected the export of tobacco products.

THE IMPACT OF REGULATORY MEASURES ON FOREIGN INVESTMENTS   173

Cancellation of a water permit or licence may be qualified as a direct expropriation only in respect to the water permit or licence itself; yet with the effect of indirectly expropriating the overall investment. Only in a few circumstances would a measure, which withdraws a licence, be assessed as a potential partial expropriation. Such a finding depends on the type of water permit and whether its use is not conditional solely to the development of the investment project, as was the case in *AbitibiBowater*.

Based on current arbitral practice and the provisions of a second generation of IIAs, the examination of a claim of indirect expropriation, under the circumstances described above, should not conclude here. As persuasively proposed by Stern: 'should a 'qualitative' approach be used in order to modify the conclusions of the 'quantitative' approach?'[68]

A negative answer, on the one hand, could imply the return of the *sole effects* approach in ascertaining claims of indirect expropriation. A positive answer, on the other, would provide full deference to the regulatory prerogative of the State and, as the tribunal in *Pope & Talbot* put it, would provide 'a blanket exception for regulatory measures,' creating 'a gaping loophole in international protections against expropriation.'[69]

The next chapter adopts a middle ground. It discusses a framework of analysis to ascertain the quality of the governmental measure; or in other words, the legitimacy of the exercise of the police power by a host State. The qualitative analysis seeks to determine whether the measure was adopted in good faith and whether it was proportional from both broad and narrow perspectives.

---

68   Stern, 'In Search of the Frontiers of Indirect Expropriation,' 44.

69   *Pope & Talbot v. Canada*, Interim Award of 26 June, 2000, para. 99.

CHAPTER 9

The Legitimacy of the Exercise of the Police Power of States

The 'Qualitative' Approach

9.1   Introduction

Due to the specific uses of water resources in every economic and human activity, regulatory measures (as an exercise of the State's police power) affecting the quantity or quality of water within a given permit may amount to an indirect expropriation of the overall investment.[1] An illustrative example is the case of a thermoelectric power plant, which requires large amounts of water for cooling. When a water permit is affected, plants may have to cut output or go offline, with significant effects on foreign investors.[2]

However, regulatory measures may also respond to less technical requirements relating to water inputs. Host States could be under pressure from local communities, such as farmers and other water users, who feel anxious about the potentially negative effects that an extractive industries project could have on their livelihoods, health and community.[3]

As discussed in Chapter 8, if such measures are analysed solely under the level of deprivation test ('quantitative' approach), they will almost always lead to the *prima facie* conclusion that the foreign investment has been expropriated. It is worth noting that even when the deprivation is substantial, as it may be when the investor lacks certain inputs necessary to develop the project, e.g. water, the investor might still be in control of the investment. As also suggested in Chapter 8, the test of control over the investment, as well duration of the governmental measure have become determinant to a finding of indirect expropriation.

---

1   The terms 'quantitative' and 'qualitative' approaches proposed to determine whether a regulatory measure constitutes or not indirect expropriation must not be confused with the notion of water management over quantity and quality. While both sets of terms are similar, they convey different concepts used in this work.

2   Kristen Averyt et al., 'Freshwater Use by U.S. Power Plants: Electricity's Thirst for a Precious Resource: A Report of the Energy and Water in a Warming World Initiative,' Cambridge, MA: Union of Concerned Scientists, 2011, 1.

3   See for instance *Saint Marys VCNA, LLC v. Government of Canada*, UNCITRAL; *Pac Rim Cayman LLC v. Republic of El Salvador*, ICSID Case No. ARB/09/12; *Bear Creek Mining Corporation v. Republic of Peru*, ICSID Case No. ARB/14/21.

© KONINKLIJKE BRILL NV, LEIDEN, 2017 | DOI 10.1163/9789004335301_010

The 'qualitative' analysis of a claim of indirect expropriation, addressed in this chapter, involves certain levels of deference for the exercise of the police power by correcting the *prima facie* conclusion that the level of deprivation has been substantial or almost total, as described above. It should be noted that such a correction is only possible to the extent that the nature and purpose of the governmental measure compllies with standards of good faith and fairness. Perhaps most importantly, a 'qualitative' analysis depends on the level of deference that the arbitral tribunal confers to the exercise of the police power in the given case.[4] For this reason, in a general context, it is argued that a 'qualitative' analysis of the governmental measure requires a determination of whether the exercise of the police power is arbitrary or not,[5] by consideration of: (i) the character of the governmental measure, (ii) the proportionality of the measure in relation to the protection owed to foreign investors, and (iii) the element of good faith as reflected in the actions of the host State. However, such a determination in the context of water and investment would be incomplete without a further consideration of: (iv) the physical characteristics of water resources, and (v) the nature of property rights in water (often precarious and insecure).

This chapter will proceed by analysing the two ambits in which the police power may be exercised, namely *strictu* and *latu sensu;* the narrow and broad scope of exercise of the police power that have been discussed and defined in Chapters 4 and 6.[6] The first ambit covers a strict scope of regulatory activity, this *conceded* sphere of regulatory action – in the words of Freund – operates by restricting individual liberties (including those of foreign investors), so as to protect public values and promote welfare objectives. Such a prerogative of the State is manifested in the protection of the environment, public health, safety and public morals; often associated to the imposition of 'obligations to refrain.' The second ambit, the police power *latu sensu*, is a broad use of the term under which host States exercise all regulatory activity. Under this *debatable* sphere, States do not restrain individual freedoms to advance welfare objectives;[7]

---

4 See Esme Shirlow, 'Deference and Indirect Expropriation Analysis in International Investment Law: Observations on Current Approaches and Frameworks for Future Analysis,' *ICSID Review* 29, no. 3 (2014), 612; also Caroline Henckels, 'Indirect Expropriation and the Right to Regulate: Revisiting Proportionality Analysis and the Standard of Review in Investor-State Arbitration,' *Journal of International Economic Law* 15, no. 1 (2012).

5 Brigitte Stern, 'In Search of the Frontiers of Indirect Expropriation,' in *Contemporary Issues in International Arbitration and Mediation*, ed. Arthur W. Rovine (Brill, The Netherlands: Martinus Nijhoff Publishers, 2007), 44.

6 See Chapter 4, Section 4.3.2 and Chapter 6, Section 6.1.

7 Freund referred to this type of police power as the 'corporate power of the State.' However, he noted that the use of the term should be confined to the power that operates by

States may sign contracts, grant licences and terminate them. In sum, the creation and distribution of welfare may fall under this type of police power.

9.2 New Treaties, Old Interpretations and Emerging Customary International Law?

As discussed in Chapter 5,[8] in the context of the police power, arbitral tribunals have sought to find a clear dividing line between indirect expropriation and legitimate regulation when interpreting expropriation provisions in IIAs.[9] The evolution of this practice is illustrated in the incorporation of the police power *latu* and *strictu sensu* in the 2004 US Model BIT (as well as its successor, the 2012 US Model BIT) and the Canadian model BIT, among others. To this end the models, and the IIAs signed on their basis, have largely adopted the US Supreme Court's *Penn Central* test to evaluate claims of expropriation for measures linked to the exercise of the police power *latu sensu*.[10] In regard to the exercise of the police power *strictu sensu,* aimed to protect welfare objectives such as public morals, health and the environment, newer IIAs have also incorporated the developments of this principle within its provisions. The arbitral tribunal in *Philip Morris*, has expressly noted this aspect, as reflecting the 'position under general international law.'[11]

Notably, the US Model BIT states that its interpretative provisions are intended to reflect customary international law.[12] The US-Korea FTA, for example, expresses:

---

restraining individual liberties (here referred to as police power *strictu sensu*). See Ernst Freund, *The police power public policy and constitutional rights* (Chicago: Callaghan & Company, 1904), 11, 17–18.

8   See specially Chapter 5, Section 5.6.2. Which submits that claims of indirect expropriation arising out of the exercise of the police power *latu sensu* may be tested under the *Penn Central* approach and those claims arising out of the exercise of the police power *strictu sensu* would rarely be deemed expropriatory, except in rare circumstances. Both type of interpretative provisions are quoted in the sections below.

9   *Philip Morris Brands SARL, Philip Morris Products S.A. and ABAL Hermanos S.A. v. Oriental Republic of Uruguay*, ICSID Case No. ARB/10/7, Award of 8 July, 2016, para. 295.

10   See for instance US' FTAS with Chile, Singapore, Morocco and the EU (TTIP still under negotiation), DR-CAFTA; Canada's FIPA, Canada with EU in CETA (not yet in force), have all adopted the *Penn Central* test.

11   *Philip Morris et al. v. Uruguay*, para 300–301.

12   This step has been expressly discussed by the arbitral in *Philip Morris et al. v. Uruguay*.

THE LEGITIMACY OF THE EXERCISE OF THE POLICE POWER OF STATES   177

[t]he Parties confirm their shared understanding that "customary international law" generally and as specifically referenced in Article 11.5 and Annex 11-B [expropriation] results from a general and consistent practice of States that they follow from a sense of legal obligation.[13]

In the case of the US for instance, this modification seeks to avoid greater protection to foreign investors than that which is afforded to national investors. As noted by constitutional experts, US law on the whole already provides a high level of protection for investments, consistent with the standards of international law.[14]

Interestingly, other States with different legal traditions have also incorporated the *Penn Central* criteria and the police power approach in their new IIAs in order to ascertain claims of indirect expropriation.[15] It is not yet conclusive whether these new provisions included in newer IIAs constitute customary international law. However, one can safely argue that the US takings doctrine has had a preponderant role in informing the emergence of customary international law in this area.[16]

Overall these provisions on expropriation suggest two different levels of deference upon a States' prerogatives to regulate. Each of them may subject a State to different tests to determine the legitimacy of the governmental measure, and ultimately whether it constitutes an indirect expropriation.

---

13   US-Korea FTA (2007).

14   See David Schneiderman, *Constitutionalizing Economic Globalization: Investment Rules and Democracy's Promise* (Cambridge–New York: Cambridge University Press, 2008), 73–74. See also the 2002 Trade Promotion Act, Section 2(b)(3)(D), where the Congress sets out the view of 'no greater protection' in the negotiation of future BITS and FTAS: 'the principal negotiating objectives of the United States regarding foreign investment are to reduce or eliminate artificial or trade-distorting barriers to foreign investment, while ensuring that foreign investors in the United States are not accorded greater substantive rights with respect to investment protections than United States investors in the United States, and to secure for investors rights comparable to those that would be available under United States legal principles and practices.'

15   Among others: China-New Zealand FTA (2008), Australia–Chile FTA (2009), India-Korea FTA (2003), China – Uzbekistan BIT (2011), China – Canada BIT (2012), China – Colombia BIT (2008).

16   As noted by Poirier: 'Acting from the position of American hegemony, it took steps to require the inclusion of the substantive U.S. domestic regulatory takings standard in all future international investment treaties. Investment protection in the generation of FTAS after NAFTA will be American indeed.' See Marc R. Poirier, 'The NAFTA Chapter 11 Expropriation Debate through the Eyes of a Property Theorist,' *Environmental Law* 33 (2003), 898.

9.2.1 *Ascertaining Indirect Expropriation: Regulatory Measures Adopted under the Police Power latu sensu*

The 2012 US Model BIT Annex B (expropriation) states:

> [t]he determination of whether an action or series of actions by a Party, in a specific fact situation, constitutes an indirect expropriation, requires a case-by – case, fact-based inquiry that considers, among other factors: (i) the economic impact of the government action [...], (ii) the extent to which the government action interferes with distinct, reasonable investment-backed expectations; and (iii) the character of the government action.[17]

Chapter 8 discussed the economic impact or the level of deprivation over investors' property rights. It concluded by illustrating the difficulties to accurately address the effects of water measures over the investment as a whole. It should also be noted that the 'quantitative' analysis developed in the previous chapter appears to be more relevant to the determination of the legitimacy of the police power *latu sensu*.

Under the umbrella of the general provisions in a relevant IIA, a fact-based analysis is bound to address the special physical, economic and social characteristics of water resources and their role within the investment in relation to other users. Property rights in water for different uses often overlap. Moreover, they are subject to an ever increasing volatile hydrological variability, which in turn, inflict on property right holders the predictable insecurity of a water right. This conclusion is of course not without controversy and requires careful consideration of the intrinsic characteristics of water (as discussed in Chapters 2 and 3).

Having devoted Chapter 8 to the discussion of the level of deprivation or economic impact of the measure over the investment (referred to as 'quantitative approach'), the next sections consider in turn the character of the government action[18] and subsequently the issue of reasonable investment backed expectations (the 'qualitative' approach).

---

17 Annex B (4) (a) 2012 US Model BIT. Available at: https://ustr.gov/sites/default/files/BIT%20text%20for%20ACIEP%20Meeting.pdf., last visited 5 July 2016. The Model is expressed in more generic terms in comparison to IIAs signed or in force, which include explanatory notes or examples to clarify the content of each criterion e.g. 'the character of the government action.'

18 Also referred to in this work as 'character of the governmental measure.'

THE LEGITIMACY OF THE EXERCISE OF THE POLICE POWER OF STATES   179

9.2.1.1   Character of the Government Action

Tribunals have considered the character of the government action or measure taken by addressing elements of analysis such as the public purpose, which justifies the measure, whether it is discriminatory and whether it was adopted under a due process of law (including the issue of good faith). Since this element is an inquiry developed by the US Supreme Court in *Penn Central,* it is useful to address the determination of the Court:

> [a] "taking" may more readily be found when the interference with property can be characterized as a physical invasion by government, than when interference arises from some public program adjusting the benefits and burdens of economic life to promote the common good.[19]

The balancing exercise the Court was confronted with is comparable to a broad proportionality analysis that investment tribunals have largely adopted in the determination of whether States – while keeping their regulatory prerogatives within the boundaries of good faith and reasonability – comply with their IIAS obligations. In *Gabčíkovo-Nagymaros*, a case initiated by Hungary against Slovakia before the International Court of Justice (ICJ),[20] Judge Weeramantry stated that the ICJ 'must *hold the balance* even between the environmental considerations and the developmental considerations raised by the respective Parties.'[21]

A proportionality analysis could be explored in two fashions within the examination of the legitimate exercise of the police power. First, proportionality is considered as a broad concept in this section as it undertakes the task of balancing competing rights and interests.[22] Proportionality has its origin in

---

19   *Penn Central Transportation Co v New York City, 366 N.E. 2d 1271 (NY 1977), affirmed 438 U.S. 104 (1978).* The US-Korea FTA, clarifies the content of this consideration as follows: 'Relevant considerations could include whether the government action imposes a special sacrifice on the particular investor or investment that exceeds what the investor or investment should be expected to endure for the public interest.' Annex 11-B 3(a)(iii) US–Korea BIT.

20   *Gabčíkovo-Nagymaros Project (Hungary/Slovakia)*, Judgment, I.C.J. Reports 1997, p. 7. The case concerned the construction of a power plant and a dam on the Danube River, under an agreement between Hungary and Slovakia. Hungary suspended the construction and terminated the treaty on the contention that Slovakia had harmed its water intake and navigation. Hungary argued, inter alia, that 'the protection of the environment precluded performance of the Treaty.'

21   *Ibid.*, Separate Opinion of Vice-President Weeramantry, 88 [emphasis added].

22   Kingsbury and Schill, 'Public Law Concepts to Balance Investors' Rights with State Regulatory Actions in the Public Interest – the Concept of Proportionality,' 79–80.

180   CHAPTER 9

German constitutional and administrative law and has been adopted by numerous civil and common-law jurisdictions.[23] Second, proportionality understood and applied in a narrow sense (in the context of the exercise of the police power *strict sensu*), which will be discussed later in this chapter.[24] It is worth noting that a vast amount of scholarship on the narrow analysis of proportionality still highlights issues of consistency among tribunals.[25] *Tecmed*[26] is one of the cases, inspired by the European Court of Human Rights (ECtHR); yet, criticised on this account.[27] It remains, however, the most influential case in which a tribunal has attempted to use a proportionality analysis in an expropriation context.[28] As a result, tribunals faced with expropriation claims have no clear analytical framework for the application of proportionality.

The broad conception of proportionality is embedded in the examination of the public purpose and discrimination analysis of the governmental measure. It is important to note that public purpose and non-discrimination (as well as due process) in the context of such examination does not refer to the conditions of lawfulness that are traditionally provided for in most provisions regulating expropriation (discussed in Chapter 5). In this context, these concepts lead to a different inquiry which seeks to respond to whether the measure has been

---

23   *Ibid.* See also Alec Stone Sweet and Jud Mathews, 'Proportionality Balancing and Global Constitutionalism,' Columbia Journal of Transnational Law 47, no. 73 (2008).

24   See Section 9.2.3 below.

25   Benedict Kingsbury and Stephan W. Schill, 'Public Law Concepts to Balance Investors' Rights with State Regulatory Actions in the Public Interest – the Concept of Proportionality,' *International Investment Law and Comparative Public Law* (2010); Alec Stone Sweet and Jud Mathews, 'Proportionality Balancing and Global Constitutionalism,' *Columbia Journal of Transnational Law* 47, no. 73 (2008); José E. Alvarez and Brink Tegan. 'Revisiting the Necessity Defense,' *New York University Public Law and Legal Theory Working Papers* 261 (2013); Kamil Gerard Ahmed et al., *Columbia International Investment Conference: The Evolving International Investment Regime – Expectations, Realities, Options* (Oxford: Oxford University Press, 2011); Alessandra Asteriti, 'Regulatory Expropriation Claims in International Investment Arbitration: A Bridge Too Far?,' in *Yearbook on International Investment Law and Policy 2012–2013*, ed. Andrea K. Bjorklund (Oxford: Oxford University Press, 2014).

26   For a discussion of *Tecmed*, see Jack Coe Jr. and Noah Rubins, 'Regulatory Expropriation and the Tecmed Case: Context and Contributions,' in *International Investment Law and Arbitration: Leading Cases from the ICSID, NAFTA, Bilateral Treaties and Customary International Law*, ed. Tod Weiler (London: Cameron May, 2005), 597–667; Asteriti, 'Regulatory Expropriation Claims in International Investment Arbitration: A Bridge Too Far?.'

27   See Henckels, 'Indirect Expropriation and the Right to Regulate: Revisiting Proportionality Analysis and the Standard of Review in Investor-State Arbitration.'

28   *Ibid.*, 234.

THE LEGITIMACY OF THE EXERCISE OF THE POLICE POWER OF STATES   181

adopted in good faith and in a reasonable manner.[29] The arbitral tribunal in *Quasar de Valores Sicab*, confronted with a case of creeping expropriation relating to the various cases brought in the context of the Russian oil company Yukos, noted:

> [i]ndirect expropriation, of course, does not speak its name. It must be deduced from a pattern of conduct, observing its conception, implementation, and effects as such, even if the intention to expropriate is disavowed at every step. *The fact that individual measures appear not to be well founded in law, or to be discriminatory, or otherwise to lack bona fides, may be important elements of a finding that there has been the equivalent of an indirect expropriation, an expropriation by other means, even though there be no need to determine whether the expropriation was unlawful.*[30]

Likewise, in *Fireman's Fund*,[31] the tribunal considered determinative factors such as public purpose, the effects of the measure over the investment, discrimination, *bona fides*, proportionality and legitimate expectations.[32]

In light of these considerations, it is relevant to briefly discuss the elements of public purpose, discrimination and due process.

a)   *Public Purpose*

In the context of this chapter, public purpose is linked to the management and protection of water resources. Therefore the public purpose in such a connection is, at least in principle incontestable, if the considerations proposed in Chapter 2 are sufficient. However, the public interest is contextual and could vary on grounds of policy preferences, societal needs and cultural background.

---

29   See for instance, the Colombia-India BIT (2009), which provides in Article 6(2)(b): '(iv) the character and intent of the measures or series of measures, whether they are for bona fide public interest purposes or not and whether there is a reasonable nexus between them and the intention to expropriate[...].'

30   *Quasar de Valores Sicav S.A., Orgor de Valores Sicav S.A., GBI 9000 Sicav S.A., ALOS 34 S.L. v. The Russian Federation* (SCC No. 24/2007), Award of 20 July, 2012, para. 45. [emphasis added] For a case comment, see Irmgard Marboe, 'Quasar De Valores Sicav Sa and Others v. the Russian Federation: Another Chapter of the Yukos Affair,' *ICSID Review* 28, no. 2 (2013).

31   *Fireman's Fund Insurance Company v. The United Mexican States,* ICSID Case No. ARB(AF)/02/01.

32   The tribunal was tasked to determine whether a measure related to the purchase of debentures benefited Mexican investors over other foreign investors, and in the context of indirect expropriation whether the measure fell within the scope of the recognised police power. See *Ibid.,* 176.

Chapters 3 and 6 consider situations in which host States may be in the process of the implementation of Integrated Water Resources Management (IWRM); principles of sustainable management may require reallocation of water resources to tackle previous allocation imbalances.[33]

It is indeed an exercise of broad proportionality that seeks to balance the rights granted to foreign investors against the development and implementation of improved water legal frameworks. As stated by Reisman:

> [t]he transformation of the United States into an industrial dynamo could not have been accomplished if the Supreme Court had not exempted much regulation from the protections of the Fifth Amendment. Any contemporary State seeking to develop is, to that extent, a regulatory State, and international investment law can hardly ignore it.[34]

The German and US Supreme Courts acknowledged the insecure nature of water rights by deferring to measures reallocating water resources, adopted presumably to improve water use.[35] The benefit is effectively transferred from private benefit to public use. This is perhaps one instance in which investment tribunals and courts could incorporate into their determination the complex and primarily *common* nature of water rights.

In the context of international investment law, the tribunal in *Methanex* held that the protection of public health and the environment (as long-term public interests) were among the main criteria in considering the legitimacy of the police power.[36] However, the immediate or shorter-term public interest was the protection of ground water resources (water quality), as a vehicle to protect health and the environment. The management of California's water resources appears to have taken into consideration principles of water law and best management practices. The US government presented evidence provided by a Report of the University of California explaining:

> [s]ince both groundwater wells and surface water reservoirs have been contaminated, alternative water supplies may not be an option for many water utilities. If MTBE continues to be used at current levels and more

---

33 See Chapter 3, Section 3.2.2 and Chapter 6, Section 6.2.1.

34 W. Michael Reisman and Rocio Digon, 'Eclipse of Expropriation?,' in *Contemporary Issues in International Arbitration and Mediation: The Fordham Papers* (Leiden: Martinus Nijhoff, 2009), 44. On the development and evolution of the police power and the US takings jurisprudence, see Chapter 4.

35 Both cases have been discussed in Chapter 7.

36 *Methanex Corp. v. United States of America*, UNCITRAL, Final Award of 3 August, 2005, Part IV – Chapter D – para. 16.

THE LEGITIMACY OF THE EXERCISE OF THE POLICE POWER OF STATES 183

sources become contaminated, the potential for regional degradation of water resources, especially groundwater basins will increase. Severity of water shortages during drought years will be exacerbated. California's water resources are placed at risk by the use of MTBE.[37]

Other investment tribunals have questioned whether the public purpose should be the sole criterion to conclude that every regulation is legitimate, thus ruling out the payment of compensation.[38]

A middle position in the scholarship notes that while there is a need for a public purpose analysis, it does not encompass a big hurdle for governments.[39] Few investment tribunals would assert the lack of relevance of the public purpose when assessing an alleged expropriatory measure.[40]

b)   *Discrimination*

This criterion is equally relevant to assess the legitimacy of regulatory measures *latu* and *strictu sensu*. One could argue, nevertheless, that the non-discrimination principle currently has greater relevance in the context of the police power *strictu sensu*. In general, the purpose of scrutinising possible discriminatory measures is to avoid the 'singling-out of aliens on the basis of national or ethnic origin.'[41] In the context of Article 1110 of NAFTA, for instance, the non-discrimination requirement for lawful expropriation pertains to an under-examined sphere of the expropriation provision, as it has been hardly addressed in NAFTA case law.[42] Higgins briefly addressed the requirement of non-discrimination in a report on expropriation, associating the examination

---

37   See *Ibid.*, Part III – Chapter A – 5. (Keller *et al.*, UC Report Vol. 1, at 11 (4 JS tab 36)) [footnote omitted].

38   *Metalclad Corporation v. The United Mexican States*, ICSID Case No. ARB(AF)/97/1; *Compañia del Desarrollo de Santa Elena S.A. v. Republic of Costa Rica*, ICSID Case No. ARB/96/1.

39   August Reinisch, 'Legality of Expropriations,' in *Standards of Investment Protection*, ed. August Reinisch (Oxford: Oxford University Press, 2008), 179.

40   See for instance in *Liamco*, where arbitrator Mahmassani noted in the context of nationalisation: 'Motives are indifferent to international law, each state being free to judge for itself what it considers useful or necessary for the public good... The object pursued by it is no the concern to third parties.' *Libyan American Oil Company (LIAMCO) v. The Libyan Arab Republic,* Ad Hoc Tribunal (Draft Convention on Arbitral Procedure, ILC 1958), Award of 12 April, 1977, 194. See also *Shufeldt Claim (US v. Guatemala)*, Award of 24 July, 1930, 2 UNRIAA 1079, 1095.

41   UNCTAD, 'International Investment Agreements: Key Issues Volume I,' Geneva: United Nations, 2004, 239.

42   Meg N. Kinnear, Andrea K. Bjorklund, and John F.G. Hannaford, *Investment Disputes under NAFTA. An Annotated Guide to NAFTA Chapter 11*, (Alphen aan den Rijn: Kluwer Law

184 CHAPTER 9

of discrimination to the analysis of public purpose, in the context of *bona fide regulations*.[43]

Discrimination might take place between foreign investors, and between foreign and domestic investors, as both types may result in differential treatment.[44] However, such a differential treatment requires a level of 'unreasonable distinction' between the two subjects.[45] This suggests that reasonable and justified distinctions between comparable investors are likely to occur and could be considered legitimate under certain conditions.[46] During the wave of nationalisations in the oil sector in the mid- to late-twentieth century, several arbitral tribunals concluded that a discriminatory taking was not unlawful, since distinctions made by States between different investors of the same nationality were not necessarily arbitrary.[47]

As regards the exercise of the police power *latu sensu*, for instance, the China-New Zealand FTA, provides in Annex 13 (4) (Expropriation):

> A deprivation of property shall be particularly likely to constitute indirect expropriation where it is either: (a) discriminatory in its effect, either as against the particular investor or against a class of which the investor forms part [...].[48]

As discussed earlier, the criterion of non-discrimination plays a more relevant role when considering the legitimacy of regulatory activity restricted to protect

---

International, 2006), 1110–32. Note however that in *Methanex v. United States* this requirement was addressed and dismissed by the tribunal.

43 See Rosalyn Higgins, 'The Taking of Property by the State. Recent Developments in International Law,' *Recueil des Cours* (*The Hague Academy of International Law*) T.176 (1982), 334.

44 Kinnear, Bjorklund, and Hannaford, *Investment Disputes under NAFTA. An Annotated Guide to NAFTA Chapter 11*, 1110–33.

45 Reinisch, 'Legality of Expropriations,' 186.

46 See *Restatement of the Law, Third, Foreign Relations Law of the United States, Comment* (f). See also *Ulysseas, Inc. v. The Republic of Ecuador*, UNCITRAL, Final Award of 12 June, 2012, para. 293, where the tribunal established that in order to make a finding of discrimination, it suffice that two similar situation were treated differently.

47 Some tribunals asserted that the alleged political motive for nationalisation was in fact not political. See *Libyan American Oil Company (LIAMCO) v. The Libyan Arab Republic*, Award, 195. See also *Kuwait v. American Independent Oil Company (Aminoil)*, Award of 24 March, 1982. In British Petroleum, the tribunal concluded that nationalisation took place for purely extraneous reasons'. See *British Petroleum v. Libya Award*, 10 October 1973 and 1 August 1974, 53 ILR 297, 329.

48 China-New Zealand FTA (2008), Annex 13, available at http://www.chinafta.govt.nz/1-The-agreement/2-Text-of-the-agreement/index.php, accessed June 2, 2016.

THE LEGITIMACY OF THE EXERCISE OF THE POLICE POWER OF STATES   185

health, the environment and safety (police power *strictu sensu*). Such measures enjoy a presumption of legitimacy, which may be rebutted if the foreign investor can show that the host State had a discriminatory intent. The requirement of non-discrimination has been expressly included in the interpretative provisions of some recent IIAs, as an example of those 'rare circumstances' under which a discriminatory measure may be found to constitute an indirect expropriation.[49]

The criterion of 'likeness' or 'similar circumstances' plays an important role in determining the presence of discrimination.[50] In the context of water management, there are different uses of water, all of which compete within the basin or other water source. Some uses may be discriminated against for reasons of prioritisation of water flows to secure human consumption or to protect of ecosystems in case of scarcity;[51] as discussed in previous chapters, prioritisation of uses has been introduced in certain national laws. However, prioritisation of water uses for different economic activities may require more complex considerations. For instance, the 2011 drought in Texas required the adoption of water management to tackle the problem of water scarcity, which created tension among farmers, cities, and power plants across the state. Some plants were forced to cut their output while others had to retrieve water from alternative sources, which increased the cost of production.[52] Such an extreme situation is presumably unlikely to arise in an investment dispute, but one may consider that such a situation of competition for water resources could originate measures that, at least on their face, appear discriminatory.

---

49   Non-discrimination included in the US Model, Canadian Model (FIPA), DR-CAFTA, among others.

50   The notion of likeness has been most used in the context of WTO Law to compare similar products offered in a given market, but also to compare products what were directly competitive; not only the manufacturing and composition of the product would be taken into account but also the perception of consumers. See for instance Michael J. Trebilcock, Robert Howse, and Antonia Eliason, *The Regulation of International Trade* (London: Routledge, 2013), 138–43. See also the analysis undertaken by the tribunal in *Methanex v. United States* on the like circumstances under the examination of the National Treatment standard: *Methanex v. United States*, Final Award, Part IV – Chapter B – paras. 11–38.

51   See Stefano Burchi, 'Trends And Developments In Contemporary Water Resources Legislation: A Comparative State-Of-The-Art Perspective,' XIV IWRA World Water Congress Governance and Water Law Theme – Sub-Theme GL1, 2012, 3.

52   Averyt et al., 'Freshwater Use by U.S. Power Plants: Electricity's Thirst for a Precious Resource,' 6.

c)   *Due Process and Good Faith*

As public purpose and discrimination, discussed above, due process is often discussed in the context of determining the lawfulness of expropriation; once it has been determined that an expropriation took place. However, the process followed by the host State to adopt a regulatory measure and the circumstances in which the measure was adopted are very telling of the *bona fide* intent of the host State. The purpose of such an inquiry is to discard the arbitrary exercise of State's regulatory power. In this vein the question proposed in *Quasar de Valores Sicab,* stated:

> [t]he questions that arise for the present Tribunal concern the bona fides of measures taken by the Respondent. Were these actions taken as part of the ordinary process of assessing and collecting taxes, or were they part of an expropriatory pattern?[53]

Due process and good faith may be approached differently in the context of ascertaining the legitimacy of the regulatory measure than in the context of determining the lawfulness of expropriation. Since some regulatory measures fall short of expropriation, investors may not be able to invoke adequate remedies from domestic judicial or administrative systems when asking for the review of the governmental measure at issue.[54] Determinations of inadequate remedies for regulatory interferences could also be interpreted in connection with inconsistent, improper and unreasonable substantiation of regulatory activity, which may result in a disguised act of expropriation.[55]

An illustrative decision within this order of ideas can be found in the case of *Metalclad,* where the construction and operation of a landfill was frustrated

---

53   *Quasar de Valores Sicav S.A. et al. v. The Russian Federation*, para. 48.

54   In *ADC*, the tribunal analysed the relevance of due process of law, in the context of expropriation, in favour of investors who should be in the position to 'raise claims against the depriving actions already taken or about to be taken against it.' See *ADC Affiliate Limited and ADC & ADMC Management Limited v. Hungary,* ICSID Case No. ARB/03/16, Award of 2 October, 2006, para. 435.

55   One should note the criticism of this approach 'Whether one reads the [Iran US Claims Tribunal] cases as addressing disguised expropriation or implicitly finding *mala fide* regulatory process, there is not much that the law of regulatory expropriation and the perspective of sustainable development can rely on: [...]to identify the required level and kind of treatment.' Martins Paparinskis, 'Regulatory Expropriation and Sustainable Development,' in *Sustainable Development in International Investment Law*, ed. Marie-Claire Cordonier-Segger, Andrew Newcombe, and Markus W. Gehring, (Alphen aan den Rijn: Kluwer Law International, 2010), 310. See also Jack Jr Coe and Noah Rubins, 'Regulatory Expropriation and the Tecmed Case: Context and Contributions,' 602–03.

THE LEGITIMACY OF THE EXERCISE OF THE POLICE POWER OF STATES   187

by the adoption of an Ecological Decree to protect a rare cactus.[56] The events that led to the enactment of this measure were alleged to lack transparency and consistency. In the context of the analysis of Article 1105 of NAFTA (fair and equitable treatment), the tribunal concluded:

> Mexico failed to ensure a transparent and predictable framework for Metalclad's business planning and investment. The totality of these circumstances demonstrates a lack of orderly process and timely disposition in relation to an investor of a Party acting in the expectation that it would be treated fairly and justly in accordance with the NAFTA.[57]

Furthermore, the tribunal also made determinations in the context of whether the Ecological Decree amounted to an indirect expropriation of the investment. It noted that by tolerating the conduct of the community of Guadalcazar against the investor and acquiescing to the frustration of the operation of the project, despite the fact that the project had been fully approved, Mexico had taken measures tantamount to expropriation.[58] The tribunal did not expressly consider – and perhaps it was not necessary to do so – whether the measure could have been held to be a disguised act of expropriation.[59] The issue of bad faith is a more serious one and it does not constitute a requirement to conclude that the host State might have breached IIAs obligations.[60]

The adoption of environmental measures, arising out of political and community pressures, are often caught in inconsistent and sometimes non-transparent procedures. Even States with highly developed, comprehensive and well-functioning judicial systems may face difficulties when dealing with sensitive resources essential to the operation of the investment. Examples of investment claims associated with the use of water resources and water services are fairly abundant, some of which have been discussed in previous chapters.[61]

---

56   *Metalclad v. Mexico*, Award of 30 August, 2000, para. 59.

57   *Ibid.*, para. 99.

58   *Ibid.,* 104.

59   In *Waste Management v. Mexico,* the tribunal recognised such a possibility, while did not find grounds to affirm the existence of a disguised expropriation. See *Waste Management, Inc. v. United Mexican States*, ICSID Case No. ARB(AF)/00/3, Award of 30 April, 2004, para. 138.

60   See *Total S.A. v. Argentine Republic*, ICSID Case No. ARB/04/1, Decision on Liability of 27 December, 2010, para. 110.

61   *Vattenfall v. Germany* (political and social pressure to cancel the project), *TECMED v. Mexico* (*social pressure*); *Aguas del Tunari S.A. v. Bolivia* (social violence and pressure of interests groups); *Bear Creeek Mining v. Peru* (social pressure and competing community

9.2.1.2 Legitimate Expectations (Reasonable Investment-Backed Expectations)

The principle of legitimate expectations has been traditionally discussed, in practice and in academic literature, in the context of the fair and equitable treatment standard.[62] This, nonetheless, has not precluded investment tribunals from addressing the principle in the context of indirect expropriation claims, as the reasonableness of an investor's expectations constitute an important element in the determination of indirect expropriation.[63]

Assurances given to foreign investors by host States signal the political, financial and regulatory stability of the legal system into which the potential foreign investor will be entering into. In addition, assurances provide investors with the necessary incentives to undertake the investment project. However, as some academics warn:

> it may be said that the fairness of such regulatory conduct towards investors cannot be judged without also assessing the conduct of investors towards the community on behalf of which the State may act.[64]

---

interests for the use of water and other natural resources. Note however this is the claim of the investor), *Metalclad v. Mexico* (inconsistencies between federal and municipal authorities).

62 '[A]s might be the case with a manifest failure of natural justice in judicial proceedings or a complete lack of transparency and candour in an administrative process. In applying this standard it is relevant that the treatment is in breach of representations made by the host State which were reasonably relied on by the claimant.' *Waste Management v. The United Mexican States*, Award, para. 98. Similarly in *Bayindir v. Pakistan*, ICSID Case No. ARB/03/29, Award of 27 August, 2009, para 252. See Peter Muchlinski, '"Caveat Investor"? The Relevance of the Conduct of the Investor under the Fair and Equitable Treatment Standard,' *International and Comparative Law Quaterly* 55 (2005), 541–42; Rudolf Dolzer, 'Fair and Equitable Treatment: Today's Contours,' *Santa Clara journal of international law* 12, no. 1 (2013).

63 Nathalie Bernasconi, 'Background paper on Vattenfall v. Germany Arbitration,' Winnipeg: IISD, 2009, 1; Rudolf Dolzer and Christoph Schreuer, *Principles of International Investment Law*, 2nd ed. (Oxford: Oxford University Press, 2012), 115; August Reinisch, 'Expropriation,' in *The Oxford Handbook of International Investment Law*, ed. Peter Muchlinski, Federico Ortino, and Christoph Schreuer (Oxford–New York: Oxford University Press, 2008).

64 Markus Perkams, 'The Concept of Indirect Expropriation in Comparative Public Law – Searching for Light in the Dark,' in *International Investment Law and Comparative Public Law*, ed. Stephan Schill (Oxford–New York: Oxford University Press, 2010). See also the analysis of arbitral tribunals in *Azurix Corp. v Argentine Republic*, ICSID Case No. ARB/01/12, Award of 14 July, 2006, paras. 316–323; *Methanex Corp. v. United States of America*, Final Award of 3 August, 2005, Part IV – Chapter D.

THE LEGITIMACY OF THE EXERCISE OF THE POLICE POWER OF STATES   189

Legitimate expectations, therefore, cannot be derived only from the 'subjective expectations' of the investor; they ought to be assessed against the social and political environment of the host State at the moment the investment is made. This was the approach of the tribunal in *EDF v. Romania*.[65]

Considering indirect expropriation, legitimate expectations as well as due process may provide some light on the determination of the legitimacy of the governmental measure. This approach has been adopted in other areas of law such as European Union (EU) Law, the ECHR and the US Constitution's Takings Clause.[66]

In the context of the protection of groundwater resources, the *Methanex* tribunal explicitly rejected a claim of expropriation by stating, among other reasons that unless the government gave specific commitments that certain regulations would be averted, *bona fide* regulatory measures would not constitute an expropriation.[67] In the award, the tribunal reminded the claimant-investor of the nature of the market that it had entered into, when it chose to invest in the US. It remarked that the US was notorious for the manner in which media, citizens and organisations scrutinise the use of chemical compounds, especially those posing a threat to the environment and public health. It further stated that this type of public scrutiny was not different from that in Methanex's home State – Canada – and that Methanex had actively participated in such processes at home.[68]

---

65   In *EDF*, the investor had negotiated a number of joint ventures with the purpose to setup sale of goods business at airports and on board aircraft. During the course of the business Romania modified the legal framework under which the investment was developed, which triggered a claim that the host State had frustrated the legitimate expectations of the investor in breach of the fair and equitable treatment standard. *EDF (Services) Limited v. Romania*, ICSID Case No. ARB/05/13, Award of 8 October, 2009, para. 219.

66   The principle of legitimate expectations under Community Law was addressed in for instance *CIRFS v. the Commission, Case C313/90, 1993 ECR I-1125*; *Ijssel Vliet v. Minister van Economische Zaken, C-311/94, 1996 ECR I-5023*; *Mulder v. Minister van Landbouw and Visserij Case 120/86, 1998 ECR 232*, among others. The ECHR has addressed the principle of legitimate expectations in the context of Article 1 of the First Protocol of the ECHR in *Pine Valley Developments Ltd and Others v. Ireland, Judgment*, 29 November 1991, ECHR Series A, No 222 and *Baner v. Sweden*, App No 11763/85, Decision, 9 March 1989, DR 60, 128., as cited by Muchlinski, '"Caveat Investor"? The Relevance of the Conduct of the Investor under the Fair and Equitable Treatment Standard,' 534. *Fredin v. Sweden, Judgment*, 18 February 1991, ECHR Series A, No 192, para. 54. Finally, the US Supreme Court included the principle of investment-backed expectations in its often used test of *Penn Central*.

67   *Methanex v. United States*, Award, Part IV – Chapter D – para. 7.

68   *Ibid.*, para. 9.

190   CHAPTER 9

Since some new IIAs' interpretative provisions invoke the term investment-backed expectations, developed according to the US takings tradition, it is worth considering the term in the context of its own development. The concept of investment-backed expectations may be compared with the notion of legitimate expectations, used in investment arbitration in relation to a particular set of property rights backed expectations of stability of social arrangements.[69]

The term was first used by Michelman,[70] who might have inspired Justice Brennan in *Penn Central.* Brennan did not define the test expressly; rather, he addressed the component of 'investment-backed' as a financial venture, 'with a view toward a specific future use.'[71] He added that:

> the decisions in which this Court has dismissed "taking" challenges on the ground that, while the challenged government action caused economic harm, it did not interfere with interests that were sufficiently bound up with the reasonable expectations of the claimant to constitute "property" for Fifth Amendment purposes.[72]

The question may be summarised as to whether the owner (or the investor in this case) had sunk capital or could expect to invest on his property on the basis of a previous regulatory regime.[73] In contrast to the 'quantitative' approach, which seeks to determine to what extent the investment was deprived of its value (Chapter 8), the question here is whether or not there was a promise of stability and security. In other words a 'distinctly perceived' or 'sharply crystallized investment backed expectation.'[74] However, the criterion alone i.e.

---

69   Marc. R. Poirier, 'The Virtue of Vagueness in Takings Doctrine,' *Cardozo Law Review* 24 (2002), 138.

70   Frank I. Michelman, 'Property, Utility, and Fairness: Comments on the Ethical Foundations of "Just Compensation" Law,' *Harvard Law Review* 80, no. 6 (1967), 1213. See also Carol Rose, 'Property and Expropriation: Themes and Variations in American Law,' *Utah Law Review* 1 (2000), 70–71.

71   See Robert M. Washburn, '"Reasonable Investment-Backed Expectations" as a Factor in Defining Property Interest,' *Washington University Journal of Urban and Contemporary Law* 49 (1996), 67.

72   *Penn Central Transportation Co v. New York City,* 366 N.E. 2d 1271 (NY 1977), affirmed 438 U.S. 104 (1978).

73   Carol Rose, 'Property and Expropriation: Themes and Variations in American Law,' 21.

74   Michelman's analysis of the test of distinct investment-backed expectations state: '[T]he test poses not nearly so loose a question of degree; it does not ask "how much," but rather (like the physical – occupation test) it asks "whether or not": whether or not the measure in question can easily be seen to have practically deprived the claimant of some *distinctly perceived, sharply crystallized, investment-backed expectation.'* Frank I. Michelman,

THE LEGITIMACY OF THE EXERCISE OF THE POLICE POWER OF STATES 191

frustration of investment-backed expectations, is not sufficient to conclude that an indirect expropriation or taking took place.[75]

The term *reasonable*, as opposed to *distinct* has been incorporated in the interpretative provisions of newer IIAS. The term *reasonable* seems to bring balancing considerations to the test, as investors may expect that the legal environment may not remain static indefinitely.

Investment tribunals addressing 'legitimate expectations' seem to propose a less strict inquiry than the US Supreme Court. Perhaps more akin to the analysis of legitimate expectations in the context of the fair and equitable treatment standard, which has more general and broad contours.[76] However, it cannot be said that investment treaty arbitration has developed a consistent test on this issue. The requirement of 'specific assurances' as expectation of a stable legal environment, discussed by the tribunals in *Methanex*[77] and *Glamis*,[78] seems to provide more deference to the host State, perhaps comparable to the term *distinct* investment-backed expectations. In contrast, the broader analysis of legitimate expectations proposes an inquiry as to 'whether the legal order in force at the time of the investment could in itself generate legitimate expectations.'[79]

9.2.2 *Ascertaining Indirect Expropriation: Regulatory Measures Adopted under the Police Power strictu sensu*

The second part of the interpretative provision of the 2012 US model BIT, states:

> ...(b) Except in rare circumstances, non-discriminatory regulatory actions by a Party that are designed and applied to protect legitimate public

---

'Property, Utility, and Fairness: Comments on the Ethical Foundations of "Just Compensation" Law,' 1233. [emphasis added] His stance seems to fall within position that strongly protects property rights. Yet, he also admits that not every regulation may require payment of compensation. *Ibid.*, 1213.

75 Daniel R. Mandelker, 'Investment-Backed Expectations: Is There a Taking?,' *Journal of Urban & Contemporary Law* 31, no. 3 (1987), 4.

76 The nature of such an inquiry has been described in the introductory part of this section.

77 *Methanex v. United States*, Award, Part IV – Chapter D – para. 16.

78 *Glamis Gold, Ltd. v. United States of America*, UNCITRAL, Award of 8 June, 2009, para. 811.

79 See *Total S.A. v. Argentine Republic*, ICSID Case No. ARB/04/1, Decision on Liability of 27 December, 2010, paras. 113–123; *Charanne and Construction Investments v. Spain*, Arbitraje No.:062/2012, bajo las reglas de SCC, Laudo Final de 21 enero 2016, para. 494 (unofficial translation by MENA Chambers). Also of interest is the separate opinion by Wälde in *International Thunderbird Gaming Corporation v. The United Mexican States*, UNCITRAL rules, Separate Opinion of December 2005.

welfare objectives, such as public health, safety, and the environment, do not constitute indirect expropriations.[80]

This provision has received different labels associated with 'exceptions,' 'carve-outs' and or a clear agreement to differentiate legitimate regulations from indirect expropriation. The term 'exception' is inadequate from both conceptual and theoretical points of view. Exceptions are often associated to a breach of the main obligation, in this case the obligation to expropriate lawfully, complying with the certain conditions set by the treaty.[81] Therefore treating this interpretative provision as an exception may require a restrictive examination of the exception to fit the conditions of such provision. An example of such a kind may be found in the General Exceptions under Article XX of the GATT 1994, and with it, one should consider the strict interpretation provided by Panels and the Appellate Body to the provisions of the *chapeau*.[82]

A 'carve-out' by contrast removes the regulatory measure in question from the scope of the provisions relating to indirect expropriation. While this term seems more connected to the purpose of the interpretative provisions, it does not appreciate the fact that such provisions are of an interpretative nature.

The third approach, 'regulatory measure' versus indirect expropriation, is the result of the interpretation of the substantive provisions to ascertain whether a regulation aimed to protect welfare objectives, as defined in the relevant measure, is equivalent to an expropriation or not. Conceptually speaking this is perhaps the most appropriate approach as it incorporates 'the shared understanding' of the contracting parties in regard to the difference between indirect expropriation and legitimate regulation.[83] For this reason, the provision is to be understood as a step towards defining the dividing line between expropriation and regulation.

The scope of the US Model BIT and similar agreements appear narrow enough to include only certain regulatory measures falling under the *conceded* sphere of the police power.[84] As discussed earlier in this chapter, as well as in Chapters 4 and 6, this type of provision restricts individual freedoms in order to protect the greater public interest by restraining activities that may affect

---

80 Annex B (4) (b), 2012 US Model BIT.

81 Such conditions are often, yet not always: the existence of a public purpose, non-discrimination due process of law, and the payment of compensation.

82 Jorge E. Viñuales, 'Foreign Investment and the Environment in International Law: The Current State of Play,' in *Research Handbook on Environment and Investment Law*, ed. Kate Miles (Cheltenham: Edward Elgar, forthcoming 2016), 19. Available at: http://papers.ssrn.com/sol3/papers.cfm?abstract_id=2661970, last visited 30 June 2016.

83 See Annex Article 9-B Expropriation of the Transatlantic Pacific Partnership.

84 See Chapter 4, Section 4.3.2.

THE LEGITIMACY OF THE EXERCISE OF THE POLICE POWER OF STATES   193

public health, morals or the environment. Therefore, considering the intention of the contracting parties to new IIAs, one could argue that such interpretative provisions confer the highest level of deference to the State's regulatory prerogatives because only in 'rare circumstances' could such regulatory measures be deemed expropriatory.

Provisions related to water quality may be more likely to fall within the scope of exercise of the police power *strictu sensu,* as they are often linked to public welfare objectives. Pollution of water flows by extractive activities could affect public health and the environment.[85] Most importantly, water for human consumption, which under some circumstances may be linked to the human right to water, must fall under the provisions elaborated in this section. As discussed earlier, most domestic legal systems prioritise water for human consumption or municipal purpose over any other uses of water resources.[86]

The condition of non-discrimination appears to be included in most IIAs, which have adopted these interpretative provisions.[87] The analysis of non-discrimination has been addressed in previous sections. The next section will analyse the criterion of narrow proportionality which constitutes an important criterion to determine whether the exercise of the police power *strictu sensu* in this context should be deemed legitimate.

9.2.3   *Narrow Application of the Proportionality Principle*

While there is currently no single coherent way of conducting a proportionality analysis, the European tradition consists of a preliminary evaluation of the legitimacy of the objective of the measure followed by three analytical

---

85   See for instance: *Glamis Gold v. United States; Chevron Corporation and Texaco Petroleum Corporation v. The Republic of Ecuador,* UNCITRAL, PCA Case No. 2009–23; *Clayton and Bilcon of Delaware Inc. v. Government of Canada,* UNCITRAL, PCA Case No. 2009–04; *Perenco Ecuador Ltd. v. The Republic of Ecuador and Empresa Estatal Petróleos del Ecuador (Petroecuador),* ICSID Case No. ARB/08/6; *Pac Rim Cayman LLC v. Republic of El Salvador,* ICSID Case No. ARB/09/12; *Commerce Group Corp. and San Sebastian Gold Mines, Inc. v. The Republic of El Salvador,* ICSID Case No. ARB/09/17; *Niko Resources (Bangladesh) Ltd. v. Bangladesh Petroleum Exploration & Production Company Limited ('Bapex') and Bangladesh Oil Gas and Mineral Corporation ('Petrobangla'),* ICSID Case No. ARB/10/18.

86   See Chapter 2, Section 2.4.2, Chapter 3 Section 3.2.1.3 in the context of the UN Watercourses Convention which accords special regard to 'vital needs' and Chapter 6, Section 6.2.1, note 11.

87   Colombia-India BIT (2009), which provides in Article 6(2)(b): 'iv c. Non-discriminatory regulatory actions by a Contracting Party [...] do not constitute expropriation or nationalization; except in rare circumstances, where those actions are so severe that they cannot be reasonably viewed as having been adopted and applied in good faith for achieving their objective'.

stages.[88] The purpose of the preliminary stage is to remove illegitimate policy objectives. For example, if the policy objective does not further or serve the interests of the public, it would not be deemed as legitimate. The first stage (i) evaluates the *suitability* of the measure in relation to its policy objective. In other words, the suitability stage requires the measure to be designed to pursue the stated objective. This is similar to the steps required by the two-tier test under the General Exceptions of Article XX of the GATT for an otherwise inconsistent trade measure under WTO law. In the second stage of the analysis, (ii) a court or tribunal must determine whether the objective of the measure in question could be achieved with less interfering measures, or indeed, whether the original measure is *necessary* to achieve the particular objective. As noted by the tribunal in *Occidental Petroleum:*

> the argument is not that the State must prove harm, but that any penalty the State chooses to impose must bear a proportionate relationship to the violation which is being addressed and its consequences. This is neither more nor less than what is encapsulated in the Respondent's own constitutional rules about proportionality.[89]

Whether the claimant or investor in this case may propose less restrictive alternative measures, as is the practice under Article XX of the GATT, would not be without controversy. In the context of international investment law (investment arbitration), such a step may be treated with caution due to the asymmetrical nature of the relationship between an individual and a sovereign State. In *Continental Casualty*, the respondent Argentina submitted before the tribunal:

> [a]n international tribunal should analyze this issue with the highest deference and should not arrogate itself the power to establish what other measures could have been taken instead.[90]

Lastly (iii), *stricto sensu* application of the police power requires a court or tribunal to balance the competing interests and conclude whether the impact

---

88 Henckels, 'Indirect Expropriation and the Right to Regulate: Revisiting Proportionality Analysis and the Standard of Review in Investor-State Arbitration,' 227.

89 *Occidental Petroleum Corporation and Occidental Exploration and Production Company v. The Republic of Ecuador*, ICSID Case No ARB/06/11, Award of 5 October, 2012, para. 416.

90 *Continental Casualty Company v. Argentina*, ICSID Case No ARB/03/9, Award of 5 September, 2008, para. 189.

THE LEGITIMACY OF THE EXERCISE OF THE POLICE POWER OF STATES

of the measure 'is proportionate to (or too severe relative to) the gain that the public policy seeks to achieve.'[91] Arguably this test could be of utmost importance in ascertaining a claim of indirect expropriation as a result of a challenge of the exercise of the police power *strictu sensu*.

9.3 'Quantitative' and 'Qualitative' Analysis in the Determination of Indirect Expropriation

Having examined academic literature and arbitral practice in relation to each inquiry, it is left to conclude whether the methodology could permit the assessment of indirect expropriations in the context of water-related measures. To this end and based on the type of measures discussed in Chapter 6, water-related measures may be linked to the following economic activities: (i) the implementation of water resources management principles in domestic legislation (including international obligations); (ii) extractive industries (mining, oil and gas); (iii) energy generation; (iv) commercial farming; (v) water trading; (vi) industry using water as a production input, including bottled water; and (vii) water supply and sanitation services.

The assessment of regulatory measures under this classification could allow a better assessment of the risks posed on each activity. For example, the extractive industries are likely to be subject to a wide array of regulatory measures deemed to protect public health and the environment (often relating to water quality). Indeed, these activities may be sensitive to environmental regulation, community and political pressure, and issues of public health and human rights. Energy generation is likely to be affected by measures linked to the allocation of water resources. For instance, power plants may compete for water with agricultural activities and water supplies for human use.[92] Commercial farming has been perceived as controversial from its beginnings. Some experts warn of potential conflicts among users in the case of water scarcity, as it appears that current land-lease agreements grant investors better conditions in the competition for water resources. For example, under commercial farming agreements negotiated between investors and Senegal, no fees will be charged for the use of water resources.[93]

---

91   *Ibid.*, 228.

92   Averyt et al., 'Freshwater Use by U.S. Power Plants: Electricity's Thirst for a Precious Resource,' 3.

93   Lorenzo Cotula provides examples of Agreements granting land-lease and water rights. For instance: 'Mali-1 grants the investor the right "to use the quantity of water necessary

In addition, the cancellation or amendment of water permits affecting previous water allocations could render the whole investment useless. Chapter 8 extensively discussed the issues on the nature of water and its impact on the development of the overall investment.

An illustrative example of such a situation is the NAFTA case of *Lone Pine.* The investor held several licences for the exploration and development of oil and shale gas in the deposits of Utica in Quebec. The River Permit Agreement relates to a Petroleum and Natural Gas Exploration Permit covering approximately 11,600 hectares of land located under the Saint Lawrence River. The claimant alleges that this licence is of paramount importance to the project. In 2010 the government of Quebec adopted a moratorium on shale gas exploration and development under the Saint Lawrence River. Furthermore, in 2011, the exploration licence for locations under the Saint Lawrence River was revoked following the coming into force of an Act to limit oil and gas activities. The Act revokes exploration licences located under the Saint Lawrence River and limits the area of those that cross the water's edge to their land portion.[94]

Canada alleges that the Act was passed in response to the findings of an environmental study that these activities in the Gulf of Saint Lawrence are not suitable for this type of environment. Canada also asserts that the measures were adopted for a public purpose and in a non-discriminatory manner. Finally, the Government of Canada disputes that the investment is even capable of expropriation. Even if this were the case, the disputed measure did not substantially deprive the investor of its investment because the Act revoked only one of the five exploration licences that are the subject of a Farmout Agreement.[95]

---

for the project without restrictions.'" Likewise, Sudan-1 'gives the investor the right to use the water needed for the project.' In addition, the contract Senegal 1 expressly states that no fee will be charged for the use of water resources; or other contracts such as Mali 1 remain silent as to fees for the use of water resources. See Lorenzo Cotula, *Land Deals in Africa: What is in the Contracts?* (London: International Institute for Environment and Development, 2011), 36. See also Carin Smaller and Howard Mann, 'A Thirst for Distant Lands: Foreign Investment in Agricultural Land and Water,' IISD, 2009; John A. Allan et al., *Handbook of Land and Water Grabs in Africa: Foreign Direct Investment and Food and Water Security* (New York: Routledge International, 2013).

94   *Lone Pine Resources Inc. v. Canada*, ICSID Case No. UNCT/15/2, Notice of Arbitration of 6 September, 2013.

95   See NAFTA Chapter 11 Investment – *Lone Pine Resources v. Canada*, available at http://www.international.gc.ca/trade-agreements-accords-commerciaux/topics-domaines/disp-diff/lone.aspx?lang=eng, accessed 5 June, 2016.

THE LEGITIMACY OF THE EXERCISE OF THE POLICE POWER OF STATES   197

It seems to be often the case that host States have second thoughts in relation to investment projects that were originally encouraged, which after closer examination or social pressure become undesirable from environmental and social perspectives. In *Saint Marys*, for example, the claimant-investor alleged that Canada had refused to provide further permits for the operation of a quarry, after conferring some initial permits, including permits to use water resources. A similar situation was also observed in *Bear Creek,* where the Peruvian government reverted to previously undertaken commitments.[96] This work has made reference to some of these examples throughout and it seems safe to conclude that this type of case will be increasingly seen in the area of investment treaty arbitration. The 'qualitative' analysis of the governmental measure discussed in this chapter may become increasingly relevant in determining the extent to which the property rights granted to an investor should be protected in its entirety; or whether the host State should bear the burden of costs relating to the implementation of new regulatory measures that negatively affect the investor's property rights.

9.4   Conclusions

Influenced by often contradictory arbitral awards and to some extent the academic literature, States have embarked on a campaign to narrow the discretion of arbitrators in the interpretation of expropriation (and other treaty) provisions. Negotiations of new IIAs adopt extensive definitions, guidance and interpretative provisions, to provide 'more certainty' in the application of substantial investment legal provisions. The provisions on indirect expropriation – embedded in a new generation of IIAs – seek now to protect States' regulatory prerogatives, having set a high threshold for a finding of indirect expropriation.

However, as suggested by some expert academics and practitioners, even with new provisions on indirect expropriation, it will still be difficult to draw a dividing line between indirect expropriation and legitimate regulation.[97] This on-going debate justifies this framework of analysis as applied to the case of water resources and its management. While it is undeniable that disputes can only be solved according to the specific facts and context of each case, it is also

---

96   See Chapter 6, Section 6.2.2.

97   See Jan Paulsson, 'Indirect Expropriation: Is the Right to Regulate at Risk?,' in *Making the Most of International Investment Aagreements: A Common Agenda,* (Paris: OECD, 2005); Vaughan Lowe, 'Regulation or Expropriation?,' *Current Legal Problems* 55 (2002).

true that specific issues of global concern, such as water resources, should be treated with consistency. In sum, this chapter concludes that the special nature of water, as analysed under specific uses i.e. mining, electricity, irrigation and others, is relevant to the overall determination of an indirect expropriation claim. Such considerations lead to a sector specific analysis that is keen to adjust the final decision to current policy needs without necessarily embarking on further considerations of normative conflicts. Such considerations have proved challenging for investment tribunals and frustrating for advocates of societal values, often at the centre of these types of disputes.

CHAPTER 10

Conclusions

10.1 Introduction

The physical, social and economic characteristics of water when approached in a holistic manner demand that this natural resource be viewed as unique. There are a number of defining features that require water to be viewed through such a lens: (i) water's physical features make it both unpredictable and variable, (ii) water's intrinsic value is rarely reflected in its price, even when it has no substitutes and (iii) water's socially sensitive status (and vital requirement for living) is such that people perceive it as a resource to which they are entitled. This basic reflection on the unique attributes of water leads one to question whether investment arbitration tribunals ought to incorporate an evaluation of this uniqueness when tasked with determining claims of indirect expropriation that involve a water-related regulatory measure. In the context of water-related measures, investment arbitration tribunals may be required to determine if a legitimate regulatory measure amounts to an indirect expropriation. In terms of guidance that can be gleaned from the analysis in this work, investment arbitration tribunals ought to consider a number of key features when evaluating a host State's water-related measure against the standards of protection provided in the applicable IIA.

10.2 A Sector-Specific Approach

(1) A sector-specific approach to water resources requires first that parties invoke the unique nature of water resources, and second that investment arbitration tribunals inquire into the specific object and purpose of the water-related measure before evaluating whether the regulatory measure negatively affects the interests of the investor-claimant.

Remarkably only a few cases, arisen in the context of water resources management, were decided on the merits by arbitral tribunals. The majority of cases have been settled, leaving one to wonder what approach arbitral tribunals might have adopted. In contrast, investment treaty disputes arising in the water services sector were in general decided in the merits stage, except in a few cases where the investor and host State settled the dispute.

© KONINKLIJKE BRILL NV, LEIDEN, 2017 | DOI 10.1163/9789004335301_011

Notably the tribunal in *Bayview Irrigation District,* albeit in an *obiter dictum,* discussed the nature of water resources and the special character of property rights in water.[1] This approach confirms the value and completeness that such reasoning provides to a decision. In contrast, the decision adopted in *Methanex*[2] focused primarily on the legality of the exercise of the police power (*strictu sensu*) by the State of California. The tribunal concluded that the measure was adopted for a public purpose and applied in a non-discriminatory manner. However, the tribunal did not make an express finding as to whether the regulatory measure was proportional to its end.[3] In other words, the tribunal failed to assess whether other alternative measures, less restrictive to the investor, were available and adequate to achieve the same goal. One also needs to consider the factual claims invoked by the investor, which in this case focused primarily on a claim for breach of the national treatment standard.[4]

Investment disputes have reached high levels of complexity, where social, economic and political aspects are intimately intertwined. So too are the actors: indigenous communities, NGOs, expert advisors, besides the parties, are all now stakeholders involved in the development of arbitration proceedings. In this connection, Chapters 2 and 3 have provided an extensive account of the nature of water and social and economic aspects of water resources. These aspects, together with water's physical characteristics, beg for a holistic approach to water management and allocation systems, as well as other legal frameworks that influence such a management in its different uses.

On this point, one could argue that it is still the task of the disputing parties to ultimately frame the terms of reference within which arbitral tribunals will expand the factual scenario that informs the final arbitral decision. Likewise, given the public nature of water-related measures, it is also important that arbitral tribunals create their own framework of analysis when assessing cases relating to water resources. Considering the implications that an arbitral decision may have on other users of water, both at the national and international levels, such a framework should look at the domestic law of the host State to

---

1   *Bayview Irrigation District et al. v. United Mexican States,* ICSID Case No. ARB (AF)/05/1, Award of 19 June, 2007.

2   *Methanex Corp. v. United States of America,* Final Award of 3 August, 2005.

3   See the test of narrow proportionality discussed in Chapter 9, Section 9.2.2.3.

4   The claimant Methanex argued that under Article 1102 NAFTA 'California and thereby the USA plainly intended to deny foreign methanol producers, including Methanex, the best treatment it has accorded to domestic *ethanol investors,* thus violating Article 1102' (emphasis added). See *Methanex Corp. v. United States of America,* UNCITRAL, Part II – Chapter D – Page 9, para. 26.

CONCLUSIONS

201

construct and shape the scope of protection of the water right. This has been extensively discussed in Chapter 7.

Of equal importance is the clarity in legal reasoning, which goes in parallel to the creation of specific frameworks to decide water-related cases; it has an internal and external function within this dispute settlement regime. First, from an internal perspective, clarity of reasoning may strengthen the regime's own internal functioning,[5] providing predictable assessments, rather than predictable outcomes. Second, from an external perspective, clarity of reasoning may also strengthen the legitimacy of the system *vis-à-vis* external stakeholders.[6] It is of general knowledge that advocates and detractors of the investment arbitration regime have long expressed the need for increased transparency and clearer rules which can assist in fostering predictability for the investment arbitration regime overall. This aspect has been a trigger for the negotiation and conclusion of IIAs of the new generation, as illustrated by the lengthy negotiations of important recent trade and investment agreements, such as CETA and the TTIP.[7] However, such clarifications are particularly relevant for those States seeking to protect their regulatory freedom for the management of natural resources. The latest text of CETA for instance includes specific provisions resembling the 1993 NAFTA Joint Statement in relation to rights and obligations relating to water resources:

---

5   Federico Ortino, 'Legal Reasoning of International Investment Tribunals: A Typology of Egregious Failures.' *Journal of International Dispute Settlement* 3, no. 1 (2012), 33.

6   *Ibid.*, 34. Professor Lalive citing Sir Frank Berman criticised the lack of reasoning in the case *Lucchetti v. Peru*, noting: 'the requirement that an award has to be motivated implies that it must enable the reader to follow the reasoning of the Tribunal on points of fact and law ... the requirement to state reasons is satisfied as long as the award enables one to follow how the Tribunal proceeds from Point A to Point B and eventually to its conclusion, even if it made an error of fact or law. See Pierre Lalive, 'On the Reasoning of International Arbitral Awards,' *Journal of International Dispute Settlement* 1, no. 1 (2010), 59. See also *Industria Nacional de Alimentos SA (Lucchetti) v. the Republic of Peru,* Decision on Annulment of September 5, 2007. Furthermore, Professor Reisman contends that arbitral awards should communicate its reasoning in a clear and succinct manner. W. Michael Reisman, '"Case Specific Mandates" Versus "Systemic Implications": How Should Investment Tribunals Decide?' – the Freshfields Arbitration Lecture.' *Arbitration International* 29, no. 2 (2013), 137.

7   UNCTAD annual report on investment and dispute settlement notes: '*Consistency of arbitral decisions.* Recurring episodes of inconsistent findings by arbitral tribunals have resulted in divergent legal interpretations of identical or similar treaty provisions as well as differences in the assessment of the merits of cases involving the same facts. Inconsistent interpretations have led to uncertainty about the meaning of key treaty obligations and lack of predictability as to how they will be read in future cases.' (UNCTAD), 'World Investment Report 2013. Global Value Chains: Investment and Trade for Development,' 112.

[t]he Parties recognise that water in its natural state, including water in lakes, rivers, reservoirs, aquifers and water basins, is not a good or a product. Therefore, only Chapters Twenty-Two (Trade and Sustainable Development) and Twenty-Four (Trade and Environment) apply to such water. 2. Each Party has the right to protect and preserve its natural water resources. Nothing in this Agreement obliges a Party to permit the commercial use of water for any purpose, including its withdrawal, extraction or diversion for export in bulk[...].[8]

This provision, as well as the 1993 NAFTA Joint Statement, reflects the importance that humans, both as individuals and communities, give to water. This is of course reflected in domestic law; the rule of non-ownership in water, as well as increasingly modern allocation systems, recognises the intertwined relations among water users, the environment and among nations.

(2) A sector-specific approach to water-related regulatory measures does not negate the fact that there are certain instances where a measure could be deemed expropriatory (in other words, the analytical framework detailed in this work does not make the case that all water-related regulatory measures should be deemed legitimate regulation as opposed to expropriations).

The second stage in the determination of indirect expropriation was discussed in Chapter 8. The 'level of deprivation' test is of a 'quantitative' nature; it seeks to ascertain whether the measure, as an expression of the exercise of the police power (generally *latu sensu*), has the effect to render the investment virtually useless. As described in Chapter 6, there are measures aimed to protect water quality and measures which may affect allocation of water quantities, the latter are arguably more relevant to this analysis. Against this background there are a number of hypothetical scenarios worth considering. The cancellation of a water permit, for instance, may be found to be a direct expropriation; after all, there is nothing indirect in such an action. The reduction of water volumes in a given permit, however, may cause comparable damage.

The measure itself does not affect other sticks of the bundle of investment rights; in other words other investment rights remain untouched. The question that follows is therefore, whether the lack of water resources, as an input of production, affects the whole operation in a manner that would render the project useless or unviable? This seems to have been the case in *Vattenfall I*,

---

8 Article 1.9 (Rights and obligations relating to water) CETA, text of the Agreement, version February 2016.

CONCLUSIONS

where the investor could not obtain a water permit to develop its power plants for electricity generation.

Certainly, there is an argument that the cancellation of a water entitlement, while only constituting one stick in the bundle of the investment rights granted to a foreign investor, is so essential to the project that its cancellation renders the whole investment useless. This has been the position adopted by an important number of investment tribunals under the 'unity of investment approach.' In addition, a water entitlement – affected by a specific measure – could not be analysed as a potential partial expropriation. Before undertaking such an analysis, arbitral tribunals may consider whether: (i) the investment can be disassembled into discrete rights, (ii) the State's measure affects rights which fall within the definition of investment under the relevant IIA and (iii) the property right could be subject to exploitation independently of the overall investment.[9]

As opposed to national investors or any other property holders, foreign investors have only one purpose in the host State, the development of its specific business. It is on this basis that the investment might have been approved in the first place. In contrast, national investors could start different economic activities or use their assets for other purposes; this is not possible in the case of foreign investors. Therefore, in a large majority of cases the water entitlement could not be exploited as an independent asset, separated from the rest of the bundle of investment rights. As such, a water entitlement serves the functioning of the whole operation and is therefore unlikely to be analysed independently of the entire investment. It is therefore likely that a reallocation (or a cancellation) of water permits gives rise to an indirect expropriation finding of the investment as a whole.

The tests of 'duration' of the measure and 'control' of the investment are relevant to this determination. Assuming the legitimacy of the governmental measure and that it is attributable to water scarcity or stress only, the capacity of the investor to endure the measure for a period of time, depends on the size of the project and its sunk costs. On the other hand, under the same assumptions, the investor is likely to remain in 'control' of the investment. This criterion, as discussed in Chapter 8, has become an important determinant in the consideration of whether the measure amounts to indirect expropriation. However, the conclusion might be again that the effects over the investment are tantamount to an expropriation.

It is important to consider that in many situations it is the physical nature of water that leads to such results and not necessarily the intent or nature of the regulatory measure.

---

9 Ursula Kriebaum, 'Partial Expropriation,' *The Journal of World Investment & Trade* 8, no. 1 (2007), 83.

All this leads to the preliminary conclusion that a 'quantitative' analysis alone is insufficient to ascertain indirect expropriation, turning every measure linked to water resources management expropriatory. As a consequence, the doctrine of the police power of States would be undermined, and the protection afforded to investors would be largely asymmetrical to the burdens that most domestic legal systems impose on water entitlements.

(3)   A sector-specific approach to water-related regulatory measures requires that arbitral tribunals scrutinise both the legitimacy and legality of the water-related measure (including the exercise of the police power).

The third and last stage in the determination – addressed in Chapter 9 – assesses the quality and nature of the measure. Its main objective in the context of the proposed framework is to asses the quality of the governmental measure, and whether such a measure, claiming to protect the public interest, does not in fact constitute a disguised act of expropriation.

There may be cases where a government measure should be deemed expropriatory. One should consider the political background of the host State in the context of the use and management of water resources against which foreign investors start the development of a project. Against this backdrop, it is appropriate to also consider those water demands associated to high moral values, e.g. environmental concerns, agriculture and food security and the human right to water. They all compete for water allocation; however, since some of these users are diffused, they cannot voice their interest, such is the case of water for environmental flows.

The protection of such values has been embraced in the provisions of the new generation of IIAs relating to indirect expropriation. They fall within the scope of the exercise of the police power *strictu sensu*. Since except in rare circumstances, a measure designed to protect the environment, public health and morals would not constitute indirect expropriation[10] one could argue that the welfare objective or public purpose of a measure enjoys a presumption of legality and needs no further scrutiny. However, there are other elements relevant to ascertain the legitimacy of the measure, such as proportionality, discrimination and good faith. The element of good faith of the governmental

---

10   See Chapter 5 on the police power in the context of international investment arbitration, and Chapter 9 which discusses the provision in more detail.

CONCLUSIONS   205

measure requires scrutiny in cases when a host State claims that a water-related measure has been adopted strictly in the face of water scarcity or to maintain the quality of the resource, but further evidence reveals that this was not in fact the primary purpose of the water-related measure.

The quality of the governmental measure is also subject to scrutiny where the measure falls outside the scope of the police power *strictu sensu*. The exercise of the police power *latu sensu* must in fact be subject to stricter scrutiny. Consequently, the determination of measures associated to wealth redistribution, such as reallocation of water resources with a view to develop new sectors of society, rezoning water-related areas, and most importantly, the improvement of water management regulation through the implementation of IWRM principles could fall within the exercise of the police power *latu sensu*. Chapter 9 adopts the interpretative provisions of the new generation of IIAS and considers each criterion of analysis, in addition to the one already discussed, namely the economic impact of the measure.[11]

The conclusion is that water does have special characteristics, which make investments more vulnerable to climate and economic changes. However, water has also a strong social component which makes governments vulnerable to social pressure. This is illustrated by a number of mining cases discussed throughout the book.

(4)   A sector-specific approach to water resources requires that tribunals be sensitive to the underlying social aspects relating to measures affecting water resources.

In addition to the three areas of analysis that arbitrators must consider under the framework suggested in this work, they must also consider the policy aspects of a water-related regulatory measure and the potential dissatisfaction stakeholders may express with having international adjudicators evaluating sensitive issues such as water-related measures. However, it is somewhat paradoxical that host States tend to settle such highly relevant investment disputes.[12] Unfortunately, this has not allowed an analysis of the extent – if

---

11   Discussed in Chapter 8.

12   See *Vattenfall AB, Vattenfall Europe AG, Vattenfall Europe Generation AG v. Federal Republic of Germany*, ICSID Case No. ARB/09/6; *Sun Belt v. Government of Canada*, NAFTA UNCITRAL rules; *Impregilo S.p.A. v. Islamic Republic of Pakistan*, ICSID Case No. ARB/03/3; *AbitibiBowater Inc., v. Government of Canada*, NAFTA case; *Aguas del Tunari S.A. v Republic of Bolivia*, ICSID Case No. ARB/02/3; *St Marys VCNA, LLC v. Government of Canada*, NAFTA UNCITRAL Rules.

any – to which arbitral tribunals would have deferred to the exercise of States' regulatory prerogatives over water resources. Whether this aspect is coincidental or not, one could argue that once a tribunal adopts a position over the regulation of water rights or the appropriateness of host States' water management, a precedent could be created with large consequences for both host States and foreign investors.

Note, however, that settlements, involving any sort of compensation are generally the equivalent to a victory for the investor-claimant and that this fact places the burden of risk and costs, in regard to the protection of water resources, on the host State.[13] Perhaps, this cautious approach seeks to keep the Pandora's Box closed because there is considerable risk associated with massive public opposition and advocacy that may arise when (and if) an arbitral tribunal finds that a water-related measure constitutes an indirect expropriation, with important economic consequences for the host State. These issues reflect the social context of water resources, and the potential conflicts it brings. Chapters 3 and 6 illustrated a handful of investment disputes arising out of investments in water services and water resources respectively, which showed the level of sensitivity and entitlement that people have over their water resources.

10.3 Water: Securely Unpredictable and Investment: Predictably Insecure?

The framework detailed in Chapters 8 and 9 suggests that the relationship between water governance and investment protection is an area of legal integration that will require intense scrutiny and diligence in the coming years. The first statement in the title of this section (water as securely unpredictable) reflects the idea that the unique nature and characteristics of water resources and increased hydrological variability, aggravated by climate change means that there is little predictability in the future allocation of water resources.

---

13   See for instance *AbitibiBowater Inc. v. Government of Canada*, NAFTA case, where the government of Canada agreed to make a payment of 130 million USD to settle the dispute. In this regard see the press release by the Government Canada, available at http://www .italaw.com/sites/default/files/case-documents/ita0235.pdf, last visited August 1, 2013. In the case *Sun Belt v. Government of Canada*, NAFTA case, the settlement arrangement remains unknown. In *Vattenfall v. Federal Republic of Germany*, the government of Germany reverted its measure, see Chapter 6, Section 6.3.2.

CONCLUSIONS

A holistic or integrated approach to water management (which may be referred to as an emerging principle of water law) may be a useful approach for governing water's unpredictability, but from an international investment law perspective may provide little assistance to host States having to defend claims dealing with changes in the regulation of thier water resources. This increases the likelihood, at least in the short-term, that host States will have to be especially careful in changing water regulations that may conflict with promises made to foreign investors. However, it is also increasingly important that foreign investors undertake not only environmental impact assessments, but also social and human rights impact assessments. Past experience in the area of water services has shown that sensitivities around water may escalate to the point where conflicts become unavoidable. A nuanced understanding about the unpredictability of water resources may assist investors in structuring investments that can survive changes in host States' water legal framework. This will of course require that the costs of due diligence as well as the risk of asymmetric information are shared by both, investors and host States. Expectations given to investors would only be considered reasonable when host States provide investors with transparent legal regimes that create a reasonably predictable investment environment.

As for the second statement (investment, as predictably insecure), the unpredictable nature of water constitutes an indication of reasonably adaptable legal frameworks. Therefore, one could argue that water users, including foreign investors, in conditions of water stress and scarcity, operate in an environment of predictable insecurity given by the nature of water resources, on one hand, but also given by the nature of the investment arbitration mechanism, on the other.

It is perhaps appropriate to note that security and predictability are not the only objectives of the investment arbitration mechanism. With over 3000 IIAs, which constitute the primary applicable law to the dispute, and 696 known disputes which are either concluded, pending or discontinued under different IIAs,[14] actors using the investor-State dispute settlement mechanism in IIAs are still debating whether there should be a case-by-case fact inquiry to decide investment disputes or whether an all encompassing legal framework promoting a general jurisprudence *constante* should be developed. This is perhaps an opportunity that was lost during the negotiations of the Multilateral Agreement

---

14   UNCTAD, Investment Dispute Settlement Navigator. Available at: http://investmentpoli-cyhub.unctad.org/ISDS, last visited July 1, 2016.

on Investment,[15] addressed in Chapter 5. Conversely, for instance the Dispute Settlement Understanding under the WTO, provides in Article 3.2 that one of the objectives of dispute settlement system of the WTO is to provide security and predictability to the trading system. Noteworthy is the fact that the WTO agreement includes 164 States under a single multilateral agreement.[16]

10.4 The Way Forward and Future Research

There are multiple aspects that could still be incorporated in the analytical framework to make it more comprehensive. One important aspect is the issue of compensation, which is beyond the scope of this work.

As it stands currently, the Hull Formula of prompt, adequate and effective compensation may hinder the interests of the investor, rather than secure the enforcement of her rights.[17] The all or nothing approach to compensation[18] may not allow for an efficient allocation of risk and costs of regulation between investors and host States. The issue of compensation needs to be addressed in the new negotiations of investment agreements, providing detailed guidelines to arbitrators as to when the costs of the effects of regulatory activity could be shared among the parties to the dispute. This aspect acquires additional relevance under the analysis of natural resources, as well as environmental and public health, in which the operation of the investor is almost always involved.

The second issue, which ought to be addressed in the light of the analytical framework proposed in this work, is the fair and equitable treatment standard. This standard has apparently turned into a blank (or catch-all) mechanism for investment protection. Failed claims of expropriation have found alternative

---

15 On the failure of the MAI negotiation see Chapter 5, Section 5.6.1. The failure to agree on a multilateral agreement on investment has had as an effect, the negotiation of numerous BITs each under different conditions and provisions.

16 See membership of the WTO, by 29 July 2016, in Understanding the WTO: The Organization Members and Observers. Available at: http://www.wto.org/english/thewto_e/whatis_e/tif_e/org6_e.htm, last visited July 30, 2016.

17 The investment agreements' provisions on compensation bind arbitrators to decide on full compensation when an expropriation occurred or zero compensation due to the inexistence of an expropriation, direct or indirect; in such case the burden of risk is fully imposed on either the investor or the host State.

18 On the issue of full compensation and the quest for a more nuanced approach see Ursula Kriebaum, 'Regulatory Takings: Balancing the Interests of the Investor and the State,' *The Journal of Word Investment & Trade* 8, no. 5 (2007).

CONCLUSIONS

redress in the standard of fair and equitable treatment.[19] As Professor Reisman notes:

> [e]xpropriation has a certain clarity, both in its precipitating event and its liquidation compensation[...] Violation of the fair and equitable treatment obligation often lack that clarity[20]

The question arises as to whether there is a relationship between the standard of fair and equitable treatment and the criterion contained in the 'qualitative' criteria to assess the nature of the governmental measure as expropriatory. It is argued that such a relationship needs further study in order to determine whether the tribunals' findings in, e.g. claims of expropriation, could inform findings of a breach of the fair and equitable treatment standard.

10.5   Final Reflections

As with many other books approaching the issue of international investment law and its relationship and interaction with other areas of law (such as environmental law or human rights law), this work aims at striking a balance between investor rights and State regulatory prerogatives. However, during the course of researching this work, the question has arisen as to whether there really is an imbalance that is in need of correction. This work submits that the protection of other societal values in the context of international investment disputes – as expressed in previous chapters – is not necessarily in danger.

While there is considerable criticism in some circles claiming that investor-State dispute settlement is slanted or biased in favour of investors, there is no

---

19   On this issue see for instance: Lucy Reed and Daina Bray, 'Fair and Equitable Treatment: Fairly and Equitably Applied in Lieu of Unlawful Indirect Expropriation?' in *Contemporary Issues in International Arbitration and Mediation*, ed. Arthur W. Rovine (Brill, The Netherlands: Martinus Nijhoff Publishers, 2007). Of interest, is also the remark made by the tribunal in *GAMI v. Mexico*, during its analysis of the expropriation claim. In this case the tribunal addressed the analysis of expropriation made by the tribunal in *S.D. Myers v. Canada*, pointing out that while the measure adopted by Canada would not be expropriatory, in view of that tribunal, redress was granted on different grounds, namely under the fair and equitable treatment standard. See *GAMI Investments v. Mexico*, under UNCITRAL Rules, Final Award, 15 November 2004, para. 124.

20   W. Michael Reisman and Digon Rocio, 'Eclipse of Expropriation?' in In Contemporary Issues in *Contemporary Issues in International Arbitration and Mediation*, ed. Arthur W. Rovine (Brill, The Netherlands: Martinus Nijhoff Publishers, 2009), 44.

conclusive evidence that such is the case.[21] In fact, some of the new empirical data indicates that investors and respondent States win and lose almost proportionally, and that when investors win, they receive much less than the amount claimed.[22]

There are of course, exceptions. In some cases, the amount of compensation awarded to investors is staggering. For example, in *Occidental*, the arbitral tribunal awarded the claimant USD 1.77 billion in damages for expropriation of an oil operation in Ecuador.[23] Yet, the highest amount of damages rendered so far was just over USD 50 billion in favour of Yukos, for several measures taken by Russia against the investor.[24] These facts perhaps explain why a large number of disputes, notably in the context of water resources, settle long before a tribunal is able to issue a final award on the merits. This could mean at least two things: (i) investors and host States do not have complete trust and faith in the way that arbitral tribunals interpret and apply investment treaties, and (ii) host States might retrospectively realise that the regulatory measures that they have instituted may not be as justifiable as they initially believed them to be, and therefore choose to repeal the measure instead of being found liable for damages by an international tribunal.[25] It is also interesting to note that

---

21   See for instance Pia Eberhardt and Cecilia Olivet, *Profiting from injustice – How law firms, arbitrators and financiers are fuelling an investment arbitration boom* (Published by Corporate Europe Observatory and the Transnational Institute, 2012). See also the *Public Statement on the International Investment Regime 31 August 2010,* proposed by several academics among which are Gus Van Harten, David Schneiderman, Muthucumaraswamy Sornarajah and Peter Muchlinski. Available at: http://www.osgoode.yorku.ca/public-statement-international-investment-regime-31-august-2010/, last visited June 30, 2016.

22   Daniel Behn, 'Legitimacy, Evolution, and Growth in Investment Treaty Arbitration: Empirically Evaluating the State-of-the-Art,' *Georgetown Journal of International Law* 46, no. 2 (2015), 405–06. See also the 2013 UNCTAD report, noting that up to 2012 from a universe of 244 investment disputes, 42 per cent were decided in favour of the State, 31 per cent in favour of the investor and 27 per cent were settled. UNCTAD, 'World Investment Report 2013. Global Value Chains: Investment and Trade for Development,' New York: United Nations, 2013, 111 and Susan Franck, 'Empirically Evaluating Claims About Investment Treaty Arbitration,' *The North Carolina Law Review* 86, no. 1 (2007): 49.

23   UNCTAD, 'World Investment Report 2013. Global Value Chains: Investment and Trade for Development,' 111.

24   *Yukos Universal Limited (Isle of Man) v. The Russian Federation,* PCA Case No. AA 227, Final Award of July 18, 2014.

25   See *supra* note 12 in this chapter.

CONCLUSIONS

several settled cases involved developed countries as defendants, rather than developing countries, as might be intuitively expected.[26]

It seems to be the threat of an investment dispute that has alerted other areas of law to speculate on potential cases whose decision by investment tribunals might bring negative consequences for environmental regulation or overwhelmingly high amounts of money for compensation. Strong advocates of the regime have asserted:

> [n]o investment tribunal has ever ordered a State to compensate an investor for simply enacting a generally applicable environmental law or for legitimately enforcing a regulation that caused an investor a loss. Very deferential standards have been applied to environmental regulatory measures.[27]

This work was originally inspired and informed by strong opinions about the negative effects that investment agreements and investment treaty arbitration could have on States' prerogative to regulate (especially in the area of water resources). Confessions aside, this work finds that international investment law has the necessary tools to approach water-related cases with adequate degree of deference to the exercise of the police power. A sector specific approach to investment disputes will indeed provide decision-makers with a detailed outlook of the specific regulatory measure at issue and the rationale behind it. The construction of property rights in water must consider constitutional, domestic and administrative laws; it should not forget the relevant of international agreements relating to water allocation in terms of both quantity and quality. This is because the provisions of international agreements are implemented at the domestic level, becoming part of the overall legal framework that shapes the water-related property right. In sum, looking at water resources specifically allows the decision-maker to identify and properly assess the specific challenges and historic development of property law relating to water resources that shape the function and object of many water regulations.

---

26 Investment treaty arbitration disputes against the US, Canada, Germany and Australia, among others, illustrate this point.

27 Charles N. Brower and Sadie Blanchard, 'From "Dealing in Virtue" to "Profiting from Injustice": The Case Against Re-Statification of Investment Dispute Settlement,' *TDM* 4 (2013), 5.

One of the outcomes of this work is in the realisation that if arbitrators are to employ the analytical tools that this book suggests, it is of equal importance for host States to be diligent in informing arbitrators of the specificities of their national laws in regard to water resources, including the object and purpose of the water-related measures. As a matter of principle, States do not want to be seen as having insecure and unpredictable investment environments; yet, from a practical perspective, States do want to avoid the payment of high compensation. In both cases, host States are required to act with great transparency and avoid confusing or conflicting internal processes, as was the case in *Metalclad*.[28]

Finally, it is important to reflect that this is not a State-centric or pro-sovereignty piece of work. Instead, this work holds that the police power of States is both an extension and a limitation on sovereignty. The police power of the State grants a sovereign State wide discretion in implementing measures that benefit the public welfare; but at the same time, that same sovereignty allows States to enter into binding international agreements that limit their own sovereign prerogatives. In other words, the police power (as an important component of State sovereignty) is not absolute. This means that the State, as sovereign, can limit its sovereignty by providing international guarantees to foreign investors in the form of treaties. It also means that the State, as sovereign, can use its police power to implement measures that benefit the public interest. It is at the nexus of these two essential components of a State's sovereignty where this book has attempted to add insight and analysis. Therefore, when one refers to the 'police power approach,' in the context of resolving disputes involving investors and host States, one may be failing to understand that the police power of the State is not absolute; it must be balanced against all of the other commitments that the State has made to itself (constitutional guarantees) and others (international commitments). Simply invoking the police power as a defence to State responsibility is as unsophisticated as it is wrong. If such a view were correct, then any measure that a State invoked under the police power would be valid – and that clearly is not the case. This is

---

28   In this case the tribunal asserted the importance of clarity and transparency to guide the actions of investors in the best possible way. 'Once the authorities of the central government of any Party [...] become aware of any scope for misunderstanding or confusion in this connection, it is their duty to ensure that the correct position is promptly determined and clearly stated so that investors can proceed with all appropriate expedition in the confident belief that they are acting in accordance with all relevant laws.'

See *Metalclad Corporation v. United States of Mexico*, ICSID Case No. ARB (AF)/97/1, Award of 30 August, 2000, para. 76.

CONCLUSIONS

something that appears to be generally recognised by investment arbitral tribunals: the State, through the use of its police power, can make promises to both foreigners and its own citizens; and sometimes a State is going to be held liable for reneging on such promises. This work attempted to assist the decision-maker in finding the appropriate balance between the duties that a State owes to its own citizens and the duties that it owes to foreign citizens through its international commitments. Obviously this is not something that is simple to delineate, but I hope that this contribution will move knowledge in this area of legal interpretation and analysis forward.

Bibliography

Primary Sources

Economic Agreements

Agreement on Technical Barriers to Trade (Annex 1A to the Marrakesh Agreement establishing the WTO).

ASEAN Comprehensive Investment Agreements, 2012.

Bilateral Investment Treaty between Bolivia and the Netherlands of 1994.

Bilateral Investment Treaty between Colombia and India of 2009.

Bilateral Investment Treaty between Colombia and UK of 2010.

Bilateral Investment Treaty between France and Argentina BIT of 1991.

Bilateral Investment Treaty between Germany and Egypt of 2005.

Bilateral Investment Treaty between Mexico and the United Kingdom of 2006.

Bilateral Investment Treaty between Mexico and Austria of 1998.

Bilateral Investment Treaty between New Zealand and China of 2008.

Bilateral Investment Treaty between United States of America and Argentina of 1994.

Bilateral Investment Treaty between United States of America and Ecuador of 1997.

Bilateral Investment Treaty between United States of America and Bolivia of 2001 (terminated in 2012).

Comprehensive Economic Cooperation Agreement between the Republic of India and the Republic of Singapore of 29 June 2005.

Comprehensive Economic and Trade Agreement between the European Union and Canada (signed in 2016).

Foreign Investment Promotion and Protection Agreement, 2004 Canada.

Free Trade Agreement between Australia and Chile of 2009.

Free Trade Agreement between China and New Zealand of 2008.

Free Trade Agreement between India and Korea 2003.

Free Trade Agreement between Korea and United States of 2012.

Free Trade Agreement between United States, Dominican Republic and Central America of 2004 (DR-CAFTA).

General Agreement on Tariffs and Trade 1994 (GATT 1994).

The *Havana Charter for an International Trade Organization (ITO)*, 24 March 1948, contained in UN Conference on Trade & Employment, UN Doc. E/CONF.2/78 (1948) (unadopted).

Transatlantic Trade and Investment Partnership (TTIP) (not yet signed)

Treaty of Friendship Commerce and Navigation between the United States and Argentina of 1855.

Treaty of Friendship, Commerce and Navigation between the United States and Japan of 1953.

United States 2004 Model Bilateral Investment Treaty.

United States 2012 Model Bilateral Investment Treaty.

Other Economic Agreements

Committee on Economic, Social And Cultural Rights, *'Substantive Issues Arising in the Implementation of the International Covenant on Economic, Social and Cultural Rights' General Comment No. 15 (2002), The right to water (arts. 11 and 12 of the International Covenant on Economic, Social and Cultural Rights)*, E/C.12/2002/11 20 January 2003, Twenty-ninth Session Geneva, 11–29 November 2002.

Convention for the Protection of Human Rights and Fundamental Freedoms (Paris: 1950) and Protocol to the Convention for the Protection of Human Rights and Fundamental Freedoms as amended by Protocol No. 11 (Paris: 1952).

General Assembly, United Nations, *'The human right to water and sanitation Resolution,'* A/RES/64/292, August 3, 2010.

Human Rights Council, *'Report of the independent expert on the issue of human rights obligations related to access to safe drinking water and sanitation, Catarina de Albuquerque,'* A/HRC/15/31, 15th Session, June 29, 2010.

Human Rights Council, *'Report of the independent expert on the issue of human rights obligations related to access to safe drinking water and sanitation, Catarina de Albuquerque,'* Addendum, Progress report on the compilation of good practices, Fifteenth session, A/HRC/15/31/Add.1, 1 July 2010.

Office of the High Commissioner of Human Rights: *'General Comment No. 15: The Right to Water (Arts. 11 and 12 of the Covenant),'* adopted at the Twenty-ninth Session of the Committee on Economic, Social and Cultural Rights, on 20 January 2003 (Contained in Document E/C.12/2002/11).

Protocol Amending the Agreement of Great Lakes Water Quality of 1978 as amended on October 16, 1983 and on November 18, 1987.

United Nations: Convention on the Law of the Non-Navigational Uses of International Watercourses (the UN Watercourses Convention) adopted in 1997.

National Laws

Australia: Environment Protection and Biodiversity Conservation (EPBC) Act 1999.

Bolivia: Decretos Supremos No.493 y No. 494, 1 May 2010.

Brazil: Constitution 1988 (as amended 2004).

Canada: Water Act RSA 2000 c. W-3 (Alberta).

Costa Rica: Ley de Aguas No. 276.

Kazakhstan: Constitution of 1995.

Mexico: Constitution 1917 (as amended in 2004).

Mexico: The Water Act (Ley de Aguas Nacionales).

BIBLIOGRAPHY

Morocco: Water Law.

Peru: Ley de Recursos Hidricos No 29338, 2009.

Peru: Reglamento de la Ley N 29338 Ley de Recursos Hidricos.

US: Arizona Groundwater Code.

US: California Senate Bill 521 of 1997.

US: The Texas Water Code.

US: Trade Promotion Act 2002.

Selected Cases

Investment Arbitration

Accession Mezzanine Capital L.P. and Danubius Kereskedohaz Vagyonkezelo Zrt v. The Republic of Hungary, ICSID Case No. ARB/12/13, Award of 17 April, 2015.

Aguas del Tunari S.A. v Republic of Bolivia, ICSID Case No. ARB/02/3.

AbitibiBowater Inc., v Government of Canada, (under Chapter II NAFTA) 2009.

Achter Daniels Midland Company and Tate & Lyle Ingredients Americas, Inc. v. Mexico, ICSID Case No. ARB(AF)/04/05, Award of 21 November 2007.

ADC Affiliate Limited and ADC & ADMC Management Limited v. Hungary, ICSID Case No. ARB/03/16, Award of 2 October 2006.

ATA Construction, Industrial and Trading Company v. Hashemite Kingdom of Jordan, ICSID Case No. ARB/08/2, Award of 18 May 2012.

Azurix Corp. v Argentine Republic, (ICSID CASE No. ARB/01/12), Award 14 July 2006.

Bayview Irrigation District et al. v United Mexican States, (ICSID Additional Facility Case No. ARB(AF)/05/1), Award 19 June 2007.

Bear Creek Mining Corporation v. Republic of Peru, ICSID Case No. ARB/14/21, Respondent's Counter-Memorial on the Merits and Memorial on Jurisdiction of 6 October, 2015.

Biloune v. Ghana, Investment Centre, ILR, 95 (1994).

Biwater Gauff (Tanzania) Limited v. United Republic of Tanzania, ICSID Case No. ARB/05/22, Award of 24 July 2008.

British Petroleum v. Libya Award of 10 October 1973 and 1 August 1974, 53 ILR 297.

Burlington Resources Inc. v. Republic of Ecuador, ICSID Case No. ARB/08/5, Decision on Liability of 14 December, 2012.

Charanne (the Netherlands) and Construction Investments (Luxembourg) v. Spain, bajo las reglas de SCC, Laudo Final de 21 enero 2016.

Chemtura Corporation v. Canada, Ad hoc—UNCITRAL NAFTA, Award of 2 August, 2010.

Chorzów Factory (Germany v. Poland), 1928 PCIJ (ser. A) No. 17.

Clayton and Bilcon of Delaware Inc. v. Government of Canada, UNCITRAL, PCA Case No. 2009–04.

CMS Gas Transmition Company v. Argentina, Case N. ARB/01/8, Award of 12 May, 2005.

Commerce Group Corp. and San Sebastian Gold Mines, Inc. v. The Republic of El Salvador, ICSID Case No. ARB/09/17.

Compañía del Desarrollo de Santa Elena, S.A. v. The Republic Of Costa Rica, ICSID Case No. ARB/96/1, Final Award of 17 February, 2000.

Continental Casualty Company v. Argentina, ICSID Case No ARB/03/9, Award of 5 September, 2008.

Deutsche Bank AG v. Democratic Socialist Republic of Sri Lanka, ICSID Case No. ARB/09/2, Award of 31 October, 2012.

EDF (Services) Limited v. Romania, ICSID Case No. ARB/05/13, Award of 8 October 2009.

Electrabel S.A. v. The Republic of Hungary, ICSID Case No. ARB/07/19, Award on Jurisdiction, Applicable Law and Liability of 30 November 2012.

Elettronica Sicula S.p.A. (ELSI) (U.S. v. Italy), 1989 I.C.J. 15 of July 20.

Empresas Lucchetti, S.A. and Lucchetti Peru, S.A. v. Republic of Peru, ICSID Case No. ARB/03/4.

En Cana Corporation v Republic of Ecuador, (under UNCITRAL Rules), Award 3 February 2006

Enron Corporation and Ponderosa Assets, L.P. v. Argentine Republic, ICSID Case No. ARB/01/3, Decision on Jurisdiction of 14 January, 2004.

Enron Corporation and Ponderosa Assets, L.P. v. Argentina, ICSID Case No. ARB/01/3, Award of 22 May, 2007.

Ethyl Corporation v. the Governments of Canada, NAFTA, under UNCITRAL Rules.

Duke Energy Electroquil Partners & Electroquil S.A. v. Republic of Ecuador, ICSID Case No. ARB/04/19, Award of 18 August 2008.

Fedax N.V. v. Republic of Venezuela, ICSID Case No. ARB/96/3, Decision on Objections to Jurisdiction of 11 July 1997.

Fireman's Fund Insurance Company v. The United Mexican States, ICSID Additional Facility Case No. ARB(AF)/02/01, Award of 17 July 2006.

GAMI Investments v. Mexico, NAFTA – UNCITRAL Rules, Final Award of 15 November 2004.

GEA Group Aktiengesellschaft v. Ukraine, ICSID Case No. ARB/08/16, Award 31 March 2011.

Glamis Gold Ltd. v. United States of America, UNICTRAL Rules NAFTA, Award of 8 June, 2009.

Harza Engineering Company v. The Islamic Republic of Iran, Award No. 19-98-2 30 of December 1982.

Holiday Inns S.A. and others v. Morocco, ICSID Case No. ARB/72/1.

Impregilo S.p.A. v. Islamic Republic of Pakistan, ICSID Case No. ARB/03/3, Decision on Jurisdiction of 22 April 2005.

Impregilo S.p.A. v. Argentine Republic, ICSID Case No. ARB/07/17.

Joy Mining Machinery Limited v. The Arab Republic of Egypt, ICSID Case No. ARB/03/11, Award on Jurisdiction of 6 August, 2004.

BIBLIOGRAPHY

Khan Resources Inc., Khan Resources B.V. and Cauc Holding Company Ltd. v. the Government of Mongolia, PCA Case No. 2011–09, Award on the Merits of 2 March 2015.

Klöckner Industrie-Anlagen GmbH and others v. United Republic of Cameroon and Société Camerounaise des Engrais, ICSID Case No. ARB/81/2, Award of 21 October, 1983.

Kuwait v. American Independent Oil Company (Aminoil), Award of 24 March, 1982.

Libyan American Oil Company (LIAMCO) v. The Libyan Arab Republic, Ad Hoc Tribunal (Draft Convention on Arbitral Procedure, ILC 1958), Award of 12 April, 1977.

Marvin Roy Feldman Karpa v. The United Mexican State, ICSID Case No. ARB(AF)/99/1, Award of 16 December, 2002.

Metalclad Corporation v. United States of Mexico, ICSID Case No. ARB(AF)/97/1, Award of 30 August, 2000.

Methanex Corp. v. United States of America, UNCITRAL rules, Final Award of 3 August, 2005.

Niko Resources (Bangladesh) Ltd. v. Bangladesh Petroleum Exploration & Production Company Limited ('Bapex') and Bangladesh Oil Gas and Mineral Corporation ('Petrobangla'), ICSID Case No. ARB/10/18.

Occidental Exploration and Production Company v. The Republic of Ecuador, London Court of International Arbitration, Case No. UN3467, under UNCITRAL Rules, Award of 1 July, 2004.

Occidental Petroleum Corporation and Occidental Exploration and Production Company v. The Republic of Ecuador, ICSID Case No ARB/06/11, Award of 5 October, 2012.

Pac Rim Cayman LLC v. Republic of El Salvador, ICSID Case No. ARB/09/12.

Perenco Ecuador Ltd. v. The Republic of Ecuador and Empresa Estatal Petróleos del Ecuador (Petroecuador), ICSID Case No. ARB/08/6.

Phelps Dodge Corp., et at. v. Islamic Republic of Iran, Award No. 217-99-2 of March 19 of 1986.

Pope & Talbot v. Canada, (NAFTA) Interim Award 26 June 2000.

Quasar de Valores Sicav S.A., orgor De Valores Sicav S.A., GBI 9000 Sicav S.A., ALOS 34 S.L. v. The Russian Federation, SCC No. 24/2007, Award of 20 July, 2012.

Railroad Development Corporation v. Republic of Guatemala, ICSID Case No. ARB/07/23, Award of 23 May, 2013.

S.D. Myers, Inc. v. Canada, NAFTA First Partial, Award of 13 November, 2000.

Salini Costruttori S.P.A. and Italstrade S.P.A. v. Kingdom of Morocco, ICSID Case No. ARB/OO/4, Decision on Jurisdiction of 23 July, 2001.

Saluka Invstments BV (The Netherlands) v. Czech Republic, Partial Award of 17 March, 2006.

Sea-Land Service, Inc. v. The Islamic Republic of Iran, Ports and Shipping Organisation. Iran–US Claims Tribunal, Case 33.

Sedco, Inc., et al. v. National Iranian Oil Co., et al., Award No. ITL 55-129-3 of October 28, 1985.

Sergei Paushok et al. v. the Government of Mongolia, under UNCITRAL rules, Award on Jurisdiction and Liability of 28 April, 2011.

Southern Pacific Properties (Middle East) Ltd v. Arab Republic of Egypt, ICSID Case No ARB/84/3.

Spence International Investments, LLC, Bob F. Spence, Joseph M. Holsten, Brenda K. Copher, Ronald E. Copher, Brette E. Berkowitz, Trevor B. Berkowitz, Aaron C. Berkowitz and Glen Gremillion v. Costa Rica, ICSID Case No. UNCT/13/2, Submission of the United States of America of 17 April, 2015.

Suez, Sociedad General de Aguas de Barcelona S.A.,and InterAgua Servicios Integrales del Agua S.A. v. Argentine Republic, ICSID Case No. ARB/03/17, Decision On Liability of 30 July, 2010.

Suez, Sociedad General de Aguas de Barcelona S.A., and Vivendi Universal S.A. v. Argentina, ICSID Case No. ARB/03/19 and under UNCITRAL Rules *AWG Group v. Argentina*, Decision on Liability of July 30, 2010.

Sun Belt Inc. v. Government of Canada, Notice of Claim and Demand for Arbitration of 12 October, 1999.

Técnicas Medioambientales Tecmed, S.A. v. United Mexican States, ICSID Case No. ARB (AF)/00/2, Award of 29 May, 2003.

Teskoslovenska Obchodni Banka, A.S. v. The Slovak Republic, ICSID Case No. ARB/97/4, Decision on Jurisdiction of 24 May, 1999.

Tidewater Inc., Tidewater Investment SRL, Tidewater Caribe, C.A., et al. v. Venezuela, ICSID Case No. ARB/10/5, Award of 13 March, 2015.

Tippetts, Abbett, McCarthy, Stratton v. Government of the Islamic Republic of Iran, Award No. 141-7-2 of 22 June, 1984.

Total S.A. v. The Argentine Republic, ICSID Case No. ARB/04/1, Decision on Liability of 27 December, 2010.

Ulysseas, Inc. v. The Republic of Ecuador, UNCITRAL Rules, Final Award of 12 June, 2012.

Philip Morris Brands SARL, Philip Morris Products S.A. and ABAL Hermanos S.A. v. Oriental Republic of Uruguay, ICSID Case No. ARB/10/7, Award of 8 July, 2016.

Vattenfall AB, Vattenfal Europe AG, Vattenfal Europe Generation AG v. Federal Republic of Germany, (ICSID Case No. ARB/09/6).

Venezuela Holdings, B.V., et al. v. Venezuela, ICSID Case No. ARB/07/27, Award of 9 October, 2014.

Waste Management v. Mexico, ICSID Case Case No. ARB(AF)/00/3, Final Award of 30 April, 2004.

Other International Cases

Barcelona Traction, Light and Power Company, Limited (Belgium v. Spain), ICJ Reports, Judgement 5 February 1970.

BIBLIOGRAPHY 221

Gabčíkovo-Nagymaros Project (Hungary v. Slovakia), Judgment, ICJ Reports 1997.
L. F. H. Neer and Pauline Neer (U.S.A.) v. United Mexican States, Volume IV pp. 60–66 United Nations, 2006 (15 October 1926).
M/V 'SAIGA' (No.2) Case – Saint Vicent and The Grenadies v Guinea, International Tribunal for the Law of the Sea, Judgement of 1 July, 1999.
Oscar Chinn Case (United Kingdom v. Belgium), December 12 1934, 1934 P.C.I.J. Reports Series A/B No. 63.
Pulp Mills on the River Uruguay (Argentina v. Uruguay), Judgment ICJ Reports, 20 April, 2010.
S.S. Wimbledon (United Kingdom, France, Italy & Japan v Germany), 1923 P.C.I.J. (ser. A) No. 1, Aug 17, 1923.

World Trade Organisation

China – Measures Affecting Imports of Automobile Parts, Panel Report WT/DS339/R, WT/DS340/R, WT/DS342/R, adopted on 12 January 2009.
India – Patent Protection for Pharmaceutical and Agricultural Chemical Products India – Patents (US), WT/DS50/AB/R, adopted on 19 January 1998.

European Court of Human Rights

Baner v. Sweden, App No 11763/85, Decision, 9 March 1989, DR 60, 128.
Pine Valley Developments Ltd and Others v. Ireland, Judgment, 29 November 1991, ECHR Series A, No 222.
The James and Others v. the United Kingdom, 21, February 1986 ECHR, Series A, No. 98.

Supreme Court of the United States of America

Arkansas Game and Fish Commission v. United States of America (Case No. 11–597).
Charles River Bridge v. Warren Bridge, 36 U.S. 420 (1837).
Dartmouth College v. Woodward, 4 Wheat. 518, 629 (U.S. 1819).
Fletcher v. Peck, 10 U.S. (6 Cranch) 87, (U.S. 1810).
Frazier v. Brown, 12 Ohio St. 294, 311 (Ohio 1861).
Gibbons v. Ogden 22 U.S. (9 Wheat.) 1(U.S.1824).
Lingle v.Chevron U.S. A. INC. (04–163) 544 U.S. 528 (2005).
Loretto v. Tele Prompter Manhattan CATV Corp., 458 U. S. 419, 426 (1982).
Mugler v. Kansas 123 U.S. 623 (1887).

Penn Central Transportation Co v New York City, 366 N.E. 2d 1271 (NY 1977), affirmed 438 U.S. 104 (1978).

Pennsylvania Coal Co. v. Mahon, 260 U.S. 393 (1922) 260 U.S. 393, Decision of December 11, 1922.

State v. Martin, 168 Ohio St. 37, 151 N.E.2d 7 (1958).

United States v. Willow River Power Co., 324 U.S. 499 (1945), 510.

Secondary Sources

Abtahi, Robert. 'Indirect Expropriations in the Jurisprudence of the Iranunited States Claims Tribunal.' *Journal of Law and Conflict Resolution* 3, no. 7 (July 2011): 80–88.

Ahmed, Kamil Gerard, Jose E. Alvarez, Karl P. Sauvant, and Gabriela P. Vizcaino. *Columbia International Investment Conference: The Evolving International Investment Regime – Expectations, Realities, Options.* Oxford: Oxford University Press, 2011.

Alexander, Gregory S. *The Global Debate over Constitutional Property: Lessons for American Takings Jurisprudence.* Chicago: University of Chicago Press, 2006.

Allan, John A., Martin Keulertz, Suvi Sojamo, and Jeroen Warner, eds. *Handbook of Land and Water Grabs in Africa: Foreign Direct Investment and Food and Water Security.* Abingdon, New York: Routledge International, 2013.

Álvarez, José E. 'A Bit on Custom.' *New York University journal of international law and politics New York University Journal of International Law and Politics* 42, no. 1 (2009): 17–80.

Álvarez, José E. 'The Return of the State.' *Minnesota Journal of International Law* 20, no. 2 (2011): 223–64.

Alvik, Ivar. 'The Hybrid Nature of Investment Treaty Arbitration – Straddling the National/International Divide.' In *The New International Law: An Anthology*, edited by Christoffer C. Eriksen and Marius Emberland. 91–97. Leiden: Martinus Nijhoff Publishers, 2010.

American Law Institute. *Restatement of the Law, Second: Foreign Relations Law of the United States. As Adopted and Promulgated by the American Law Institute at Washington D.C. In May 26 1962.* St. Paul, Minn.: American Law Institute Publishers, 1965.

Anghie, Antony. *Imperialism, Sovereignty, and the Making of International Law,* Cambridge, UK; New York, NY: Cambridge University Press, 2005.

Asteriti, Alessandra. 'Regulatory Expropriation Claims in International Investment Arbitration: A Bridge Too Far?.' In Yearbook on International Investment Law and Policy 2012–2013, edited by Andrea K. Bjorklund. Oxford: Oxford University Press, 2014.

BIBLIOGRAPHY

Ball, Jane. 'The Boundaries of Property Rights in English Law.' *Electronic Journal of Comparative Law: Report to the XVIIth International Congress of Comparative Law* 10, no. 3 (July 2006).

Barlow, Maude, and Tony Clarke. *Blue Gold the Battle against Corporate Theft of the World's Water.* London: Earthscan Publications Ltd., 2003.

Barnes, Richard. *Property Rights and Natural Resources: Studies in International Law No. 19.* Oxford, Portland: Hart Publishing, 2009.

Baron Jane B., 'Rescuing the Bundle-of-Rights Metaphor in Property Law,' *University of Cincinnati Law Review* 82, no. 1, 2013.

Bates, Bryson C., Zbigniew Kundzewicz, Shaohong Wu, and Jean Palutikof. 'Climate Change and Water. Ipcc Technical Paper Iv.' Geneva: Intergovernmental Panel on Climate Change, 2008.

Martin Beniston, Markus Stoffel, and Margot Hill, 'Impacts of Climatic Change on Water and Natural Hazards in the Alps: Can Current Water Governance Cope with Future Challenges? Examples from the European "Acqwa" Project,' *ENVSCI Environmental Science and Policy* 14, 7 (2011), 738–39.

Bernasconi, Nathalie. 'Background Paper on Vattenfall V. Germany Arbitration.' Winnipeg: International Institute for Sustainable Development (IISD), 2009.

Bishop, R. Doak, and E. Etri James. 'International Commercial Arbitration in South America' *Available at:* http://www.kslaw.com/library/pdf/bishop3.pdf, last visited June 9, 2011.

Biswas, Asit K., and Cecilia Tortajada. *Impacts of Megaconferences on the Water Sector.* Berlin: Springer, 2009.

Bjorklund, Andrea K. 'Investment Treaty Arbitral Decisions as "Jurisprudence Constante".' In *International Economic Law: The State and Future of the Discipline* edited by Colin B. Picker, Isabella D. Bunn and Douglas W. Arner. 265–80. Oxford: Hart, 2008.

Bjorklund, Andrea K. 'Emergency Exceptions to International Obligations in the Realm of Foreign Investment: The State of Necessity and Force Majeure as Circumstances Precluding Wrongfulness.' *UC Davis Legal Studies Research Paper No. 99*

Bjorklund, Andrea K. 'Emergency Exceptions: State of Necessity and Force Majeure.' Chap. 12 In *The Oxford Handbook of International Investment Law*, edited by Peter Muchlinski, Ortino Federico and Christoph Schreuer. 459–523. New York: Oxford University Press, 2008.

Blackstone, William. *Commentaries on the Laws of England.* Vol. 1 – Books I & Ii. Chapter I. Vol. Available at: http://oll.libertyfund.org/index.php?option=com_content&task=view&id=1415&Itemid=262,1893.

Bodansky, Daniel. 'The Legitimacy of International Governance: A Coming Challenge for International Environmental Law?.' *American Journal of International Law* 93 (1999): 593–624.

Boehm, Frédéric. 'Regulatory Capture Revisited – Lessons from Economics of Corruption.' *Working Paper* (2007).

Boisson de Chazournes, Laurence, Christina Leb and Mara Tignino, eds. *International Law and Freshwater. The multiple challenges.* Cheltenham: Elgar Publishing, 2013.

Borchard, Edwin. 'The "Mininmum Standard" of the Treatment of Aliens.' *American Society of International Law: Proceedings. Thirty-Third Annual Meeting. April 27–29* 33 (1939): 52–63.

Borquin, Juliane R., and A. Matthews. 'Modern Approach to Groundwater Allocation Disputes: Cline V. American Aggregates Corporation.' *J. Energy Law Policy* 7:2 (1986): 361–76.

Brower, Charles N., and Sadie Blanchard. 'From "Dealing in Virtue" to "Profiting from Injustice": The Case against Re-Statification of Investment Dispute Settlement – 2013 Harvard International Law Journal Symposium Keynote Address.' *TDM Journal* 10, no. 4 (2013).

Brown Weiss, Edith, Laurence Boisson de Chazournes, and Nathalie Bernasconi-Osterwalder, eds. *Fresh Water and International Economic Law.* Oxford; New York: Oxford University Press, 2005.

Brownlie, Ian. *Principles of Public International Law*, 7th ed. Oxford: Oxford University Press, 2008.

Buckley, Neil. 'Russia's Yukos threats signal a lurch away from international law,' Financial Times, 5 August 2015.

Burke-White, William W., and Andreas Von Staden. 'Investment Protection in Extraordinary Times: The Interpretation and Application of Non-Precluded Measures Provisions in Bilateral Investment Treaties.' *University of Pennsylvania Law School* Public Law and Legal Theory Research Paper Series, no. Research Paper No. #07-14 (2007).

Callies, David L., and Calvert G. Chipchase. 'Water Regulation, Land Use and the Environment.' *University of Hawai'i Law Review* 30 (2007): 49–96.

Camacho, Alejandro. 'Adapting Governance to Climate Change: Managing Uncertainty through a Learning Infrastructure.' *Emory Law Journal* 59 (2009).

Caponera, Dante A. 'Possible Contents of and Reasons for Water Law.' Chap. 7 In *Principles of Water Law and Administration: National and International*, edited by Dante A. Caponera and Marcella Nanni. 133–59: Routledger – Taylor & Francis, 2007.

Caponera, Dante Augusto *Principles of Water Law and Administration: National and International.* Rotterdam: A.A. Balkema, 1992.

Carlston, Kenneth S. 'Concession Agreements and Nationalization.' *The American Journal of International Law* 52, no. 2 (1958): 260–79.

Chang, Howard F. 'Risk Regulation, Endogenous Public Concerns, and the Hormones Dispute: Nothing to Fear but Fear Itself?' *Public Law and Legal Theory Research Paper Series* Research Paper No. 39.Available at SSRN: http://ssrn.com/

BIBLIOGRAPHY

abstract=432220 or http://dx.doi.org/10.2139/ssrn.432220, last visited July 12, 2013 (2003).

Chiati, A.Z. El. *Protection of Investment in the Context of Petroleum Agreements*. Recueil Des Cours. Vol. 204, The Hague: The Hague Academy of International Law, 1987.

Christie, G.C. 'What Constitutes a Taking of Property under International Law.' *The British Yearbook of International Law* 38 (1964): 307–38.

Ciriacy-Wantrup, S.V., and Richard C. Bishop. '"Common Property" as a Concept in Natural Resources Policy.' *Natural Resources Journal* 15 (1975): 713–28.

Coe, Jack J. Jr. 'Denial of Justice and Nafta Chapter Eleven the Mondev Award.' *International Arbitration News* Winter/ Spring 3, no. 2 (2003).

Coe, Jack Jr., and Noah Rubins. 'Regulatory Expropriation and the Tecmed Case: Context and Contributions.' In *International Investment Law and Arbitration: Leading Cases from the ICSID, NAFTA, Bilateral Treaties and Customary International Law* edited by Tod Weiler. 597–667. London: Cameron May, 2005.

Conca, Ken. *Governing Water: Contentious Transnational Politics and Global Institution Building*. Cambridge: MIT Press, 2005.

Cordonier Segger, Marie-Claire, Markus W. Gehring, and Andrew Newcombe, eds. *Sustainable Development in World Investment Law*, Global Trade Law Series. Alphen aan den Rijn Kluwer Law International, 2011.

Costamagna, Francesco. 'Investor's Rights and State Regulatory Autonomy: The Role of the Legitimate Expectation Principle in the CMS v. Argentina Case' in *Transnational Dispute Management* 3, no. 2 (2006).

Cotula, Lorenzo. *Land Deals in Africa: What Is in the Contracts?* London: International Institute for Environment and Development, 2011.

Cotula, Lorenzo, 'Stabilization Clauses and the Evolution of Environmental Standards in Foreign Investment Contracts.' *Yearbook of International Environmental Law* 17 (2006): 111–38.

Crawford, James, *The International Law Commission's Articles on State Responsibility* (Cambridge: Cambridge University Press, 2002).

Crawford, James. 'Continuity and Discontinuity in International Dispute Settlement: An Inaugural Lecture.' *Journal of International Dispute Settlement* 1, no. 1 (2010): 3–24.

Cullet, Philippe. 'Water Law in a Globalised World: The Need for a New Conceptual Framework.' *Journal of Environmental Law* Advance Access published 18 May 2011 (2011).

Cumming, Joseph, and Robert Froehlich. 'Nafta Chapter Xi and Canada's Environmental Sovereignty: Investment Flows, Article 1110 and Alberta's Water Act.' *University of Toronto Faculty of Law Review* 65 (2007): 107–35.

Dalhuisen, H. Jan, and Andrew T. Guzman. 'Expropriatory and Non-Expropriatory Takings under International Investment Law.' *UC Berkeley Public Law Research Paper No. 2137107* (2012).

Declaration of the High-Level Conference on World Food Security: The Challenges of Climate Change and Bioenergy. edited by FAO, WFP and IFAD. Rome, June 5 2008.

Dellapenna, Joseph W. 'United States: The Allocation of Surface Waters.' Chap. 12 in *The Evolution of the Law and Politics of Water*, edited by Joseph W. Dellapenna and Joyeeta Gupta. Springer, 2009.

Dellapenna, Joseph, and Joyeeta Gupta. 'Toward Global Law on Water.' *Global Governance* 14 (2008): 437–53.

Delmon, Jeffrey. 'Understanding Options for Public-Private Partnerships in Infrastructure Sorting out the Forest from the Trees: Bot, Dbfo, Dcmf, Concession, Lease....' Washington: Finance Economics & Urban Department Finance and Guarantees Unit – World Bank, 2010.

Demsetz, Harold. 'Toward a Theory of Property Rights.' *The American Economic Review* 57, no. 2 (1967): 347–59.

Denny, Collins. 'The Growth and Development of the Police Power of the State.' *Michigan Law Review* 20, no. 2 (1921): 173–214.

Desierto, Diane A. 'Conflict of Treaties, Interpretation, and Decision-Making on Human Rights and Investment During Economic Crises.' *Transnational Dispute Management* 1 (2013).

Dimple Roy, Jane Barr, and Henry David Venema. 'Ecosystems Approaches in Integrated Water Resources Management (IWRM). A Review of Transboundary River Basins' (International Institute for Sustainable Development (IISD) and UNEP-DHI Centre for Water and Environment, August 2011).

Dolzer, Rudolf. 'New Fundations of the Law of Expropriation of Alien Property.' *American Journal of International Law* 75 (1981): 553–89.

Dolzer, Rudolf. 'Indirect Expropriations: New Developments?.' *New York University Environmental Law Journal* 11 (2002): 64–93.

Dolzer, Rudolf, and Christoph Schreuer. *Principles of International Investment Law* [in English]. 2nd ed. Oxford: Oxford University Press, 2012.

Dolzer, Rudolf, and Felix Bloch. 'Indirect Expropriation: Conceptual Realignments?.' *International Law Forum du Droit International* (2003): 155–65.

Dolzer, Rudolf, and Margrete Stevens. *Bilateral Investment Treaties*. The Hague: Martinus Nijhoff, 1995.

Dolzer, Rudolph, and Christoph Schreuer. *Principles of International Investment Law*. Oxford: Oxford University Press, 2008.

Doremus, Holly. 'Takings and Transitions.' *Journal of Land Use* 19, no. 1 (2003): 1–46.

Douglas, Zachary. 'The Hybrid Foundations of Investment Treaty Arbitration.' *The British Yearbook of international Law* 74 (2003): 151–289.

Douglas, Zachary. *The International Law of Investment Claims*. Cambridge: Cambridge University Press, 2009.

Douglas, Zachary. 'Property, Investment and the Scope of Investment Protection Obligations.' In *The Foundations of International Investment Law*, edited by Joost

BIBLIOGRAPHY

Pauwelyn and Jorge E. Viñuales Zachary Douglas. Oxford Oxford University Press, 2013.

Dukhovny, Victor and Vadim I. Sokolov. *Integrated Water Resources Management: Experience and Lessons Learned from Central Asia – Towards the Fourth World Water Forum*. Tashkent: GWP–CACENA, 2005.

Eberhardt, Pia, and Cecilia Olivet. *Profiting from Injustice – How Law Firms, Arbitrators and Financiers Are Fuelling an Investment Arbitration Boom*. Published by Corporate Europe Observatory and the Transnational Institute, 2012.

Ellickson, Robert C. 'Property in Land.' *Yale Law Journal* 102 (1992–1993): 1315–400.

Emmerich, Vattel. *The Law of Nations of the Principles of Natural Law*. Available at http://www.lonang.com/exlibris/vattel/vatt-208.htm, last visited 2 June 2011, 1758.

Epstein, Richard A. 'The Historical Variation in Water Rights.' In *The Evolution of Markets for Water: Theory and Practice in Australia*, edited by Jeff Bennett. New Horizons in Environmental Economics. Cheltenham: Edward Elgar, 2005.

Fennell, Lee Anne. 'Ostrom's Law: Property Rights in the Commons.' *International Journal of the Commons* 5, no. 1 (February 2011): 9–27.

Finger, Matthias, and Geremy Allouche. *Water Privatisation*. London: Spon Press, 2002.

Finnegan, William. 'Letter from Bolivia. Leasing the Rain: The Race to Control Water Turns Violent,' (The New Yorker, April 8, 2002): 43–53.

Fischel, William A. *Regulatory Takings: Law, Economics and Politics*. Cambridge: Harvard University Press, 1995.

Fortier, L. Yves, and Stephen L. Drymer. 'Indirect Expropriation in the Law of International Investment: I Know It When I See It, or Caveat Investor.' *ICSID review: Foreign investment law journal* 19, no. 2 (2004): 293–327.

Foster, Vivien, and Tito Yepes. 'Is Cost Recovery a Feasible Objective for Water and Electricity? The Latin American Experience.' *World Bank Policy Research* Working Paper 3943 (2006).

Francioni, Francesco. 'Compensation for Nationalisation of Foreign Property: The Borderland between Law and Equity.' *The International and Comparative Law Quarterly* 24, no. 2 (1975): 255–83.

Franck, Thomas M. *Fairness in International Law and Institutions*. Oxford: Oxford University Press, 1995.

Franck, Susan D. 'The Legitimacy Crisis in Investment Treaty Arbitration: Privatizing Public International Law through Inconsistent Decisions.' *Fordham Law Review* 73 (March 2005): 1521–38.

Franck, Susan D. 'Empirically Evaluating Claims About Investment Treaty Arbitration.' *The North Carolina Law Review* 86, no. 1 (2007): 1–87.

Freund, Ernst. 'The Police Power Public Policy and Constitutional Rights.' Chicago: Callaghan & Company, 1904.

Gleick, Peter H., and Jon Lane. 'Large International Water Meetings: Time for a Reappraisal.' *Water International* 30, no. 3 (2005): 410–14.

Grant, Douglas L. 'Esa Reductions in Reclamation of Water Contract Deliveries: A Fifth Amendment Taking of Property?' *Environmental Law* 36, no. 4 (2006): 1331–82.

Gray, Janice. 'Legal Approaches to the Ownership, Management and Regulation of Water from Riparian Rights to Commodification.' *Transforming Cultures* 1, no. 2 (2006): 64–96.

Green, C. 'If Only Life Were That Simple; Optimism and Pessimism in Economics.' *Physics and Chemistry of the Earth* 25, no. 3 (2000): 205–12.

Griffin, Ronald C. *Water Resources Economics. The Analysis of Scarcity, Policies and Projects.* Cambridge, Mass.: MIT Press, 2006.

Gross, Leo. 'The Peace of Westphalia, 1648–1948.' *American Journal of International Law* 42, no. 1 (1948): 20–41.

Guasch, J. Luis, Jean Jacques Laffont, and Stéphane Straub. 'Concessions of Infrastructure in Latin America: Government-Led Renegotiation.' *Journal of Applied Econometrics* 22, no. 7 (2007): 1267–94.

Hall, David, and Emanuele Lobina. 'Water as a Public Service.' Public Services International, 2006.

Heiskanen, Veijo. 'The Contribution of the Iran-United States Claims Tribunal to the Development of the Doctrine of Indirect Expropriation.' *International law FORUM du droit international: The Journal of the International Law Association International Law Forum du droit international* 5, no. 3 (2003): 176–87.

Henckels, Caroline. 'Indirect Expropriation and the Right to Regulate: Revisiting Proportionality Analysis and the Standard of Review in Investor-State Arbitration.' *Journal of International Economic Law* 15, no. 1 (2012): 223–55.

Hendry, Sarah Marjorie. 'An Analytical Framework for Reform of National Water Law.' PhD Thesis, Water Law, Dundee, 2008.

Henkin, L. 'That "S" Word: Sovereignty, and Globalization, and Human Rights, Et Cetera.' *Fordham Law Review* 68, no. 1 (1999): 1–14.

Higgins, Rosalyn. 'The Taking of Property by the State. Recent Developments in International Law.' *Recueil des Cours (The Hage Academy of International Law)* T. 176 (1982): 259–392.

Hirsh, Moshe. 'Sources of International Investment Law.' In *International Investment Law and Soft Law*, edited by Andrea K. Bjorklund and August Reinisch. Cheltenham, UK; Northampton, MA: Edward Elgar Pub., 2012.

Hodgson, Stephen. 'Modern Water Rights. Theory and Practice.' Rome: Development Law Service FAO Legal Office, Food and Agriculture Organization of the United Nations, 2006.

Hoffmann, Anne. 'Indirect Expropriation.' In *Standards of Investment Protection*, edited by August Reinisch. Oxford; New York: Oxford University Press, 2008.

BIBLIOGRAPHY

Howland, Douglas, and Luise White. 'The State of Sovereignty Territories, Laws, Populations.' Indiana University Press, available at: http://public.eblib.com/EBLPublic/PublicView.do?ptiID=437616, last visited 10 July 2011.

Hughes, D.A., and S.J.L. Malloryb. 'The Importance of Operating Rules and Assessments of Beneficial Use in Water Resource Allocation Policy and Management.' *Water Policy* 11 (2009): 131–41.

International Conference on Freshwater. 'Bonn Recomendations for Action.' Bonn, 3–7 December, 2001.

International Law Commission. 'Yearbook of the International Law Commission 1959 – Volume II. Documents of the Eleventh Session Including the Report of the Commission to the General Assembly.' New York: United Nations, 1959.

Jackson, John H. 'Dispute Settlement and the WTO. Emerging Problems.' *Journal of International Economic Law* 1, no. 3 (1998): 329–52.

Joskow, Paul L. 'Regulation of Natural Monopolies.' In *05–008 WP*. Boston: Center for Energy and Environmental Policy Research, 2005.

Kahn, Alfred E. *The Economics of Regulation. Principles and Institutions.* London: Massachusetts Institute of Technology, 1988.

Kantor, Mark. 'Little Has Changed in the New US Model Bilateral Investment Treaty.' *ICSID review: Foreign investment law journal* 27, no. 2 (2012): 335–78.

Kinnear, Meg N., Andrea K. Bjorklund, and John F.G. Hannaford. *Investment Disputes under Nafta. An Annotated Guide to Nafta Chapter 11.* Alphen aan den Rijn Kluwer Law International, 2006.

Klabbers, Jan. 'Clinching the Concept of Sovereignty: Wimbledon Redux.' *Austrian Review of International and European Law* 3, no. 3 (1998): 345–67.

Klein, Michael. 'Economic Regulation of Water Companies.' Washington: World Bank, 1996.

Kolo, Abba, and Thomas Waelde. 'Environmental Regulation, Investment Protection and "Regulatory Taking" in International Law.' *International and Comparative Law Quarterly* 50, no. 4 (2001): 811–48.

Koskenniemi, Martti. *The Gentle Civilizer of Nations: The Rise and Fall of International Law, 1870–1960* Cambridge, UK; New York: Cambridge University Press, 2002.

Koskenniemi, Martti. *From Apology to Utopia* New York: Cambridge University Press, 2005.

Koskenniemi, Martti. 'What Use for Sovereignty Today?' *Asian Journal of International Law* I (2011): 61–70.

Krajewski, Markus. 'Role of Sustainable Development in the Context of Expropriation,' in *Shifting Paradigms in International Investment Law: More Balanced, Less Isolated, Increasingly Diversified*, ed. Steffen Hindelang and Markus Krajewski (Oxford: Oxford University Press, 2016): 84–96.

Kriebaum, Ursula. 'Partial Expropriation.' [In English]. *The journal of world investment & trade The Journal of World Investment & Trade* 8, no. 1 (2007): 69–84.

Kriebaum, Ursula. 'Regulatory Takings: Balancing the Interests of the Investor and the State.' *The Journal of Word Investment & Trade* 8, no. 5 (October 2007): 717–44.

Kuhn, Arthur K. 'The International Conference on the Treatment of Foreigners.' *The American Journal of International Law* 24, no. 3 (1930): 570–73.

Kuks, Stefan M.M. 'The Privatisation Debate on Water Services in the Netherlands: Public Performance of the Water Sector and the Implications of Market Forces.' *Water Policy* 8 (2006): 147–69.

Kundzewicz, Z.W., L.J. Mata, N.W. Arnell, P. Döll, P. Kabat, B. Jiménez, K.A. Miller, T. Oki, Z. Sen and I.A. Shiklomanov, *2007: Freshwater resources and their management*, in M.L. Parry, O.F. Canziani, J.P. Palutikof, P.J. van der Linden and C.E. Hanson, eds, *Climate Change 2007: Impacts, Adaptation and Vulnerability. Contribution of Working Group II to the Fourth Assessment Report of the Intergovernmental Panel on Climate Change* (Cambridge: Cambridge University Press, 2007).

Lalive, Pierre. 'The First "World Bank" Arbitration (Holiday Inns V. Morocco): Some Legal Problems.' *British Yearbook of International Law* 51 (1982): 123–61.

Lalive, Pierre. 'On the Reasoning of International Arbitral Awards.' *Journal of International Dispute Settlement* 1, no. 1 (2010): 55–65.

Lang, Andrew. 'The Gats and Regulatory Autonomy: A Case Study of the Social Regulation of the Water Industry.' *Journal of International Economic Law* 7, no. 4 (December 2004).

Lehavi, Amnon. 'Mixing Property.' *Seton Hall Law Review* 38, no. 1 (2007): 137–212.

Lehavi, Amnon, and Amir N. Licht. 'Bits and Pieces of Property.' *The Yale Journal of International Law* 36, no. 1 (2011): 115–66.

Lentini, Roberto. 'Servicios De Agua Potable y Saneamiento: Lecciones De Experiencias Relevantes.' Santiago: CEPAL and Ministerio Federal de Cooperacion Economica y Desarrollo, 2011.

Leshy, John D. 'A Conversation About Takings and Water Rights.' *Texas Law Review* 83, no. 7 (2005): 1985–2026.

Levesque, Celine. 'Investment and Water Resources: Limits to Nafta.' Chaper 17 In *Sustainable Development in World Investment Law*, edited by Marie-Claire Cordonier Segger, Markus W. Gehring and Andrew Newcombe. Global Trade Law Series, 409–28. Alphen aan den Rijn: Kluwer Law International 2011.

Lewis, Kristen, ed. *Water Governance for Poverty Reduction: Key Issues and the Undp Response to Millenium Development Goals*. New York: Water Governance Programme, Bureau for Development Policy, UNDP, 2004.

Lowe, Vaughan. 'Regulation or Expropriation?.' *Current legal problems* 55 (2002): 447–66.

BIBLIOGRAPHY

Lowe, Vaughan. 'Changing Dimensions of International Investment Law.' *Oxford Legal Studies* Research Paper No. 4/2007 (March 2007).

Mann, Howard. 'Implications of International Trade and Investment Agreements for Water and Water Services: Some Responses from Other Sources of International Law.' available at: http://www.idrc.ca/en/ev-102451-201-1-DO_TOPIC.html.

Mann, Howard. 'The Right of States to Regulate and International Investment Law.' In *Expert Meeting on the Development Dimension of FDI: Policies to Enhance the Role of FDI in Support of the Competitiveness of the Enterprise Sector and the Economic Performance of Host Economies, Taking into Account the Trade/Investment Interface, in the National and International Context.* Geneva, 2002.

Mann, Howard. 'Who Owns "Your" Water? Reclaiming Water as a Public Good under International Trade and Investment Law.' *International Institute for Sustainable Development* (2003).

Mann, Howard. 'International Economic Law: Water for Money's Sake.' *International Institute for Sustainable Development* (2004).

Mann, Howard and Konrad von Moltke. 'Nafta's Chapter 11 and the Environment: Addressing the Impacts of the Investor-State Process on the Environment.' *International Institute for Sustainable Development, Publication Centre* (1999).

Marboe, Irmgard. 'Quasar De Valores Sicav Sa and Others v. the Russian Federation: Another Chapter of the Yucos Affair.' *ICSID Review* 28, no. 2 (2013): 247–53.

Marin, Philippe. 'Public-Private Partnerships for Urban Water Utilities a Review of Experiences in Developing Countries.' Washington: World Bank, 2009.

Marrella, Fabrizio. 'On the Changing Structure of International Investment Law: The Human Right to Water and ICSID Arbitration.' *International Community Law Review* 12, no. 3 (2010): 335–59.

McCrudden, Christopher. *Regulation and Deregulation. Policy and Practice in the Utilities and Financial Services Industries.* Oxford: Clarendon Press, 1999.

McLachlan, Campbell. 'The Principle of Systemic Integration and Article 31(3) (C) of the Vienna Convention.' *International and comparative law quarterly.* 54, no. 2 (2005): 279–319.

McLachlan, Campbell. 'Investment Treaties and General International Law' *International and Comparative Law Quarterly* 57 (April 2008): 361–401.

McLachlan QC, Campbell, Laurence Shore, Matthew Weiniger, and Loukas Mistelis. *International Investment Arbitration: Substantive Principles.* Edited by Oxford International Arbitration Series New York: Oxford University Press, 2007.

Mendelson, Wallace. 'New Light on Fletcher V. Peck and Gibbons v. Ogden' *The Yale Law Journal* 58, no. 4 (1949): 567–73.

Millennium Ecosystem Assessment. 'MA Conceptual Framework' Chap. 1 In *Ecosystems and Human Well-Being: Current State and Trends, Volume 1: Findings of the*

Condition and Trends Working Group of the Millennium Ecosystem Assessment, edited by Rashid Hassan, Robert Scholes and Neville Ash. Washington, Covelo, London: Island Press, 2003.

Montt, Santiago. *State Liability in Investment Treaty Arbitration. Global Constitutional and Administrative Law in the BIT Generation*. Portland: Hart Publishing, 2009.

Muchlinski, Peter. "'Caveat Investor'"? The Relevance of the Conduct of the Investor under the Fair and Equitable Treatment Standard.' *International and Comparative Law Quarterly* 55 (July 2005): 527–58.

Muñoz, Hugo A. 'La Administración Del Agua Y La Inversión Extranjera Directa ¿Cómo Se Relacionan?.' In *Estudios En Homenaje Al Dr. Rafael González Ballar*, edited by Universidad de Costa Rica (UCR). San Jose: Isolma S.A., 2009.

Nagan, Winston P., and Craig Hammer. 'The Changing Character of Sovereignty in International Law and International Relations.' *Columbia Journal of Transnational Law* 43, no. 1 (2004): 141–87.

Navajas, Sergio. 'El Servicio De Agua Potable y Desagues Cloacales En Buenos Aires.' In *La Regulación De La Competencia y De Los Servicios Públicos. Teoria y Experiencia Argentina Reciente* Buenos Aires: Fundación de Investigaciones Economicas Latinoamericanas, 1999.

Neuman, Janet C. 'Adaptive Management: How Water Law Needs to Change.' *Envtl. L. Rep.* 31 (2001): 11432–37.

Newcombe, Andrew. 'The Boundaries of Regulatory Expropriation in International Law.' *ICSID Review* 20, no. 1 (2005).

Newcombe, Andrew, and Lluís Paradell. *Law and Practice of Investment Treaties: Standards of Treatment* Alphen aan den Rijn: Kluwer Law, International. Wolters Kluwer, 2009.

Newcombe, Andrew, Lluís Paradell, and International Kluwer Law. *Law and Practice of Investment Treaties: Standards of Treatment* Alphen aan den Rijn: Wolters Kluwer, 2009.

Nikièma, Suzy H. 'Best Practices Indirect Expropriation.' Winnipeg, Man. International Institute for Sustainable Development, 2012.

North, Douglas. 'Economic Performance through Time.' *American Economic Review* 84, no. 3 (1994): 369–68.

Nowrot, Karsten. *International Investment Law and the Republic of Ecuador from Arbitral Bilateralism to Judicial Regionalism*. Halle (Saale): Institute of Economic Law, 2010.

O'Neill, Timothy. 'Water and Freedom: The Privatization of Water and Its Implications for Democracy and Human Rights in the Developing World.' *Colorado Journal of International Environmental Law and Policy* 17, no. 2 (2006): 357–83.

OECD Draft Convention on Foreign Property, 12 October 1967.

OECD Directorate for Financial and Enterprise Affairs. '"Indirect Expropriation" and the "Right to Regulate" in International Investment Law.' Paris: Organisation for Economic Co-operation and Development, 2004.

OECD Secretariat. 'Draft OECD Principles for International Investor Participation in Infrastructure.' In *OECD Global Forum on International Investment. Enhancing the Investment Climate: the Case of Infrastructure*. Istanbul, Turkey: OECD, 2006.

Ogus, Anthony. *Regulation. Legal Form and Economic Theory*. Oxford: Clarendon Press, 1994.

Organisation for Economic Co-operation and Development. 'Managing Water for All: An Oecd Perspective on Pricing and Financing. Key Messages for Policy Makers.' Paris: OECD, 2009.

Orr, Stuart, Anton Cartwright, and Dave Tickner. 'Understanding Water Risks a Primer on the Consequences of Water Scarcity for Government and Business.' World Wildlife Fund, 2009.

Ortino, Federico. 'Legal Reasoning of International Investment Tribunals: A Typology of Egregious Failures.' Journal of International Dispute Settlement 3, no. 1 (2012): 31–52.

Ostrom, Elinor. 'Private and Common Property Rights.' In *Encyclopedia of Law and Economics: Civil Law and Economics*, edited by Gerrit De Geets and Bouckaert Boudewijn. Gent: Cheltenham, Edward Elgar, 2000.

Owen, David Lloyd *Pinsent Masons Water Yearbook 2007–2008*. London: Pinsent Masons, 2007.

Pahl-Wostl, Claudia, Joyeeta Gupta, and Daniel Petry. 'Governance and the Global Water System: A Theoretical Exploration.' *Global Governance* 14 (2008): 419–35.

Palaniappan, Meena, and Peter H. Gleick. 'Peak Water.' Chap. 1 In *The World's Water 2008–2009: The Biennial Report on Freshwater Resources*, edited by Peter H. Gleick, Heather Cooley, Michael Cohen, Mari Morikawa, Jason Morrison and Meena Palaniappan. Washington: Pacific Institute for Studies in Development, Environment and Security, 2009.

Paparinskis, Martins. 'Regulatory Expropriation and Sustainable Development.' In *Sustainable Development in International Investment Law*, edited by M.C. Cordonnier-Segger and A. Newcombe M.W. Gehring. Kluwer Law International, 2010.

Park, William W. Yanos Alexander A. 'Treaty Obligations and National Law: Emerging Conflicts in International Arbitration.' *The Hastings Law Journal* 58, no. 2 (2006): 251.

Parvanov, Parvan, and Mark Kantor. 'Comparing U.S. Law and Recent U.S. Investment Agreements: Much More Similar Than You Might Expect.' In *Yearbook on International Investment Law and Policy*, edited by Karl P. Sauvant. New York: Oxford University Press, 2010–2011.

Paulsson, Jan. 'Arbitration without Privity.' *Foreign Investment Law Journal* 10, no. 2 (1995): 232–57.

Paulsson, Jan. 'Indirect Expropriation: Is the Right to Regulate at Risk?' In *Making the Most of International Investment Aagreements: A Common Agenda*, edited by Organisation for Economic Co-operation and Development. Paris, 2005.

Pauwelyn, Joost. *Conflict of Norms in Public International Law: How Wto Law Relates to Other Rules of International Law* Cambridge, UK; New York: Cambridge University Press, 2003.

Perkams, Markus. 'The Concept of Indirect Expropriation in Comparative Public Law – Searching for Light in the Dark.' Chap. 4 In *International Investment Law and Comparative Public Law*, edited by Stephan Schill. Oxford; New York: Oxford University Press, 2010.

Pindyck, Robert S., and Daniel L. Rubinfeld. *Microeconomics*. Sixth ed. New Delhi: Prentice Hall of India, 2006.

Poirier, Marc. R. 'The Virtue of Vagueness in Takings Doctrine.' Cardozo Law Review 24 (2002): 93–192.

Poirier, Marc R. 'The Nafta Chapter 11 Expropriation Debate through the Eyes of a Property Theorist.' *Environmental law* 33 (2003): 851–928.

Porterfield, Matthew. 'International Expropriation Rules and Federalism.' *Stanford Environmental Law Journal* 23, no. 3 (2004).

Postel, Sandra L. 'Securing Water for People, Crops, and Ecosystems: New Mindset and New Priorities.' *Natural Resources Forum* 27, no. 2 (2003): 89–98.

Poulos, Andrew 'Australia: Senate Passes Economic Protection and Biodiversity Conservation "Water Trigger" Bill.' *Mondaq*, 2013.

Public-Private Infrastructure Advisory Facility. World Bank. *Approaches to Private Participation in Water Services: A Toolkit*. Washington, DC: International Bank for Reconstruction and Development/World Bank, 2006.

Rahaman Mizanur, Muhammad, and Olli Varis. 'Integrated Water Resources Management: Evolution, Prospects and Future Challenges.' *Sustainability: Science, Practice, & Policy* – http://ejournal.nbii.org 1, no. 1 (2005).

Reed, Lucy, and Daina Bray. 'Fair and Equitable Treatment: Fairly and Equitably Applied in Lieu of Unlawful Indirect Expropriation?.' In *Contemporary Issues in International Arbitration and Mediation: The Fordham Papers 2007*, edited by Arthur W. Rovine. 13–27. Leiden; Boston: Martinus Nijhoff Publishers, 2008.

Reidy, Joseph M. 'Cline V. American Aggregates Corp. An Ohio Waterloo?.' *Capital University Law Review* 13 (1983–1984): 683–98.

Reinisch, August. 'Expropriation.' Chap. 11 In *The Oxford Handbook of International Investment Law*, edited by Peter Muchlinski, Federico Ortino and Christoph Schreuer. Oxford; New York: Oxford University Press, 2008.

Reinisch, August. 'Legality of Expropriations.' Chaper 9 In *Standards of Investment Protection*, edited by August Reinisch. Oxford: Oxford University Press, 2008.

Reinisch, August, ed. *Standards of Investment Protection*. Oxford: Oxford University Press, 2008.

Reisman, W. Michael. 'The Evolving International Standard and Sovereignty.' Paper presented at the The Future of International Law, Washington DC, 2007.

Reisman, W. Michael. '"Case Specific Mandates" Versus "Systemic Implications": How Should Investment Tribunals Decide? – the Freshfields Arbitration Lecture.' *Arbitration International* 29, no. 2 (2013): 131–52.

Reisman, W. Michael and Digon Rocio. 'Eclipse of Expropriation?.' In *Contemporary Issues in International Arbitration and Mediation: The Fordham Papers, ed by Arthur W Rovine* Leiden: Nijhoff, 2009: 27–46.

Reisman, W. Michael, and Sloane Robert D. 'Indirect Expropriation and Its Valuation in the BIT Generation.' *British Yearbook of International Law* (2004): 115–50.

Rieu-Clarke, Alistair, and Flavia Rocha Loures. 'Still Not in Force: Should States Support the 1997 Un Watercourses Convention?.' *Review of European Community & International Environmental Law* 18, no. 2 (2009): 185–97.

Roberts, Anthea. 'The Next Battleground: Standards of Review in Investment Treaty Arbitration.' *International Council for Commercial Arbitration Congress Series* 16 (2011): 170–80.

Rogers, Peter, and Alan W. Hall. 'Effective Water Governance.' Stockholm: Global Water Partnership. Technical Committee (TEC), 2003.

Root, Elihu. 'The Basis of Protection to Citizens Residing Abroad.' *American Journal of International Law* 4, no. 3 (1910): 517–28.

Rose, Carol. 'Property and Expropriation: Themes and Variations in American Law.' *Utah Law Review* 1 (2000): 1–38.

Sacerdoti, Giorgio. 'Bilateral Treaties and Multilateral Instruments on Investment Protection.' In *Recueil Des Cours: Collected Courses of the Hague Academy of International Law*, edited by The Hague Academy of International Law. The Hague: Martinus Nijhoff Publishers, 1997.

Sadoff, Claudia W., and Mike Muller. 'Perspectives on Water and Climate Change Adaptation. Better Water Resources Management – Greater Resilience Today, More Effective Adaptation Tomorrow.' Stockholm: Global Water Partnership, 2009.

Salman, Salman M.A. 'The United Nations Watercourses Convention Ten Years Later: Why Has Its Entry into Force Proven Difficult?' *Water International.* 32, no. 1 (2007): 1.

Salman, Salman M.A. 'Downstream Riparians Can Also Harm Upstream Riparians: The Concept of Foreclosure of Future Uses.' *Water International* 35, no. 4 (2010): 350–64.

Salman, Salman M.A., and Daniel D. Bradlow. *Regulatory Frameworks for Water Resources Management: A Comparative Study.* Washington: The World Bank, 2006.

Sampliner, Gary H. 'Arbitration of Expropriation Cases under U.S. Investment Treaties: A Threat to Democracy or the Dog Didn't Bark?' *ICSID Review: Foreign investment law journal* 18, no. 1 (2003): 1–43.

Sánchez-Moreno, Maria, and Tracy MacFarland Higgins. 'No Recourse: Transnational Corporations and the Protection of Economic, Social, and Cultural Rights in Bolivia.' *Fordham International Law Journal* 27, no. 5 (2004): 1663–805.

Sands, Philippe. 'Litigating Environmental Disputes: Courts, Tribunals and the Progressive Development of International Environmental Law.' Paper presented at the Global Forum VII on International Investment, Paris, 27–28 March, 2008 (2007).

Sauvant, Karl P. *Yearbook on International Investment Law & Policy 2010–2011*. New York: Oxford University Press, 2012.

Savenije, Hubert H.G. 'Why Water Is Not an Ordinary Economic Good, or Why the Girl Is Special.' *Physics and Chemistry of the Earth* 27 (2002): 741–44.

Sax, Joseph L. 'Takings and the Police Power.' *Yale Law Journal* 74, no. 36 (1964): 36–76.

Sax, Joseph, 'The Limits of Private Rights in Public Waters.' *Environmental Law* 19 (1989):473–83.

Sax, Joseph. 'The Constitution, Property Rights and the Future of Water Law.' *University of Colorado Law Review* 61 (1990): 257–82.

Saxer, Shelley Ross 'The Fluid Nature of Property Rights in Water.' *Pepperdine University School of Law. Legal Studies Research Paper Series* Paper Number 2010/13 (July 2010).

Schill, Stephan. *The Multilateralization of International Investment Law* Cambridge, UK: Cambridge University Press, 2009.

Schill, Stephan W. 'Enhancing International Investment Law's Legitimacy: Conceptual and Methodological Foundations of a New Public Law Approach.'*Virginia Journal of International Law* 52, no. 1 (2011): 57–102.

Schlager, Edella, and Elinor Ostrom. 'Property-Rights Regimes and Natural Resources: A Conceptual Analysis.' *Land Economics* 68, no. 3 (1992): 249–62.

Schouten, Marco. 'Strategy and Performace of Water Supply and Sanitation Providers. Effects of Two Decades of Neo-Liberalism.' UNESCO-IHE, Erasmus Universiteit Rotterdam, 2009.

Schreiber, William. 'Realizing the Right to Water in International Investment Law: An Interdisciplinary Approach to Bit Obligations.' *Natural Resources Journal* 48, no. 1 (2008): 431–78.

Schreuer, Christoph. 'The Concept of Expropriation under the ECT and Other Investment Protection Treaties.'(2005).

Schreuer, Christoph. 'Introduction: Interrelationship of Standards.' Chapter I in *Standards of Protection*, edited by August Reinisch. Oxford: Oxford University Press, 2008.

Schreuer, Christoph, Loretta Malintoppi, August Reinisch, and Anthony Sinclair. *The ICSID Convention: A Commentary on the Convention on the Settlement of Investment Disputes between States and Nationals of Other States* Cambridge [England]; New York: Cambridge University Press, 2009.

Schwarzenberger, Georg. *International Law as Applied by International Courts and Tribunals*. London: Stevens, 1957.

Scott, Anthony, and Georgina Coustalin. 'The Evolution of Water Rights.' *Natural Resources Journal* 35 (1995): 821–980.

BIBLIOGRAPHY

Shaw, Malcolm N. *International Law*. Fifth ed. Cambridge, UK: Cambridge Univesity Press, 2003.

Shelton, Dinah. 'Righting Wrongs: Reparations in the Articles on State Responsibility.' *Symposium: The ILC's State Responsibility Articles. The American journal of international law* 96, no. 4 (2002): 833–56.

Simma, Bruno, and Theodore Kill. 'Harmonizing Investment Protection and International Human Rights: First Steps Towards Methodology.' Chap. 36 In *International Investment Law for the 21st Century Essays in Honour of Christoph Schreuer*, edited by Ursula Kriebaum Christina Binder, August Reinisch, and Stephan Wittich. Oxford, New York: Oxford University Press, 2009.

Smaller, Carin, and Howard Mann. 'A Thirst for Distant Lands: Foreign Investment in Agricultural Land and Water.' International Institute for Sustainable Development (IISD), http://epe.lac-bac.gc.ca/100/200/300/iisd/2009/thirst_for_distant_lands.pdf.

Smaller, Carin, and Howard Mann. 'A Thirst for Distant Lands: Foreign Investment in Agricultural Land and Water.' *International Institute for Sustainable Development. Foreign Investment for Sustainable Development Program* (May 2009).

Sohn, Louis B., and R.R. Baxter. 'Responsibility of States for Injuries to the Economic Interests of Aliens.' *American Society of International Law* 55 (1961): 545–84.

Solanes, Miguel. 'Water Services and International Investment Agreements.' Chap. 11 In *Global Change: Impacts on Water and Food Security*, edited by Claudia Ringler, Asit K. Biswas and Sarah Cline. Water Resources Development and Management, 209–34. Berlin/Heidelberg: Springer 2010.

Solanes, Miguel, and Andrei Jouravlev. 'Revisiting Privatization, Foreign Investment, International Arbitration and Water.' *Serie Recursos Naturales e Infrastructura* 129 (2007).

Soloway, Julie A., and Chris Tollefson. *NAFTA's Chapter 11 Investor Protection, Integration and the Public Interest* Montreal: Institute for Research on Public, Policy (IRPP), 2003.

Sornarajah, M. 'State Responsibility and Bilateral Investment Treaties.' *Journal of World Trade Law* 20, no. 1 (1986): 79–98.

Sornarajah, M. *The International Law of Foreign Investment*. Third ed. Cambridge: Cambridge University Press, 2010.

Spronk, Susan, and Carlos Crespo. 'Water, National Sovereignty and Social Resistance: Bilateral Investment Treaties and the Struggles against Multinational Water Companies in Cochabamba and El Alto, Bolivia.' *Law, Social Justice & Global Development (LGD)* 1 (9 October 2008).

Stanton Kibel, Paul. 'Grasp on Water: A Natural Resource That Eludes Nafta's Notion of Investment.' *Ecology Law Quarterly* 34, no. 2 (2007): 655–72.

Stanton, Paul, and Jon Schutz. 'Two Rivers Meet: At the Confluence of Cross-Border Water and Foreign Investment Law.' Chapter 29 In *Sustainable Development in*

World Investment Law, edited by Marie-Claire Cordonier Segger, Markus W. Gehring and Andrew Newcombe. Global Trade Law Series, 749–467. Alphen aan den Rijn: Kluwer Law International, 2011.

Stern, Brigitte. 'In Search of the Frontiers of Indirect Expropriation.' In *Contemporary Issues in International Arbitration and Mediation The Fordham Papers 2007*, edited by W. Arthur Rovine Brill, the Netherlands: Martinus Nijhoff Publishers, 2007.

Steven Shupe, J., Gary D. Weatherford, and Elizabeth Checchio. 'Western Water Rights: The Era of Reallocation.' *Natural Resources Journal*, 29, 2 (1989).

Subedi, Surya P. *International Investment Law: Reconciling Policy and Principle*. Oxford; Portland, OR: Hart, 2008.

Sutton, William R., Jitendra P. Srivastava, and James E. Neumann. 'Looking Beyond the Horizon: How Climate Change Impacts and Adaptation Responses Will Reshape Agriculture in Eastern Europe and Central Asia.' Washington D.C.: Directions in development: Agriculture and Rural Development, World Bank, 2013.

Tanzi, Attila. 'On Balancing Foreign Investment Interests with Public Interests in Recent Arbitration Case Law in the Public Utilities Sector.' *The law and practice of international courts and tribunals: A Practioners' Journal* 11, no. 1 (2012): 47–76.

Tarlock, Dan A. 'National Water Law: The Foundations of Sustainable Water Use.' *Journal of Water Law* 15 no. 3–4 (2004): 120–26.

Technical Advisory Committee (TAC), Global Water Partnership. 'Integrated Water Resources Management.' Stockholm: Global Water Partnership (GWP), 2000.

The International Federation of Private Water Operators (AquaFed). 'Bilateral Investment Treaties and the Right to Water: The Case of the Provision of Public Water Supply and Sanitation Services.(Submission by Aquafed).' In *Office of the UN High Commissioner for Human Rights: Consultation on business and human rights: Operationalizing the 'Protect, Respect, and Remedy' framework on business and human rights*. Geneva, 2009.

The World Bank. 'Water Resources Management.' Washington: The World Bank, 1993.

Thompson, Barton H. Jr. 'Water Law as a Pragmatic Exercise: Professor Joseph Sax's Water Scholarship.' *Ecology Law Quarterly* 25 (1998–1999): 363–84.

Trachtman, Joel P. 'Transcending "Trade And..." an Institutional Perspective.' (2001). In, *SSNR. Available at:* http://papers.ssrn.com/sol3/papers.cfm?abstract_id=271171.

Treanor, William Michael. 'The Original Understanding of the Takings Clause.' *Columbia Law Review* 95 (1995): 782–887.

Trebilcock, Michael J., Robert Howse, and Antonia Eliason. *The Regulation of International Trade*. London: Routledge, 2013.

Triantafilou, Epaminontas E. 'No Remedy for an Investor's Own Mismanagement: The Award in the ICSID Case Biwater Gauff V. Tanzania.' In, *International Disputes Quarterly. Focus: An Arbitrator's Perspective* Winter, (2009). http://www.whitecase.com/files/Publication/cc5f123c-0700-4b93-aef0-a628ebb05bd1/Presentation/PublicationAttachment/b81f3439-af93-4aab-9f45-7c2dee791bc1/IDQ_Winter_2009.pdf.

BIBLIOGRAPHY

Troell, Jessica and Greta Swanson, 'Adaptive Water Governance and the Principles of International Water Law,' Chapter Two. In *Transboundary Water Governance: Adaptation to Climate Change*, edited by Juan Carlos Sanchez and Joshua Roberts, (Gland: International Union for Conservation of Nature, 2014).

Tuckness, Alex 'Locke's Political Philosophy.' In *The Stanford Encyclopedia of Philosophy*, edited by Edward N. Zalta http://plato.stanford.edu/archives/win2012/entries/locke-political/ Winter 2012.

Turner, Kerry, Stavros Georgiou, Rebecca Clark, Roy Brouwer, and Jacob Burke. 'Economic Valuation of Water Resources in Agriculture: From the Sectoral to a Functional Perspective of Natural Resource Management.' Rome: Food and Agriculture Organization of the United Nations (FAO), 2004.

United Nations. 'Yearbook of the International Law Commission. Volume II.' 1959.

United Nations. 'Report of the United Nations Water Conference: Mar Del Plata, 14–25 March 1977.' New York, Sales No. E.77.II.A.12 and corrigendum, 1977.

United Nations. 'Report of the World Summit on Sustainable Development.' Johannesburg, 2002.

United Nations. 'The Millennium Development Goals: Report 2010.' New York: United Nations, 2010.

United Nations Conference on Environment Development. 'United Nations Conference on Environment and Development: Rio De Janeiro, 3–14 June 1992: Item 9 of the Provisional Aganda: Adoption of Agreements on Environment and Development: Agenda 21.' New York, 1992.

United Nations Conference on the Human Environment. 'Report of the United Nations Conference on the Human Environment, Stockholm, 5–16 June, 1972.' New York, 1973.

United Nations Conference on Trade and Development (UNCTAD), 'International Investment Agreements: Key Issues Volume I.' Geneva: United Nations, 2004.

United Nations Conference on Trade and Development (UNCTAD) 'International Investment Agreements: Key Issues Volume II.' Geneva: United Nations, 2004.

United Nations Conference on Trade and Development. *Investor-State Dispute Settlement and Impact on Investment Rulemaking*. New York, Geneva: United Nations, 2007.

United Nations Conference on Trade and Development (UNCTAD) *World Investment Report 2009: Transnational Corporations, Agricultural Production and Development*. Geneva: UNCTAD, 2009.

United Nations Conference on Trade and Development (UNCTAD). 'World Investment Report 2010: Investing in a Low-Carbon Economy.' New York: United Nations, 2010.

United Nations Conference on Trade and Development (UNCTAD) 'World Investment Report 2011: Non-Equity Modes of International Production and Development.' Geneva: United Nations, 2011.

United Nations Conference on Trade and Development (UNCTAD), 'Expropriation: A Sequel. UNCTAD Series on Issues in International Investment Agreements II.' New York, Geneva: United Nations, 2012.

United Nations Conference on Trade Development. *World Investment Report 2012: Towards a New Generation of Investment Policies*. New York; Geneva: United Nations, 2012.

United Nations Conference on Trade and Development (UNCTAD), 'World Investment Report 2013. Global Value Chains: Investment and Trade for Development.' Geneva: UNCTAD, 2013.

United Nations Conference on Trade and Development (UNCTAD), 'IIA Issues Note. Recent Developments in Investor – State Dispute Settlement (ISDS).' Geneva: UNCTAD, 2013.

United Nations Conference on Trade and Development (UNCTAD), 'Reform of Investor-State Dispute Settlement: In Search of a Roadmap (Updated for the Launching of the World Investment Report (WIR), 26 June 2013).' Geneva: UNCTAD, 2013.

United Nations Conference on Trade and Development (UNCTAD) 'Towards a New Generation of International Investment Policies: UNCTAD's Fresh Approach to Multilateral Investment Policy – Making.' Geneva: United Nations, 2013.

United Nations Conferences on Trade Development (UNCTAD), *World Investment Report 2015: Reforming International Investment Governance*, (New York, Geneva: United Nations, 2015).

United Nations Development Programme. 'Global Consultation on Safe Water and Sanitation for the 1990s: 10–14 September 1990, New Delhi, India.' New York, 1990.

United Nations Development Programme. 'Human Development Report 2006. Beyond Scarcity: Power, Poverty and the Global Water Crisis.' New York: United Nations, 2006.

United Nations Development Programme. 'Human Development Report 2010. 20th Anniversary Edition. The Real Wealth of Nations: Pathways to Human Development.' New York: United Nations, 2010.

United Nations Educational, Scientific, Cultural Organization,. 'The United Nations World Water Development Report (WWDR4).' Paris: UNESCO, United Nations 2012.

United Nations Environment Programme (UNEP). 'Geo: Year Book 2003.' In *GEO: Global Environment Outlook*. Washington: United Nations, 2003.

United Nations Environment Programme (UNEP), (UNWater). 'Status Report on the Application of Integrated Approaches to Water Resources Management.' Nairobi, Kenya: UNEP, GWP, SIWI, UNDP, UNEP-DHI Centre for Water and Environment, 2012.

United Nations: General Assembly. 'Proclaming of the International Drinking Water Supply and Sanitation Decade, Resolution 35/18. 55th Plenary Meeting.' New York, 10 November 1980.

BIBLIOGRAPHY

United Nations. World Summit Sustainable Development. 'Report of the World Summit on Sustainable Development Johannesburg, South Africa, 26 August–4 September, 2002. A/Conf.199/20.' Johannesburg, 2002.

Van der Kamp, Garth. 'The Hydrology of Springs in Relation to the Biodiversity of Spring Fauna: A Review.' *Journal of the Kansas Entomological Society* 68, no. 2 (1995): 4–17.

Van der Zaag, P., and H.H.G. Savenije. 'Water as an Economic Good: The Value of Pricing and the Failure of Markets.' *Value of Water* Research Report Series No. 19 (2006).

Van Harten, Gus. 'Five Justifications for Investment Treaties: A Critical Discussion.' *Trade, law and development Trade, Law and Development* 2, no. 1 (2010): 19–58.

Van Harten, Gus. *Investment Treaty Arbitration and Public Law.* New York: Oxford Univesity Press, 2007.

Vandevelde, Kenneth J. *Bilateral Investment Treaties. History, Policy, and Interpretation.* Oxford: Oxford University Press, 2010.

Varady, Robert G. and Matthew Iles-Shih. 'Global Water Initiatives: What Do the Experts Think? Report on a Survey of Leading Figures in the World of Water.' In *Workshop on Impacts of Megaconferences on Global Water Development and Management.* Bangkok Third World Centre for Water Management (Mexico) with support from the Sasakawa Peace Foundation (USA and Japan), January 29–30, 2005.

Viñuales, Jorge E. 'Access to Water in Foreign Investment Disputes.' *The Georgetown International Environmental Law Review* 21 (2009): 733–59.

Viñuales, Jorge E. 'Iced Freshwater Resources: A Legal Exploration.' *Yearbook of International Environmental Law* 20, no. 1 (2011): 188–206.

Viñuales, Jorge E. *Foreign Investment and the Environment in International Law* Cambridge: Cambridge University Press, 2012.

Viñuales, Jorge E. 'Foreign Investment and the Environment in International Law: The Current State of Play' in Kate Miles (ed.), *Research Handbook on Environment and Investment Law* (Cheltenham: Edward Elgar, forthcoming 2016), Chapter 2.

Von Rosenvigne, D. Alison. 'Creating a Working Vocabulary of Sovereignty Language at the International Court of Justice.' *Comparative Research in Law & Political Economy, Network. CLPE Research Paper 05/2010* 6, no. 2 (2010).

Von Staten, Andreas. 'Deference or No Deference, That Is the Question: Legitimacy and Standards of Review in Investor-State Arbitration.' In, *Investment Treaty News* 19 July, (2012). http://www.iisd.org/itn/2012/07/19/deference-or-no-deference-that-is-the-question-legitimacy-and-standards-of-review-in-investor-state-arbitration.

Wade, Jeffory S. 'Privatization and the Future of Water Services.' *Florida Journal of International Law* 20 (2008).

Wälde, Thomas, and Stephen Dow. 'Treaties and Regulatory Risk in Infrastructure Investment. The Effectiveness of International Law Disciplines Versus Sanctions by Global Markets in Reducing the Political and Regulatory Risk for Private Infrastructure Investment.' *Journal of World Trade* 34, no. 2 (2000): 1–61.

Wälde, Thomas and Abba Kolo. 'Environmental regulation, investment protection and "Regulatory taking" in international law.' *International and Comparative Law Quarterly* 50, no. 4 (October 2001): 811–48.

Wälde, Thomas W. and Todd Weiler. 'Investment Arbitration under the Energy Charter Treaty in the Light of New Nafta Precedents: Towards a Global Code of Conduct for Economic Regulation.' *Transnational Dispute Management* 1 (February 2004).

Weeramantry, J. Romesh. *Treaty Interpretation in Investment Arbitration*. Oxford: Oxford University Press, 2012.

Weil, Prosper. 'Les Clauses De Stabilisation Ou D'intangibilité Insérées Dans Les Accords De Développement Economiques.' In *Mélanges Offerts À Charles Rousseau: La Communauté Internationale*, edited by Mélanges Rousseau Charles. Paris: Editions A. Pedone, 1974: 301–28.

Weston, Burns H. '"Constructive Takings" under International Law: A Modest Foray into the Problem of "Creeping Expropiation".' *Virginia Journal of International Law* 16, no. 1 (1975): 103–75.

Weston, Burns H. 'The Charter of Economic Rights and Duties of States and the Deprivation of Foreign-Owned Wealth.' *American Journal of International Law* 75, no. 3 (1981): 437–75.

WHO/UNICEF Joint Monitoring Programme for Water Supply and Sanitation (JMP). 'Progress on Sanitation and Drinking Water. 2010 Update.' Geneva: WHO/UNICEF, 2010.

Wilson, Robert R. 'A Decade of New Commercial Treaties.' *American Journal of International Law* 50, no. 4 (1956): 927–33.

Wilson, Robert R. 'Property-Protection Provisions in United States Commercial Treaties.' *American Journal of International Law* 45, no. 1 (1951): 83–107.

Winpenny, James 'Financing Water for all.' Report of the World Panel on Financing Water Infrastructure, 2003.

World Bank. 'World Development Report 2011: Conflict, Security, and Development.' Washington: World Bank, 2011.

World Economic Forum. 'Global Risks 2011. Sixth Edition. An Initiative of the Risk Response Network.' Geneva: World Economic Forum, 2011.

World Economic Forum Water Initiative. 'The Bubble Is Close to Bursting: A Forecast of the Main Economic and Geopolitical Water Issues Likely to Arise in the World During the Next Two Decades. Draft for Discussion at the World Economic Forum Annual Meeting 2009.' World Economic Forum, 2009.

World Health Organization. 'Progress on Drinking Water and Sanitation. 2012 Update.' Geneva: World Health Organization, 2012.

World Water Assessment Programme. 'The United Nations World Water Development Report 2: Water a Shared Responsibility.' Paris–New York: United Nations, 2006.

BIBLIOGRAPHY

World Water Assessment Programme. 'The United Nations World Water Development Report 3: Water in a Changing World.' Paris–London: United Nations, 2009.

World Water Assessment Programme. 'The United Nations World Water Development Report 4: Managing Water under Uncertainty and Risk.' Paris–London: United Nations, 2012.

Wouters, Patricia, Sergei Vinogradov, and Magsig Bjoern-Oliver. 'Water Security, Hydrosolidarity, and International Law: A River Runs through It.' *Yearbook of International Environmental Law* 19 (2010): 97–134.

Zaunbrecher, Katie. 'Pac Rim Cayman V. Republic of El Salvador: Confronting Free Trade's Chilling Effect on Environmental Progress in Latin America.' *Houston Journal of International Law* 33, no. 2 (2011): 489–502.

Zellmer, Sandi, and Jessica Harder. 'Unbundling Property in Water.' In, *College of Law, Faculty Publications* available at: http://digitalcommons.unl.edu/lawfacpub, (2007).

Other Sources

Poulos, Andrew. 'Australia: Senate passes Economic Protection and Biodiversity Conservation "water trigger" Bill,' *Mondaq* 2013.

BBC News, '*Estamos recuperando la propiedad y la gestión de estas áreas estratégicas,*' BBC World.com, 27 February 2007.

BBC News, '*Chavez Nacionaliza Campos Petroleros,*' BBC World.com, 27 February 2007.

International Law Reporter, '*Bolivia's Denunciation of the ICSID Convention,*' 8, July, 2007. Available at: http://ilreports.blogspot.com/2007/07/bolivias-denunciation-of-icsid.html, last visited 12 June, 2013.

Investment Arbitration Reporter (IA Reporter), '*Ecuador becomes Second State to Exit ICSID; Approximately two-thirds of Ecuador's BIT Claims were ICSID-based,*' 17 July 2009. Available at: http://www.iareporter.com/articles/EcuadorExit.

Investment Arbitration Reporter (IA Reporter), '*Argentina by the numbers: Where Things Stand with Investment Treaty Claims arising out of the Argentine Financial Crisis,*' February 1, 2011. Available at: http://www.iareporter.com/articles/20110201_9.

La Republica, '*Proyecto Majes Siguas II ya no represará aguas del Apurímac,*' Tuesday, 14 August 2012.

Public Statement on the International Investment Regime 31 August 2010, proposed by several academics among which are Gus Van Harten, David Schneiderman, Muthucumaraswamy Sornarajah and Peter Muchlinski.

OOSKA News, 'Bolivia Needs Another $32.5 Million to Complete Misicuni Project,' March 21, 2014. Available at: http://www.ooskanews.com/story/2014/03/bolivia-needs-another-325-million-complete-misicuni-project_159851.

Region Sur, 'Tarucani sí afectará inversión en Majes II,' by Elizabeth Huanca, 23 May 2013.

The Democracy Center On-Line, *Bechtel VS. Bolivia: The People Win!!* (2006), http://www.democracyctr.org/newsletter/vol69.htm.

The Democracy Center, 'Water Revolt: The World Bank Letters,' June 2002, available at http://democracyctr.org/bolivia/investigations/bolivia-investigations-the-water-revolt/bechtel-vs-bolivia-role-of-the-world-bank/water-revolt-the-world-bank-letters/

The Prague Post, *Residents reject shale gas drilling, May 16* 2012. Available at: http://www.praguepost.com/business/13127-residents-reject-shale-gas-drilling.html.

UNCTAD, Investment Dispute Settlement Navigator, available at: http://investmentpolicyhub.unctad.org/ISDS/FilterByBreaches.

Index

Agenda 21   32*n69*, 40, 40*n14*, 119*n9*

Bilateral Investment Treatie (BIT)   10*n24*, 13, 14, 60, 61, 63*n121*, 65*n1*, 70*n16*, 70*n17*, 71*n22*, 75, 75*n33*, 97*n38*, 98, 105, 106*n78*, 107*n87*, 108*n89*, 113, 147, 151, 155, 155*n3*, 161, 176, 177*n15*, 178, 178*n17*, 181*n29*, 191, 192*n80*, 193*n87*

climate change   18, 20, 22, 22*n23*, 22*n25*, 23, 27–9, 30*n66*, 41, 43*n27*, 47, 47*n39*, 47*n40*, 47*n42*, 48, 48*n43*, 48*n44*, 68*n8*, 132, 206

conventions. *See* treaties

Dublin Statement, the   18*n6*, 23*n28*, 24*n31*, 39, 39*n11*, 40, 40*n12*, 54*n76*

energy
  coal   125, 128
  hydropower   25, 163, 171
  renewable   48, 48*n45*
  thermoelectric   174

Energy Charter Treaty   2*n3*, 7*n16*, 8*n18*, 48, 95*n30*, 148, 148*n56*

expropriation
  compensation   4, 10, 56, 61, 62, 89, 90–4, 90*n6*, 90*n8*, 94*n21*, 94*n22*, 94*n25*, 96, 103, 104, 120*n11*, 127, 128, 154, 183*n17*, 183*n18*, 202, 208, 208*n17*, 209
  direct expropriation   6, 91, 93–7, 95*n31*, 98, 101, 113, 130, 144, 154, 161, 163, 165, 166, 168, 169, 173
  definition   93, 94
  discrimination   92, 103, 109, 114, 184, 186, 192*n81*
  indirect expropriation   2*n3*, 6, 6*n11*, 7, 7*n14*, 9, 9*n20–n22*, 13–16, 45, 64–87, 87*n74*, 88–114, 89*n3*, 95*n31*, 97*n38*, 97*n41*, 98*n42*, 99*n45*, 100*n50*, 100*n55*, 101*n57*, 101*n59*, 103*n62*, 105*n76*, 108*n89*, 110*n95*, 114*n109*, 131*n48*, 131*n49*, 154*n2*, 155, 156*n4*, 156*n5*, 157*n10*, 157*n11*, 158, 158*n13*, 159*n17*, 159*n20*, 160, 160*n22*, 161–74, 184*n19*, 202–206
  definition   78, 89, 97, 98, 99*n45*, 100
    US Model BIT   10, 14, 70*n17*, 98, 105, 107*n87*, 155, 155*n3*

determination of
  deprivation, level of   86, 113, 162, 164, 172, 202
  legitimate expectations   111
  Penn Central criteria   81, 82, 106
  qualitative analysis or approach   131, 161, 173, 174–198
  quantitative analysis or approach   131, 131*n48*, 154 –173, 174*n1*, 178, 190, 204
  sole effects   131, 156, 158, 173
  water-related measures   161, 199, 204
legitimate regulation (also lawful)   6, 9, 13, 45, 56, 93, 95, 101, 106, 108, 110, 111, 176, 183, 192, 197, 199, 202
partial expropriation   150, 150*n62*, 165, 165*n39*, 165*n44*, 166, 167, 169*n56*, 173, 178*n9*, 203
  water permits   150, 167, 173

fair and equitable treatment   12*n33*, 13, 61, 61*n109*, 62, 88, 88*n2*, 114*n109*, 184*n19*, 187, 188, 189*n65*, 191, 208, 209
foreign investors. *See also* International Investment Agreements; Bilateral Investment Treaties
  in relation to property rights   11, 36, 41*n22*, 86, 87, 98, 101, 102, 211, 121, 148, 158
  rights   65, 66, 209
Free Trade Agreement   1, 10, 13, 67*n7*, 76, 88*n1*, 105, 106*n77*, 107*n84*, 107*n87*, 124*n26*, 149*n57*

Global governance   28, 28*n51*, 38*n7*, 69, 76
Global Water Partnership, the   22*n25*, 38, 38*n5*, 43*n27*, 46*n34*, 47*n42*

Human Rights   15, 25, 26, 27, 31, 38, 61, 63, 63*n121*, 102, 117, 118, 193, 195, 204

International Centre for Settlement of Investment Disputes   1, 2*n3*, 3*n5*, 4*n6*, 6*n10*, 7*n13*, 9, 10*n25*, 32*n73*, 33*n74*, 35*n1*, 49*n47*, 58*n99*, 59, 59*n100*, 60*n105*, 60*n107*, 61*n111*, 61*n113*, 62*n115*, 62*n119*, 63*n121*, 66*n3*, 71*n18*, 71*n21*, 75*n34*, 75*n35*,

246   INDEX

International Centre for Settlement of
Investment Disputes (cont.)
    86*n73*, 95*n31*, 96*n32*, 96*n33*, 100*n50*,
    100*n51*, 100*n53*, 100*n54*, 101*n57*, 108*n90*,
    112*n99*, 115*n3*, 115*n4*, 116*n5*, 124*n23*,
    128*n43*, 129*n44*, 139*n22*, 144*n38*, 147*n50*,
    150, 150*n60*, 151*n63*, 151*n64*, 152, 157*n6*,
    157*n10*, 158*n13*, 160*n21*, 160*n23*, 169*n57*,
    170*n60*, 170*n61*, 171*n65*–*n67*, 175*n4*,
    180*n12*, 185*n25*, 186*n54*, 187*n28*, 188*n64*
International Investment Agreements 1,
    1*n1*, 3*n6*, 9*n23*, 36*n1*, 37, 37*n2*, 64, 88, 92,
    95*n27*, 97*n40*, 110*n92*, 110*n95*, 153*n70*,
    158*n14*, 178, 183*n41*, 199, 203. *See also*
    Bilateral Investment Treaties;
    Free Trade Agreements
  generations
    first generation 10, 64, 65, 88, 109,
    113, 160
    second (new) generation 10, 13, 16,
    82, 173
  North America Free Trade Agreement
    2*n3*, 3*n6*, 8*n8*, 12*n29*–*n33*, 35*n1*, 65*n1*,
    67*n7*, 71, 71*n20*, 76, 87*n74*, 95*n26*,
    95*n28*, 100*n52*, 101, 111, 112, 126, 127,
    127*n35*, 129, 141, 141*n28*, 145*n40*, 155–7,
    159, 159*n16*, 160, 165, 165*n40*, 166,
    166*n47*, 175*n4*, 180*n12*, 181*n12*, 186*n25*,
    201, 202
  case law 3, 183
  standards of protection 61, 61*n109*, 62, 66,
    70, 74, 88, 88*n2*, 89, 91, 109, 114, 141, 157,
    199, 208, 209
International Investment Law 1, 2*n3*, 3*n6*,
    4*n7*, 6, 8, 9, 9*n21*, 9*n22*, 10*n25*, 14–16,
    16*n40*, 23*n27*, 35, 35*n1*, 36, 37*n3*,
    41*n22*, 45, 48, 63*n121*, 65*n1*, 66, 76,
    78, 82, 87*n74*, 88*n2*, 90, 93, 97*n41*,
    103*n62*, 105*n76*, 110*n93*, 110*n94*, 118, 121,
    126–7, 134, 135–9, 142*n31*, 143*n33*, 154*n2*,
    159*n15*, 166, 175*n4*, 180*n25*, 182, 186*n55*,
    188*n63*, 194, 207, 209, 211
  Customary International Law (under
  the term International Investment
  Law) 45, 90, 112, 176, 177
  regime 1, 66, 180, 210
    concerns over 74, 124
International Law Commission 44, 44*n31*,
    54*n76*, 91, 91*n15*, 94*n22*, 103*n63*, 135*n6*,
    135*n6*, 136*n9*

investment
  definition 49, 131, 131*n48*, 134, 135, 135*n7*,
    138, 141, 141*n26n28*, 148-152, 153, 161, 166, 168
  bundle of investment rights 162, 163-165,
    166, 172, 202, 203

nationalisation
  definition 93–7
  expropriation 8, 93–5, 94*n24*, 97

police power
  definition 79
  doctrine
    latu sensu 11, 106, 106*n81*, 114–16, 123,
    175, 176, 178, 184, 202, 205
      in relation to water 114–16, 205
    legitimate exercise of (*also sover-*
    eignty) 4, 6, 12, 14, 64, 66, 85, 91, 111,
    113, 179, 193
    strictu sensu 11, 13, 106*n81*, 107, 108,
    114, 115, 122, 126, 176, 183, 185, 191–3, 195,
    200, 202, 204
      in relation to water 13, 114, 115, 116,
      122, 126, 193, 200, 205
  International Law 11, 66, 76, 82, 85, 102,
    112, 176, 177
    International Investment Arbitra-
    tion 180*n26*, 204*n10*
  investment rights, deprivation of 86, 92,
    103, 111, 162, 171, 184, 202, 203
  legitimacy of
    discrimination/non-discrimination
    85, 114, 180, 181, 183–185, 193, 204
    due process 3, 179, 180, 182, 186, 189,
    192*n81*
    good faith 11, 108, 126, 132, 173, 179
    legitimate expectations 11, 66, 85, 111,
    181, 188, 189, 189n65, 190, 191
    proportionality 85, 114, 126, 132,
    156n5, 179, 181, 182
      narrow analysis 175*n3*, 180
    public purpose 87, 179–183, 204
  origin of term 77–9
  public interest, relation to 64–6, 74, 79,
    83, 85, 93, 101–5, 107, 181, 182
  scope of 82–5, 102, 122, 175, 193, 204, 205
  US law, influence of 78
property
  alien protection 7, 89–91, 90*n9*, 92, 102,
    103. *See also* expropriation

INDEX

customary international law   91, 103
Hull Formula   90, 208
definition   52, 133, 144
domestic law
   Case law   3n6, 36n1, 183
   construction of   134, 135, 137, 139, 140, 143, 146, 147, 152, 153, 161, 162, 211
   as facts   135, 136, 139, 152
International Investment Agreements   37n3, 92, 110n95, 183
water, relation to   133. *See also* water ownership
proportionality. *See* police power

regulatory chill   12, 37
'stall implementation of regulation'   10

sustainable development   2n3, 3n6, 4n6, 9, 9n22, 15n39, 18n6, 23n28, 30n66, 32n69, 35n1, 39n11, 40, 41, 41n20, 61, 61n112, 119n8, 159n15, 186n55, 202
sovereignty. *See also* police power
definition   64, 67, 69, 72n24, 73, 76
international obligations
   economic integration   28, 67, 70, 72, 86, 86n71, 102, 113
   international law   92n18, 108
nationality   137, 184
public interest   3n6, 74, 85, 181, 182, 212
regulatory chill   12
theories   77
treaty negotiations
   ex ante   68–72
   ex post   68–72

treaties
negotiation of
   Convention on the Protection and Use of Transboundary Watercourses and International Lakes   43, 45, 118n7
   United Nations Convention on the Law of the Non-Navigational Uses of International Water Courses   43

United Nations
General Assembly   26, 26n45, 27n47, 39n10, 67, 70n13, 90, 90n9, 91, 91n15
   resolutions   26n45, 27n47, 39n10, 67, 90, 90n9

United Nations Conference on the Human Environment   39, 39n8
United Nations Conference on Trade and Development   1n1, 2n2, 9, 9n23, 37, 37n2, 68n7, 70n15, 88n1, 94n24, 95n27, 97n40, 99, 99n47, 105n77, 110n92, 113n105, 113n106, 114n108, 115n11, 153n70, 158n14, 159n15, 159n17, 176n7, 182n14, 185n22, 185n23
United Nations Convention on the Law of the Non-Navigational Uses of International Water Courses   43, 44, 45, 54, 68n8, 69, 70, 117, 193n86
United Nations Development Programme   19, 22, 25, 27n50, 28n53, 29n59, 30n63, 32n68, 37n4, 57n93
UN Water   41, 43, 43n27, 44, 44n29, 44n30, 45n33, 54, 68n8, 69, 69n11, 70, 117, 118n7, 193n86
United Nations World Water Development Report   7n2, 19n9, 21n21, 22n22, 22n23, 27n50, 28n53, 30n63, 32n68, 37n4

water
climate change   18, 20, 22, 22n25, 23, 27–9, 41, 43n27, 47, 47n40, 48n43, 206
conferences
   International Conference on Freshwaters   40, 40n17, 46, 46n37
   International Conference on Water and the Environment   39
   United Nations Conference on Environment and Development   40, 40n14 (*see also* Agenda 21)
   World Summit on Sustainable Development   32n69, 41, 41n20
   World Water Congress   42
   World Water Forums   42
Customary International Law   44, 52
ecosystem   20, 20n15, 21, 21n15, 22, 23, 24, 30n64, 39, 43n27, 44, 46, 117, 121n15, 123, 150n61, 185
governance of
   pollution   18, 21, 21n21, 23, 28, 29, 30, 31, 123, 124, 130, 132, 144, 150, 193
   soil   19n11, 53, 125, 162
   water quality   21, 45, 115, 117, 118n7, 121n15, 123–6, 125n32, 130, 144, 182, 193, 195, 202

248 INDEX

water (cont.)

water supply   29, 36, 39, 39n10, 40, 42, 57, 58, 58n99, 59, 195

human right   3n6, 25–7, 27n47, 31, 35n1, 63, 63n121, 193, 195, 204, 209

hydrological cycle   18, 19, 47, 53, 55, 111, 153, 178, 206

law

customary   52

domestic   14, 55, 118, 121, 133–53, 162, 200, 202

international   14, 37n4, 38n7, 44n31, 54n76, 69, 200

management of

integration of   206

international   38, 42n25, 45, 46, 62, 140, 200, 205

local   37, 42, 46, 62

national   45–7, 62, 185, 212

public purpose   11, 65n1, 181, 200

quality   21, 29, 40, 45, 115, 117, 118, 118n7, 121n15, 123–6, 125n32, 130, 144, 174, 182, 193, 195, 202, 205, 211

quantity   27n49, 30n66, 117, 118–23, 144, 174, 195n93, 211

resources

allocation of   23, 32, 37, 45, 47, 48, 49n49, 51, 56, 119, 129, 133, 182, 195, 202, 205, 206

conflicts   1, 20, 25, 34, 35, 47, 54, 120, 126, 132, 195, 206, 207

disputes, investment   1, 4, 7, 36n1, 58, 58n99, 77, 121, 161, 183n42, 184n44, 200, 205, 206

Case law   3n6, 36n1, 183

economic value   23, 23n28, 24, 40, 164

entitlements   6, 23, 38, 47, 56, 63, 119, 121, 130, 132, 143, 144, 144n37, 146, 148, 150, 152, 153, 155, 161–3, 165, 167, 203, 204

exploitation   29, 123, 167, 203

foreign investment   4n6, 23n27, 30n65, 34, 36n1, 120n12, 132n50, 174, 177n14, 192n82

risk   66, 116

monitoring   26, 31n67, 121, 121n15

Human Development Index   119n8, 119n10, 120, 121

ownership of (see also Expropriation)

bundle of rights   6n10, 133, 133n1, 142, 143n34, 149, 151n64, 153

common property   49, 49n50, 50, 50n52–n56, 51, 51n57, 51n62

foreign investment   4n6, 23n27, 30n65, 34, 36n1, 120n12, 132n50, 174, 196n93

groundwater   17n1, 116, 122n19, 124, 182, 183, 189

intangible right   144

International Investment Agreements   1, 1n1, 3n6, 9n23, 36n1, 37, 37n2, 64, 88, 92, 183n41

open-access   49, 49n50, 50

physical asset   139, 144, 163, 166, 175, 178

permits   48, 55–7, 111, 116, 128, 130, 144, 145n44, 150, 162, 163, 167, 168, 193, 197, 203

pollution   124, 132, 193

public interest   63, 66, 181, 182

use of

agriculture   25, 25n37, 30n66, 59, 132, 204

consumption, human   13, 18, 20, 25, 25n37, 30, 31, 32, 59, 120n11, 185, 193

cultural   25, 26, 29, 181

energy   7n16, 17, 174n2

scarcity of

causes   31, 53, 55

energy security, relationship to   43n27

food security, relationship to   3n6, 28, 30, 30n66, 36n1, 43n27, 204

inequality   26, 26n42

poverty   26, 26n42, 27n49, 29n59, 30

stress   22, 27, 27n49, 29, 31, 34, 132, 207

substitutes, lack of   24, 98, 149, 172

types

drinking water

access to   4n6, 23n28, 24–6, 26n46, 27n48, 29, 29n59, 31–4, 36n1, 42, 57, 60, 61, 128, 132

services

investment disputes   31, 32, 33, 162, 185, 206

regulation of   31, 34, 57

frozen water   19

groundwater   17, 19, 19n11, 20, 44n31, 53, 53n74, 54, 54n76, 54n79, 122n19, 124, 142, 142n32, 182, 183, 189

World Trade Organization

General Agreement on Tariffs and Trade   86, 86n72

General Agreement on Trade in Services   108

WTO Agreement   67, 70, 208

Printed in the United States
By Bookmasters